W9-BXD-682

TUDOR TRACTS

AN ENGLISH GARNER

TUDOR TRACTS

1532-1588

WITH AN INTRODUCTION BY

A. F. POLLARD, M.A., F.R. Hist. S.

Author of *England under Protector Somerset* and of *Henry VIII.*

NEW YORK

COOPER SQUARE PUBLISHERS, INC.

1964

PUBLISHERS' NOTE

THE texts contained in the present volume are reprinted with very slight alterations from the *English
Garner* issued in eight volumes (1877-1890, London,
8vo) by Professor Arber, whose name is sufficient
guarantee for the accurate collation of the texts
with the rare originals, the old spelling being in
most cases carefully modernised. The contents of
the original *Garner* have been rearranged and now
for the first time classified, under the general
editorial supervision of Mr. Thomas Seccombe.
Certain lacunae have been filled by the interpolation
of fresh matter. The Introductions are wholly
new and have been written specially for this issue.
The references to volumes of the *Garner* (other than
the present volume) are for the most part to the
editio princeps, 8 vols. 1877-90.

Published by
Cooper Square Publishers, Inc.
59 Fourth Avenue, New York, N. Y. 10003
Library of Congress Catalog Card No. 64-16741
Printed in the United States of America

CONTENTS

INTRODUCTION

OF all the forms and methods of historical representation, the best is said to be that which echoes original voices. But it is not echoes we hear in this and its fellow-volumes; it is the original voices themselves. They speak in no borrowed accents; no interpreter mars their meaning; no medium muffles their tones. History is a glass through which we behold the past; but the glass is coloured by the historian's mind, and we see through it sometimes darkly. Contemporary writings are a glass of truth, a mirror of the age in which they are written. If we seek to know how men thought, and felt, and talked in the days of bluff King Hal, or of Good Queen Bess, it is a sorry expedient to take down from the shelf the volumes of this or of that historian, however learned and accurate, brilliant or imaginative he may be. The golden rule is to ascend to the fountain-head, to imbibe historical truth at its source before it has lost its original purity in its tedious passage across the dusty arena of religious and secular controversy.

Not that these Tudor Tracts contain the whole truth or nothing but the truth. They are perhaps as full of misrepresentations as the news-sheet and review of to-day, and errors of fact may crowd their pages as closely as those of the most brilliant of modern historians. Their writers were no more exempt than we from a human delight in error. Nay, since they cared more than we do for what they believed, they were even more anxious than we to prove that each other's opinions were the outcome, not merely of perverted intelligence, but also of evil hearts. There are in these tracts striving and crying and jangling enough; the din of battle is never far off, and the passions of war have not subsided in the breasts of those who record it. There may be more heat than light, but heat is a proper subject of scientific investigation; it produces more than light, and he who would understand history must know something of the causes of popular passions. These tracts reflect many phases of popular feeling in Tudor times; they are real phenomena, whatever the truth of their contentions may be. Of that the reader must judge for himself. He stands in the position of the audience at an Attic theatre, while the editor, like a Greek chorus, may give an occasional hint. As the messengers of the Greek stage came on to relate what they had seen and heard of the battles, murders, and sudden deaths, which Greek sensitiveness would not suffer to be enacted on the boards, so in these pages each pamphleteer comes forward in turn to tell of ancient deeds of which himself was witness or partaker. The use of messengers was the nearest approach to dramatic realism which the Greeks would tolerate; the perusal of these tracts will best enable modern minds to realise the conditions of a bygone age.

Metaphors from the drama are naturally suggested by the contents of this volume, for these tracts illustrate a period, of which the dramatic unity is complete, and the dramatic interest unsurpassed. Within the fifty odd years between 1532 and 1588 there was fought the greatest struggle in English history, the battle for spiritual independence between England and the forces of the Roman

Catholic Church. Our first piece marks the inception of the contest, our last is a song of triumph. The tide of victory flows and ebbs and flows again; reaction succeeds to reform and fails; and for half a century the issue hangs in the balance. Henry VIII. throws down the challenge to Rome by marrying Anne Boleyn in 1533, and in 1588 Anne Boleyn's daughter defeats the last effort made by Rome to rivet again by force the bonds which Henry had burst.

The interview between Francis I. and Henry VIII. described in *The Manner of the Triumph at Calais and Boulogne*,[1] was not the first occasion on which those two doughty monarchs had met. Twelve years before, amid surroundings of unparalleled splendour, they had pledged eternal friendship on the Field of Cloth of Gold; but the display which flaunted over that scene was not more portentous than the perfidy which it concealed. Henry VIII. went from his interview with Francis I. to negotiate that secret alliance with the Emperor Charles V., which in five years' time made Charles dictator of Europe and the Pope little more than his chaplain. Wolsey, the prime mover in the deception, was one of the first to suffer from the Nemesis which dogged its steps. Clement VII. amid the clash of imperial arms was deaf to the mutterings of the storm in England; and, helpless in the Emperor's hands, he refused Henry VIII.'s petition for divorce from the Emperor's aunt. The refusal precipitated Wolsey's fall, and Henry determined to effect by other means that divorce which he had for five years begged in vain from the Pope. He had made up his mind that the power of

---

[1] First printed London, 1532, 4to; it was reprinted the same year, and then not again till 1884, when it appeared in E. M. Goldsmid's *Bibliotheca Curiosa*. Its authorship is unknown.

Rome was but an imposing image. For twenty years he had seen its authority spurned by the most Christian and Catholic kings, whenever it stood in the way of their secular interests; he had watched a humble monk of Wittenberg defy all the weapons of the Papal armoury; and he had observed the steady growth in England of contempt for the Papacy and dislike for the Church. For fifteen years Wolsey had staved off the revolution by allowing Parliament no voice in the government, and lay-men as little as possible, and by plunging the king into the maelstrom of foreign war and foreign intrigue. But at last that game was played out; the treasures amassed by Henry VII. were spent; the enthusiastic loyalty with which Henry VIII. had been greeted on his accession was turned to discontent; heavy taxation was demanded and refused; and England stood no higher in 1529 in the councils of Europe than she had done when Wolsey first grasped the reins. From his own point of view Wolsey had been right; a Cardinal of the Roman Church could not desire a breach with Rome; he had tried the only possible means of averting it, and he had failed, as he was bound to do.[1]

In 1529, with or without the fall of Wolsey, with or without the divorce of Catherine of Aragon, an attack on the Church and the Papacy was imminent. The only question was, in which ranks would the crown be found fighting? The importance of the divorce was that it determined Henry VIII. to side against the Papacy. It brought over to the cause of reform that royal influence, the hostility of which had paralysed the anti-ecclesiastical movement in the early years of the fifteenth century. The

---

[1] See the present writer, *Henry VIII.*, 1902, cap. iii.-iv.

extent of Henry's power was largely due to the fact that
he stood between opposing and well-matched forces,
and that comparatively little was required to turn the
balance. No one, whose perceptions were not dulled by
theological bias, would now maintain that in one scale
were the forces of the Papacy, the wishes of the English
laity, and the influence of the English Church; and in the
other nothing but Henry VIII. and his evil passions. To
believe that the divorce of Catherine of Aragon was the
sole cause of the breach with Rome is to be blind not
merely to the facts of Tudor history, but to the fundamental
conditions which govern human affairs. No ruler can effect
anything except by using forces which exist independently
of his personal will, and Henry VIII. would have been
powerless against the Church of Rome without the help
of collaborating tendencies. One man cannot alter a
nation's character, and it is not possible to believe that,
but for Henry VIII., England would have remained per-
manently within the Roman Catholic communion.

But, if the divorce was not the sole cause of the breach
with Rome, neither was Anne Boleyn the sole cause of the
divorce. Henry VIII. had had mistresses before Anne,
without their existence giving rise to the least hint
of a separation from Catherine of Aragon. They were
recognised royal institutions, with which Popes no more
thought of interfering than they expected kings to meddle
with equally delicate questions of Papal morals. Henry
did not want a divorce because his marriage with Catherine
stood in the way of his passion for Anne Boleyn, but
because it stood in the way of his having a wife who should
bear him an heir to the throne. He might have had Anne
as his mistress, he desired her as his wife; and, if the

difference was not due to the need of an heir, it was due to scruples with which we are not inclined to credit Henry VIII. But to marry Anne Boleyn meant a complete repudiation of the Pope's authority, and—what seemed more important to men of that time—it involved the risk of a quarrel with Charles V. Not that any personal insult to Catherine would have moved her imperial nephew; but the divorce of Catherine implied the destruction of Hapsburg influence at the English court, the ruin of Mary's hopes of the English crown and of the prospect of adding England to the already monstrous Hapsburg empire. Charles's view of the divorce was purely political; Henry's marriage with Anne Boleyn meant that, in the great struggle for predominance in Europe, England's weight would be transferred from the scale of Charles V. to that of Francis I. For that same reason the divorce was popular in France, and the interview at Calais in 1532 was marked by a genuine desire for friendship which had been absent from the meeting on the Field of Cloth of Gold. The French king was once more a match for the Emperor, and Henry could with impunity brave the Pope so long as there was no fear that Charles and Francis would combine to carry out the Pope's decrees.

No allusion to such matters of high policy is, however, allowed to transpire in the popular account of the meeting. Our tract is confined exclusively to its spectacular aspect; and the only symbolical incident appears to be the wrestling match in which the Englishmen overthrew a band of priests—a possible mimicry of the struggle between Church and State then raging in England. It is probable, however, that the two monarchs came to a sufficient understanding. At any rate, events followed each other rapidly after Henry's return. In January 1533 Anne Boleyn

was pregnant; her issue must at all costs be legitimate.
It could only be legitimate if the English king were
divorced from Catherine and married to Anne. Warham,
Archbishop of Canterbury, had died in the previous
August; a successor willing to execute the royal wishes
was found in Thomas Cranmer. By threatening to deprive
the Roman curia of the first-fruits of English sees, Henry
induced the Pope to grant Cranmer his bulls, though
Clement must have known for what purpose they were
wanted. As soon as they arrived Cranmer was con-
secrated, and a few days later he opened his court at
Dunstable to determine the validity of Henry's marriage
with his deceased brother's wife. His verdict was a
foregone conclusion, as was his pronouncement that Henry
and Anne were legally husband and wife, though the date
and manner of their union remain doubtful to this day.
On Whitsunday, the 1st of June 1533, took place *The
noble triumphant Coronation of Queen Anne, wife unto the
most noble King, Henry the VIIIth.*[1] The reason of the
honour done her is plainly indicated in the verses recited
before her; she was expected to bear the king a son; then
the terror of a disputed succession would cease, and the
golden age would come to an anxious people (pp. 17, 20,

[1] This tract, which was originally printed in quarto in 1533, has only been
reprinted in Goldsmid's *Bibliotheca Curiosa*, 1884. It is obviously an officially
inspired account, and for a more impartial description the reader is referred to
the *Letters and Papers of Henry VIII.*, vol. vi. No. 584, where many interesting and curious details will be found. Anne's popularity was by no means so
great as this tract would lead us to suppose; the people as a whole sympathised
with Catherine, and at times even the royal influence could scarcely protect
Anne Boleyn from insult. Nicholas Udall, the writer of the verses appended to
the tract, is famous as the author of the earliest known English comedy; he was
also headmaster of Eton and Westminster, his connection with the former school
being terminated by a very scandalous episode. See *Dict. Nat. Biogr.*, lviii. 6.
The MS. of Udall's verses is in the British Museum, Royal MS. 18 A LXIV.

21). The nation had not long to wait for the expected issue, but it was not a son. On 7th September following Anne gave birth to a child at Greenwich. Chapuys, the Spanish ambassador, scarcely deigned to notice the event in his despatches to his master. The king's mistress had borne a daughter, a matter of no moment to so mighty a monarch as the Hapsburg emperor. Yet the child thus ushered into a contemptuous world lived to be Queen Elizabeth, to humble the pride of Spain, and to bear to a final triumph the banner which Henry had raised.

So the curtain rings down on the first act of the drama. It rises on a different scene. The interest of the next tract lies in the religious and not the political aspect of the Reformation, and the contest is domestic rather than foreign. It need hardly be repeated that the motives of the separation from Rome were in a very slight degree doctrinal; and few of those who assisted Henry VIII. to break the Roman yoke had any taste for a tincture of Lutheran dogma. That redoubtable monarch had, indeed, digested many formulas and swallowed not a few scruples; he was keeping an open and receptive mind for new truth and fresh support from whatever quarter it might come; and more than once, when a Catholic storm was brewing, he signalled for Protestant help by professing his anxiety for the preaching of the Word and pretending to be a true evangelical. But this was only *in extremis*; if the Pope and the Catholic powers would let him enjoy his peculiar conscience in peace, he would abstain from Lutheran gods, if not from Lutheran goddesses; and although the imperial ambassador described Anne Boleyn and her relatives as the real apostles of the new sect, they failed to make a convert of their king. New doctrines began, however, to spread in England; even the guarded precincts of the court were not free from infection, and in the privy council itself the two most prominent members from 1532 to 1540 were Thomas Cromwell and Thomas Cranmer. The archbishop was gradually leaning towards Lutheran doctrine, and Cromwell believed in a Lutheran policy if not in the Lutheran creed. But they were in a minority ; their colleagues, headed by Norfolk and Bishop Gardiner, had no love for the two arch-heretics, and their enmity often threatened Cranmer and proved fatal to Thomas Cromwell. It was almost on the eve of his fall that Cromwell was able to do Cranmer the service described in the amusing extract here reprinted from Foxe (pp. 29-35).[1]

From ecclesiastical and domestic questions, we turn to a real imperial issue, the Union between England and Scotland. That design was the uppermost thought in Henry's mind for the last six years of his reign, and, indeed, it occupied the attention of Tudor monarchs during the whole of the time they sat on the English throne. Henry VII. no doubt had it in view when he married his daughter Margaret to the Scottish king ; but in the earlier years of Henry VIII. English interests in Scotland had been sacrificed to Wolsey's passion for playing a prominent part in European politics. As soon as Henry VIII. had emancipated himself from Wolsey's and other clerical control, and had triumphantly asserted his authority over Church and

---

[1] *How the Lord Cromwell helped Archbishop Cranmer's Secretary*; the secretary was Ralph Morice, whose anecdotes of Cranmer constitute one of the best authorities for the Archbishop's life. As Morice furnished Foxe with information for his ecclesiastical works, there is little doubt that this story comes from Morice's own lips. It affords some interesting glimpses at the court and manners of Henry VIII.'s time.

State at home, he turned his energy towards the extension
of England's dominion beyond her borders. He first com-
pleted the union of England and Wales, he then brought
Ireland into better order than it had enjoyed since the days
of Poynings, and finally he set about the reduction of Scotland. The age was one of national expansion and consolida-
tion, and nature seemed to have designed the formation of
the British Isles into one empire, quite as clearly as she had
the union of Castile and Aragon, or of France and Brittany.
Moreover, the inconvenience of an independent Scotland
had been forcibly brought home to Henry during his
struggle with Rome. James v. of Scotland, although, or
perhaps because, he was Henry's nephew, had been regarded
by Pope and by Emperor as the most promising instrument
of their schemes against the schismatic king. Beaton had
been made a Cardinal and sent from Rome to Scotland
with the express object of publishing the papal bull of
deposition on the Borders, and inciting the northern
counties to revolt; James himself had been urged to
claim the English throne; and a Scots invasion might
generally be reckoned on, whenever England found itself in
difficulties. The last and most reckless of these inroads had
ended in 1542 with the rout of the Scots at Solway Moss,
the death of James v., and the succession to the throne of a
week-old infant, Mary, Queen of Scots. The time seemed
apt for Henry's intervention; nearly half the nobility of
Scotland had been killed or captured at Solway Moss; and
before the prisoners were released, they were made to swear
allegiance to Henry as sovereign of Scotland, and to promise
their co-operation in effecting a marriage between Queen
Mary and Henry's son, Prince Edward. But dealing with
the Scottish Government was no easy task; there was an

English faction in Scotland and a French faction, and the two were constantly fighting for control of Scottish policy; when an understanding had been reached with a foreign state, the opposite faction often expelled its rival and reversed its acts. Such was the case in 1543; the disastrous effects of the war with England had brought the English party into power, and mainly through Henry's abating his terms, a treaty was actually signed for the marriage alliance. But the arrival of French ships, men, and money produced its effect; the French party was once more in the ascendant. The treaty with England was repudiated, and one with France was substituted.[1] To Englishmen, the Scots Government appeared to have been guilty of the grossest perfidy, and to repay it the expedition described in the next tract was despatched against Scotland in May 1544.[2]

The object of this invasion, and of the devastation which marked its course, is not at once apparent. A desire for revenge was the ostensible motive, and partly no doubt the real one, but the ultimate end in view was to convince the Scots that England could make herself more unpleasant as an enemy than France, and therefore that the English alliance was the better policy for Scotland to pursue. Henry VIII. never attempted to *conquer* Scotland, for the simple reason that he had not the means to hold it when conquered. The only union with Scotland effected by force was Oliver Cromwell's; the conquest of Scotland was possible to him and to no one else, because Cromwell was head of an efficient and permanent army. He ruled Scotland by the methods of a military despot, but a military despotism was

---

[1] For the negotiations during that year, see the latest volume (XVIII.) of the *Letters and Papers of Henry VIII.*, ed. GAIRDNER.

[2] See pp. 39-51; this tract, which was almost certainly published in 1544, has never been reprinted except for this *Garner*.

b

an impossibility in Tudor times, and Henry's standing army was limited to a few gentlemen-pensioners and yeomen of the guard. Hence he had to resort to coercion by methods of barbarism, to the slow and feeble policy of repeated and ruthless raids, which in the end failed of their purpose. Henry VIII., however, had come within measurable distance of success, when he was baulked by the treachery of his friend and ally, the Emperor. The experience of 1543 had taught him that Scotland would never yield so long as she could look for effective assistance from France. So, with the object of putting France *hors de combat*, Henry had joined Charles V. in an alliance which was to crush for generations the French King's power. Both monarchs led powerful armies into France in 1544, but when Charles was in the heart of the French dominions, he made peace and left the English in the lurch.[1] All thoughts of beating Scotland to her knees had now to be abandoned; and England in 1545 had to bend all her energies towards resisting a threatened French invasion. Peace was made in 1546, and in the midst of his preparations for a renewed attack on Scotland, Henry died.[2]

His successor, the Protector Somerset, was as resolute as Henry had been to effect the union with Scotland by means of the marriage between Queen Mary and Edward VI., but he approached his task in a somewhat different spirit. He first made strenuous efforts to persuade the Scots by peaceful means to carry out the treaty of 1543. On their failure, he determined to prove by an overwhelming display

---

[1] See for the latest information on these events vol. vii. of the *Calendar of Spanish State Papers*, ed. M. A. S. HUME.

[2] That Henry was resolved to renew his attempt on Scotland, is clear from the despatches in the *Correspondance Politique d'Odet de Selve*, published in 1886 by the French Government.

of force the hopelessness of Scots resistance. A large and well-equipped army was collected on the Borders in August 1547 ; a fleet under Clinton sailed up the coast to co-operate with the land forces ; and at Pinkiecleugh or Musselburgh, the Protector inflicted on the Scots one of the most crushing defeats in the whole of their history.[1] Somerset, however, was no great believer in coercion, and he next set to work to secure Scottish consent to the union with England. He promised the Scots autonomy ; he suggested that the use of the names England and Scotland should be discontinued, that the united kingdom should be called by the 'old indifferent name' of the Empire of Great Britain, and that there should be complete freedom of trade between the two.[2] But these offers proved unavailing. The French faction controlled the Government; zealously aided by the Church, it prevented Somerset's terms from reaching the ears of the people, and fanned to a flame the inveterate hatred of the Scots for their English neighbours. French

[1] The account of this expedition here printed (pp. 53-157) is one of the earliest, most interesting, and most detailed of military tracts ; it is even furnished with sketch maps and plans. The author, William Patten, had excellent opportunities for writing a history of the campaign ; he was one of the 'judges of the marshalsea,' that is, one of those appointed to administer martial law in the provost-marshal's court. His colleague was William Cecil, afterwards the great Lord Burghley, who assisted Patten in his literary as well as in his judicial work. Patten's book was reprinted in Dalzell's *Fragments of Scottish History*, 1798 ; it was also largely used by Holinshed and by Hayward in his *Reign of Edward VI*. There are, however, several *lacunae* in Patten's story ; he makes scarcely any allusion to the importance of the presence of the English fleet. Other accounts by eyewitnesses are that by the Sieur de Barteville (mentioned on pp. 90, 95), a French adventurer in the English service, whose narrative was printed by the Bannatyne Club in 1825 ; the descriptions given to the French ambassador by Jean Ribauld, another Frenchman in English service, and by the Scots chancellor, Huntly, which may be found in the *Correspondance d'Odet de Selve*, pp. 220 *sqq.* ; the best Scots accounts are in the *Diurnal of Occurrents* (Bannatyne Club), pp. 44-5, and Lesly's 'History' (Bannatyne Club), pp. 195-9. See the present writer's *England under Protector Somerset*, pp. 155-160.

[2] *Ibid.* pp. 163-5.

gold was lavished among the nobility, French arms and French soldiers were poured into the country, and eventually France herself declared war upon England. Nor was that all. At the same time the social discontent, which troubled England throughout the Tudor period, came to a head;[1] revolts of the commons broke out in the east and in the west; levies intended for the Scottish Borders, or for service in France, had to be diverted to Norfolk and Devon. The Protector, whose attempts to alleviate the distress had been frustrated by the Council, was held responsible for risings due to the rejection of his policy. He was driven from office, and his successor, the Duke of Northumberland, made an ignominious peace with France and with Scotland, in the hope that France would abet him in his unprincipled scheme for placing his daughter-in-law on the English throne.[2]

But, before we come to that pitiful tragedy, we must refer to the predominant factor in the reign of Edward VI., the struggle between the old faith and the new. The Reformation in England had originally little to do with dogma ; no doctrine played the part in England that justification by faith did in Germany, or predestination in Switzerland. The English movement arose from antagonism to the privileges, powers, and possessions of the clergy, and began with an attack on clerical fees. When, in the reign of Edward VI., theological questions came to the front of the political stage, the doctrine round which controversy waged most furiously was, for an obvious reason, the doctrine of the Eucharist. For, if priests could perform daily miracles, there was something more than human about them, something which raised them above their fellow men and justified

---

[1] *England under Protector Somerset*, cap. viii.   [2] *Ibid.*, caps. ix. and x,

their claim to exceptional privileges and exceptional
authority ; and, in their hatred of these clerical claims, men
began to attack the doctrinal basis upon which they rested.
The controversy was fierce, and in its popular manifestations
at any rate was not very edifying, though the materialistic
views of the sacrament of the altar expounded by not very
literate priests were to some extent responsible for the
coarseness with which they were attacked. The dialogue
between *John Bon and Master Parson*[1] is no doubt typical
of many an argument in the tavern and at the street corner,
when the leniency of Protector Somerset had opened the
floodgates of that diversity of opinion which Henry VIII.
had striven by means of his royal supremacy and his
statute of Six Articles to keep shut.

It was not, however, religious motives which precipitated
the downfall of the Duke of Northumberland and of that
innocent traitress, Lady Jane Grey. The Duke had earned
a well-nigh universal detestation by a government that was
more violent than that of Henry VIII. and more pusillanimous
than that of Mary. Even his daughter-in-law declared
that he was 'hated and evil spoken of by the commons.'
His judicial murder of his rival, the Duke of Somerset, his
revival and extension of the harsh laws of Henry VIII., and
his attempts to pack parliament and the privy council had
offended three-quarters of the nation before his insane plot

[1] This metrical tract was published by Luke Shepherd, M.D., in 1548 ;
Professor Arber from a misapprehension of Underhill's remarks on pp. 194-5
assigned the tract to 1551, but there is a copy in the British Museum dated 1548,
there was no Protector in 1551 (see p. 195), and Sir John Gresham (p. 194) was
Lord Mayor in 1547-8; these facts make the date certain. The tract was
reprinted in facsimile in 1807 from the only copy known to be extant, and in
1852 was re-edited for the Percy Society. Bale's opinion that Dr. Shepherd's
verse was not inferior to Skelton's is scarcely borne out by *John Bon and
Master Parson*. The doctor appears to have been imprisoned in Mary's reign
for his authorship of this work.

to alter the succession alienated the rest. It was no question of Protestant against Catholic; the issue was decided against Northumberland by the most Protestant parts of the country before the Catholics had time to stir. East Anglia and the city of London were hotbeds of the new learning, yet the men of Norfolk and Suffolk flocked to Mary's standard, and London gave her such a welcome as had not been seen in the memory of man.[1] Even Edward Underhill, the Hot Gospeller and author of our next tract,[2] would not raise a finger for Lady Jane Grey. The people had already suffered enough under Northumberland; that alone would have made them side with Mary, and there were powerful reasons besides. Then, and throughout the sixteenth century, men saw in the Tudor dynasty their only bulwark against a recurrence of the Wars of the Roses, and they will submit to much from a government when the only alternative is anarchy. There were, no doubt, objections to Mary as the protégée of Rome and Spain, but those who felt these objections most keenly were not partisans of Lady Jane Grey, but of the daughter of Anne Boleyn. Elizabeth was as effectually excluded as Mary from the throne by Northumberland's plot; hence its speedy and ignominious collapse.

Mary's accession was welcomed as a relief from the tyranny of Northumberland's rule, and at first she did something to justify the high hopes with which she had been received. The worst of the treason laws enacted after Somerset's fall were repealed, and although there was

---

[1] See the present writer's *England under Protector Somerset*, 1900, pp. 311-13.

[2] Underhill's *Narrative* was partly printed by Strype, and also in the *Chronicles of Queen Jane and Queen Mary* (Camden Society); but it was first printed in full in *Narratives of the Reformation* (Camden Society); it was used by Miss Strickland for her *Queens of England* and by Harrison Ainsworth for his *Tower of London*; see *Dict. Nat. Biogr.*, lviii. 29-30.

naturally a return to the old religion, there was not at first
any great persecution of the devotees of the new. Though
Edward Underhill's *Narrative* is a graphic description of the
perils to which Protestants[1] were liable, it also shows that
escape was comparatively easy even for 'Hot Gospellers'
so long as they had taken no active part in the 'rebellion'
of Lady Jane Grey. But this fair promise soon withered
away ; the threatened marriage of Mary with Philip of Spain
revived all those apprehensions upon which Henry VIII. had
played so successfully when he pleaded the necessity of a
male heir to the throne as a justification for his divorce
from Catherine of Aragon. No Queen had ever wielded the
English sceptre in peace ; one only had tried to seize it—
the Empress Matilda—and the effects of that attempt
had been such as to make Englishmen shrink from the
prospect of its repetition. It was a popular impression
in England, based on the experience of four centuries, that
women were excluded from the English throne, as they
were from that of France. If a woman succeeded, she must
either marry or she would leave the kingdom without heirs ;
if she married, she must wed either an English noble or a
foreign prince. If she chose an English noble, she would
provoke a repetition of those jealousies which had led to
the Wars of the Roses ; and if she preferred a foreign prince,
she might endanger the nation's independence. By marriage,
Brittany had been merged in France ; by marriage, the
Netherlands had been brought under the yoke of Spain,
with results soon to be luridly illustrated ; by marriage,
Hungary had come under the sway of the same Hapsburg

---

[1] The employment of this term by Underhill, pp. 174, 179, 188, is one of the
earliest occasions on which it is used to denote a religious party in England;
cf. Dixon, *Church History*, v. 262, 338, vi. 92.

family, had been torn by civil war and left a prey to the Turk. Was it so groundless a fear that by marriage to a Hapsburg, Mary might entail upon England the disasters that had attended similar unions in other countries? So the prospect of a Spanish marriage evoked a storm of protest which no religious reaction could produce, and only a total want of preparation robbed Wyatt's rebellion of the success to which it so nearly attained.[1]

It was probably well for England that the rising did fail, for the capture of London by the insurgents would almost certainly have been followed by a religious civil war, which might have devastated England for a generation, like the wars of religion in France. But the results of the failure were bad enough. The rebellion gave Mary and her episcopal advisers an excuse for maintaining that treason was a natural development of heresy, and that there could be no peace until the heretics had been extirpated. Then began the bloodiest persecution with which England has ever been cursed ; neither old nor young, man nor woman, bishop nor parish priest was spared, unless he would abjure his faith, or seek safety in craven silence and cowardly compliance with the powers that were. Attempts

---

[1] In this volume we have accounts of Wyatt's rebellion from two different points of view. Underhill's *Narrative* relates to the experience of a gentleman-pensioner who helped to defeat the rebels, while Proctor's *History* is obviously compiled from facts supplied by eyewitnesses who accompanied Wyatt's forces. John Proctor, who was an ardent adherent of the Roman Catholic faith, had already dedicated to Mary, when Princess, a work entitled *The Fall of the Late Arian*, written on Somerset's deposition from the Protectorate. The *History of Wyatt's Rebellion*, originally published in 1554, and here reprinted from the second edition of 1555, was largely used by Holinshed, and is described by the learned antiquary, Hearne, as 'a book of great authority.' In spite of his Romanism, Proctor was in Elizabeth's reign rector of St. Andrew's, Holborn, dying in 1584. Tennyson's *Queen Mary* embodies an interesting dramatisation of Wyatt's story.

have been made to shift from one to another the responsibility for the blood of the martyrs, enumerated in the pages of Foxe and in Brice's *Register*.[1] Clerical writers have pretended that the bishops, like Gardiner and Bonner, were ever on the side of mercy; and that it was a 'recklessly base legislature' which caused the holocaust. Others have sought to lighten the burden which lies so heavy on Mary's memory. Yet even Mary may claim some Protestant gratitude; though the good she did was undesigned. It was not Henry VIII., it was not Edward VI., nor even Queen Elizabeth who made certain the triumph of the Reformation in England. It was the champion of the Roman Church herself, whose cruelties planted an ineradicable detestation of Rome in the average Englishman's heart.

The final overthrow of the Roman Catholic cause was not the only unrehearsed effect of Mary's reign. She not merely alienated men's minds from the faith she professed, but from the temporal policy she pursued. She had tied England to the chariot wheels of Spain, and plunged her into war with France to serve the purposes of the Hapsburg family. The result was the loss of Calais, which had been in England's unbroken possession since its capture by Edward III. two centuries before. It was a sore blow to English pride; feebleness abroad was no compensation for Mary's ferocity at home. But the ultimate results were all for England's good; the alliance with Spain was

[1] This doggerel tract was published at London in 1559 in duodecimo, and another edition was issued in 1597. As it was written some years before Foxe's *Book of Martyrs*, and almost immediately after Mary's death, it is probably the most trustworthy list we possess, though the attacks made by S. R. Maitland and others on Foxe have not materially impaired the martyrologist's reputation for accuracy. See *Dict. Nat. Biogr.*, *s.v.* FOXE, JOHN; and Canon Dixon's *Church History*, vol. v. p. 327.

hopelessly discredited, and England was relieved from the
Continental embarrassments in which the retention of
Calais would have perpetually involved her. Here again
the responsibility for disaster has been removed from
Mary's shoulders to those of her privy council. Her
council, it is true, was most incompetent; Wentworth, the
deputy of Calais, was a man of no ability, though even he
had repeatedly demanded reinforcements which the council
refused to send.[1] But Mary had chosen her own privy
council; and if she had made the best selections possible,
the result illustrates the astonishing intellectual sterility
which seems to have smitten the party of reaction in England. To Mary, indeed, must be ascribed the principal part
in the blunders and crimes of her reign, as well as in the
unpremeditated blessings which ultimately flowed from
them. Yet it is impossible not to feel the pathos of Mary's
last hours; she died fully conscious that her life had been
a failure; she, like her mother, had lost the love of her
husband; to her, as to her mother, the longed-for son was
denied; the throne would pass to the daughter of her
mother's supplanter; and the faith for which she and her
mother had suffered so much would become anathema

---

[1] The story of the loss of Calais is here (pp. 289-330) told in great detail from
the original sources; the two main narratives are those of George Ferrers and
Thomas Churchyard, both of them poets of some repute. Churchyard's account
is only accessible in Grafton's *Chronicle*, published in 1569, if so rare a volume
can be called accessible; and Churchyard's *General Rehearsal of Warres*, 1579,
is quite out of the reach of any but the most lucky or most lavish of book-
collectors. The rest of the account is made up from the MS. correspondence of
the deputy of Calais and his subordinates. So sensational an event—a modern
parallel might be supplied by the capture of Gibraltar—evoked quite a literature on the Continent; a volume entitled *La Reduction de Calais* appeared at
Paris, and an Italian account, *Discorso sopra la presa della inespugnabile città di
Calès*, was published at Rome, both in 1558; and two centuries later a novel by
Guerin de Tencin, dealing with the subject, was published at the Hague, and
attained a wide popularity (2nd ed. 1739; 3rd ed. 1740; 4th ed. 1749).

unto her people. Well might men say 'that she died of thought and sorrow,' and believe, with Mary herself, that 'Calais would be found in her heart.'[1]

But sombre reflections were little in harmony with men's mood when they heard of Mary's death. It was an event for which the majority of Englishmen had been eagerly watching for years; and the private grief of the few was drowned in the public joy of the multitude. The fear of Spanish dominion passed away; the nation breathed again, and its pulse began to beat with a vigour it had never known before. The new queen was not half-Spanish like her sister; she was the most English of all English monarchs since the Norman Conquest. To trace a drop of foreign blood in her veins, men had to go back more than a century to her great-great-grandmother, Catherine of France, the widow of Henry V., and wife of Owen Tudor. No wonder she appealed to 'all English hearts.'[2] It was well for her and for England that she established her throne in the hearts of her people, for no sovereign inherited a more doubtful position or essayed a more arduous task. She was beset by perils at home and perils abroad. The mere fact that Anne Boleyn's daughter should have ascended the throne at all would seem to indicate that the stars in their courses fought on her side. Branded, by the strangest and most erratic of her father's acts,[3] with the stigma of

---

[1] P. 331; the passage relating Queen Mary's death, which is here reprinted from Foxe, is the origin of the well-known story about Mary and Calais, which was told to Foxe by 'Master Ryse and Mistress Clarentius,' attendants on the queen; from Foxe it was adopted by Holinshed; Froude, who was apparently unaware of its origin, describes the story as 'having come somehow into existence.'

[2] See p. 395.

[3] No satisfactory explanation of Henry VIII.'s motive in divorcing as well as beheading Anne Boleyn has yet been suggested; he gained little or nothing by it, while he added enormously to the difficulties with which Elizabeth was surrounded at her accession. See the present writer's *Henry VIII.* pp. 232-3.

bastardy from the third year of her childhood, she had been to Catholic Europe, and to many of her own people, the emblem of the prevailing of the gates of hell ; she was the fruit of that passion which was thought to have led her father into the sin of schism ; and the repudiation and shameful death of her mother left her with no support but the somewhat capricious will of Henry VIII. She had suffered ignominy enough in his reign, and in that of her brother Edward VI., though she escaped the religious persecution which troubled her sister Mary ; she was brought into greater peril by the intrigues of her bold, bad lover, Lord Seymour of Sudeley.[1] Mary's accession placed Elizabeth in an even worse case ; that queen was never forgiving, and the temptation was strong to visit on Anne Boleyn's daughter the wrongs which Anne had inflicted on Mary's mother. The desire was inflamed by Mary's suspicion that Elizabeth was the real centre of all the plots against her throne, and after Wyatt's rebellion Elizabeth's life hung by a slender thread. She was only saved by her consummate caution and assumed acquiescence in Mary's religious policy. Therein her conduct seems to compare unfavourably with Mary's stout resistance to the reforming measures of Edward VI. ; but no one in Edward's reign thought of sending Mary to the block or even to the Tower, while Mary would have given her sister short shrift had she displayed the religious obstinacy on which Mary had prided herself.

---

[1] The somewhat compromising relations between Elizabeth and the Lord High Admiral are discreetly passed over by Foxe, from whose pages we reprint the account of Elizabeth's early years and imprisonment. The curious about such matters will find full details in Haynes' *Burghley State Papers*, from which Lingard has printed such particulars as would most damage Elizabeth's character. Foxe's encomiums must be received with caution ; he would not be likely to say anything disagreeable to the queen in 1563 ; nor would she have let him, had he been so minded.

At length there came a happy issue out of all her afflictions, and Elizabeth was no worse a queen for the bread of bitterness she had eaten for twenty years. She ascended the throne the last of the Tudors; there was no rival to divide the confidence and affection which the people lavished on that dynasty, as they did on no other before or since. 'Remember old King Henry VIII.,' shouted one in the throng as Elizabeth rode to her coronation[1] in Westminster Abbey on the 14th of January 1559; and the queen, we are told, 'rejoiced at his name whom this Realm doth hold of so worthy memory,' while the people hoped she would 'in her doings resemble the same.'[2] The hope was signally fulfilled; Elizabeth avoided some errors which Henry VIII. committed, and she was saved by her council from some risks which Henry would not have provoked; but on the whole she carried out with remarkable success the work which he had begun. She was a true daughter of her father; and when we speak of Tudor characteristics, we really mean those of Henry VIII. and Elizabeth, whose reigns covered nearly eighty years of the sixteenth century. Elizabeth had not perhaps the majestic force of Henry, but in subtlety of intellect, consummate and unprincipled statecraft, indomitable courage and superb self-confidence she was little, if at all inferior; and the two together stand in a class apart from the rest of England's monarchs.

Both needed all their qualities for the work they had to do. Elizabeth came to the throne in a blaze of popular

[1] The tract describing Elizabeth's coronation is reprinted from Tottel's edition of 1558, 4to; another edition appeared in the same year, printed by 'S. S. for John Bury'; neither seems to have been reprinted except for this *Garner*.

[2] See p. 393.

favour largely due to Mary's blunders; and her coronation
was the occasion of rejoicings in striking contrast with the
sullen disapproval, which had greeted her mother twenty-
five years before. But the curtain was raised on the final
act of the great sixteenth century drama amid omens that
boded ill for England's victory. Mary had left her country
well-nigh defenceless, and our second extract[1] dealing with
Elizabeth's reign describes the measures she took to repair
the condition of English arms. It was not merely weapons
but ships and money which England needed; for the navy,
of which Henry VIII. has been called the father, had been
suffered to decay, and the currency consisted of more than
half alloy.[2] Abroad, too, a formidable rival appeared; one
Mary succeeded another as the champion of Roman
Catholicism. The second was Mary Stuart, the infant who had
been left Queen of Scotland by the death of James V., who
was now Queen of France by her marriage to Francis II., and
who claimed to be Queen of England by reason of Elizabeth's bastardy and of her own descent from Margaret,
sister to Henry VIII.   So began the contest which ended in
the tragic scene at Fotheringay.

But of all the problems that Elizabeth had to solve, the
hardest was that of religion.   The exact proportion of
Protestants to Catholics in England at the time of her
accession was probably unknown to the queen herself, and
it has been a matter of dispute ever since. It is reasonable
to suppose that the two parties were not unevenly matched;
and it is almost certain that the complete estrangement of

---

[1] Pp. 396-400; for its author, William Harrison, see *Dict. Nat. Biog.*
xxv. 46.
[2] For the debasement of the English coinage in the sixteenth century, see
England under Protector Somerset, pp. 45-52.

either at any time within the first five years of her reign would have wrecked Elizabeth's throne. Fortunately, there was a large class which belonged to neither of the extreme parties, and more fortunately still, all but a very few were willing, in default of any practicable alternative, to put up for a time with the Elizabethan settlement ; they regarded it as merely temporary, and hoped, the Puritans for a speedy extirpation of papistical remains, and the Catholics for an early return to the Roman fold. The object of Elizabeth and her council was to keep both in a state of tolerable suspense. Uniformity was considered essential to national unity, but articles of religion were to be worded so as to admit of as many interpretations as possible. Adherents of the old learning were persuaded to subscribe the Articles because they were Catholic; adherents of the new, because they were Protestant. The same studied ambiguity pervaded the rules about rites and ceremonies; and it is probable that the famous Ornaments Rubric itself, which still puzzles the priest and the lawyer, was vague and obscure with deliberate intent. It prescribed such ornaments as were in use by authority of Parliament in the second year of Edward VI. But it is not clear that there were any such ornaments, for Parliament did not interpose its authority in the matter of ornaments until the third year of Edward VI., and the ornaments in use in the second year were the result of ancient custom and canon law, and not of Parliamentary definition. The net result of the Ornaments Rubric must have been practically an order to 'go as you please,' so long as the peace was kept. That, indeed, was the first requisite; it was Elizabeth's boast that she 'made no windows into men's hearts.' There were plenty of Catholics at her court ; one commanded her fleet against the Armada;

and Essex's friends were described as 'a damnable crew of atheists.' People could believe what they liked, so long as they respected the persons of bishops and went to church on Sundays. The settlement was not at the time regarded as more than a makeshift, and many were indignant at what they considered to be paltering with the truth. They thought it would bring down on England the wrath of Heaven, and interpreted disasters like the burning of St. Paul's as divine judgments either for going too far along the path of religious change, or else not far enough.[1]

The makeshift was none the less successful; and however much opposing parties to-day may lament the indefiniteness of the Elizabethan settlement, it is that very indefiniteness which keeps them now and kept them then within one Church. It saved England from becoming a prey to civil war, as France was at that moment, as the Netherlands were to become within ten years, and Germany two generations, later. What religious wars could mean was vividly brought home to Englishmen by the *Spoil of Antwerp*,[2] an event comparable to the Sack of Rome, the Massacre of St. Bartholomew, and the Sack of Magdeburg. It was a valuable object-lesson; it warned Englishmen of what they might expect if ever Spanish soldiery gained a foothold on English shores; it contributed not a little to the zeal with which they rallied

[1] See p. 407. Bishop Pilkington's sermon is not now extant. See Pilkington's *Works* (Parker Soc.), pp. 481 *sqq.* A facsimile reprint of this tract on the burning of St. Paul's was included in *Genealogica Curiosa*, vol. iii. 1885. The extract from Foxe which here follows is a piece of pure comedy placed a little out of chronological order because of its natural connection with the fire at St. Paul's; the incident must have taken place during Mary's reign.

[2] This tract has only been printed in this *Garner*; the documents prefixed to it prove conclusively that its author was Gascoigne, and not a hypothetical Gaston, as stated in *Dict. Nat. Biogr.*, xxi. 38.

round their Queen when danger became acute; and it made them tolerant of the strong measures which Elizabeth and her council took to parry plots against the government. Genuine Englishmen would look with little patience on the schemes of men like the Northern Earls, whose punishment is now said to prove Elizabeth more 'bloody' than Queen Mary, but whose efforts, if successful, would then have involved England in the throes of civil war, and have left her a prey to foreign foes. It is easy to say that the conditions which prevailed on the continent could not have been repeated in England; but it is difficult to say why not, unless it was because the strong right arm and the iron will of the Tudors withstood the beginnings of debate.

The necessity for rigorous rule is not to be denied, but necessity is after all the tyrant's facile plea, and it will scarcely be held to justify all the steps which Elizabeth took to secure her throne. Religious toleration was not a popular idea in the sixteenth century, but the cruelties they had suffered under Mary made Protestants a little ashamed to persecute for religious opinion. At the same time, they instinctively regarded Jesuits and other emissaries of the Roman Church as enemies to whom no mercy could be shown. It was a ready escape from the dilemma to represent them not as martyrs to their faith, but as traitors to their queen. And, indeed, it was not always easy to distinguish religion from politics, especially when a religious person like the Pope was also a great political power. Had not the Pope excommunicated and deposed Elizabeth? Was it not the duty of a faithful Roman Catholic to respect and further the decrees of the Holy Father? Then, how could a true son of the Church be a loyal subject of Queen Elizabeth? The problem was not an easy one to solve; but of all the Catholic sufferers under Elizabeth, none has better title to the martyr's crown than Edmund Campion. He was a saint far removed from political intriguers [1] like Parsons, for the Jesuits had not yet become the instruments of Spanish policy in England, and Campion was purely and simply a missioner of his faith. The conduct of George Elliot [2] in using his former intimacy with Roman Catholics to effect Campion's arrest has been described as patriotic, but it was the kind of patriotism which Dr. Johnson defined as the last refuge of scoundrels.

Another head more illustrious, but less innocent, than that of the Jesuit martyr was next to fall on the scaffold. The execution of Mary, Queen of Scots, was as illegal as that of Charles I., for in neither case had the court which tried the prisoner any jurisdiction. But then monarchs are not subject to courts of law; they may murder and plot and steal to their hearts' content, and the law cannot touch them. Hence it has sometimes happened that not only expediency, but also justice has demanded that the law should be overridden. It is not so easy to believe that Mary's execution was unjust as that it was illegal, and we are less indignant with Elizabeth for signing Mary's death-warrant than for the infamous means she took to shift the responsibility from her own to subordinate shoulders.[3] By

[1] For the political intrigues of the Jesuits of Elizabeth's later years, see *The Archpriest Controversy* (Camden Soc.), Taunton's *History of the Jesuits*, and Hume's *Treason and Plot*.

[2] See pp. 451-474, *A very true Report of the apprehension and taking of that Arch-Papist, Edmund Campion*. The official record of the payment to Elliot and Jenkins for their services will be found in the *Acts of the Privy Council*, ed. Dasent, 1581-2, p. 398.

[3] See Hume, *The Great Lord Burghley*, 1898, pp.417-22, where the plot which ruined Secretary Davison is exposed; the wretched man was made to suffer under the imputation that he had forged the warrant, in order to save Elizabeth from the resentment of the Catholic powers.

a strange coincidence Mary was buried[1] in Peterborough
Cathedral, where fifty-one years before another unfortunate
queen had been laid to rest. Catherine of Aragon was
the earliest, as Mary was the latest, crowned victim in the
strife between England and Rome; but even in the battle
of the creeds spotless purity of life counts for little against
feminine beauty, and Catherine has found no such band of
defenders as the noble army of writers who have risen to
champion the doubtful character of the Scottish queen.
Charles V. believed that his aunt had been poisoned, but no
imperial hosts flew to avenge the crime. Mary was more
fortunate; the greatest fleet that the modern world had
seen sailed from the ports of Spain to exact retribution for
her death. Was Philip a truer son of the Church than
Charles? It may be, but Mary had also bequeathed him
her claim to the English throne, and he had thus a more
substantial motive than mere religious zeal for seeking the
conquest of England. Possibly, too, he was not so wise as
his father. Henry VIII. had hinted that a Spanish fleet
might come to English waters and might not perhaps
return. 'Surely,' writes Gascoigne of the Spaniards in
1576 in *The Spoil of Antwerp*, 'their boasting and bragging
of iniquity is over great to escape long unscourged'; and
again, 'I leave the scanning of their deeds unto God, who
will bridle their insolency when He thinketh good and convenient.' Twelve years later the hour struck, and the
Spanish Armada sailed. No Spaniard, except its com-

---

[1] This description (pp. 475-484) of Mary's funeral does not seem to have
been reprinted except in this *Garner*. For Robert Scarlett, see *Dict. Nat.
Biogr.* xl. 6. The fact that they were buried by the same sexton creates one
more curious link between Catherine of Aragon and Mary Queen of Scots.

mander, doubted of its success ; according to Deloney,[1] the expedition was even furnished with instruments of torture to be applied to the vanquished heretics. The Pope had blessed the crusaders, but ' God blew and they were scattered.' So ran the inscription on the medal struck to commemorate the victory, and so Englishmen loved to think. But the winds and the waves only help those who help themselves ; they buffet English ships as well as Spanish galleons ; in September 1588 they proved fatal to the one and not to the other because English arms had already beaten the Spaniards from off the English shores. But for that ten days' running fight up the English channel, the storm would have swept harmlessly over the Spanish Armada as it lay snug in Plymouth Sound, in Portsmouth Harbour, or under the lee of the Downs.

With the defeat of the Spanish Armada, the work of the Tudors was done. Elizabeth lingered a few more years on the stage, but she was losing touch with her people. No sooner was the peril from abroad averted than the voice of domestic discontent began to be heard in the land. Parliament was girding itself for its hundred years' war with the Crown. England had proved in the sixteenth century that no foreign power should have dominion or jurisdiction over her ; she was to prove in the seventeenth that she would govern herself in the way that pleased her best, caring no more for tyrannous kings than she had done for absolute Popes.

A. F. POLLARD.

[1] These three ballads are only accessible in the original broadsides, in a limited edition of thirty copies issued by Halliwell-Phillipps in 1860, and in this *Garner*.

⸿The manner of the triumph at Calais and Boulogne.

The second printing. With more additions as it was done indeed.

Cum privilegio Regali.

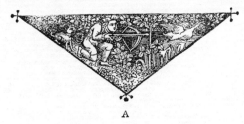

A

❧ The names of the Noblemen of France.

❧ First, the French King.

The King of NAVARRE.

The Dauphin, FRANCIS, Duke de BRETAGNE.

HENRY, Duke D'ORLEANS.

CHARLES, Duke D'ANGOULEME.

CHARLES, Duke DE VENDÔME.

The Duke DE GUISE.

The Duke DE LONGUEVILLE.

The Cardinal DE BOURBON.

The Cardinal DE LORAINE.

The Legate, and Cardinal Chancellor of France, ANTONY DE PRAYT.

The Cardinal TOURNON.

The Cardinal GRAMOND.

The Marquis DE LORAINE DE PONT.

The Marquis DE ROCHELINE.

The two sons of the Duke DE VENDÔME.

The son of the Duke DE GUISE, Comte D'AUMALLE.

The Comte DE SAINT PAUL, FRANCOIS DE BOURBON.

The Comte DE NEVERS.

The Comte LOUIS DE NEVERS, Comte DANSEORE.

The Lord Marshal, Seigneur DE FLORAINE.

The Lord MIREPOIS, *Maréchal de la Foy*.

The Comte DE PORSEAN.

The Comte DE BRENE.

The Comte DE TONNORE.

The Comte DE SENSARE.

The Comte DE GRAND PRÉ.

The Comte D'APREMONT.

The Lord Great Master, ANNE DE MONTMERANCY.

The Lord Admiral, PHILIPPE CHABOT.

The Lord Grand Esquire, GALLIOT.

The Prince of MOLSE.

The Comte DE TANDE.

The Comte DE VILLARS.

The Comte D'ESTAMPES, JEAN DE LA BERRE.

The Comte DE CHAMBRE.

The Lord CANAMPLES.

The Lord BARBELVIEZ.

The Lord HUMMERES.

The Lord ROCHEPIOT.

The Lord of SAINT ANDREWS.

The Lord MONTIGUE.

The Lord PIENNES.

The Lord PONTREMY.

Monsieur DE LANGE.

Monsieur DE BELLAY.

The Archbishop of ROUEN.

The Archbishop of VIENNE.

The Bishop of LISIEUX.

The Bishop of LANGRES.

The Bishop of CHARTRES.

The Bishop of LIMOGES.

The Bishop of BEAUVAIS.

The Bishop of AUVERGNE.

The Bishop of MACON.

The Bishop of CASTRES.

The Bishop of PARIS.

The Bishop of ANGOULÊME.

❧ And as concerning the nobles and royal states of this realm; it needeth not to be express by name.

 WILL certify you of our news in the parts of Calais.

First, the 11th day of October [1532], which was Friday; in the morning at five o'clock, the King's Grace took his ship called the *Swallow* : and so came to Calais by ten o'clock.

And there he was received with procession, and with the Mayor and the Lord Deputy, and all the spears [*knights*] and the soldiers in array; with a great peal of guns: and lay in Calais till the Sunday se'nnight after [the 20th of October].

And on the 16th day of October, my lord of NORFOLK, accompanied with my lord of DERBY and a great number of gentlemen besides, met with the Great Master of France six miles from Calais at the "English Pale:" the said Great Master having two great lords in his company of their order, and a hundred gentlemen attending upon them. And there my lord of NORFOLK and the Great Master devised the place where the two kings should meet : which was at Sandingfield. And that so done; they went both to Calais with their companies.

And the said Great Master, with divers other strangers, dined that day with the King: and after dinner, my lord of NORFOLK brought them forth of their way a mile or two; and so departed for that time.

And on the Monday, the 21st day of October, the King of England took his way to meet with the French King at the place before appointed, with seven score [gentlemen] all in velvet coats afore him, lords and knights; and forty of his guard, and others to the number, as we think, of six hundred horse, and as well horsed as ever was seen.

And the King, our Master, met with the French King at Sandingfield, within the English Pale three miles. There the French King tarried for our Master the space of an hour or two : the French King being accompained with the King of NAVARRE, the Cardinal DE LORRAINE, the Duke DE VENDÔME; with divers others noblemen well and richly appointed, being of like number as our King was of, that is to say, six hundred persons.

There was the lovingest meeting that ever was seen; for the one embraced the other five or six times on horseback; and so did the lords on either party each to other : and so did ride hand in hand with great love the space of a mile.

At the meeting of these two noble Kings, there were [*English*] sakers and sakrets cast off: and at divers flights [*of shot*], two kites were beaten down, which were soaring in the air, with such like pastime, which greatly pleased all the nobles of both parties. And then they did light off their horses, and drank each to other. The French King drank first to our King : and when they had drunk they embraced each other again with great love ; and so rode towards Boulogne, our King on the right hand.

And when they came within a mile of Boulogne, there met with the Kings, the Dauphin, being accompanied with his two brethren the Duke D'ORLEANS and the Duke D'ANGOU-LÊME; very goodly children : and attending on them, four Cardinals ; with a thousand horse, very well beseen.

And when they came near the town, the French King caused our Master to tarry, while the gunshot was shot; which was heard twenty English miles from Boulogne : and so entered the town.

Where stood the Captain with the soldiers in good order. And above them stood a hundred Switzers of the French King's Guard, in their doublets and their hose of yellow velvet cut, goodly persons ; and above them, stood two hundred more of the French King's Guard, Scots and Frenchmen, in coats of yellow, blue, and crimson velvet, bearing halberts in their hands ; and above them stood two hundred gentlemen, being in their gowns well and richly beseen, every man having a battle axe in his hand, and their captains standing by them.

And so they tarried in Boulogne ; Monday, Tuesday, Wednesday, and Thursday all day.

The Tuesday, being the second day of this their being there, the French King gave our King rich apparel wrought with needle work purled [*fringed*] with gold ; in the which like apparel both the Kings went to our Lady's Church at Boulogne. At that time, our King obtained release and liberty from the French King, for all prisoners at that time prisoners in Boulogne. And in like wise, did the French King in Calais of our King and Master at his being there ;

and obtained grace for all banished men that would make
suit for their pardon. And to esteem the rich traverses
[*low curtains*] that were in our Lady's Church in Boulogne, and
in our Lady's Church in Calais likewise, for both the Kings;
the rich ordinances and provision for the same: it is too
much to write!

And as for the great cheer that was there, no man can
express it. For the King's Grace was there entertained all
at the French King's cost and charges. And every day
noblemen of France desired our nobles and gentlemen home
to their lodgings: where they found their houses richly
hanged [with tapestry], great cupboards of plate, sumptuous
fare, with singing and playing of all kinds of music. And
also there was sent unto our lodgings great fare with all
manner of wines for our servants; and our horses' meat was
paid for: and all at their charges.

And every day the French king had at dinner and supper
with him certain noblemen of England: and the King's
Grace had in like wise certain of their nobles at dinner and
supper; during the time of their being at Boulogne. And
this continued with as great cheer and familiarity as might be.
And as concerning ladies and gentlewomen, there were none.

And on the Friday following, the Kings came towards
Calais. And the Dauphin, with the Cardinals and all their
gentlemen, brought the Kings unto the place where they
first met them; and then departed. The French King had
great carriage [*baggage*]; for there came more than three
hundred mules laden with stuff.

And so coming towards Calais, the Duke of RICHMOND,
accompanied with Bishops, and many other noblemen that
were not with the King at Boulogne; and all the King's
Guard, which were with all others marvellously well horsed
and trimmed; they stood in a place appointed, in array and
good order in the way, two miles out of Calais where the
French King should come: who saluted the French King
with great honour, in like manner as the King our Master
was saluted at Boulogne, with amicable and goodly salutations
as ever were seen. They were saluted with great melody;
what with guns, and all other instruments [!]: and the order
of the town, it was a heavenly sight for the time!

First at Newnam Bridge, 400 shot; at the Block House,

30 shot; at Risbank Tower [*in Calais harbour*] 300 shot; within the town of Calais 2,000 shot, great and small; besides the ships. It was all numbered at 3,000 shot. And at Boulogne, by estimation, it passed not 200 shot; but they were great pieces [*cannon*].

Also for the order of the town there was set all serving men on the one side, in tawny coats; and soldiers on the other side, all in coats of red and blue, with halberts in their hands.

And so the Kings came riding in the midst: and so the French King went to Staple Hall; which is a princely house.

And upon Saturday, both the Kings rode to our Lady's Church to mass; and in the afternoon both their councils sat together.

And upon Sunday, both the Kings heard mass in their lodgings. And at afternoon, the King of England rode to Staple Hall to the French King; and there was both bear-baiting and bull-baiting till night.

And at night, the French King supped with our King, and there was great banqueting.

After supper, there came in a Masque, my Lady Marquess of PEMBROKE [*i.e.*, ANNE BOLEYN], my Lady MARY [BOLEYN], my lady DERBY, my lady FITZ-WALTER, my lady ROCHFORD, my lady L'ISLE, and my lady WALLOP, gorgeously apparelled, with visors on their faces: and so came and took the French King, and other lords of France, by the hand; and danced a dance or two.

After that, the King took off their visors; and then they danced with gentlemen of France an hour after: and then they departed to their lodgings.

As for the apparel of the French lords, my tongue cannot express it, and especially the French King's apparel passeth my pen to write; for he had a doublet set over all with stones and rich diamonds, which was valued by discreet men at a £100,000 [= £800,000 *in the present day*]. They far passed our lords and knights in apparel and richesse.

They had great cheer in Calais, and loving also; and all at our King's costs and charges.

Also the same day that the Kings came from Boulogne, the French King made the Duke of NORFOLK, and the Duke of SUFFOLK, of the Order of Saint Michael. And upon Monday, which was the 29th day of October, at Calais; our King made the Great Maister of France and the Admiral of France, Knights of the Garter.

And that day, there was a great wrestling between Englishmen and Frenchmen, before both the Kings. The French King had none but priests that wrestled, which were big men and strong (they were brethren); but they had most falls.

As concerning the abundance and liberal multitude of gifts that were so lovingly and cordially given on both parties (to the great honour of both the Kings) my pen or capacity cannot express it : as well among the great lords as with the lowest yeoman that bare any office in either King's house; and specially the King's gifts, on both parties, always rewarded the one like unto the other.

And all other gifts were nothing but rich plate, and gold coin—silver was of no estimation—besides raiments, horses, geldings, falcons, bears, dogs for the game : with many other, which were too much to write.

And upon the 29th day of October, the French King departed from Calais to Paris ward : and our King brought him as far as Morgyson, which is from Calais, seven miles; and so came to Calais again.

And he purposeth, GOD willing, to be at Canterbury the 8th day of November, and so home. Whom GOD, of His goodness, ever preserve! and send good passage, and safe again into England. Amen.

❡ God save the King.

❡ Imprinted by Wynkyn de Worde, under the grace and privilege of our most royal and redoubted Prince, King Henry the viijth, for John Gough dwelling at Paul's gate in Cheap
[i.e. Cheapside].

Cum privilegio.

❡ The noble triumphant Coronation of Queen Anne, Wife unto the most noble King Henry the viiith.

IRST, the 29th day of May [1533], being Thursday; all the worshipful Crafts and Occupations in their best array, goodly beseen, took their barges which were splayed [*displayed*] with goodly banners fresh and new, with the cognizance and arms of their faculty; to the number of fifty great barges, comely beseen, and every barge had minstrels making great and sweet harmony.

Also there was the Bachelors' Barge comely beseen, decked with innumerable banners and all about hanged with rich cloth of gold; and foists [*swift boats*] waiting upon her, decked [*adorned*] with a great shot of ordnance: which descended the river afore all the barges; the Batchelors' Barge foremost. And so following in good order, every Craft [*i.e., City Company*] in their degree and order, till they came to Greenwich, and there tarried; abiding the Queen's Grace: which was a wonderful and goodly sight to behold.

Then at three o'clock, the Queen's Grace came to her barge: and incontinent [*immediately*] all the citizens with that goodly company set forth towards London in good array, as is before said. And to write what number of gun shots—what with chambers, and great pieces of ordnance—were shot off as she passed by, in divers places, and especially at Ratcliff and at Limehouse out of certain ships; it passeth my memory to write or to tell the number of them! And so the Queen's Grace, being in her rich barge among her nobles, the citizens accompanied her to London, unto the Tower wharf.

Also ere she came near the Tower, there were shot off innumerable pieces of ordnance, as ever there was there by any men's remembrances : where the King received her Grace with a noble loving countenance; and so gave thanks and praise to all the citizens for all their great kindness and loving labour and pains taken in that behalf, to the great joy and comfort of all the citizens.

Also to behold the wonderful number of people that ever was seen, that stood on the shore on both sides of the river; it was never seen, in one sight, out of the City of London. What in goodly lodgings and houses that be on the river side between Greenwich and London; it passeth all men's judgements to esteem the infinite number of them : wherein her Grace with all her ladies rejoiced much.

❧ Knights made at Greenwich the Sunday before Whit-sunday.

❧ And the Sunday before this Triumph, being the 25th day of May [1533]; the King made at his Manor of Greenwich all these knights.

Sir CHRISTOPHER DANBY.	Sir THOMAS BUTTELLER.
Sir CHRISTOPHER HYLARD.	Sir WILLIAM WALGRAVE.
Sir BRIAN HASTINGS.	Sir WILLIAM FIELDING.
Sir THOMAS METHEM.	

❧ The Friday, were made Knights of the Bath, nineteen ; whose names followeth.

❧ Also on Friday the 30th day of May, the king created and made in the Tower of London, nineteen noblemen, Knights of the Bath : whose names follow.

The Lord Marquis DORSET.
The Earl of DERBY.
The Lord CLIFFORD, son and heir to the Earl of CUMBER-LAND.
The Lord FITZ-WALTER, son and heir to the Earl of SUSSEX.
The Lord HASTINGS, son and heir to the Earl of HUNTINGDON.
The Lord BERKELEY.

The Lord MONTEAGLE.
The Lord VAUX.
Sir HENRY PARKER, son and heir to the Lord MORLEY.
Sir WILLIAM WINDSOR, son and heir to the LORD WINDSOR.
Sir JOHN MORDAUNT, son and heir to the Lord MORDAUNT.
Sir FRANCIS WESTON.
Sir THOMAS ARUNDELL.
Sir JOHN HUDLESTON.
Sir THOMAS PONINGS.
Sir HENRY SAVILLE.
Sir GEORGE FITZWILLIAM, of Lincolnshire.
Sir JOHN TYNDALL.
Sir THOMAS JERMEY.

❧ Also Saturday, the last day of May, the King made those Knights of the sword, in the Tower of London, whose names follow :

Sir WILLIAM DRURY.
Sir JOHN GERNINGHAM.
Sir THOMAS RUSH.
Sir RANDOLPH BUERTON.
Sir GEORGE CALVERLEY.
Sir EDWARD FYTTON.
Sir GEORGE CONYERS.
Sir ROBERT NEDHAM.
Sir JOHN CHAWORTH.
Sir GEORGE GRESLEY.
Sir JOHN CONSTABLE.
Sir THOMAS UMPTON.
Sir JOHN HORSLEY.
Sir RICHARD LYGON.
Sir John SAINT CLERE.
Sir EDWARD MAIDISON.
Sir HENRY FERYNGTON.
Sir MARMADUKE TUNSTALL.
Sir THOMAS HALSALL.
Sir ROBERT KIRKHAM.
Sir ANTHONY WINDSOR.
Sir WALTER HUBBERT.
Sir JOHN WILLOUGHBY.
Sir THOMAS KITSON.
Sir THOMAS MYSSEDEN.
Sir THOMAS FOULEHURST.
Sir HENRY DELVES.
Sir PETER WARBURTON.
Sir RICHARD BULKELEY.
Sir THOMAS LAKING.
Sir WALTER SMITH.
Sir HENRY EVERYNGHAM.
Sir WILLIAM UVEDALL.
Sir THOMAS MASSINGBERD.
Sir WILLIAM SANDON.
Sir JAMES BASKERVYLLE.
Sir EDMOND TRAFFORD.
Sir ARTHUR EYRE.
Sir HENRY SUTTON.
Sir JOHN NORIES.
Sir WILLIAM MALORY.
Sir JOHN HARCOURT.
Sir JOHN TYRELL.
Sir WILLIAM BROWNE.
Sir NICHOLAS STURLEY.
Sir RANDOLPH MANERING.

¶ Also the Sunday after Whit-sunday, being Trinity Sunday, and the 8th day of June; were made at Greenwich, these Knights following.

Sir CHRISTOPHER CORWEN.
Sir GEOFREY MYDLETON.
Sir HUGH TREVYNEON.
Sir GEORGE WEST.
Sir CLEMENT HERLESTON.
Sir HUMPHREY FERIES.

Sir JOHN DAWN.
Sir RICHARD HAUGHTON.
Sir THOMAS LANGTON.
Sir EDWARD BOWTON.
Sir HENRY CAPEL.

¶ Also all the pavements of the City, from Charing Cross to the Tower, were covered over and cast with gravel.

And the same Saturday, being Whitsun Eve, the Mayor with all the Aldermen and the Crafts of the City prepared array in a good order to stand and receive her Grace; and with rails for every Craft to stand and lean, from the press of people.

The Mayor met the Queen's Grace at her coming forth of the Tower. All his brethren and aldermen standing in Cheap [*Cheapside*].

And upon the same Saturday, the Queen came forth from the Tower towards Westminster, in goodly array; as hereafter followeth.

She passed the streets first, with certain strangers, their horses trapped with blue silk; and themselves in blue velvet with white feathers, accompanied two and two. Likewise Squires, Knights, Barons, and Baronets, Knights of the Bath clothed in violet garments, edged with ermine like judges. Then following: the Judges of the law, and Abbots. All these estates were to the number of two hundred couple and more: two and two accompanied.

And then followed Bishops, two and two; and the Archbishops of York and Canterbury; the Ambassadors of France and Venice; the Lord Mayor with a mace: Master Garter the King of Heralds, and the King's coat armour upon him, with the Officers of Arms, appointing every estate in their degree.

Then followed two ancient Knights with old fashioned hats, powdered on their heads, disguised, who did represent the Dukes of NORMANDY and of GUIENNE, after an old custom: the Lord Constable of England for the time, being the

Duke of SUFFOLK; the Lord WILLIAM HOWARD, the Deputy for the time to the Lord Marshal, the Duke of NORFOLK.

Then followed the Queen's Grace in her litter, costly and richly beseen, with a rich canopy over her: which was borne by the Lords of the Five Ports [*i.e., Barons of the Cinque Ports*]. After her, following the Master of her Horse with a spare white palfrey richly appointed, and led in his hand.

Then followed her noble Ladies of Estate richly clothed in crimson powdered with ermines; to the number of twelve.

Then the Master of the Guard, with the guard on both sides of the streets in good array; and all the Constables well beseen in velvet and damask coats with white staves in their hand; setting every man in array and order in the streets until she came to Westminster.

Then followed four rich chariots with Ladies of Honour. After them followed thirty Ladies and gentlewomen richly garnished: and so the serving men after them.

And as she was departed from the Tower a marvellously great shot of guns [*cannonade*] was there fired, and shot off.

So this most noble company passed, till her Grace came to Fenchurch; where was a pageant fair and seemly, with certain children who saluted her Grace with great honour and praise, after a goodly fashion: and so passed forth to Gracechurch. Where was a rightly costly pageant of APOLLO, with the Nine Muses among the mountains, sitting on the mount of Parnassus: and every of them having their instruments and apparel according to the description of poets, and namely [*particularly*] of VIRGIL; with many goodly verses to her great praise and honour.

And so she passed forth through Gracious [*Gracechurch*] Street unto Leaden Hall where was built a sumptuous and costly pageant in manner of a castle wherein was fashioned a heavenly roof and under it upon a green was a root or a stock, whereout sprang a multitude of white and red roses curiously wrought. So from the heavenly roof descended a white falcon, and lighted upon the said stock and root: and incontinent [*immediately*] descended an angel with goodly harmony, having a close crown between his hands, and set it on the falcon's head. And on the said floor sat Saint ANNE in the highest place. And on that one side, her progeny with Scripture, that is to wit, the three MARIES with their issue,

that is to understand, MARY, the mother of Christ, MARY
SALOME the mother [*or rather the wife*] of ZEBEDEE with the
two children of them. Also MARY CLEOPHAS with her
husband ALPHEUS, with their four children on the other side.
With other poetical verses [*see p.* 20] said and sung ; and with
a ballad in English [*see p.* 22] to her great praise and honour,
and to all her progeny also.

And so she passed forth from thence, through Cornhill ;
and at the Conduit was a sumptuous pageant of the Three
Graces. At the coming of the Queen's Grace a poet declared
the nature of all those three Ladies ; and gave high praises
unto the Queen. And after this preamble finished, each
Lady in particular spake great honour and high praise of the
Queen's Grace.

And so she passed forth with all her nobles till she came in
Cheap [*Cheapside*]. And at the Great Conduit was made a
costly fountain, where out ran white wine, claret, and red
wine, in great plenty, all that afternoon. And there was
great melody, with speeches.

And so passed forth through Cheap to the Standard, which
was costly and sumptuously garnished with gold and azure,
with [coats of] arms and stories [? *galleries*] : where was
great harmony and melody.

And so passed she forth by the Cross in Cheap, which was
new garnished : and so through Cheap towards the lesser Conduit. And in the midway between, the Recorder of London
received her before the Aldermen ; with great reverence and
honour saluting her Grace, with a loving and humble proposi-
tion, presenting her Grace with a rich and costly purse of gold,
and in it a thousand marks [= £666 *or about* £5,000 *in present
value*] in gold coin; given unto her as a free gift of honour.
To whom she gave great thanks both with heart and mind.

And so her Grace passed a little further, and at the lesser
Conduit was a costly and rich pageant ; whereat was goodly
harmony of music and other minstrels, with singing. And
within that pageant were five costly seats, wherein were
set these five personages, that is to wit, JUNO, PALLAS,
MERCURY, VENUS, and PARIS ; who having a ball of gold
presented it to her Grace with certain verses of great honour
[*see p.* 25]: and children singing a ballad [*see p.* 27] to her
Grace, and praise to all her ladies.

And so passed forth to Paul's Gate, where was a proper and sumptuous pageant, that is to wit, there sat three fair ladies, virgins, costly arrayed, with a fair round throne over their heads; where about was written, *Regina ANNA prospere! procede! et regna!* that is in English, "Queen ANNE prosper! proceed! and reign!" The lady that sat in the midst having a table of gold in her hand, written with letters of azure, *Veni amica coronaberis,* "Come my love! thou shalt be crowned!" And two angels having a close crown of gold between their hands. And the lady on the right hand had a table of silver, whereon was written, *DOMINE! dirige gressos meos!* "LORD GOD! direct my ways!" The other on the left hand had in another table of silver written, this *Confide in DOMINO!* "Trust in GOD!" And under their feet was a long roll wherein was written this, *Regina ANNA novum regis de sanguine natum, cum paries populis aurea secula tuis.* "Queen ANNE when thou shalt bear a new son of the King's blood; there shall be a golden world unto thy people!" And so the ladies cast over her head a multitude of wafers with rose leaves; and about the wafers were written with letters of gold, this posy. [*Not given by the Writer.*]

And so her Grace passed forth into Paul's Churchyard. And at the East end of the Church against the [*i.e., Saint Paul's*] School was a great scaffold, whereon stood the number of two hundred children, well beseen: who received her with poet's verses to her noble honour. When they had finished, she said "Amen," with a joyful smiling countenance.

And so passed forth through the long Churchyard; and so to Lud Gate, which was costly and sumptuously garnished with gold, colours, and azure; with sweet harmony of ballads to her great praise and honour; with divers sweet instruments.

And thus her Grace came through the City with great honour and royalty, and passed through Fleet Street till she came to the Standard and Conduit where was made a fair tower with four turrets with vanes. Therewithin was a great plenty of sweet instruments, with children singing. The Standard, which was of mason work, costly made with images and angels, costly gilt with gold and azure, with other colours, and divers sorts of [coats of] arms costly set out, shall there continue and remain: and within the Standard a vice with a

B   1 chime. And there ran out of certain small pipes great plenty of wine all that afternoon.

And so her Grace passed through the city to Temple Bar; and so to Charing Cross: and so through Westminster into Westminster Hall, that was well and richly hanged with cloth of Arras [*tapestry*], with a marvellous rich cupboard of plate: and there was a void [*collation*] of spice-plates and wine.

And that done, the Queen's Grace withdrew her into the White Hall for that night; and so to York Place by water.

¶ The Sunday, in the morning, at eight o'clock, the Queen's Grace with noble ladies in their robes of estate, assembled with all the nobles apparelled in Parliament robes, as Dukes, Earls, Archbishops and Bishops, with Barons and the Barons of the Five Ports; with the Mayor of the City and the Aldermen in their robes, as mantles of scarlet.

The Barons of the Five Ports bare a rich canopy of cloth of gold, with staves of gold, and four bells of silver and gilt. The Abbot of Westminster with his rygals [? *regalia*] came into the Hall *in pontificalibus*, with his monks in their best copes; the [members of] the King's chapel in their best copes: with the Bishops, richly adorned *in pontificalibus*.

And the blue 'ray cloth spread from the high dosses [? *dais*] of the King's Bench unto the high altar of Westminster.

And so every man proceeding to the Minster in the best order, every man after his degree appointed to his order and office as apperteineth; came unto the place appointed: where her Grace received her crown, with all the ceremonies thereof, as thereunto belongeth. And so all ceremonies done, with the solemn Mass: they departed home in their best orders; every man to the Hall of Westminster: where the Queen's Grace withdrew for a time into her chamber appointed.

And so after a certain space, Her Grace came into the Hall. Then ye should have seen every nobleman doing their service to them appointed, in the best manner that hath been seen in any such ceremony.

The Queen's Grace washed. The Archbishop of CANTERBURY [CRANMER] said grace. Then the nobles were set to the table. Therewith came the Queen's service with the service of the Archbishop. A certain space, three men with the Queen's Grace's service.

Before the said service, came the Duke of SUFFOLK (High Constable that day, and Steward of the feast) on horseback, and marvellously trapped in apparel with richesse. Then with him came the Lord WILLIAM HOWARD, as Deputy to the Duke of NORFOLK, in the room [*office*] of the Marshal of England, on horseback.

The Earl of ESSEX, Carver. The Earl of SUSSEX, Sewer. The Earl of DERBY, Cupbearer. The Earl of ARUNDEL, Butler. The Viscount LISLE, Panterer. The Lord BRAYE, Almoner.

These noble men did their service in such humble sort and fashion, as it was a wonder to see the pain and diligence of them : being such noble personages.

The service borne by Knights, which were to me too long to tell in order : the goodly service of kinds of meat ; with their devices from the highest unto the lowest : there have not been seen a more goodly nor more honourably done in no man's days.

❡ There were four tables in the great Hall, along the said hall.

The noblewomen, one table : sitting all on that one side.

The noblemen another table.

The Mayor of London another table, with his brethren.

The Barons of the [*Cinque*] Ports, with the Master of the Chancery, the fourth table.

And thus all things nobly and triumphantly done at her Coronation ; her Grace returned to White Hall, with great joy and solemnity.

And on the morrow, there were great justs at the tilt done by eighteen Lords and Knights, where were broken many spears valiantly ; and some of their horses would not come at their pleasure, near unto the tilt ; which was displeasure to some that there did run.

❡ Thus endeth this triumph.

Imprinted at London in Fleet Street by Wynkyn de Worde, for John Gough. Cum privilegio.

Nicholas Udall.

English Verses and Ditties at the Coronation Procession of Queen Anne Boleyn.

[*Royal MS.* 18. A. Lxiv.]

At the Pageant representing the Progeny of Saint ANNE, exhibited at Cornhill, besides Leadenhall.

Were pronounced unto the Queen's Grace, these words following.

By a Child.

Ost excellent Queen, and bounteous Lady!
Here now to see your gracious Goodness,
With such honour entering this City;
What joy we take, what hearty gladness,
No pen may write, nor any tongue express!
For of you, depend the sure felicity
And hope, both of us and our posterity.

For like as from this devout Saint ANNE
Issuèd this holy generation,
First CHRIST, to redeem the soul of man;
Then JAMES th'apostle, and th'evangelist JOHN;
With these others, which in such fashion
By teaching and good life, our faith confirmed,
That from that time yet to, it hath not failed:

Right so, dear Lady! our Queen most excellent!
Highly endued with all gifts of grace,
As by your living is well apparent;
We, the Citizens, by you, in short space,

Hope such issue and descent to purchase ;
Whereby the same faith shall be defended,
And this City from all dangers preserved.

Which time that we may right shortly see,
To our great comfort, joy and solace ;
Grant the most high and blessed Trinity !
Most humbly beseeching your noble Grace,
Our rude simpleness showed in this place
To pardon ; and, the brief time considering,
To esteem our good minds, and not the thing.

This spoken, opened a cloud, and let down a White
Falcon, in the descending of which was pronounced, as
followeth :

BY ANOTHER CHILD.

EHOLD and see the Falcon White !
How she beginneth her wings to spread,
And for our comfort to take her flight.
　　But where will she cease, as you do read ?
　　A rare sight ! and yet to be joyed,
　　On the Rose ; chief flower that ever was,
　　This bird to 'light, that all birds doth pass !

Then out of the same cloud descended an Angel, and
crowned the same Falcon with a Crown Imperial : at which
doing, was pronounced as followeth :

BY ANOTHER CHILD.

ONOUR and grace be to our Queen ANNE !
For whose cause an Angel celestial
Descendeth, the Falcon as white as swan,
To crown with a Diadem Imperial !
　　In her honour rejoice we all.
　　For it cometh from GOD, and not of man.
　　Honour and grace be to our Queen ANNE !

Then, at the departing of the Queen's said Grace, was sung this ballad following.

HIS White Falcon,
Rare and geason,
    This bird shineth so bright;
Of all that are,
No bird compare
    May with this Falcon White.

The virtues all,
No man mortal,
    Of this bird can write.
No man earthly
Enough truly
    Can praise this Falcon White.

Who will express
Great gentleness
    To be in any wight;
He will not miss,
But call him this
    The gentle Falcon White.

This gentle bird
As white as curd
    Shineth both day and night;
Nor far ne near
Is any peer
    Unto this Falcon White.

Of body small,
Of power regal,
    She is, and sharp of sight;
Of courage hault
No manner fault
    Is in this Falcon White.

In chastity,
Excelleth she,
    Most like a virgin bright :
And worthy is
To live in bliss
    Always this Falcon White.

But now to take
And use her make
    Is time, as troth is plight ;
That she may bring
Fruit according
    For such a Falcon White.

And where by wrong,
She hath fleen long,
    Uncertain where to light ;
Herself repose
Upon the Rose,
    Now may this Falcon White.

Whereon to rest,
And build her nest ;
    GOD grant her, most of might !
That England may
Rejoice alway
    In this same Falcon White.

*At the Conduit in Cornhill was exhibited a Pageant
of the Three Graces* [see p. 16.]

In which a Child, apparelled like a Poet, pronounced
unto the Queen's Grace these verses:

QUEEN ANNE, behold your servants, the Three
    Graces!
Giving unto your Grace faithful assistance.
With their most goodly amiable faces,
They attend with their continual presence,
Where your Grace goeth.   Absent in your absence.
While your Grace is here, they also here dwell
About the pleasant brinks of this live well.

Now here to be, they thought it their duty,
And presently to salu[t]e you, gracious Queen!
Entering this day into this noble City,
In such triumphant wise as hath not been seen:
Which thing, to your honour and joy may it been!
These Three Sisters thought it their rebuke and shame,
This day to be slack in honouring their Dame.

Then immediately followed the speeches of the Three
Graces, in this wise:

AGLAIA.   HEARTY GLADNESS.

QUEEN ANNE! whom to see, this City doth rejoice;
We three Graces, ladies of all pleasance,
Clasped hand in hand, as of one mind and voice,
    With our three gifts in all good assurance,
Shall never fail your Grace, to t'endue and enhance!
For I, HEARTY GLADNESS by my name called,
Shall your heart replenish with joy unfeigned.

THALEIA. STABLE HONOUR.

ND I, STABLE HONOUR, gracious Queen ANNE!
Joying in your joy, with this noble City,
In honour and dignity, all that I can,
    Shall you advance! as your Grace is most worthy.
You to assist, I am bound by my duty.
For your virtues being incomparable,
You cannot but live, aye, most honourable.

EUPHROSYNE. CONTINUAL SUCCESS.

ND FOR the great virtues, which I perceive
To be in your Grace, so high and excellent!
By me, CONTINUAL SUCCESS, ye receive
    Long fruition, with daily increasement
Of joy and honour, without diminishment.
Never to decay, but always to arise!
All men, women, and children pray the same wise.

*At the Little Conduit in Cheapside was exhibited the
Judgement of PARIS* [see p. 16],
  In manner and form following:

MERCURY. UPITER, this apple unto thee hath sent,
Commanding, in this cause, to give
    true judgement!

PARIS. JUPITER, a strange office hath given me,
    To judge which is fairest of these ladies three.

JUNO. All riches and kingdoms be at my behest,
    Give me the apple! and thou shalt have the best!

PALLAS.   Adjudge it to me! and for a kingdom,
             I shall give thee incomparable wisdom!

VENUS.   Prefer me! and I shall reward thee, PARIS!
             With the fairest lady that on the earth is.

PARIS.   I should break JUPITER's high commandment,
             If I should for mede or reward give judgement.

             Therefore, lady VENUS! before both these twain,
             Your beauty much exceeding; by my sentence,
             Shall win, and have this apple. Yet, to be plain!
             Here is the fourth Lady, now in presence,
             Most worthy to have it of due congruence,
             As peerless in riches, wit, and beauty;
             Which are but sundry qualities in you three.
             But for her worthiness, this apple of gold
             Is too simple a reward a thousand fold!

The conclusion of this Pageant pronounced by
A CHILD.

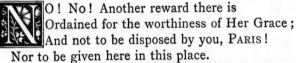

NO! No! Another reward there is
Ordained for the worthiness of Her Grace;
And not to be disposed by you, PARIS!
Nor to be given here in this place.
Queen ANNE! most excellent that ever was,
For you is ready a Crown Imperial!
To your joy, honour, and glory immortal.

GOD, that of His goodness all things doth us send,
Hath sent us your Grace, our hearts to make glad.
Wherefore with as much humbleness we intend
Your noble Grace to serve, as ever Queen had.
For nothing there is, that may now make us sad,
Having your noble Grace, our refuge and rest,
Provided by Him, that knoweth what is best.

All joy, wealth, and honour, with long space of life,
Be to your Grace ; with succession royal !
And He, that hath power of all prerogative,
The most blessed Trinity, GOD eternal,
Save our King HENRY in his estate royal !
Thus pray all the citizens, wife, child, and man,
GOD save King HENRY, and his Spouse Queen ANNE !

At the departing of the Queen's said Grace was sung
this ballad following :

UEEN ANNE so gent,
Of high descent.
ANNE excellent
        In nobleness !
Of ladies all,
You principal
Should win this ball
        Of worthiness !

Passing beauty
And chastity,
With high degree,
        And great riches ;
So coupled be
In unity,
That chief are ye
        In worthiness.

When JUPITER
His messenger
Sent down hither,
        He knew certes
That you, victrice
Of all ladies,
Should have the prize
        Of worthiness.

And wise PARIS
Made judge in this;
Anon, I wis,
    Most high Princess!
Well understood
Your virtues good,
Your noble blood
    And worthiness.

Your dignity
When he 'gan see,
The Ladies Three,
    Queen ANNE peerless!
He bade give place
Unto your Grace;
As meet it was
    In worthiness.

The golden ball,
Of price but small,
Have VENUS shall,
    The fair goddess!
Because it was
Too low and base
For your good Grace
    And worthiness!

JOHN FOX, the Martyrologist.

[*The Ecclesiastical History, containing the Acts and Monuments, &c.* and Ed., II., pp. 1355-6, 1570.]

How the Lord CROMWELL helped Archbishop CRANMER's Secretary.

[July 1539.]

ENTION was made before how King HENRY, in the 31st year [1539-1540] of his reign, caused the *Six Articles* [31. *Hen. VIII.*, c. 14. *An Act abolishing diversity in opinions*] to pass [in June 1539]; much against the mind, and contrary to the consent of the Archbishop of CANTERBURY, *The Archbishop CRANMER disputeth three days in Parliament against the Six Articles.*

THOMAS CRANMER: who had disputed three days against the same in the Parliament House, with great reasons and authorities. Which *Articles*, after they were granted and passed by the Parliament, the King, for the singular favour which he ever bare to CRANMER and reverence to his learning (being desirous to know what he had said and objected in the Parliament against these *Articles*; or what could be alleged by Learning against the same) required a Note of the Archbishop's doings, what he had said and opposed in the Parliament touching that matter. And this word was sent to him from the King by CROMWELL and other Lords of the Parliament, whom the King then sent to dine with him at Lambeth: somewhat to comfort again his grieved mind and troubled spirits: as hath been above recited at page 1,298.

[The passage referred to runs thus :

After the Parliament was finished and that matter concluded; the King (considering the constant zeal of the Archbishop in defence of his cause; and partly also weighing the many authorities and reasons whereby he had substantially confirmed the same) sent [in July 1539] the Lord CROMWELL (which within a few days after [*or rather on* 10*th June* 1540] was apprehended), the two Dukes of NORFOLK and SUFFOLK, and all the Lords of the Parliament, to dine with him at Lambeth: where they signified to him, That it was the King's pleasure that they all should, in His Highness's behalf, cherish comfort and animate him as one that, for his travail in that Parliament, had declared himself both greatly learned, and also a man discreet and wise: and therefore they willed him not to be discouraged in anything that was passed in that Parliament contrary to his allegations.

He most humbly thanked, first the King's Highness of his singular good affection towards him; and them, for all their pains: adding moreover that he so hoped in GOD that hereafter his allegations and authorities should take place, to the glory of GOD and commodity of the realm.]

Whereupon, when this dinner was finished [in July 1539], the next day after the Archbishop (collecting both his arguments, authorities of Scripture, and Doctors [*i.e. the Fathers of the Church*] together) caused his Secretary to write a fair Book thereof for the King, after this order :

The name of this Secretary was Master RALPH MORICE, being yet alive [*i.e., in* 1570].

First, the Scriptures were alleged.

Then, the Doctors.

Thirdly, followed the arguments deduced from those Authorities.

This book was written in his Secretary's Chamber [at Lambeth Palace]; where, in a by-chamber, lay the Archbishop's Almoner.

When this Book was fair written, and while the Secretary was gone to deliver the same unto the Archbishop his Master, who was, as it chanced, ridden to Croydon; returning back to his chamber, he found his door shut, and the key carried away to London by the Almoner.

At this season also [it] chanced the father of the said
Secretary to come to the city; by whose occasion it
so fell out, that he [RALPH MORICE] must needs go to
London. The Book he could not lay in his chamber, neither
durst he commit it to any other person to keep; being
straitly charged, in any condition, by the Archbishop his
master, to be circumspect thereof: so he determined to go
to his father, and to keep the Book about him.

And so, thrusting the Book under his girdle, he went
over [the Thames] unto Westminster Bridge, with a
sculler; where he entered into a wherry that went to
London: wherein were four of the Guard, who meant to
land at Paul's Wharf; and to pass by the King's Highness
who was then in his barge, with a great number of barges
and boats about him, then baiting of bears in the water,
over against the Bank [Side in Southwark].

The aforesaid Yeomen of the Guard, when they came
against the King's barge, they durst not pass by towards
Paul's Wharf, lest they should be espied: and therefore
entreated the Secretary to go with them to the Bearbaiting;
and they would find the means, being of the Guard, to
make room and to see all the pastime.

The Secretary perceiving no other remedy, assented
thereto.

When the wherry came nigh the multitude of boats;
they with poleaxes got the wherry so far that, being
encompassed with many other wherries and boats, there
was no refuge if the bear should break loose and come upon
them: as, in very deed, within one *Paternoster* while,
the bear brake loose; and came into the boat where the
Yeomen of the Guard were, and the said Secretary.

The Guard forsook the wherry, and went into   Tall Yeomen,
another barge; one or two of them leaping short,   but ill Keepers.
and so fell into the water.

The bear and the dogs so shaked the wherry wherein
the Secretary was, that the boat being full of water sank
to the ground; and being also, as it chanced, an ebbing
tide, he sat there in the end of the wherry up to   A Bearbaiting
the middle in water. To whom came the bear   upon [the]
                                                Thames before
and all the dogs. The bear, seeking as it were   the King.
aid and succour of him, came back with his hinder parts

upon him ; and so, rushing upon him, the Book was loosed from the Secretary's girdle, and so fell into the Thames out of his reach.

The Book of Dr CRANMER against the Six Articles lost in the Thames.

The flying of the people, after that the bear was loose, from one boat to another, was so cumbrous that divers persons were thrown into the Thames : the King commanding certain men, that could swim, to strip themselves naked ; and to help to save them that were in danger.

This pastime so displeased the King, that he bade, " Away, away with the bear ! and let us go all hence ! "

The Secretary, perceiving his Book to fleet away in the Thames, called to the Bearward to take up the Book.

When the Bearward had the Book in his custody, being an arrant Papist, far from the religion of his Mistress (for he was the Lady ELIZABETH'S Bearward, now the Queen's Majesty), ere that the Secretary could come to land, he had delivered the Book to a Priest of his own affinity in religion standing on the bank : who, reading in the Book, and perceiving that it was a manifest Refutation of the *Six Articles,* made much ado ; and told the Bearward that whosoever claimed the Book, should surely be hanged.

This Bearward was Princess ELIZABETH'S servant.

Dr CRANMER's Book against the Six Articles delivered to a Popish Priest.

Anon, the Secretary came to the Bearward for his Book.

" What," quoth the Bearward, " dare you challenge this Book ? Whose servant be you ? "

" I am servant to one of the [Privy] Council," said the Secretary, " and my Lord of CANTERBURY is my master."

" Yea, marry," quoth the Bearward, " I thought as much. You be like, I trust, to be both hanged for this Book."

" Well," said he " it is not so evil as you take it : and, I warrant you, my Lord will avouch the book to the King's Majesty. But I pray you let me have my Book, and I will give you a crown [6s., *or in present value about £2*] to drink."

" If you will give me 500 crowns, you shall not have it," quoth the Bearward.

With that the Secretary departed from him : and, understanding the malicious forwardness of the Bearward, he learned that BLAGE the Grocer in Cheapside might do much with him. To whom the Secretary brake this matter,

requiring him to send for the Bearward to supper; and
he would pay for the whole charge thereof: and besides
that, rather than he would forego his Book after this
sort, the Bearward should have 20s. [*in present value about*
£6] to drink.

The supper was prepared. The Bearward was sent for,
and came. After supper, the matter was intreated; and 20s.
offered for the Book.

But do what could be done; neither friendship, acquaintance, nor yet reward of money, could obtain the Book
out of his hands: but that the same should be delivered
unto some of the [Privy] Council, that would not so slightly
look on so weighty a matter as to have it redeemed for
a supper, or a piece of money. The honest man, Master
BLAGE, with many good reasons would have persuaded him
not to be stiff in his own conceit: declaring that in the end
he should nothing at all prevail of his purpose, but be
laughed to scorn; getting neither penny nor praise for
his travail. He, hearing that, rushed suddenly out of
the doors from his friend Master BLAGE; without any
manner of thanksgiving for his supper: more like a
Bearward than like an honest man.

When the Secretary saw the matter so extremely to
be used against him; he then thought it expedient to
fall from any farther practising of entreaty with the Bearward, as with him that seemed rather to be a bear himself
than master of the beast: determining the next morning to
make the Lord CROMWELL privy of the chance that
happened.

So, on the next day, as the Lord CROMWELL went to
the Court, the Secretary declared the whole matter unto
him; and how he had offered the Bearward 20s. for the
finding thereof.

"Where is the fellow?" quoth the Lord CROMWELL.

"I suppose," said the Secretary, "that he is now in
the Court, attending to deliver the book unto some of the
Council."

"Well," said the Lord CROMWELL, "it maketh no matter.
Go with me thither, and I shall get you your book
again.!"

When the Lord CROMWELL came into the Hall of the

The Bearward waiting to give CRANMER's Book to the Council. Court, there stood the Bearward with the Book in his hand ; waiting to have delivered the same unto Sir ANTHONY BROWNE or unto [STEPHEN GARDINER] the Bishop of WINCHESTER, as it was reported.

To whom the Lord CROMWELL said, "Come hither, fellow! What Book hast thou there in thy hand?" and The Lord CROMWELL getteth the Book from the Bearward. with that snatched the Book out of his hand : and looking in the Book, said, "I know this hand well enough. This is your hand," said he to the Secretary.

"But where hadst thou this Book?" quoth the Lord CROMWELL to the Bearward.

"This Gentleman lost it two days ago in the Thames," said the Bearward.

"Dost thou know whose servant he is?" said the Lord CROMWELL.

"He saith," quoth the Bearward, "that he is my Lord of CANTERBURY's servant."

"Why then didst thou not deliver to him the Book when he required it?" said the Lord CROMWELL. "Who made thee so bold as to detain or withhold any Book or writing from a Councillor's servant, especially being his Secretary? It is more meet for thee to meddle with thy bears, than with such writing : and were it not for thy Mistress's sake, I would set thee fast by the feet, to teach such malapert knaves to meddle with Councillors' matters. Had not money been well bestowed upon such a good fellow as this is, that knoweth not a Councillor's man from a cobbler's man!"

And with those words, the Lord CROMWELL went up into the King's Chamber of Presence, and the Archbishop's Secretary with him : where he found, in the Chamber, the Lord of CANTERBURY.

To whom he said, "My Lord, I have here found good The words of the Lord CROMWELL to the Archbishop CRANMER. stuff for you," showing to him the paper book that he had in his hand, "ready to bring both you, and this good fellow your man, to the halter : namely [*especially*] if the knave Bearward, now in the Hall, might have well compassed it."

At these words, the Archbishop smiled, and said, "He that lost the Book is like[ly] to have the worst bargain: for, besides that he was well washed in the Thames, he must write the Book fair again."

And, at these words, the Lord CROMWELL cast the Book unto the Secretary, saying, "I pray thee, MORICE, go in hand therewith, by and bye, with all expedition: for it must serve a turn."

"Surely, my Lord, it somewhat rejoiceth me," quoth the Lord CROMWELL, "that the varlet might have had of your man 20s. for the Book: and now I have discharged the matter with never a penny; and shaken him well up for his overmuch malapertness."

"I know the fellow well enough," quoth the Archbishop, "there is not a ranker Papist within this realm than he is; most unworthy to be a servant unto so noble a Princess."

And so, after humble thanks given to the Lord CROMWELL, the said MORICE departed with his Book: which, when he again had fair written it, was delivered to the King's Majesty by the said Lord CROMWELL, within four days after.

The late expedition in Scotland,

made by the King's
Highness' army, under the conduct of the Right Honourable the Earl of Hertford, the year of our LORD GOD

1544.

Londini.

Cum privilegio ad imprimendum solum.

The late Expedition in Scotland.

Sent to the Right Honourable Lord RUSSELL, Lord Privy Seal; from the King's army there: by a friend of his.

FTER long sojourning, my very good Lord! of the King's Majesty's army at Newcastle, for lack of commodious winds, which long hath been at North East and East North East, much to our grief; as your Lordship, I doubt not, knoweth: the same—as God would, who doth all things for the best— the first of May [1544], the 36th year of His Majesty's most prosperous reign, veered to the South and South South West so apt and propice [*propitious*] for our journey; being of every man so much desired, that there was no need to hasten them forwards. To be brief; such diligence was used that in two tides the whole fleet, being 200 sail at the least, was out of the haven of Tynemouth towards our enterprise.

The third day after, we arrived in the Firth of Forth, a notable river in Scotland; having the entry between two islands, called the Bass and the May. The same day, we landed divers of our boats at a town named Saint Mynettes, on the north side of the Frith, which we burnt; and brought from thence divers great boats, that served us afterwards to good purpose for our landing.

That night, the whole fleet came to an anchor, under the

island called Inchkeith, three miles from the haven of Leith. The place where we anchored hath, of long time, been called the English road: the Scots now take the same to be a prophesy of the thing which has now happened.

The next day, being the 4th day of May, the said army landed two miles by west of the town of Leith, at a place called Grantham Crag : every man being so prompt thereunto, that the whole army was landed in four hours. And, perceiving our landing to be so quiet, which we looked not for; having our guides ready, we put ourselves in good order of war marching forwards towards the town of Leith in three battles—whereof my Lord Admiral led the Vanguard, the Earl of SHREWSBURY the Arrieregard; and the Earl of HERTFORD being Lord Lieutenant, the Battle—having with us certain small pieces of artillery, which were drawn by force of men : which enterprise we thought necessary to be attempted first of all other, for the commodious lodging of our navy there, and the landing of our artillery and victail.

And in a valley, upon the right hand, near unto the said town, the Scots were assembled to the number of 5,000 or 6,000 horsemen, besides a good number of footmen ; to impeach [*prevent*] the passage of our said army: in which place, they had laid their artillery at two straits [*passes*] through which we must needs pass, if we minded to achieve our enterprise. And seeming, at the first, as though they would set upon the Vanguard : when they perceived our men so willing to encounter with them, namely, the Cardinal, who was there present, perceiving our devotion to see his holiness to be such as we were ready to wet our feet for that purpose, and to pass a ford which was between us and them ; after certain shot of artillery on both sides : they made a sudden retreat ; and leaving their artillery behind them, fled towards Edinburgh. The first man that fled was the holy Cardinal [BEATON] like a valiant champion ; and with him the Governor, the Earls of HUNTLEY, MURRAY and BOTHWELL, with divers other great men of the realm. At this passage, were two Englishmen hurt with the shot of their artillery ; and two Scottish men slain with our artillery.

The Vanguard having thus put back the Scots, and eight pieces of their artillery brought away by our hackbutters [*harquebussiers*], who in this enterprise did very manfully employ themselves; we marched directly towards the town of Leith; which before we could come to, we must of force [*necessity*] pass another passage, which also was defended a while with certain ensigns [*companies*] of footmen and certain pieces of artillery; who being sharply assailed, having three of the gunners slain with our archers, were fain to give place; leaving also their ordnance behind them, with which ordnance they slew only one of our men and hurt another.

And in this brunt, the victory being earnestly followed; the town of Leith was entered perforce and won with the loss only of two men of ours and hurt of three: where the Scots had cast great trenches and ditches purposely to have defended it. The same night, the army encamped in the said town of Leith; and by reason of the said ditches and trenches, we made there a strong camp.

The morrow, being the 5th of May, we caused our ships ladened with our great artillery and victuals to be brought into the haven; where we discharged the same at our pleasure. In the said haven, we found many goodly ships, specially two of notable fairness: the one called the *Salamander* given by the French king at the marriage of his daughter into Scotland; the other called the *Unicorn*, made by the late Scottish king [JAMES V.] The town of Leith was found more full of riches than we thought to have found any Scottish town to have been.

The next day, the 6th, the army went towards Edinburgh, leaving the Lord STURTON in Leith with 1,500 men, for the defence of the same. And the army being come near to Edinburgh; the Provost accompanied with one or two burgesses and two or three Officers at Arms, desired to speak with the King's Lieutenant; and—in the name of all the town —said, "that the keys of the town should be delivered unto his Lordship; conditionally, that they might go with bag and baggage, and the town to be saved from fire." Whereunto answer was made by the said Lord Lieutenant, "that whereas the Scots had so many ways fals[ifi]ed their faiths; and so manifestly had broken their promises, confirmed by oaths and seals, and certified by their whole parliament, as is evidently known unto all the world: he was sent thither by the King's Highness to take vengeance of their detestable falsehood, to declare and show the force of His Highness' sword to all such as should make any resistance unto His Grace's power sent thither for that purpose. And therefore being not sent to treat or capitulate with them, who had before time broken so many treaties : " he told them resolutely; " that unless they would yield up their town unto him frankly, without condition, and cause man, woman, and child to issue into the fields, submitting themselves to his will and pleasure; he would put them to the sword, and their town to the fire." The Provost answered, " that it were better for them to stand to their defence than to yield to that condition." This was rather a false practice of the Provost and the Heralds, thereby to espy the force and order of our camp, than for any zeal they had to yield their town; as it appeared afterwards. Whereupon commandment was given to the said Provost and Officers at Arms, upon their peril, to depart.

In the meantime, word was brought by a Herald of ours— whom the Lord Lieutenant had sent to summon the Castle —that the Earl BOTHWELL and the Lord HUME with the number of 2,000 horsemen were entered the town, and were determined to the defence thereof. Upon which knowledge, the Lord Lieutenant sent with diligence to the Vanward, that they should march towards the town. And Sir CHRISTOPHER MORICE, Lieutenant of the Ordnance, was commanded to approach the gate called the Cany gate [*Canongate*], with certain battery pieces : which gate lay so, that the ordnance must be brought up a broad street of the suburbs, directly against the said Cany gate ; which was the occasion of the loss of certain of our gunners. And before that any battery could be made by the said ordnance, divers of the captains of the Vanward—the better to comfort their soldiers— assailed the said gate with such courage, that they repulsed the Scottish gunners from the loupes [*embrasures*] of the same, and there slew and hurt sundry of their gunners, and by force drew one piece of artillery out of one of the said loupes.

Our archers and hackbutters shot so hotly to the battlements of the gate and wall, that no man durst show himself at the defence of the same : by reason whereof, our gunners had good leisure to bring a cannon hard to the gate, which, after three or four shots, made entry to our soldiers; who at their breaking in, slew 300 or 400 Scots of such as were found armed. In the meantime, the Earl BOTHWELL and the Lord HUME with their company, fled, and saved themselves by another way issuing out towards the Castle of the said town. The situation whereof is of such strength that it cannot be approached, but by one way; which is by the High Street of the town; and the strongest part of the same Castle lieth to beat the said street: which was the loss of divers of our men with the shot of the ordnance out of the said Castle, which did continually beat along the said High Street. And considering the strength of the said Castle, with the situation thereof; it was concluded not to lose any time, nor to waste and consume our munition about the siege thereof. Albeit the same was courageously and dangerously attempted; till one of our pieces, with shot out of the said Castle, was struck and dismounted.

And finally it was determined by the said Lord Lieutenant utterly to ruinate and destroy the said town with fire: which for that the night drew fast on, we omitted thoroughly to execute on that day; but setting fire in three or four parts of the town, we repaired for that night unto our camp.

And the next morning, very early, we began where we left off, and continued burning all that day and the two days next ensuing continually, so that neither within the walls nor in the suburbs was left any one house unburnt: besides the innumerable booty, spoil and pillage that our soldiers brought from thence; notwithstanding the abundance which was consumed with fire. Also we burnt the Abbey called Holy Rood House, and the Palace adjoining the same.

In the meantime, while we held the country thus occupied; there came unto us 4,000 of our light horsemen from the Borders, by the King's Majesty's appointment: who after their coming, did such exploits in riding and devastating the country that within seven miles every way of Edinburgh, they left neither pile, village, nor house standing unburnt, nor stacks of corn; besides great numbers of cattle, which they brought daily in to the army, and met also with much good stuff which the inhabitants of Edinburgh had for the safety of the same, conveyed out of the town.

In this mean season, Sir NICHOLAS POINTZ, by order of my Lord Lieutenant, passed the river, and won by force the town of Kinghorn; and burnt the same with certain other towns on that side.

After these exploits done at Edinburgh, and all the country thereabouts devastated; the King's said Lieutenant thinking the Scots not to be condignly punished for their falsehood used to the King's Majesty, determined not to return without doing them more] displeasure.   He therefore gave orders to the said Sir CHRISTOPHER MORICE for the reshipping of the great artillery; reserving only certain small pieces to keep the field : giving also commandment to every captain to receive victuals out of the said ships for their companies for six days.   And for the carriage of the same, caused one thousand of our worst horsemen to be set on foot; and the same horses divided equally to every captain of hundreds, for the better carriage of their victuals.   The men that rode upon the said horses being appointed to attend upon the said victuals.   Which was done.   Besides there were divers small carts, which we recovered [*captured*] in the country; the which with such cattle as we had there, did great service in drawing of our victuals, tents, and other necessaries.

These things being supplied, the 14th day of May, we brake down the pier of the haven of Leith, and burnt every stick of it ; and took forth the two goodly ships, manned them, and put them in order to attend upon the King's Majesty's ships.   Their ballast was cannon shot of iron ; which we found in the town to the number of 80,000.   The rest of the Scottish ships meet to serve, we brought away : both they and our own being almost pestered [*encumbered*] with the spoil and booty of our soldiers and mariners.

That done, we abandoned ourselves clearly from the ships : having firm intent to return home by land.   Which we did. And to give them [*the Scots*] better occasion to show them-selves in the field against us ; we left neither pile, village, town, nor house in our way homewards, unburnt.

In the meantime of the continuance of our army at Leith, as is aforesaid ; our ships upon the seas were not idle ; for they left neither ship, crayer, nor boat belonging to either village, town, creek or haven of either side of the Frith between Stirling and the mouth of the river, unburnt or not brought away ; which containeth in length fifty miles.   Continuing of time, they also burnt a great number of towns and villages on both sides the said water ; and won a fortress situated on a strong island called Inchgarve, which they razed and destroyed.

The 15th of May, we dislodged our camp out of the town of Leith; and set fire in every house, and burnt it to the ground.

The same night, we encamped at a town of the Lord SEATON's where we burnt and razed his chief castle, called Seaton, which was right fair; and destroyed his orchards and gardens, which were the fairest and best in order that we saw in all that country. We did him the more despite, because he was the chief labourer to help their Cardinal out of prison : who was the only [sole] author of their calamity.

The same day, we burnt a fair town of the Earl BOTHWELL, called Haddington, with a great nunnery and a house of friars.

The next night after, we encamped besides Dunbar, and there the Scots gave a small alarm to our camp; but our watches were in such a readiness that they had no vantage there, but were fain to recoil without doing any harm.

That night, they looked for us to have burnt the town of Dunbar; which we deferred till the morning, at the dislodging of our camp: which we executed by 500 of our hackbutters, being backed with 500 horsemen. And by reason that we took them in the morning — who, having watched all night for our coming, and perceiving our army to dislodge and depart, thought themselves safe of us, were newly gone to their beds: and in their first sleeps closed in with fire —the men, women and children were suffocated and burnt.

That morning [the 17th] being very misty and foggy, we had perfect knowledge by our espials, that the Scots had assembled a great power, in a strait [pass] called "the Pease." The chiefs of this assembly were the Lords SEATON, HUME and BUCCLEUCH : and with them the whole power of the [Scotch] Marches and Teviotdale. This day in our marching, divers of their prickers [scouts] by reason of the said mist gave us alarm, and came so far within our army, that they unhorsed one between the Vanward and the Battle; being within two hundred feet of the Lord Lieutenant. At that alarm, one of their best prickers, called JOCK HOLLY BURTON was taken: who confessed that the said Scottish lords were ready at the passage [pass] with the number of 10,000 good men. And forasmuch as the mist yet continued and did not break, being past noon, the Vanward being within a mile of the said passage, entering into dangerous ways for an army to march in such weather that one could not descry another twenty yards off: we concluded if the weather did not break up, to have encamped ourselves upon the same ground; where we did remain for the space of two hours. And about two of the clock at afternoon, the sun brake out, the fog went away, and a clear day was left us: whereof every man received as it were a new courage, longing to see the enemy; who, being ready for us at the said passage, and seeing us come in good order of battle, as men determined to pass through them or to leave our bones with them, abode us but two shots of a falcon, but scaled every man his way to the high mountains, which were hard at their hands, and covered with flocks of their people. The passage was such, that having no let [*impediment*]; it was three hours before all the army could pass it.

The same night, the army encamped at a pile called Ranton, eight miles from our borders: which pile was a very ill neighbour to the garrison of Berwick. The same we razed and threw down to the ground.

The next day, being the 18th of May, the whole army entered into Berwick, and ended this voyage; with the loss unneth [*of scarcely*] forty of the King's Majesty's people, thanks be to our Lord.

The same day, at the same instant, that the army entered into Berwick, our whole fleet and navy of ships, which we sent from us at Leith, arrived before Berwick: as GOD would be known to favour our master's cause. Who ever preserve his most royal Majesty with long and prosperous life, and many years to reign in the imperial seat of the monarchy of all Britain.

⁋ The names of the chief burghs, castles and towns burnt and desolated by the King's army, being lately in Scotland: besides a great number of villages, piles, and [home]steads which I cannot name.

HE burgh and town of Edinburgh, with the Abbey called Holy Rood House, and the King's Palace adjoining to the same.

The town of Leith burnt, and the haven and pier destroyed.

The castle and village of Craigmillar.
The Abbey of New Battell.
Part of Musselburgh town, with the Chapel of our Lady
of Lawret [*Loretto*].
Preston town and castle.
Haddington town, with the friary and nunnery.
A castle of OLIVER SANCKLER's [*SINCLAIR's*].
The town of Dunbar.
Lawreston, with the grange.

Drylawe.
Wester Craig.
Enderleigh, the pile and
the town.
Broughton.
Thester Felles.
Crawnend.
Duddingstone.
Stanhows.
The Ficket.
Beverton.
Tranent.
Shenstone.

Markle.
Trapren.
Kirkland hill.
Hatherwike.
Belton.
East Barnes.
Bowland.
Butterden.
Quickwod.
Blackborne.
Raunton.
Byldy, and the tower.

❡ Towns and villages burnt by the fleet, upon the seaside;
with a great number of piles and villages which I
cannot name nor rehearse, which be all devastated and
laid desolate.

Kinkorne.
S. Minetes.
The Queen's ferry.

Part of Petynwaynes
[*Pittenweem.*]
The Burnt Island.

Other new and prosperous adventures of late against the Scots.

FTER the time that the Earl of HERTFORD, Lieutenant to the King's Majesty in the North parts of the realm, had dissolved the army, which lately had been within Scotland ; and repaired to the King's Highness: the Lord EURE, with many other valiant wise gentlemen — abiding in the Marches of the North part—intending not by idleness to surcease in occasions convenient, but to prove whether the Scots had yet learned by their importable [*unbearable*] losses lately chanced to them, to tender their own weals by true and reasonable uniting and adjoining themselves to the King's Majesty's loving liege people—took consultation by the advice of Sir RALPH EURE his son, and other sage forward gentlemen ; upon the 9th day of June [1544], at a place named Mylnefeld ; from whence by common agreement, the said lord with a good number of men, made such haste into Scotland, that by four of the clock after the next midnight, he had marched within a half mile of the town whereunto they tended, named Jedworth."

After their coming, a messenger was sent unto the Provost of the said town, letting him to know " that the Lord EURE was come before the town to take it into the King's allegiance, by means of peace if thereunto the Scots would truly agree, or else by force of arms to sack the same if therein resistance were found." Whereunto the Provost—even like to prove himself a Scot—answered by way of request, " that they might be respected upon their answer until the noontide or else to maintain their town with defence : " having hope that in tracting [*treating*] and driving off time they might work some old cowardly subtilty. But upon his declaration made, the snake crawling under the flowers easily appeared to them, which had experience : knowledge also being had, that the townsmen had bent seven or eight pieces of ordnance in the market-stead. Wherefore the Lord EURE — part of his company being into three bands divided, and abiding at three several coasts of the same town, to the end that there might be three entries at one time made into the town—appointed and devised that the gunners, which had battered certain places plain and open, should enter in one side, and the kernes on another side, and Sir RALPH EURE's, of the third side. But it fortuned that, even upon the approachment of the men to their entries, the Scots fled from their ordnance, leaving them unshot, into the woods thereabout, with all other people in the same town. In which flight was slain above the number of 160 Scots, having for that recompense thereof, the loss of six Englishmen only. The people thus fled, and the town given to Englishmen by chance of war: the gunners burned the Abbey, the Grey Friars, and divers bastel and fortified houses, whereof there were many in that town: the goods of the same town being first spoiled, which laded, at their departing, 500 horses; besides seven pieces of ordnance.

In their return likewise, as they passed, burning divers places, towers and castles: as the Tower of Calling Craige, the Castle of Sesforth, Otterburn, Cowboge, Marbottle church, with many other like; until they came to a place called Kirkyettham, being ten miles from certain villages within English ground, named Hetton, Tylmouth and Twysell, which appeared to them burning. For the which cause Sir RALPH EURE and the Captain of Norham, accompanied with 500 horsemen, rode in such haste towards the fire, that at what time the said Sir RALPH did set upon the Scots which had burned the village, he had not with him above 200 horsemen. Nevertheless the Scots, upon the only sight of the standards, used for their defence their light feet, and fled in so much haste that divers English horses were tired in the pursuit: but overtaken there was a great number, whereof many were slain, partly by the fierceness of the Englishmen, partly by the guilty cowardice of the Scots. And truly to speak in a few words; in this act doing, reason will scarcely suffice to persuade the truth: insomuch that there were divers Englishmen whereof every man had eight or nine prisoners, besides such as were slain whose number

is certainly known to have been a hundred or more. And
yet in this skirmish, not one Englishman taken, neither
slain : thanks be to GOD ! Also further here is to be
remembered that the Englishmen in their return from the
sack of Jedworth, drave and brought out of Scotland into
England, a great number of cattle, both note [*neat*] and sheep.

Furthermore to the apparent continuance of GOD's favour
unto the purposes of the Englishmen, it is to be certainly
known, that on the 15th day of June [1544] there was another
raid made by divers Englishmen to a town called Synlawes,
whereas divers bastel houses were destroyed, eight Scots
taken, and 60 oxen brought away. For the return [*recovery*]
whereof, a number of Scottish men pursued very earnestly ;
who for their coming, lost six of their lives, and fifty of their
horsemen [prisoners].

And upon the Tuesday next following, Sir GEORGE
BOWES, Sir JOHN WITHERINGTON, HENRY EURE, and
LIONEL GRAYE rode to the Abbey of Coldingham, and
demanded the same ; but it was denied earnestly, insomuch
that after an assault made for five hours, it was burnt all
saving the church, which having fire in the one end smoked
so by the drift of the wind towards the Englishmen that
it could not be conveniently then be burned. The store of
the cattle and of the other goods there, served well for the
spoil of the soldiers. In this Abbey were slain one monk and
three other Scots. And amongst the English was one only
gunner slain by a piece of ordnance shot out of the steeple.

Since this journey, the 20th of June [1544], a company of
Tynedale and Redesdale with other valiant men, ventured
upon the greatest town in all Teviotdale, named Skraysburgh,
a town of the Lord HUNTHILL's ; whereas besides rich spoils
and great plenty of note [*neat*] and sheep, 38 persons were
taken. Adding thereunto, that which is a marvellous truth,
that is to say, these prisoners being taken, three Scots being
slain, with divers wounded : not one Englishmen was either
hurt or wounded.

In these victories, who is to be most highest lauded but
GOD ? by whose goodness the Englishmen hath had of a

great season notable victories and matters worthy of
triumphs. And for the continuance of GOD's favour toward
us, let us pray for the prosperous estate of our noble good
and victorious Lord Governor and King &c. : for whose sake
doubtless, GOD hath spreaded his blessing over us, in peace
to have mirth, and in wars to have victory.

Imprinted at London in Paul's
Church yard, by Reynold
Wolf; at the sign of the
Brazen Serpent.
Anno 1544.

Cum privilegio ad imprimendum solum.

 # THE

**Expedition into Scotland of the most
worthily fortunate Prince Edward, Duke of
Somerset, uncle unto our most noble sove‐
reign Lord, the King's Majesty** Edward **the
VI., Governor of His Highness's person, and
Protector of His Grace's realms, dominions
and subjects; made in the First year of His
Majesty's most prosperous reign: and
set out by way of Diary by
W. Patten, Londoner.**

VIVAT VICTOR.

UNTO the Right Honourable Sir WILLIAM PAGET, Knight of the most noble Order of the Garter, Comptroller of the King's Majesty's Household, one of His Highness's Privy Council, Chancellor of the Duchy of Lancaster ; and his most benign fautor and patron: WILLIAM PATTEN most heartily wisheth felicity.

(?)

AVING *in these last wars against Scotland, that never were any with better success achieved, made notes of* [the] *acts there done, and disposed the same, since my coming home, into order of Diary, as followeth; as* one *that would show some argument of remembrance, Right Honourable Sir! of your most benign favour that, as well while I was with the Right Honourable my very good Lord and late master, the Earl of* ARUNDEL, *as also since, ye have vouchsafed to bear me: I have thought meetest to dedicate my travail unto your Honour.*

How smally I either am or have been, by any means, able to merit the same your gentleness, by so much the less have I need here to show; as your humane generosity, your willing benignity and promptness to profit all men, is unto all men so commonly known: for the which, your name and honour is so familiar and well esteemed with foreign princes abroad, and so worthily well beloved of all estates at home.   For who was he, of any degree or country, that had any just suit or other ado with our late sovereign Lord, the King's Majesty deceased, (when His Highness, in these his latter years, for your approved wisdom, fidelity, trust, and diligence, had committed the special ministry and despatch of his weighty affairs unto your hands) that felt not as much then, as I have found since? or who findeth not, still, a constant continuance thereof, where the equity of his suit may bear it?   Right many, sure[ly], *of the small knowledge I have, could I myself reckon both of then and since, which here all willingly I leave unattempted to do; both because my rehearsal should be very unnecessary and vain to you that know them better than I; and also that I should tell the tale to yourself. Whom, for the respect of your honour, as I have a reverence, with vanities from your grave occupations* [not] *to detain; so have I, for honesty's sake, a shame to be suspect*[ed], *by any means, to flatter.*

That same, your singular humanity wherewith ye are wont also so gently to accept all things in so thankful a part, and wherewith ye have bound me so straightly to you, did first, to say the truth now, embolden me in this theme to set pen to the book; and now after, in this wise, to present my work unto you. The which if it shall please your Honour to take well in worth, and receive into your tuition, as the thing shall more indeed be dignified by having such a patron than your dignity gratified by receiving so unworthy a present; even so what fault shall be found therein I resume, as clearly coming of myself. But if ought shall be thought to be aptly said, pleasant, anything savouring of wit or learning, I would all men should know it as I acknowledge it myself, that it must wholly be referred to you, the encouraging of whose favour hath ministered such matter to my wit, that like as OVID *said to* CESAR *of his, so may I say to you of mine—*

Fastor. 1.   Ingenium vultu statque caditque tuo.

But now no further, with my talk, to trouble you.

Thus, with increase of honour unto your Worthiness, most heartily, I wish the same continuance of health and wealth.

Your most bounden client and pupil,

W. PATTEN.

A PREFACE

serving, for much part, instead of Argument, for the matter of the Story, ensuing.

LTHOUGH it be not always the truest means of meeting, to measure all men's appetites by one man's affection: yet hereof, at this time, dare I more than half assure me, that (even as I would be, in like case, myself) so is every man desirous to know of the manner and circumstances of this our most valiant victory over our enemies, and prosperous success of the rest of our journey. The bolder am I to make this general judgement, partly for that I am somewhat by learning, ARISTOTLE. *Metaph.* i. but more by nature instruct[ed] to understand the thirsty desire that all our kind hath to Know: and then, for that in every company, and at every table, where it hath been my hap to be, since my coming home, the whole communication was, in a manner, nought else but of this Expedition and wars in Scotland. Whereof, many to me then have ministered so many Interrogatories as would have well cumbered a right ripe tongued Deponent readily to answer; and I indeed thereto, so hastily, could not. Yet, nevertheless, I blame them no more for quickness of question, than I would myself for slowness of answer. For considering how much in every

narration, the circumstances do serve for the perfect instruc-
tion of them that do hear, I can easily think the same were
as much desired of them to be heard, as necessary of me to be
told.   And specially of this, to say chiefly, of the battle, being
such a matter as neither the like hath been seen with eyes
by any of this age now, nor read of in story of any years past.
So great a power, so well picked and appointed, so restful
and fresh, so much encouraged by hope of foreign aid, at their
own doors, nay, in the midst of their house, and at the worst,
so nigh to their refuge; to be beaten, vanquished, put to
flight, and slain, by so small a number, so greatly travailed
and weary, so far within their enemies' land, and out of their
own; without hope, either of refuge or rescue.   The circumstances hereof, with the rest of our most Triumphant Journey,
which otherwise aptly, for unaptness of time, I could not
utter by word of mouth, here mind I, GOD willing! now to
declare by letter of writing : not, as of arrogancy, taking upon
me the thing which I myself must confess many can do
better; but as, of good will, doing mine endeavour for
that in me lieth, to make all men privy of that whereof it
were meet no man were ignorant.   As well because they may
the rather universally be moved to pray, praise, and glorify
the most merciful LORD, whose clemency hath so continually, of these late years, vouchsafed to show His most benign
favour towards us : as also to worship, honour, and have in
veneration the reverend worthiness of our most honourable
Council, by whose general sage consultations and circumspect wisdoms, as friendship with foreign princes, and provision for the enemy, hath been continued and made abroad;
we guarded from outward invasion or disturbance at home;
no prince, with obedience and diligence more nobly served;
nor no communalty with justice and mercy more sagely governed.   Even so, by the special invincible virtue and valiant
policy of my Lord Protector's Grace, we have first, and as it
were in the entry of this most honourable and victorious
Voyage, overturned many of our enemies' rebellious Holds;

and then overcome the double of our number and strength in open field, by plain dint of sword; slain so great a multitude of them, with so small a loss of our side; taken of their chiefest, prisoners; won and keep a great sort [*number*] of their strongest forts; built many new; taken and destroyed their whole navy; and brought the townships in the hither parts of their bounds, above twenty miles in compass, into an honest obedience unto the King's Majesty. By the martial courage of his undaunted hardiness was this Expedition so boldly taken in hand; by the presence and adventure of his own person was the same so warily and wisely conducted; by the virtuous policy of his circumspect prowess was this Victory, or rather Conquest so honourably achieved: unto whose valiance and wisdom, I can entirely attribute so much, as to the furtherance of Fortune, nothing at all; which, as CICERO proveth, is either a vain name, or not at *De divinat.* ii. all, or if there be, is ever subject, as the Platonics affirm, to wisdom and industry. The which indeed did so manifestly appear in the affairs of this Voyage, that like as in accounts, the several numbers of ten, twenty, thirty, forty, being cast together, must needs make up the just sum of an hundred: even so, such his Grace's providence, circumspection, courage, and order (do Fortune what she could) must needs have attained to such success of victory: that if the Romans were content to allow the honour of a Triumph to SCIPIO TIT. LIVIUS. *Africanus* for overcoming HANNIBAL and SYPHAX; and to M. ATTILIUS REGULUS, for vanquishing the Salentines; and, thereto, to set up images, the highest honour they had, for a perpetual memory of M. CLAUDIUS MARCELLUS and MUTIUS SCEVOLA (the one but for killing VIRIDOMAX the French king in [the] field at the river of Padua, and for devising how HANNIBAL might be vanquished, and overcoming but of VALERI. *lib.* i. *et* ii. the only city of Sarragossa: and the other but for PLINI, *de vir.* *illust.* his attempt to slay King PORSENNA that besieged Rome): what thanks then, what estimation, what honour and reverence condign, for these his notable demerits [*merits*] ought our Protector to receive of his? Nay, what can we worthily give him?

Howbeit, if we call to mind, how first Allhallowentide was five year, [*November*] 1542, his Grace, lying as Lord Warden in our Marches against Scotland, by the drift of his device, both the great invasion of the late Scottish King JAMES V. was stoutly then withstood at Solmon Moss [*Solway Moss*], the King's death's wound given him, and the most part of all his nobility taken. How, the next year after, [1544] he, being accompanied by my Lord of WARWICK and with but a handful [of men], to speak of, did burn both Leith and Edinburgh [*see* pages 39-47] and returned thence triumphantly home; but with an easy march travelling forty-four long miles through their mainland. Whose approved valiance, wisdom, and dexterity in the handling of our Prince's affairs, how can we be but sure that it did not smally advance or cause [*bring*] about the conclusion of an honourable peace between France and us, although it did not then strait ensue? when his Grace in the same year, soon after his return out of Scotland, was deputed Ambassador to treat with the Bishop of BELLAY and others the French King's Commissioners, at Hardilow Castle.

In the year [1545] how his Grace, about August, so invaded the Scottish borders, wasted and burnt Teviotdale and their Marches, that even yet they forthink [*grieve over*] that inroad.

In February [1545] then next, how, being appointed by our late sovereign Lord to view the fortifications in the Marches of Calais, the which his Grace having soon done with diligence accordingly, he so devised with my Lord the Earl of WARWICK, then Lieutenant of Boulogne, and took such order with the garrisons there, that with the hardy approach of but seven thousand men he raised [the camp of] an army of twenty-one thousand Frenchmen that had encamped themselves over the river by Boulogne, and therewith then wan all their ordnance, carriage, treasure, and tents in their camp, wholly as it stood; with the loss but of one man. And from thence, returning by land to Guisnes, wan in his way, within the gunshot and rescue of Ardes, the Castle of Outings, called otherwise, the Red Pile.

How hereto, by his force, 1545, was Picardy invaded and spoiled, the forts of Newhaven, Blaknestes, and Boulogne-berg begun, built, and so well plied in work; that in a few weeks, ere his departing thence, they were made and left defensible.

Calling to mind, I say, (I speak not of his unwearied diligence in the mean time) these his valiant incursions, his often overthrowings and notable victories over our enemies. And yet though this his last be far to be preferred above them all, having been so great, and achieving so much in so little time, the like not heard nor read of; and, but that there be so many witnesses, half incredible : yet is it none other sure but such as makes his Grace's virtue rather new again than strange, and rather famous than wonderful. We wonder not, ye wot! but at things strange and seldom seen or heard; but victory to his Grace seems no less common and appropried [*appropriate*] than heat to the fire, or shadow to the body. That, like as the well keeping of the Pallady in Troy was ever the conservation and defence of the city; even so in warfare the presence of his person is a certain safeguard of the host and present victory over the enemy; for the which I have heard many, of right honest behaviour, say that "for surety of themselves, they had rather, in [the] field, be a mean soldier under his Grace than a great captain under any other." And, sure[ly], but that by my profession I am bound, and do believe all things to be governed, not by fortune or hap (although we must be content, in common speech to use the terms, of our formers [*predecessors*] devised) but by the mighty power of Almighty GOD, without whose regard a sparrow

Palladium was an ancient wooden image in Troy, where-upon Apollo by oracle did prophesy that then should Troy be destroyed, when that was had out of the city. This not unknown to the Greeks; DIOMEDES and ULYSSES, in the time of the siege there, scaled the tower walls where the image was kept, killed the warders, and brought the image away with them. Whereupon, the city was soon after destroyed.

Matt. x.

lighteth not upon the ground, I could count his Grace a prince that way most fortunate of any living.

But now remembering my religion, and what Fortune's force is, and hereto seeing his Grace's godly disposition and behaviour, in the fiercest time of war seeking nothing more than peace, neither cruel upon victory, nor insolent upon good success, but with most moderate magnanimity, upon the respect of occasion, using, as the poet saith,

VIRGIL. *Parcere subjectis et debellare superbos.*

In peace again, wholly bent to the advancement of GOD's glory and truth, the King's honour, and the common's quiet and wealth. And herewith conferring the benefits and blessings Psa. cxi. and cxxvii. that, by the prophet DAVID, the Lord assureth to all them that so stand in love and dread of Him: I am compelled to think his Grace, as least happy by Fortune, so most blessed by GOD ; and sent to us, both King and commons, as a Minister by whom the merciful majesty of the LORD, for our entire comfort, of both soul and body, will work His divine will. That, if, without offence, I may openly utter that which I have secretly thought, I have been often at a great muse with myself whether the King's Majesty, of such an uncle and Governor ; we, of such a Mediator and Protector, or his Grace again, of such a Prince and cousin, might most worthily think themselves happiest.

But since I am so certain the excellency of his acts, and the baseness of my brain to be so far at odds, as ought that I could utter in his praise, should rather obscure and darken them, and, as it were, wash ivory with ink ; than give them their due light and life : let no man look that I will here enterprise to deal with the worthiness of his commendations, who, both have another matter in hand, and they again being such as might by themselves be an ample theme for a right good wit ; wherein to say either little or insufficiently were better, in my mind, left unattempted and to say nothing at all.

Marry, an epigram made upon the citizens receiving of
his Grace, and for gratulation of his great success and safe
return, the which I had, or rather (to say truth and shame
the devil, for out it will) I stole, perchance more familiarly
than friendly, from a friend of mine ; I thought it not much
amiss (for the neatness of making and fineness of sense, and
somewhat also to serve, if reason would bear it, in lieu of my
lack) to place here.

Auspice nobilium (Dux inclyte) turba virorum.
Utque alacris latos plebs circumfusa per agros.
Te patriæ patrem communi voce salutent.
Scilicet et Romam victo sic hoste CAMILLUS,
Sic rediit victor domito POMPEIUS Iarba
Ergo tuus felix reditus, præsentia felix.
Utque Angli, fusique tua gens effera Scotti
Dextra, qua nunquam visa est victoria major
Det DEUS imperium per te coeamus in unum :
Simus et unanimes per secula cuncta Britanni.

Though I plainly told ye not that my friend's name was
ARMIGIL WADE ; yet, ye that know the man his good
literature, his wit and dexterity in all his doings, and mark
the well couching of his clue, might have a great guess, of
whose spinning the thread were.

But why these wars by our late sovereign Lord, the King's
Majesty deceased (a Prince most worthy of eterne fame,
whose soul GOD have !), were, in his days. begun ; and yet
continued ? Forasmuch as by sundry publications of divers
writings, as well then as since, the just title of our King unto
Scotland, and the Scots often deceits, untruths of promise,
and perjury hath been among other [things] in the same
writings so manifestly uttered ; I intend not here now
to make it any part of my matter, which is but only a
Journal or Diary of this Expedition into Scotland : wherein
I have digested out every day's deeds orderly, as they were

done, with their circumstances, so nigh as I could, from the time of my Lord Protector's Grace's coming to Newcastle until our breaking up of the camp from Roxburgh. And herein I doubt not but many things, both right necessary and worthy to be uttered, I shall leave untold; but, sure[ly], rather of ignorance than of purpose. Although indeed I know it were meetest for any writer in this kind to be ignorant of fewest and writing of most, yet trust I again it will be considered that it is neither possible for one man to know all, nor shame to be ignorant in that he cannot know. But as touching deeds well done, being within the compass of my knowledge; as, so GOD help me! I mind to express no man's for flattery, so will I suppress no man's for malice.

Thus battle and field now, which is the most principal part of my matter, the Scots and we are not yet agreed how it shall be named. We call it Musselburgh Field, because that is the best town, and yet bad enough, nigh the place of our meeting. Some of them call it Seaton Field, a town there-nigh too, by means of a blind prophecy of theirs, which is this, or some such toy.

> *Between Seaton and the sea*
> *Many a man shall die that day.*

Some will have it Fauxside Bray Field, of the hill (for so they call a *Bray*) upon the side whereof our Foreward stood, ready to come down and join. Some others will have it Under-esk [*Inveresk*] Field; in the fallows whereof, they stood and we met. Some will have it Walliford Field: and some no "Field" at all, for that they say "there were so few [English] slain, and that we met not in a place by certain appointment, according to the order and manner of battle," with such like fond arguments. Marry, the hinderers of this meeting, I think for their meaning, have small sin to beshrew. They, of this haste, hoped to have had the whole advantage. For what they did appoint upon: without warning, then so early to dislodge, and so hastily to approach, who cannot judge? And whether they meant to make a Field of their fight, or meant to fight at all or not, judge ye! by this that after ye hear.

Certain it is that against their assembly and our encounter (for they were not un[a]ware of our coming) in the former part of the year, they had sent letters of warning to the Estates of their realm; and then caused the Fire Cross in most places of their country to be carried: whereof the solemnity is never used but in an urgent need, or for a great power, either for defence of themselves or invasion of us. And this is a Cross, as I have heard some say, of two brands' ends carried across upon a spear's point, with Proclamation of the time and place when and whither they shall come, and with how much provision of victail. Some others say, it is a Cross painted all red, and set for certain days in the fields of that Barony, whereof they will have the people to come; whereby all, between sixty and sixteen, are peremptorily summoned, that if they come not, with their victail according, at the time and place then appointed, all the land there is forfeited straight to the King's use, and the tarriers taken for traitors and rebels.

By reason of which letters and Fire Cross, there were assembled in their camp, as I have heard some of themselves, not of the meanest sort, to confess, above twenty-six thousand fighting footmen, beside two thousand horsemen, " prickers " as they call them: and hereto four thousand Irish archers brought by the Earl of ARGYLE. All of which, saving certain we had slain the day before, came out of their camp to encounter with us. Now, where they will have it no Field, let them tell their cards, and count their winning! and they shall find it a Field. Howbeit, by mine assent, we shall not herein much stick with them: since both without them the truth shall have place; and also, by the courtesy of gaming, we ought somewhat to suffer, and ever let the losers have their liberty of words.

But whatsoever it were, Field or no Field, I dare be bold

E   I

to say, not one of us all is any whit prouder of it than would be the tooth that hath bit the tongue, otherwise than in respect that they were our mortal enemies, and would have done as much or more to us; nor are nothing so fain to have beaten them as enemies, as we would rejoice to receive them as friends; nor are so glad of the glory of this Field, as we would be joyful of a steadfast atonement [at-one-ment (of one mind)]: whereby like countrymen and countrymen, like friend and friend, nay, like brother and brother, we might, in one perpetual and brotherly life, join, love, and live together, according as thereto, both by the appointment of GOD at the first, and by continuance of Nature since, we seem to have been made and ordained; separate by seas, from all other nations; in customs and conditions, little differing; in shape and language, nothing at all. The which things other nations viewing in charts [maps] and reading in books; and therewith hearing of this tumult, this fighting, these incursions and intestine wars between us, do thereat no less marvel, and bless them, than they would, to hear Gascoigny fight with France; Arragon, with Spain; Flanders, with Brabant; or (to speak more near and naturally) friend with friend, brother with brother, or rather hand with hand.

That no little, both wonder and woe it is to me, my To the Scots. countrymen! for I can vouchsafe ye well the name! to consider what thing might move ye? what tale might incense ye? what drift, force ye? what charm, enchant ye? or what fury, conjure ye? so fondly to fly from common sense, as ye should have need to be exhorted to that for the which it were your parts chiefly to sue; so untowardly to turn from human reason as ye will be the hinderers of your own weals; and so untruly to sever from the bonds both of promise and covenant as ye will needs provoke your friends to plain revengement of open war!

Your friends indeed, nay, never wink at the word! that have so long before these wars foreborn our quarrels so just that were so loath to begin, and since, that suffered so many injuries unrevenged, entreating [*treating*] your men taken, not as captives of our mortal enemies, but as ambassadors of our dearest friends!

O, how may it be thought to be possible that ye should ever forget, or else not ever remember the great munificence of our most magnificent Prince, our late King! that when, with most cruelty, by slaughter of subjects and burning of towns, your last king, JAMY, with all your nobility, At Allhallow-had invaded his realm; and, soon after, the invin- entide 1542. cible policy of my Lord Protector's Grace, the lying at Alnwick, as Lord Warden of our Marches, by the sufferance of GOD's favour (which, thanks to His Majesty! hath not yet left us), at Solom Moss, made them captive and thrall to our Prince's own will. With whom, for their deeds, if His Highness had dealt then as they had deserved, what should have blamed him? or who could have controlled? since what he could do, they could not resist: and what he should do, they had set him a sample [*an example*].

But his Majesty, among the huge heap of other his princely virtues (being ever of nature so inclined to clemency as never, of will, to use extremity), even straight forgetting who they were, and soon forgiving what they had done; did not only then receive them into His Highness's grace; place every of them with one of his nobility or council, not in prison like a captive; pardon them their raundsommes [*ransoms*], wherewith, if they be ought worth, some Prince might have thought himself rich; and hereto most friendly, for the time they were here, entertain them: but also, of his princely liberality, imparting treasure at their departing to each of them all, did set them frank and free at their own doors! Touching their silks, their chains, and their cheer beside; I mind not here, among matters of weight, to tarry on such trifles. Marry, there be among us that saw their habit [*dress*] and port [*state, or attendance*], both at their coming and at their departing! Take it not, that I hit you here in the teeth, with our good turns! (yet know I no cause, more than for humanity's sake, why ye should be forborne!) but as a man may sometimes, without boast of himself, say simply the thing that is true of himself, so may the subject without obbraid [*upbraiding*] of benefits, recount the bounty of his Prince's largesse : although, perchance, it were not much against manners flatly to break courtesy with them, who, either of recklessness forget their friends' benignity, or else of ingratitude will not acknowledge it.

To my matter now! What would CYRUS, DARIUS, or HANNIBAL, (noble conquerors, and no tyrants) in this case, have done? But why so far off? What would your own King JAMY have done? Nay, what King else would have done as our King did? But somewhat to say more. As our Prince in cases of pity, was, of his own disposition, most merciful; so wanted there not then of Councillors very near about His Highness, that showed themselves their friends; and furthered his affects in that behalf to the uttermost: being thus persuaded, that as ye of the Nobility appeared men, neither rude of behaviour, nor base of birth; so ye would never show yourselves inhuman and ingrate towards him, to whom ye should be so deeply bound.

And though since that time, GOD hath wrought His will upon His Majesty (a loss to us, sure[ly], worthy never enough to have been lamented; but that His mercy hath again so bountifully recompensed us with an image so nigh representing his father's majesty and virtues, and of so great hope and towardness); yet be there left us most of the Councillors we had, who, upon occasion, will bend both power and will to show you further friendship. In part of proof thereof, hcw many means and ways hath my Lord Protector's Grace, within his time of governance, under the King's Majesty that now is, attempted and used to shun these wars, and show himself your friend? What policy hath he left unproved? What shift unsought? or what stone unstirred?

Touching your weals now! Ye mind not, I am sure, to live lawless and headless, without a Prince! but so to bestow

your Queen, as whose mate must be your King! And is it
then possible ye can so far be seduced and brought to believe,
that in all the world there should be any so worthy a Prince
as our King? as well for the nobility of his birth, for his rare
comeliness of shape, his great excellency of qualities, his
singular towardness to all godliness and virtues! any likely
to be so natural a Prince for you, as His Majesty born, bred
and brought up under that hemisphere and compass of ele-
ment, and upon that soil that both ye and we be all, any so
meet for her, as your Princess's own countryman, a right
Briton, both bred and born? a Prince also by birth, of so
great a power, and of so meet an age? the joining of whom
both the Kings, their fathers, did vow in their lives; and ye,
since, agreed upon in parliament, and promised also after their
deaths?

Than which thing, taking once effect, what can be more
for your universal commodities, profits, and weals? whereby,
even at once, of foreign foes, ye shall be accepted as familiar
friends! of weak, ye shall be made strong! of poor, rich! and
of bond, free! And whether this now be rather to be offered
of us or sued for by you, I make yourselves the judges!
What we are able alone to do, both in peace and war, as
well without you as against you, I need not here to brag.
Yet seek we not the Mastership of you, but the Fellowship!
for if we did, we have, ye wot, a way of persuasion of the
rigorous rhetoric, so vengeably vehement (as I think ye have
felt by an Oration or two) that if we would use the extremity
of argument, we were soon able so to beat reason into your
heads or about your heads, that I doubt not ye would quickly
find what fondness it were to stand in strife for the mastery
with more than your match.

We covet not to keep you bound, that would so fain have
you free, as well from the feigned friendship of France (if I may
call it any friendship at all, that for a few crowns do but stay
you still in store for their own purpose) whereunto now, both
ye seem subject, and your Queen ward (which friendship,

nevertheless, whatsoever it be, we desire not ye should break with them, for the love of us; but only in case where ye should be compelled to lose either them or us, and, in that case, perchance, we may be content again to lose them for you); as well from the semblance or rather dissembling of this feigned friendship, I say, we covet to quit ye! as also from the most servile thraldom and bondage under that hideous monster, that venemous *aspis* and very ANTICHRIST, the Bishop of ROME, in the which, of so long time, ye have, and yet do most miserably abide! Whose importable pride and execrable arrogancy, as well most presumptuously against all the sacred Estates of Princes upon earth, as also most contumeliously against the High Majesty of GOD Himself; with fastidious and utter contempt, both of GOD and man, both the context and tenour of his own decrees, *decretals*, *canons*, and *Extravagants* (made and conspired at the Congregations, Councils, and Synods, at sundry times, for the maintenance and augmenting of his Antichristian authority, in his Holiness's name assembled) [demonstrate]. And hereto his wicked blasphemy against GOD, his devilish dispensations against His Divine laws, his obstinate rebellion against all powers, his outrageous usurpation in Prince's lands, his cruel tyranny for keeping of his kingdom, his covert hypocrisy at at home, his crafty conspiracies abroad, his insatiable avarice, his subtle superstition, his mischievous malice, his privy theft, his open rapine, his sacred simony, his profane whoredom, his ambition, sacrilege, extortion, idolatry, and poisonings; with many other his cardinal virtues besides. And also the undoubted witness of Holy Writ, in both the Testaments, doth most certainly show, and plainly make clear to the eyes of all, if ye will not wilfully wink at that ye should

Capi. xi.   willingly see! Of him, hardily spake the prophet DANIEL. *He shall be lift up a high, and magnified against all that is GOD ; and shall speak presumptuous words, and shall be set in a course until wrath be fulfilled against him.* In the same chapter. *He shall set at nought the GOD of their fathers ; and shall be in the daliances and desires of women, and shall pass nought for GOD; but shall obstinately be stubborn, and rise against all.* And the holy prophet EZEKIEL. *Thy heart was lift up very high, and saidest, "I am GOD, and sit in GOD's* Cap. xxviii. *seat;" where thou art but man, and not GOD, and nevertheless hast framed thy heart like the heart of GOD!* The apostle Saint PAUL also, in whom the gracès of GOD did so plentifully abound, seemed not utterly to forget this prelate, when, in his *Epistle to the Thessalonians*, he said, *The Lord* 2 Thess. ii. *JESU shall not come till first there be a failing, and that wicked man be discovered, the Child of Perdition; who is adversary and exalted against all that is called GOD, in such sort, as he sticks not to sit in the temple, vaunting himself that he is GOD.* And addeth, a little after, *Whom the Lord JESU shall quell with the spirit of His holy mouth.*

Of him and his abominable behaviour is there much in both the Holy Testaments; and a great deal more, Jer. xxiii. I must confess, than I know my cunning can Ezek. xxiii. Apo.xiv.,xvii., recite; so plain in sense, and easy to be under- xix. stood, that if ye confer the words of the same with the acts of his life, ye shall have no more cause to doubt whether he be the only ANTICHRIST; than ye may have whether He were the only CHRIST, of whom Saint JOHN the Baptist said, *Behold the Lamb of GOD!* and the Centurion, *This* John i. *was, sure[ly], the very Son of GOD!* Matt. xv.

I speak neither of spite, nor of speciality of this precious prelate, PAUL IV., that now is alone; but of him and his whole ancestry, of these many years past. Of whom, sure[ly], who list to say aught, it were meet they said truth; and who list to say truth, can say no good. For their acts by their office, and their lives by their profession, are not less certainly known unto all the world to be thus, than is the lion, as they say, by the paw; or the day, by the sunshine. The trees of that stock never bear other fruit. And therefore was it that neither the Greeks, the Ruthens [*Russians*], nor many nations in the East parts besides (whom we cannot but count

Christians) could never be brought once so much as to taste
of it: and would never abide the presumptuous
usurpation of his insolent Impery ; but utterly, at
the first, did wisely refuse the unwieldy weight of
so heavy a burden, and the painful wringing of so
uneasy a yoke.

*Contrary to
CHRIST's;
whose burden
is light, and
yoke easy.*
Matt. xi.

The Bohemians and Germans, of later years, have quite
rejected, and cast him up.

And we, at last, not so much led by the example of others'
well doing, as moved by the mere mercy and grace of
Almighty GOD; who (as, by DAVID, He hath promised) *is
Psa. cxlv.   ever at hand, and nigh to all them that call upon him
in truth,* and always ready to do that He came for, that is, to
Matt. xviii.   *save that [which] was forelorn.*   Through the aid
and goodness of His mighty power and eterne wisdom
strengthening his worthy Champion, our late sovereign
Lord; and instructing his circumspect Council : have we,
most happily, exterminated, and banished him our bounds.
Whereby, as we have now the grace to know and serve but
one GOD, so are we subject but to one King.   He naturally
knoweth his own people ; and we obediently know him our
only Sovereign.   His Highness's Estate brought and reduced
from perdition, and in a manner subjection unto the old
princely entire and absolute power again: and ours, redeemed
from the doubt as to whom we should obey.   The great
polling and intolerable taxes of our money, yearly, both from
His Majesty and us, now saved clear[ly] within his realm.
Not fain, now, to fetch justice so unjustly ministered, as he
that bids most (like Calais market), whatsoever be the cause,
shall be sure of the sentence ; and that so far from home,
and with so great cost of money and danger of life.   Our
consciences, now, quite unclogged from the fear of his vain
terriculaments and rattle-bladders ; and from the fondness of
his trimtrams and gugaws [*gewgaws*], his interdictions, his
cursings, his damning to the devil, his pardons, his [as]soilings,
his plucking out of purgatory, his superstitious sorts of sects

of religion, his canonization of saints, forbidding and licensing the eating of meat, singing and saying and wot not a word! roving a procession, gadding a pilgrimage, worshipping of idols. Oblations and offerings of meats, of otes, images of Saint UNCUMBER. wax, bound pens and pins for deliverance of bad SaintMUDWIN. husbands, for a sick cow, to keep down the belly, Saint AGNES. Saint SYTH. and when " KIT had lost her key." Setting up candles to saints in every corner, and knakkynge [*knocking*] of bead-stones [*beads*] in every pew, tolling of bells against tempests, *Scala cœli* masses, pardon beads, " Saint Anthony's bells," Tauthrie laces, rosaries, collets, charms for every disease, and sovereign *suffrages* for every sore : with a thousand toys else, of his devilish devices, that lack of opportunity doth let [*hinder*] me here to tell.

We are, now, no more by them so wickedly seduced, to the great offence of GOD's dignity, and utter peril of our souls. Now, have we, by His divine power, wound ourselves out of the danger of His just indignation that we worthily were in for our former obstinacy and turning from His truth: and have received, with most humble thanksgiving, His Holy Word, whereof we have the free use in our own tongue.

These goodly benefits, or rather GOD's blessings, if ye will yourselves! shall we, with GOD's assistance, bring you to enjoy as well as ourselves! but if ye will not, but be still stubborn in your ungodliness, refuse His graces that He daily offereth, wilfully wry so far from His truth, and be utterly obstinate in upholding the ANTICHRIST! as, first, DANIEL the prophet doth declare what ye are, and show you the state ye stand in by these words, *They shall magnify Him ! as many as have drunk of the wine of the wrath of GOD, and whose names are not written in the book of life !* Even so, think ye hardily that the just judgement, which the Head Priests and Seniors of the Jews (in answering CHRIST, unawares to themselves) did give of themselves, unto your confusion, shall be verified upon you ! which is, *Without mercy, shall the LORD*

Matt. xxi. *undo* [destroy] *the evil, and set out his vineyard to other good husbands* [husbandmen], *that will yield him fruit in due times.* And that soon after himself said to them, Exod. c. *Therefore the kingdom of GOD shall be taken from you, and be given to the nation that will do profit!* And hereto the sharp sentence of Saint PAUL to be pronounced specially against you! *The Lord JESU, with the angels of his bliss,* 1 Thess. ii. *shall come from heaven in a flame of fire; taking vengeance upon all them that will not know GOD, and obey the gospel of him our Lord JESU CHRIST. They shall be punished by death for ever, from the glory of his virtue; when he shall come to be glorified among his holy, and be wonderful in the eyes of all that believe.*

As well, nevertheless, that ye may be delivered from the dreadful danger of this most terrible sentence, as also that the LORD, of His immeasurable mercy, will once vouchsafe to open your eyes, and waken you out of this drowsy ENDYMION's dream*, or rather this mortal Lethargy†, wherein by the biting of this most venemous *aspis* ‡, the Pope I say, ye do lamentably lie a slumber, being benumbed of all the limbs of your soul and lacking the use of all your spiritual senses. However, of grace, ye shall be moved to do, we shall of charity most heartily pray: for we do not so much remember our quarrel and forget our profession, but that we can wish rather your amendment than your destruction!

And hereto that once also, ye may see the miserable subjection whereunto ye are thrall! and have the grace, to pray for grace to the LORD that ye may be quitted of that captivity, and be made apt to receive the truth and His Holy Word, and then to know who be your friends, and whether we will you well! With whom by so many means, since GOD, of good will, hath so nigh joined you, seem not you, of frowardness, to sever asunder against the

* ENDYMION, beloved of the Moon, was laid by her into a continual sleep, in a den of Mount Latmus in Caria, where she kissed him. CIC. i, *Tusc. Quest.*

† A disease coming of burnt choler, compelling the patient to covet nought but drowsy sleep, to forget all things, and to be, as it were, in a trance. CŒLIUS, *lib.* xiii.

‡ Bitten with this serpent are cast in a deadly slumber, with a stiffling and benumbing of all parts ; and with a yoxe, do soon die.

thing that should be a general wealth and common concord,
the provision of Nature, and ordinance of GOD! And against
His Holy Word, which not all unaptly, perchance, here may
be cited.

Quos DEUS conjunxit, homo ne separet !   Matt. xix.

The great mischiefs rising by this disunion and severing,
and the manifold commodities coming by the contrary, being
shortly by you had in considerance; this marriage, I doubt
not, between our Princes shall be consummated, all causes of
quarrel ceased, atonement made between us, and a firm
alliance of friendship for ever concluded. The which thing,
as most heartily, for my part, I daily wish for; so have I good
hope shortly to see, and herewith betake you to GOD!

But now to return out of my digression, for though I have
been long a talking to my countrymen abroad in the North:
yet were I loath to seem to forget my friends at home in the
South; and fare like the diligent servant that walks so
earnestly on his master's errand, that, in the midst of his way,
he forgets whither he goeth.

Howbeit I might well, perchance, think it, even here, high
time to leave [off]; were it not that since I am in hand to utter,
in this case, what I know, and nooseld [*nourished*] of my
nurse never to be spare of speech: though I be but a bad
evangelist, yet will I leave as few unwritten verities as I can.

As my Lord's Grace, my Lord of WARWICK, the other
estates of the Council there, with the rest of the dignity of
the army did, at our setting outward, tarry a few days at
Berwick; the well-appointing of the noblemen for their
bands, and of the knights and gentlemen for themselves and
servants, I mean specially of the horsemen; which though,
but at musters, was never showed of purpose, yet could it not,
at that time, be hid, but be bright and apparent in every
man's eye: and was, if I can ought judge, I assure you, for
the goodly number of the likely men and ready horses; for
their perfect appointment of sure armour, weapons, and

apparel; and their sumptuous suits of liverers [*serving-men*] beside (whereof I must of duty, if I must of duty say truth, most worthily prefer and give the chiefest price and praise to my Lord Protector Grace's train, and to my Lord of WARWICK'S), was, I say, so generally such, and so well furnished: that both their duty toward their Prince, their love toward their country and to the rulers were there; and hereto the ancient English courage and prowess, might have easily in this assembly been viewed. Men going out, never better, at any time, in all points, appointed; never better beseen, with more courage and gladder will: whereof with speed (for no doubt our enemies had factors at this mart among us, though, as wisdom was, they did not openly occupy) the Scots had soon knowledge. And as they are merry men, and feat jesters hardily, they said, as we heard, "that we were very gay, and came belike a wooing." The which, though they spake dryly more to taunt the sumpt [*sumptuousness*] of our show than to seem to know the cause of our coming; yet said they therein more truly than they would kindly consider. For, indeed, even as they were ascertained by my Lord Grace's *Proclamation*, as well at and before our entry into their country, that the cause of our coming then, was nothing else but touching the performance of covenants, on both sides, about this marriage, that had been before time, on both sides, agreed upon; which should be greatly for the wealths of us both: and not to make war, sure[ly], nor once to be enemy, but only to such as should appear to be hinderers of so godly and honourable a purpose. Even so, according to the promise of the Proclamation, neither force nor fire was used wittingly against any other, during all our time of abode in the country. Howbeit, the truth was so, that having doubt of the worst, it was wisely consulted so to go to commune with them as friends, as nevertheless, if needs they would, we might be able to meet them as foes: the which thing proved, after, not the worst point of policy.

But what a marvellous unkind people were they, that where

we came, as wooers come, not otherwise, but for good love and quiet; they to receive us with hatred and war! It was too much ungentleness and inhumanity, sure[ly], in such a case to be showed. Yet since we so quit [*requited*] them their kindness; and departed so little in their debt; let us bear somewhat with them! Marry, I wot they were not all so well content with the payment. For the Earl HUNTLEY (a gentleman of a great sobriety and very good wit, as by his very presence is half uttered), being asked of a man of Estate with us, by way of communication, as I heard, how "he bare his affection towards the joining of the two Princes?" "In gude faith," quoth he, "I wade it sud gae furth, and haud weil with the marriage: but I like not this wooing."

But now lest I may worthily be doubted by the plot of my Prologue to have made the form of my book* like the proportion of Saint PETER's man; I will here leave off further process of Preface, and fall to the matter.

* [There is a tale, indeed beside [*outside*] the *Bible*, that Saint PETER having gotten leave of our Lord to make a man; made one first with a very great head, then with an exceeding little neck: and so forth, with such inequality of proportion.

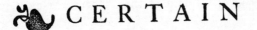

FINIS.

CERTAIN

Noble men and others, being special

Officers in this Expedition.

 HE DUKE of SOMERSET, my Lord Protector's Grace, General of the Army: and Captain of the Battle [*the main body*], having in it 4,000 footmen.

The Earl of WARWICK, Lord Lieutenant of the Army; and having the Foreward, of 3,000 footmen.

The Lord DACRES, the Rereward, of 3,000 footmen.

The Lord GREY of Wilton, Lord Lieutenant of Boulogne, High Marshal of the Army, and Captain General of all the Horsemen there.

Sir RALPH SADLER Knight, Treasurer of the Army.

Sir FRANCIS BRYAN Knight, Captain of the Light Horsemen, being in number, 2,000.

Sir RALPH VANE Knight, Lieutenant of all the Men of arms and Demi-lances, being in number, 4,000.

Sir THOMAS DARCY Knight, Captain of all the King's Majesty's Pensioners and Men of arms.

Sir RICHARD LEE Knight, Devisor [*i.e., Engineer*] of the fortifications to be made.

Sir PETER MEWTYS Knight, Captain of all the Hackbutters a foot, being in number, 600.

Sir PETER GAMBOA Knight, a Spaniard, Captain of 200 Hackbutters on horseback.

Sir FRANCIS FLEMING Knight, Master of the Ordnance.

Sir JAMES WILFORD Knight, Provost Marshal.

Sir GEORGE BLAGUE and Sir THOMAS HOLCROFT, Commissioners of the Musters.

EDWARD SHELLEY, my Lord GREY; Lieutenant of the Men of arms of Boulogne.

JOHN BREN, Captain of the Pioneers, being 1,400.

❡ Officers upon the Sea.

❡ The Lord CLINTON, Lord Admiral of the Fleet : which was of sixty vessels; whereof the Galley and thirty - four more good ships were perfectly appointed for war, and the residue for carriage of munition and victail.

Sir WILLIAM WOODHOUSE Knight, his Vice Admiral.

There in the Army, of great ordnance, drawn forth with us, by horses, Fifteen pieces.

And of carriages; 900 carts, besides many waggons.

THE STORY

and process of the Journey.

Saturday,
the 27th of
August [1547].

Y Lord Protector's Grace, (whom neither the length nor weariness of the way did any whit let [*hinder*], speedily to further that he had deliberately taken in hand) riding all the way from London, his own person, in post, accompanied by [Lord GREY] my Lord Marshal, and Sir FRANCIS BRYAN, was met a six mile on this side of Newcastle by my Lord Lieutenant [the Earl of WARWICK], and Master Treasurer [Sir RALPH SADLER] (who for the more speedy despatch of things were come to town there, three or four days before), and all the nobles, knights, and captains of the army, on horseback, attending upon them.

And coming thus to town, my Lord's Grace was honourably, for the dignity of the place, with gun shot and the presence of the Mayor, Aldermen, and commoners there, about three o'clock in the afternoon, received and welcomed : and lay at the house of one PETER RYDDELL.

Sunday, the
28th of August.

HIS day morning, in the fields in the north-east side of the town, muster was made of such Demi-lances and Light Horsemen as were come; whereat my Lord's Grace was himself, with my Lord Lieutenant and other of the council of the army.

In the afternoon, came the Laird of Mangerton, with a forty Scottish gentlemen of the East borders, and presented themselves to my Lord, at his lodging : whom his Grace did gently accept.

It should not be forgotten, and it were but for example's sake, how a new pair of gallows were set up in the market place ; and a soldier hanged for quarrelling and fighting.

Monday, the
29th of August.

LL Captains with their bands, that had been mustered, were commanded forward. My Lord's Grace himself did early also then depart the town ; dined at Morpeth, twelve miles on the way ; and lay that night at Alnwick Castle, with Sir ROBERT BOWES Knight Lord Warden of the Middle Marches ; being twelve miles further. Where neither lacked any store of guests, nor of good cheer to welcome them with ; in the provision whereof, a man might note great cost and diligence, and in the spending, a liberal heart.

Tuesday, the
30th of August.

HIS day, his Grace, having journeyed in the morning a ten mile, dined at Bamborough Castle ; whereof one Sir JOHN HORSLEY Knight is Captain. The plot of this castle standeth so naturally strong, that hardly can anywhere, in my opinion, be found the like. Inaccessible on all sides, as well for the great height of the crag whereon it standeth ; as also for the outward form of the stone whereof the crag is, which, not much amiss perchance, I may liken to the shape of long bavens [*a brush faggot bound with only one withe*] standing on end with their sharper and smaller ends upward. Thus is it fenced round about : and hath hereto, on the east side, the sea, at flood, coming up to the hard walls. This castle is very ancient, and was called in ARTHUR's day, as I have heard, *Joyous Gard.*

Hither came my Lord CLINTON from shipboard to my Lord.

In the afternoon, his Grace rode to Berwick, fourteen miles further; and there received with the Captains, garrisons, and with the officers of the town, lay in the Castle, with Sir NICHOLAS STRELLEY Knight, the Captain there.

Wednesday, the last of August. UCH part of this day, his Grace occupied in consultation about orders and matters touching this Voyage and army.

This day, to the intent we might save the store of the victail we carried with us in the army by cart, and to be sure rather, among us, to have somewhat too much than any whit too little; and also that we should not need to trouble our ships for victail till we came to the place, by my Lord's Grace appointed: every man of the army, upon general commandment, made private provision for himself, for four days' victail.

Thursday, the first of September. Is Grace, with not many more than his own band of horsemen, rode to a town in the Scottish borders, standing upon the sea coast, a six mile from Berwick, and is called Eyemouth: where there runneth a river [*Eye Mill water*] into the sea, the which he caused to be sounded; and perceiving then the same to be well able to serve for a haven, hath since caused building to be made there, whereof both Master and Captain is THOMAS GOWER, Marshal of Berwick.

Friday, the 2nd of September. PON commandment generally given, by sound of trumpet, all save the council, departed the town; and encamped a two flight-shots off, upon the sea-side, toward Scotland.

This day, my Lord CLINTON with his fleet took the seas from Berwick toward Scotland, and herefore the rather, that though they might not have always wind at will to keep their course still with us; yet, and it were but with the driving of tides, they might, upon any our need of munition or victail, not be long from us.

My Lord Lieutenant and Master Treasurer, who remained at Newcastle after my Lord's Grace, for the full despatch of the rest of the army, came this day to Berwick.

Saturday, the 3rd of September. MY LORD Lieutenant, from out of the town, did camp in the field with the army. To the intent, the excuse of ignorance either of the cause of my Lord Grace's coming, or of his goodness to such of the Scots as should show themselves to favour the same coming, might quite be taken from them; his Grace's *Proclamation*, whereof they could not but hear, was openly pronounced by Herald, after sound of trumpet, in three several places of our camp.

Besides the mere matter of the journey, I have here to touch a thing, which seem it ever so light to other, yet is it of more weight to me, than to be let pass unspoken of.

In the morning of this day, my Lord's Grace, walking upon the rampart of the town walls on the side towards Scotland, did tell, I remember, that, not many nights before he dreamt he was come back again to the Court, where the King's Majesty did heartily welcome him home, and every Estate else [*also*] : but yet him thought he had done nothing at all in this voyage: which when he considered the King's Highness's great costs, and the great travail of the great men and soldiers, and all to have been done in vain, the very care and shamefast abashment of the thing did waken him out of his dream. What opinion might we conceive of his waking thoughts? that even, dreaming, was moved with so pensive a regard of his charge towards his Prince, and with so humane a thought toward all men else!

Howbeit, my mind is rather to note the prognostication and former advertence of his future success in this his enterprise, the which, I take it, was hereby then most certainly showed him : although, of right few, or rather of none, the same be so taken. That if, for ensample like to this, I should rehearse Gen. xli. to you out of the *Old Testament*, how the seven plentiful years, and the seven years of famine in Egypt were plainly signified afore to PHARAOH by his dreams of seven fat oxen, and seven full ears of corn ; and by seven lean oxen that devoured the fat, and seven withered ears consuming the full ears. JUSTINI *li.* 1. And hereto, out of profane authors, how ASTYAGES,

King of the Medians, was, many a day before, admonished
that he should be overcome by a nephew* of his, as *His name was
yet then ungotten and unborn, and lose his kingdom, CYRUS.
and this by a dream also, wherein he thought there sprang
out of the womb of his daughter MANDANE, JOSEPHUS *de
a vine, by the spreading of whose branches *antiquit. lib.*
all Asia was shadowed. And how ARCHELAUS, *ultimo.*
King of Cappadocia, was warned afore of his ban- De Divin. i.
ishment out of his country and kingdom by his VALER. *li.* i.
dream of ten wheat ears, full ripe, that were eaten *ca.* vii.
of oxen. And hereto the multitude of ensamples *illustr. cap.*
besides touching this case in TULLY, VALERIUS CŒLIUS *An-*
MAXIMUS, PLINY the second, [L.] CŒLIUS [RICHE- *tig. lect. li.* xiv.
RIUS] *Rodiginus*, SUETONIUS, and in infinite authors SUETONIUS *in*
more; they should be too cumberous and irksome both for me *cap.* xxiii.
to write and you to read.

The natural cause of which kind of prophecying, as I may
call it, whether it come, as astronomers hold opinion, by the
influence of the air or by constellation; or else by sobriety of
diet, and peculiar to the melancholic, as both *SOCRATES*
PLATO and also physicians affirm; or by gift of *apud* PLATO
GOD as divine judge: I trust I shall be borne with,
although I do not here take upon me to discuss, but leave it
for a doubt among them as I found it.

Yet that there is such dignity and divinity in man's soul,
as sometimes in dreams, we be warned of things to come;
both the learning of ancient philosophers, IAMBLICUS
PLOTINUS, IAMBLICUS, MERCURIUS, TRISME- *Ægypt.*
GISTUS, with many other doth avow; Holy MERCURIUS
Scripture and profane stories do prove; and in *Pymand.*
experience to them that do mark it, doth also show.

But to this now, that my Lord's Grace dreamt one thing,
and the contrary came to pass; writers upon the exposition of
dreams, and specially ARTEMIDOROUS do make two Lib. i. *cap.* ii.
special kinds of dreams. The one, Speculative, whereby we
see things, the next day after (for the most part), much like as
we saw them in dream: the other Allegoric, which warneth
us, as it were by riddle, of things more than a day, at the least,
after to come. And in these Allegoric dreams, he saith,
" the head betokeneth the father, the foot the servant, the
right hand signifieth the mother, the left, the wife," and so

Lib. ii. *cap.* lxv. forth. And sometimes one contrary is meant by the other, as to seem for some cause to weep or be sorry is a token of gladness to come; and again to joy much is a *Lib.* iii. *cap.* sign of care; to see foul water coming into the xxvii. house is a sign to see the house burning. APOLLO-*Lib.* iv. *cap.* NIDES, a surgeon, thought he went out, and wounded iii. many: and soon after he healed many.

Of which sort of dreams, this of my Lord's Grace was, that showed that he had done nothing, and signified, as we may now be held to conster, he should do so much as it were scant possible to do more. Howbeit, as I would have no man so much to note and esteem dreams, as to think there are none vain, but all significative; a thing indeed, both fondly superstitious, and against the mind of GOD uttered in the Deut. xviii. Old Law: so would I have no man so much to contemn them as to think, we can at no time, be warned by them; a thing also both of too much incredulity, and Acts ii. against the promise of GOD rehearsed in the New Joel ii. Law, by PETER out of the prophet JOEL.

But least, with my dreams, I bring you a sleep [*asleep*]; I shall here leave them, and begin to march with the army.

Sunday, the 4th of September.

Y LORD's Grace came from out of the town, and the army raised from out of the camp.

And after this disposition of order. That Sir FRANCIS BRYAN, the Captain of Light Horsemen, with a four hundred of his band, should tend to the scout, a mile or two before; the carriage to keep along by the sea-coast; and the Men of arms and the Demi-lances (divided into three troops, answering the three Wards) so to ride, in array, directly against the carriages a two flight shot asunder from them.

Our three Battles kept order in pace between them both. The Foreward, foremost; the Battle, in the midst; and the Rereward, hindermost: each Ward, his troop of horsemen, and guard of ordnance; and each piece of ordnance, his aid of Pioneers, for amendment of ways, where need should be found.

We marched a six mile, and camped by a village called Roston [*Reston*], in the barony of Bonkendale.

Monday, E MARCHED a seven mile, till we came to
the 5th of a place called The Peaths [*Pease Bridge*].
September. It is a valley running from a six mile
west, straight eastward and toward the
sea ; a twenty score [400 *yards*] broad from bank to bank
above, and a five score [100 *yards*] in the bottom, wherein
runs a little river. So steep be these banks on either side,
and deep to the bottom, that he who goeth straight down
shall be in danger of tumbling; and the comer up so sure
of puffing and pain. For remedy whereof, the travellers that
way, have used to pass it, not by going directly, but by paths
and footways leading slopewise : from the number of which
paths they call it, somewhat nicely indeed, "The Peaths."

A bruit [*rumour*], a day or two before, was spread among
us, that hereat the Scots were very busy a working ; and
how we should be stayed and met withal by them : whereunto, I heard my Lord's Grace vow that "he would put it in
proof, for he would not step one foot out of his appointed
course."

At our coming, we found all in good peace. Howbeit the
sideways, on either side, most used for ease, were crossed
and cut off in many places with the casting of traverse
trenches, not very deep indeed, and rather somewhat hinder-
ing than utterly letting [*preventing*]. For whether it were
more by policy or diligence, as I am sure neither of both did
want, the ways, by the Pioneers, were soon so well plained,
that our army, carriage, and ordnance were quite set over,
soon after sunset, and there as then we pight [*pitched*] our camp.

But while our army was thus in passage, my Lord's Grace
(willing to lose no time, and that the Scots, as well by deed as by
bruit, should know he was come) sent a Herald to summon a
castle of GEORGE DOUGLAS, called Dunglas, that stood at
the end of the same valley, nearer the sea, and a mile from
the place of our passage.

The Captain thereof, MATTHEW HOME, a brother's son of
Lord HOME, upon this summons, required to speak with my
Lord's Grace. It was granted, and he came. To whom,
quoth his Grace, " Since it cannot be, but that ye must be
witting, both of our coming into these parts, and of our
Proclamation sent hither before and proclaimed also since ;
and ye have not yet come to us, but keep this Hold thus : we

have cause to take you as our mere enemy. And therefore, be ye at this choice (for we will take none advantage of your being here now)! whether ye and your company will render your Hold, and stand, body and goods, at the order of our will! or else to be set in it, as ye were : and we will assay, to win it as we can."

The Captain, being brought in great doubt, about this riddle, what answer well to make, and what best to do; at last, stricken with the fear of cruelty that by stubbornness he should well deserve, and moved, again, with the hope of mercy that by submission he might hap to have, was content to render [*surrender*] all at his Grace's pleasure : and thereupon commanded to fetch his company, returned to the castle.

In the time of tarrying for fetching his guard, we saw our ships, with a good gale and fair order, sailing into their Frith; which is a great arm of the sea, and runneth westward into their country above four mile. Upon this standeth Leith, Blackness, Stirling, and Saint John's road; and all the best towns else in the south part of Scotland.

This Captain came, and brought with him his band to my Lord's Grace, which was of twenty-one sober soldiers, all so apparelled and appointed, that, so GOD help me ! I will say it for no praise, I never saw such a bunch of beggars come out of one house together in my life. The Captain, and six of the Worshipful of the Company were stayed, and com· manded to the keeping of the Provost Marshal, more, (hardly), to take " Monday's handsell " than for hope of advantage. The residue were licensed to " gae their gate," with this lesson that if they were ever known to practice or do aught against the army, while it was in the country, and thereupon taken, they should be sure to be hanged.

After this surrender, my Lord JOHN GREY, being Captain of a number (as for his approved worthiness, right well he might be) was appointed to seize and take possession of the Manor " with all and singular the appurtenances in and to to the same belonging." With whom, as it hapt, it was my chance to go thither. The spoil was not rich, sure[ly], but of white bread, oaten cakes, and Scottish ale ; whereof was indifferent good store, and soon bestowed among my Lord's soldiers accordingly. As for swords, bucklers, pikes, pots, pans, yarn, linen, hemp, and heaps of such baggage besides, they were scant stopped for, and very liberally let alone : but yet, sure, it would have rued any good housewife's heart to have beholden the great unmerciful murder that our men made of the brood geese and good laying hens that were slain there that day; which the wives of the town had penned up in holes in the stables and cellars of the castle ere we came.

In this meantime, my Lord's Grace appointed that the house should be overthrown. Whereupon [JOHN BREN] the Captain of the Pioneers, with a three hundred of his labourers were sent down to it ; whom he straight set a digging about the foundation.

In the town of Dunglas, which we left unspoiled and unburnt, we understood of their wives (for their husbands were not at home) that it was GEORGE DOUGLAS's device and cost to cast those cross trenches at The Peaths ; and it stood him in four Scottish pounds, which are as much sterling as four good English crowns of five shillings a piece [=*almost* £10 *in all, now*]. A meet reward for such a work !

 Tuesday, the 6th of September. UR Pioneers were early at their work again about the castle; whose walls were so thick and foundation so deep, and thereto set upon so craggy a plot, that it was not an easy matter soon to underdig them.

Our army dislodged, and marched on. In the way we should go, a mile and a half from Dunglas northwards, there were two Piles or Holds, Thornton and Anderwick, [*Inner-wick*] both set on craggy foundation, and divided, a stone's cast asunder, by a deep gut, wherein ran a little river.

Thornton belonged to the Lord HOME, and was kept then by one TOM TROTTER. Whereunto, my Lord's Grace, over night, for summons, sent SOMERSET his Herald. Towards whom, four or five of this Captain's prickers [*Light horseman*], with their gads ready charged, did right hastily direct their course : but TROTTER both honestly defended the herald, and sharply rebuked his men ; and said, for the summons, " he would come and speak with my Lord's Grace himself."

Notwithstanding, he came not ; but straight locked up a sixteen poor soldiers, like the soldiers of Dunglas, fast within the house, took the keys with him, and commanding them they should defend the house and tarry within (as they could not get out) till his return, which should be on the morrow with munition and relief; he, with his prickers, pricked quite his ways.

Anderwick [*Innerwick*] pertained to the Lord of HAMBLE-TON [*i.e.* HAMILTON], and was kept by his son and heir (whom, of custom, they call, the Master of Hamble-ton), and eight more with him; gentlemen, for the most part, we heard say.

To be known that the Scots call the son and heir of every Lord, the Master of the house whereof his father is called Lord.

My Lord's Grace, at his coming nigh, sent unto both these Piles; which, upon summons, refusing to render, were straight assailed. Thorn-ton, by a battery of four of our great pieces of ordnance, and certain of Sir PETER MEWTYS's hackbutters to watch the loopholes and windows on all sides; and Ander-wick, by a sort [*company*] of these hackbutters alone. Who so well bestirred them[selves], that where these keepers had rammed up their outer doors, cloyed and stopped up their stairs within, and kept themselves aloft for defence of their house about the battlements; the hackbutters got in, and fired the underneath, whereby being greatly troubled with smoke and smother, and brought in desperation of defence, they called pitifully, over their walls, to my Lord's Grace, for mercy: who, notwithstanding their great obstinacy and the ensample others of the enemy might have had by their punishment, of his noble generosity, and by these words, making half excuse for them, "Men may sometimes do that hastily in a gere [*business*], whereof, after, they may soon repent them," did take them to grace, and therefore sent one straight to them. But, ere the messenger came, the hack-butters had got up to them, and killed eight of them aloft. One leapt over the walls, and, running more than a furlong after, was slain without, in a water.

All this while, at Thornton, our assault and their defence was stoutly continued: but well perceiving how on the one side they were battered, mined at the other, kept in with hackbutters round about, and some of our men within also occupying all the house under them, for they had likewise shopped [*shut*] up themselves in the highest of their house, and so to do nothing, inward or outward, neither by shooting of base [*small cannon*], whereof they had but one or two, nor tumbling of stones, the things of their chief annoyance,

whereby they might be able any while to resist our power or
save themselves; they plucked in a banner that afore they
had set out in defiance, and put out over the walls, a white
linen clout tied on a stick's end, crying all, with one tune,
for "Mercy!" but having answer by the whole voice of
the assailers, "They were traitors! It was too late!" they
plucked in their stick, and sticked [stuck] up the banner of
defiance again, shot off, hurled stones, and did what else
they could, with great courage on their side, and little hurt
of ours. Yet then, after, being assured by our earnesty
that we had vowed the winning of their hold before our
departure, and then that their obstinacy could deserve no
less than their death, they plucked in their banner once
again, and cried upon "Mercy!" And being generally
answered, "Nay, nay! Look never for it! for ye are arrant
traitors!" then, made they petition that "If they should
needs die, yet that my Lord's Grace would be so good to
them, as they might be hanged: whereby they might somewhat reconcile themselves to GOD, and not to die in malice,
with so great danger of their souls!" A policy, sure[ly], in
my mind, though but of gross heads, yet of a fine device,
Sir MILES PARTRIDGE being nigh about this Pile, at the
time, and spying one in a red doublet, did guess he should
be an Englishman; and, therefore, the rather came and
furthered this petition to my Lord's Grace. Which then
took effect. They came and humbled themselves to his
Grace: whereupon, without more hurt, they were but commanded to the Provost Marshal.

It is somewhat here to consider, I know not whether the
destiny or hap of man's life. The more worthy men, the
less offenders, and more in the Judge's grace, were slain;
and the beggars, the obstinate rebels that deserved nought
but cruelty, were saved.

To say on now. The house was soon after so blown with
powder, that more than one half fell straight down to
rubbish and dust, the rest stood, all to be shaken with rifts
and chinks. Anderwick was burned, and all the houses of
office [servants' rooms], and stacks of corn about them both.

While this was thus in hand, my Lord's Grace, in turning
but about, saw the fall of Dunglas, which likewise was
undermined and blown with powder.

This done, about noon, we marched on, passing soon after within gunshot of Dunbar, a town standing long-wise upon the seaside : whereat is a castle, which the Scots count very strong, that sent us divers shots as we passed; but all in vain.

Their horsemen showed themselves in their fields beside us ; towards whom BARTEVILLE, with his eight men, all hackbutters on horseback (whom he had right well appointed), and JOHN DE RIBAUDE, with divers others, did make: but no hurt on either side, saving that a man of BARTEVILLE's slew one of them with his piece. The skirmish was soon ended.

We went a four mile further, and having travelled that day a ten mile, we camped nigh Tantallon ; and hath, at night, a blind [*false*] alarm.

Here had we, first, certain advertisement that the Scots were assembled in camp at the place where we found them.

Wednesday, the 7th of September. ARCHING this morning a two mile, we came to a fair river called Lyn [*now called Tyne*], running all straight eastward towards the sea. Over this river there is a stone bridge, that they name Linton Bridge, of a town thereby on our right hand, and eastward as we went, that stands on the same river.

Our horsemen and carriages passed through the water, for it was not very deep : our footmen over the bridge. The passage was very straight for an army ; and therefore the longer in setting over.

Beyond this bridge, about a mile westward, for so me-thought, as then we turned, upon this same river, on the south side, stands a proper house and of some strength be-like. They call it Hailes Castle. It pertaineth to the Earl BOTHWELL; but was kept, as then, by the Governor's appointment, who held the Earl in prison.

Above the south side of this castle lieth a long hill east and west, whereupon did appear, in divers plumps, about three hundred of their prickers : some making towards the passage to be in wait there to take up stragglers and cut off the tail of our host. My Lord's Grace and my Lord Lieutenant did stay awhile [over] against the castle, upon a hill over which we should pass; as well for the army, that was not all come, as also to see a skirmish that some of these prickers by coming over the river towards us, began to make, but did not maintain. Whereupon our Foreward marching softly afore, his Grace then took his way after : at whom, out of the Castle there were roundly shot off, but without hurt, six or seven pieces ; which before that (though some of our men had been very nigh) yet kept they all covert.

In this meantime, did there arise a very thick mist, my Lord the Earl of WARWICK, then Lord Lieutenant, as I told you, of the Army, did so nobly quit himself upon an adventure that chanced then to fall, as that his accustomed valiance might well be acknowledged; whereby first, and first of all men (a little but not without purpose now to digress) being Lord Lieutenant of Boulogne next after it was won [in 1544]— beaten [*battered*] on all sides, weak without, ill harbour within, and (now to say truth, for the danger is past) scant tenable as it was—did so valiantly defend it against the Dauphin then, and all his power; that, as I remember, was reckoned at fifty-two thousand. Of whom, in a camisado [? *night attack*] then, as they had slain many of our men and won the base [*lower*] town ; his Lordship killed above eight hundred, counted [*accounted*] of the best soldiers in all France ; drave the rest away ; and recovered the town from them again.

And the next year after [1545], occupying his Office of Lord Admiral upon the sea, in person himself, what time the great Fleet of France, with all their galleys, which was no small power, came to invade our coasts ; he proferred battle unto the French Admiral and all his navy : which fight, I will not say how cowardly, he utterly refused. His Lordship repelled their force, and made them fain to fly back again home with their brags and cost in vain.

And, the same year, but with a seven thousand, whereof not five thousand landed, maugre all France, he burnt Treport and divers villages there beside; and returned to ship again, with the loss but of one DAVID GOOGAN, and no more.

And the year then next after, 1546, his diligence so well showed among the rest of the Commissioners, that an honourable and friendly peace was concluded between France and us; his Lordship was sent over, by our late sovereign Lord, to receive the oath of the late French King, for confirmation of the same peace. In which journey, how nobly, he did advance his port [*state*] for the King's Majesty's honour and estimation of the realm, and yet not above his degree, all men that saw it will easily confess with me, that it was too much then to be showed in few words here.

Very few things else, to say truth, that have been anywhere in these wars, against the enemy either nobly attempted or valiantly achieved, wherein his Lordship hath not been, either the first there in office or one of the foremost in danger; that if it fell so fit for my purpose to speak of his Lordship's honour at home, as it hath done somewhat to touch [on] his prowess abroad; I could, sure[ly], for commendation thereof, move myself matter, wherein I were able to say rather liberally much, than scarcely enough.

But omitting that therefore, and to turn to my tale again, his Lordship regarding the danger our Rereward was in, by reason of the disorder, caused at this passage, by the thickness of this mist, and nighness of the enemy; himself, with scant a sixteen horse (whereof BARTEVILLE and JOHN DE RIBAUDE were two; seven or eight light horsemen more, and the rest of his own servants), returned towards the passage, to see to the array again.

The Scots perceiving our horsemen to have passed on before (and thinking, as the truth was, that some Captain of honour did stay for the looking to the order of his Rereward) keeping the south side of the river, did call over to some of our men to know, " Whether there were any nobleman nigh there ? "

They were asked, " Why they asked ? "

One of them answered that " he was" such a man (whose name our men knew to be honourable among them), "and would come in to my Lord's Grace ; so that he might be sure to come in safety."

Our young soldiers, nothing suspecting their ancient falsehood, told him that "my Lord Lieutenant, the Earl of WARWICK was nigh there; by whose tuition, he should be safely brought to my Lord Grace's presence ! "

They had conned their lesson, and fell to their practice ; which was this.

Having come over the water, in the way that my Lord should pass, they had couched behind a hillock about a two hundred of their prickers, a forty had they sent beside, to

search where my Lord was: whom when they found, part of
them pricked very nigh; and, these again, a ten or twelve of
my Lord's small company, did boldly encounter, and drave
them well nigh home to their ambush, flying, perchance, not
so much for fear of their force, as for falsehood to trap
[*entrap*] them.

But hereby informed that my Lord was so nigh, they sent
out a bigger number, and kept the rest more secret: upon
this purpose, that they might either, by a plain onset, have
distressed him; or that not prevailing, by feigning of flight,
to have trained him under their ambush. And thus instruct[ed], they came pricking towards his Lordship apace.

"Why," quoth he, "and will not these knaves be ruled?
Give me my staff [*spear*]!" With the which, then, with so
valiant a courage, he charged at one, (as it was thought,
DANDY CAR, a Captain among them) that he did not only com-
pel CAR to turn, but himself chased him above twelve score,
[*i.e.*, 240 *yards*] together, all the way, at the spear point; so
that if CAR's horse had not been exceeding good and wight
[*swift*], his Lordship had surely run him through in this race.
He also, with his little band, caused all the rest to flee amain.

After whom then, as HENRY VANE, a gentleman of my
Lord's, and one of this company, did fiercely pursue; four
or five Scots suddenly turned, and set upon him. And though
they did not altogether 'scape his hands, free; yet by hewing
and mangling his head, body, and many places else, they did
so cruelly intreat [*treat*] him, as if rescue had not come the
sooner, they had slain him outright. But saved as he was,
I dare be bold to say, many a thousand in war or elsewhere,
have died with less than half the less hurt.

Here was BARTEVILLE run at sideling [*sideways*] and
hurt in the buttock: and one of our men slain. Of Scots
again, none slain; but three taken: whereof one was
RICHARD MAXWELL, hurt in the thigh. Who had been
long in England, not long before, and had received right
many benefits, as I heard himself confess, both of the late
King's Majesty, and of my Lord Lieutenant, and of many
other nobles and gentlemen in the Court beside; and therefore for his ingratitude and traiterous untruth threatened to
be hanged. But as otherwise he had a great deal too much
more than he deserved, so had he here somewhat too little:

for how my Lord's Grace bestowed him, I wot not; but hanged indeed he was not.

To make my tale perfect: it is certainly thought that if my Lord Lieutenant had not thus valiantly encountered them ere they could have warned their ambush how weakly as he was warded, he had been beset round about by them, ere ever he could have been [a]ware of them or rescued of us; where now hereby his Lordship showed his wonted worthiness, saved his company, and discomfited the enemy.

Soon after, he overtook my Lord Protector, being as then set at dinner; to whom he presented these prisoners, and recounted his adventures.

Whose Grace, in the meantime, had happed upon a fellow like a man, but I wot not of what sort; small of stature, red headed, curled round about and shedded [*parted*] afore, of a forty year old, and called himself KNOCKES. To say somewhat of his [be]haviour, his coat was of the colour of a well burnt brick (I mean not black), and well worth twenty pence a broad yard. It was prettily fresed, half with an ado; and hemmed round about very suitably with pasmain lace of green caddis [*worsted ribbon*]. Methought, he represented the state of a sumner in some city or of a pedler in some borough. How far soever he had travelled that day, he had not a whit filed [*defiled*] his boots; for he had none on. Harmless, belike, for he wore no weapon. He rode on a trotting tit [*horse*], well worth a couple of shillings; the loss whereof, at his taking, he took very heavily: yet did my Lord's Grace cause him to be set on a better.

I take his learning was but small, but his utterance was great, sure[ly], for he never leaved babbling, very moist mouthed, and somewhat of nature disposed to slaver; and therefore fain, without a napkin to wipe his lips, to supp at every word. Some said it was no fault in the man; but the manner of the country. Indeed they have many moist mists there. No lack of audacity or store of wit; for being taken, and brought in for a spy, and posed in that point, whither he went: neither by the honesty of his errand, nor goodness of his wit was he able to make any likely excuse. The tenour of his talk so tempered throughout, and the most of his matter so indifferently mingled, as, if they make him not both, it was hard for any there to judge whether they might

count him a foolish knave or a knavish fool.   At whom, my
Lord's Grace and others had right good sport.

As BARTEVILLE, that day, had right honestly served, so did
the Lord's right honourably quite [*requite*] it.   For straight
upon the overtaking of my Lord's Grace, my Lord Lieutenant did get him a surgeon.   Dressed he was, and straight
after laid and conveyed in my Lord Grace's own chariot, that
was both right sumptuous for cost, and easy for carriage.
The rest that were hurt, Scots and others, were here also
dressed.

We had marched that day a nine mile, and camped at
night, by a town upon the Frith, called Lang Nuddrey
[*Longniddry*].

Here we found a gentlewoman, some said a Lady, the wife
of one HUGH DOUGLAS.   She was great with child, and, in
a house of hers, there abode her good time of deliverance;
and had with her, an ancient gentlewoman her mother, a
midwife, and a daughter: whose estate, the council understanding, my Lord's Grace and my Lord Lieutenant took
order, that all night, without danger or damage, she was well
preserved.   But soon after our departure in the morning, I
heard that some of our northern prickers had visited her;
not much for her profit, nor all for their honesty; that had
they then been caught with their kindness, they should have
been sure of thanks accordingly.   Good people be they; but
given much, as they say, to the spoil.

Thursday, the
8th of Septem-
ber; being our
Lady Day.
THIS morning, in the time of our dislodging, sign was made to some of our
ships (whereof the most part and
chiefest [*biggest*] lay a ten or twelve
mile in the Frith beyond us, over against Leith and Edinburgh) that the Lord Admiral should come ashore to speak
with my Lord's Grace.

In the meantime, somewhat early, as our Galley was coming
towards us, about a mile or more beyond our Cape, the Scots
were very busy a wafting her ashore towards them, with a
banner of Saint George that they had.   But my Lord
Lieutenant soon disappointed that policy: for making towards
that place where my Lord Admiral should land, our men

on the water, by the sight of his presence, did soon discern their friends from their foes.

By and by then, my Lord CLINTON, the Admiral, came to land: who, with my Lord Lieutenant rode back to my Lord's Grace; among whom order was taken, that our great ships should remove from before Leith, and lie before Musselburgh, and their camp: and our smaller vessels, that were victuallers, to lie nearer us. This thus appointed, my Lord Admiral rode back to take the water again.

And as our army had marched onward a mile or two, there appeared upon a hill that lay longwise east and west, and on the south side of us, a six hundred of their horsemen prickers, whereof some were within a two flight shot directly against us, upon the same hill: but the most further off. Towards these, over a small bridge, for there ran a little river also by us, very hardily did ride about a dozen of our hackbutters on horseback, and held them at bay so nigh to their noses, that whether it were by the goodness of our men or badness of theirs, the Scots did not only not come down to them, but also very courteously gave place, and fled to their fellows. And yet I know they lack no heart; but they cannot so well away with these cracks.

Our army went on, but so much the slower, because our way was somewhat narrow, by means of the Frith on the one side, and certain marshes nigh on the other.

The Scots kept always pace with us, upon their hill; and showed themselves, upon sundry brunts, very crank and brag. At whom, as our captains did look to the ordering and arraying again of the Battles; my Lord Protector's Grace appointed two field pieces to be turned. Each piece shot off twice, whereof one GOLD, the Master Gunner there, discharged one, and did so well direct it, that, at his former shot, he struck off the leg of a black horse, right fair, and as it was thought the best in the company; and, at his next shot, he killed a man.

Hereby, rather somewhat calmed than fully content, they went their ways; and we saw no more of them, till the time of our camping.

Then showed they themselves very lordly aloft upon this hill again, over against us, as though they stood there to take a view of our camping and muster of our men. My

Lord Marshal [Lord GREY] minding to know their commission, did make towards them with a band of horsemen : but they went wisely their way, and would never abide the reasoning of the matter.

In the way, as we came, not far from this place, GEORGE FERRERS, a gentleman of my Lord Protector's, and one of the Commissioners of the Carriages in the army, happened upon a cave in the ground ; the mouth whereof was so worn with the fresh print of steps, that he seemed to be certain there were some folk within : and having gone down to try, he was readily received with a hackbut or two. Yet he left them not till he had known, whether they would be content to yield and come out. Which they fondly [*foolishly*] refusing : he went to my Lord's Grace, and upon utterance of the thing, got licence to deal with them as he could ; and so returned to them, with a score or two of pioneers.

Three vents had their cave, which we were [a]ware of. He first stopped up one. Another he filled full of straw and set it a fire ; whereat they within did cast water apace : but it was so well maintained without, that the fire prevailed, and they within, fain to get them, belike, into another parlour.

Then devised we, for I happened to be with him, to stop the same up ; whereby we should either smother them, or find their vents, if they had any more. As this was done, at another issue, about a twelve score [240 *yards*] off, we might see the fume of our smoke to come out. The which continued with so great a force and so long a while, that we could not but think they within, must needs get them out or smother. And forasmuch, as we found not that they did the one : we thought it for certain, they were sure of the other. So we had done that we came for, and so left them.

By this time, our ships (taking mannerly their leave of Leith with a score of shot or more ; and, as they came by, saluting the Scots, in their camp, also with as many) came and lay, according to appointment.

We had gone this day about a five mile, and camped, towards night, nigh a town they call Salt Preston by the Frith [*Prestonpans*]. Here one CHARLETON, a man, before time, banished out of England, and continuing all the while in Scotland, came in, and submitted himself to my Lord's Grace ; who took him to mercy.

Friday, the 9th of September.

HIS day is marked in the Calendar with the name of Saint Gorgon; no famous saint, sure[ly]; but either so obscure that no man knows him, or else so ancient as every man forgets him. Yet were it both pity and blame that he should lose his estimation among us. And, methinks, out of that little that I have read, I could somewhat say to bring him to light again: but then I am in doubt what to make of him, a He-Saint, a She-Saint, or a Neuter; for we have all in our Calendar. Of the male and female saints, every leaf there showeth samples enough: and, as for the neuter, they are rather, I wot, unmarked than unknown, as Saint Christmas, Saint Candlemas, Saint Easter, Saint Whitsuntide; and sweet Saint Sunday comes once a week.

Touching my doubt, now. If the day bear name in the worship and memory of him whom the Preacher HORACE doth mention in his first book of Sermons, by these words

1 *Satira* ii.　*Pastillos* RUFILLUS *olet,* GORGONIUS *hircum.*

then may we be bold to believe it was a He-Saint; but yet a very sloven saint, and, belike, a nesty.

If this name were calendared of MEDUSA *Gorgon* * that had the hair of her head turned into adders, whom PERSEUS overcame and killed, as Doctor OVID declares in his fourth book *Of changes*

[*Lib.* iv.]　GORGONIS *anguicomæ* PERSEUS *superator,*

then may we be sure it was a She-Saint. But if it were in the honour of PALLAS's shield, wherein this MEDUSA *Gorgon's* head was graven, as TITUS STROZZA (a devout Doctor, but of later days) doth say

* PHORCUS, King of the isles Corsica and Sardinia, had four daughters, SCYLLA, MEDUSA, STENIO, and EURIALE, called *Gorgons.* Of whom, as NEPTUNE had ravished MEDUSA *Gorgon* in the temple of PALLAS: this goddess for displeasure of the fact, changed all the hair of her head into snakes and adders; and gave her a further gift of that whosoever saw her should be turned straight into stone.

PERSEUS coveting to kill this monster, borrowed of MERCURY his wings and falchion; and struck off her head as she slept, and brought it with him; which PALLAS did after set in her shield: and it had the same power still after, as it had while she lived.

GORGONIS *anguicomæ cœlatos ægide vultus,* STROZ. *pr.*
        PALLAS habet.   *Æolo* iv.

Then was it neither a He, nor a She, but a plain Neuter-
Saint. And thus with the ancient authority of mere poetical
Scriptures, my conscience is so confounded, as I wot not in
the world what saint to make of him.

JAMES * of the Sink-hole, saving your reverence ! a friar, · JACOBUS DE
forsooth, that wrote the Legendaury, telleth me a VORAIGNE.
very preposterous order in good cookery, of one
GORGON † and his fellow DOROTHEUS that were first † *Legenda*
sauced with vinegar and salt, and after that, then *aurea*
broiled on a girdiron [*grid-iron*]. But to be plain, as it is best *cap.* cxxviii.
for a man to be with his friends, he hath farced [*stuffed*] his
book so full of lies, that it is quite out of credit in all honest
company. And, for my part, I am half ashamed to say that
I saw it : but since it is said, and somewhat to tell you what
I saw, he makes me THOMAS the traitor, LUPUS the lecher,
PETER the knave, if I may call a conjuror so, all *THOMAS*
to be his high and holy saints in heaven ; and that *Cantuar* ca. xi.
with such prodigal impudency, and so shameless *LUPUS* ca:
lying, as I may safely think he had either a *Bull* to *Exorcist.*
make saints of devils, or else a *Placard* to play the knave as ca. lxxiiii.
he list.

But as for GORGON, be he as he may be, it makes no great
matter : for he shall have my heart while he stands in the
calendar ; he hath been ever so lucky ! But what saint soever he be, he is, sure[ly], no Scotsman's friend : but a very
angry saint towards them.

For, upon his day, thirty-four years past, they had a great
overthrow by us at Flodden Field, and their King JAMY the
FOURTH slain : and therefore is this day not smally marked
among them.

To tell our adventures that befell now upon it, I think it
very meet that first I advertise how as we here lay.

Our camp and theirs were either [*each*] within the sight
and view of others [*each other*] ; and, in distance, as I guessed,
a two mile and [a] little more asunder. We had the Frith
on the north ; and this hill, last remembered, as I said, on
the south ; the west end whereof is called Fauxside Bray
[*now Falside Brae*], whereupon standeth a sorry castle and

half a score of houses of like worthiness by it.   We had west
ward, before us, them lying in camp.

Along this hill, being about a mile from us, were they very
busy pranking up and down, all the morning : and fain would
have been of counsel with the doings of our camp.   We,
again, because their army seemed to sit to receive us, did
diligently prepare that we might soon go to them ; and therefore kept our camp all that day : my Lord's Grace and the
council sitting in consultation ; and the captains and officers
providing their bands with store of victail and furniture of
weapons, for furtherance whereof, our vessels of munition
and victuals were here already come to the shore.

The Scots continued their bravery on the hill ; the which
we not being so well able to bear, made out a band of Light
Horsemen and a troop of Demi-lances to back them.   Our
men gat up on the hill, and thereby, of even ground with the
enemy, rode straight towards them, with good speed and
order ; whom, at the first, the Scots did boldly countenance
and abide ; but, after, when they perceived that our men would
needs come on, they began to prick [*ride away*], and would
fain have begone ere they had told their errand.   But our
men hasted so speedily after, that, even straight, they were at
their elbows, and did so stoutly then bestir them, that, what
in the onset at the first, and after in the chase, which lasted
a three mile, well-nigh to as far as the furthest of their camp
on the south side, they had killed of the Scots, within a three
hours, above the number of thirteen hundred, and taken the
Master of Home, Lord HOME's son and heir, two priests and
six gentlemen (whereof one, I remember, by Sir JACQUES
GRANADO) : and all, upon the highest, and well nighest
towards them, of the hill ; within the full sight of their whole
camp.

Of our side, again, one Spanish hackbutter was hurt : and
Sir RALPH BULLMER Knight, THOMAS GOWER, Marshal of
Berwick, and ROBERT CROUCH (all Captains of several
bands of our Light Horsemen, and men of right good courage
and approved service) were taken at this time ; distressed by
their own forwardness, and not by the enemy's force.

After this skirmish, it was marvelled on their side, that we
used so much cruelty ; and doubted, on ours, that we had
killed so many.   Their marvel was answered, that they had

picked the quarrel first themselves, and showed us a precedent at Paniarhough [*Penial Heugh*]; where, of late years,
without any mercy, they slew the Lord EVERS and a great
company with him. Our doubt was cleared by the witness
of their own selves, who confessed that there were two thousand that made out of their camp (fifteen hundred horsemen
for skirmish and five hundred footmen to lie close in ambush,
and be ready at need) and that of all these, for certain, not
seven hundred returned home.

After this skirmish, we also heard that the Lord HOME
himself, for haste in this flight, had a fall from his horse, and
burst so the canell bone [*collar bone*] of his neck, that he
was fain to be carried straight to Edinburgh, and his life was
not a little despaired of.

Then, also, my Lord's Grace, my Lord Lieutenant, and other
of the council, with but a small guard, did take, upon this
Fauxside Bray (where the slaughter, as I said, was made),
about half a mile south-east of them, full view of their camp:
whereof the tents, as I noted them, were divided into four
several orders and rewes [*rows*] lying east and west, and a
prickshot asunder; and mustered not unlike, as methought,
unto four great ridges of ripe barley.

The plot where they lay was so chosen for strength, as in
all their country, some thought there was not a better. Safe
on the south, by a great marsh; and on the north by the
Frith; which side also they fenced with two field pieces and
certain hackbuts a crock, lying under a turf wall. Edinburgh,
on the west, at their backs: and eastward, between us and
them, they were strongly defended by the course of a river,
called the Esk, running north into the Frith; which, as
[*though*] it was not very deep of water, so [*yet*] were the
banks of it so high and steep (after the manner of the Peathes
mentioned in our Monday's journey), as a small sort [*company*]
of resistants might have been able to keep down a great
number of comers-up.

About a twelve score [240 *yards*] off from the Frith, over
the same river, is there a stone bridge, which they did keep
also; well warded with ordnance.

From this hill of Fauxside Bray, my Lord's Grace, my
Lord Lieutenant, and the others descended along before their
camp; within less than two flight shots into a lane or street

of a thirty foot broad, fenced on either side with a wall of turf, an ell in height; which way did lead straight northward, and nigh to a church called Saint Michael's of Underesk [*Inveresk*], standing on a mean rising hill somewhat higher than the site of their camp.

Thus this viewed, they took their return directly homeward to our tents. At whom, in the way, the Scots did often shoot: but with all their shots, and of all our company, they killed but one horse in the midst of three, without any hurt of the rider.

And as my Lord's Grace was passed well nigh half the way homeward, a Scottish Herald, with a coat of his Prince's arms upon him as the manner is, and a trumpeter with him, did overtake his Grace, we thought, upon some errand; and therefore every man gave them place to come, and say their errands: which, as I might guess, partly by the answers as follow, were these or to this effect.

The Herald, first: "My Lord the Governor hath sent me to your Grace to inquire of prisoners taken, and therewith to say, that for the pity he hath of the effusion of Christian blood, which, by battle, must needs be shed; and because your Grace hath not done much hurt in the country; he is content ye shall return, as ye came, and will proffer your Grace honest conditions of peace."

And, then, the trumpeter: "My Lord and master, the Earl of HUNTLEY hath willed me to show your Grace that because [*in order that*] this matter may be the sooner ended, and with less hurt; he will fight with your Grace for the whole quarrel, twenty to twenty, ten to ten, or else himself alone with your Grace, man to man."

My Lord's Grace, having kept with him my Lord Lieutenant, had heard them both thoroughly, and then, in answering, spake somewhat with a louder voice than they had done their messages; whereupon we, that were the riders by, thinking his Grace would have it no secret, were somewhat the bolder to come the nigher. The words whereof, as it seemed to me, were uttered so expeditely with honour, and so honourably with expedition as I was, for my part, much moved then to doubt whether I might rather note in them the promptness of a singular prudence, or the animosity [*bravery*] of a noble courage. And they were thus:

" Your Governor may know that the special cause of our
coming hither, was not to fight, but for the thing that should
be the weal of both us and you : for, we take GOD to record !
we mind no more hurt to the realm of Scotland, than we do
to the realm of England ; and therefore our quarrel being so
good, we trust GOD will prosper us the better.   But as for
peace, he hath refused such conditions at our hands as we will
never proffer again, and therefore let him look for none till,
this way we make it !

" And thou, Trumpet ! say to thy master ! he seemeth to
lack wit, to make this challenge to me, being, by the sufferance of GOD, of such estate, as to have so weighty a charge
of so precious a jewel, the Governance of a King's person, and,
then, the Protection of all his realms : whereby, in this case,
I have no power of myself ; which, if I had, as I am true
gentleman ! it should be the first bargain I would make.
But there be a great sort [number] here among us, his
equals, to whom he might have made this challenge without
refusal."

Quoth my Lord Lieutenant to them both.   " He showeth
his small wit to make challenge to my Lord's Grace, and he so
mean ! but if his Grace will give me leave, I shall receive it ;
and, trumpeter ! bring me word thy master will so do, and
thou shalt have of me a hundred crowns " [= £30 *then* = *about*
£300 *now*].

" Nay," quoth my Lord's Grace, " the Earl HUNTLEY is not
meet in estate with you, my Lord !   But, Herald ! say to the
Governor and him also that we have been a good   *Sober* is the
season in this country ; and are here now but with a   proper term
whereby the
sober company, and they a great number : and if   Scots do sig-
they will meet us in field, they shall be satisfied   *little, easy,* or
with fighting enough. And, Herald ! bring me word   *slender.*
they will so do, and, by my honour ! I will give thee a thousand crowns [= £300 *then* = *about* £3,000 *now*].

" Ye have a proud sort among you, but I trust to see their
pride abated shortly, and of the Earl of HUNTLEY's too.   I
wis his courage is known well enough : but he is a glorious
young gentleman."

This said, my Lord Lieutenant continued his requests that
he might receive this challenge : but my Lord's Grace would,
in no wise, grant to it.

These messengers had their answers, and therewith leave to depart.

It is an ancient order in war, inviolably observed, that the Heralds and trumpeters, at any time, upon necessary messages, may freely pass to and fro between the enemies, without hurt or stay of any, as privileged with a certain immunity and freedom of passage : likewise that, during the time of any such message, hostility on both sides should utterly cease.

The Scots, notwithstanding (what moved them, I know not, but somewhat besides the rules of *stans puer ad mensam*) shot three or four shot at us, in the midst of this message doing ; but as hap was, wide enough.

On the morrow after, they had every one of their guns taken from them ; and put into the hands of them that could use them with more good manners.

It becometh me not, I wot, apertly [*openly*] to tax their Governor, with the note [*slur*] of Dissimulation : for however he be our enemy, yet is he a man of honourable estate, and worthy, for aught I know, of the office he bears.

Howbeit, touching this message sent by the Herald, to say as I think, I am fully persuaded he never sent it either because he thought it would be received by my Lord's Grace, whose courage, of custom, he knew to be such that would never brook so much dishonour as to travel so far to return in vain ; or else that he meant any sparing or pity of us, whom, in his heart, he had already devoured. But only to show a colour [*appearance*] of kindness, by the refusal whereof he might first, in his sight, the more justly, as he should list, use extremity against us ; and then, upon victory, triumph with more glory. For he thought himself no less sure of victory than he was sure he was willing to fight. And that which makes me, in this case, now to be so quite out of doubt, were these causes; whereof I was after certainly informed.

And they were, first, his respect of our only strength, as he thought, our horsemen : which (not so much upon policy to make his men hardy against us, as for that he plainly so took it) he caused to be published in his host, that "they were wholly but of very young men, unskilful of the wars, and easy to be dealt withal."

And, then, his regard to the number and place of our power and his : the which, indeed, were far unequal.

And hereto, his assured hope of twelve galleys and fifty ships that he always looked to be sent out of France, to come in at our backs.

He, with his host, made themselves hereby so sure of the matter, that in the night of this day, they fell aforehand to playing at dice for certain of our noblemen and captains of fame. For as for all the rest, they thought quite to despatch us, and were of nothing so much afraid as lest we should have made away out of the country ere they and we had met; bruiting among them, that our ships, the day before, removed from before Leith only to take in our footmen and carriages, to the intent our horsemen then, with more haste and less cumber, might thence be able to hie them homeward. For the fear hereof also, they appointed, this night, to have given us a camisado [*night attack*] in our camp, as we lay : whereof, even then, we happened to have an inkling ; and therefore late in the night, entrenched our carriages and waggon-borough, and had good scout without and sure watch within : so that if they had kept appointment (as what letted [*hindered*] them, I could not learn) they should not have been un-welcomed nor unlooked for.

Yea, the great fear they had of our hasty departure made them so hasty, as the next morrow, being the day of the battle, so early to come towards us, out of their camp: against whom, then, though they saw our horsemen readily to make ; yet would they not think, but that it was for a policy to stay them, while our footmen and carriage might be stowed a shipboard.

Marvellous men ! They would not believe there were any bees in the hive, till they came out and stang them by the nose. They fared herein (if I may compare great things to small, and earnesty to game) like as I have wist a good fellow, ere this, that hath come to a dicing board, very hastily thrusting, for fear lest all should be done ere he could begin ; and hath soon been shred [*stripped*] of all that ever he brought : but, after, when he hath come from the board with his hands in his bosom, and remembered there was never a penny in his purse, he could quickly find that the fondness was not in tarrying too long, but in coming too soon.

We are warned, if we were wise, of these witless brunts, by the common proverb that saith, "It is better to sit still, than rise up and fall." But, belike, they know it not.

In the night of this day, my Lord's Grace appointed that early in the next morning, part of our ordnance should be planted in the lane I spake of, under the turf wall next to their camp; and some also to be set upon the hill, nigh to Underesk Church, afore remembered: and these to the intent we should, with our shot, cause them either wholly to remove their camp or else much to annoy them as they lay. It was not the least part of our meaning, also, hereby to win from them certain of their ordnance that lay nearest this Church.

It will be no great breach of order I trust; though here I rehearse the thing that not till after, I heard touching the trumpeter's message from the Earl HUNTLEY: which was, as I heard the Earl himself say, that he never sent the same to my Lord's Grace, but GEORGE DOUGLAS, in his name. And this was devised by him, not so specially for any challenge sake, as that the messenger should maintain, by mouth, his talk to my Lord's Grace, while his eyes were rolling to toote [*glance*] and pry upon the state of our camp, and whether we were packing or not: as, indeed, the fellow had a very good countenance to make a spy.

But my Lord's Grace (of custom, not using so readily to to admit any kind of enemy to come so nigh) had despatched them both, with their answers, as I said, ere ever they came within a mile of our camp.

As I happed, soon after, to rehearse the excuse of the Earl, and this drift of DOUGLAS, a gentleman Scot that was a prisoner and present, sware " By the mis [*mass*]! it was like enough: for he kenned GEORGE full well," and said " he was a meet man to pick quarrels for other men to fight for."

To the intent I would show my good will to make all things as easy to the sense of the reader as my knowledge could instruct: and forasmuch as the assault, especially of our horsemen at the first; their retire again: and our last onset, pursuit, and slaughter of the enemy cannot all be showed well in one plot: I have devised and drawn, according to my cunning, three several views of them [*see pp.* 114, 115, 118, 119], placed in their order, as follow in the battle. Wherein are also other towns and places remembered, such at that time, I thought meet to mark; and in my memory could since call to mind. No fine portraiture indeed, nor yet any exquisite observance of geometrical dimension; but yet neither so gross nor far from the truth, I trust, but they may serve for some ease of understanding.

But since the scantness of room will not suffer me plainly and at length to write there every place's name, I am therefore fain instead of a name to set up a letter. The reader must be content to learn his A. B. C. again; such as I have there devised for the expounding of the same views.

They that list to learn; I trust, in this point will not much stick with me: considering also that

> *Ignoratis terminis, ignoratur et ars.*   ARISTOTLE.

If they know not my A. B. C., they cannot well know my matter: like as he that knows not RAYMOND'S *In practica testi. suis* Alphabet shall never come to the composition of *ca. vi.* his quintessence; what he shall do though, some practitioners do doubt.

And minding to interrupt the process of the battle that followeth, with as few mean matters as I may; I have thought good, to have written this here before.

*Saturday, the 10th of September. The day of the battle.** His day morning, somewhat before eight o'clock, our camp dislodged: and our host march straight towards the Church of Underesk, as well for intent to have camped nigh the same, as for placing our ordnance, and other considerations afore remembered.

The Scots, I know not whether more for fear of our departing or hope of our spoiling, were out of their camp; coming towards us, passed the river, gathered in array, and well nigh at this Church ere we were half way to it.

They had quite disappointed our purpose; and this, at the first, was so strange in our eyes, that we could not devise what to make of their meaning: and so much the stranger, as it was quite beside our expectation or doubt, that they would ever forsake their strength [*strong position*], to meet us

---

* This day was long after known in Scotland as "Black Saturday": and the battle then fought, was the last conflict between the Scotch and the English, as separate *nations*. E. A.

in field. But we, after, understood that they did not only thus purpose to do : but also to have assailed us in our camp, as we lay, if he had not been stirring the timelier.

And to the intent, at this time, that as well none of their soldiers should lurk behind them in their camps, as also that none of their captains should be able to flee from their enterprise : they had first caused all their tents to be let flat down to the ground ere they came out; and they that had horses (as well nobles as others, a few expected), that were not horsemen, appointed to leave their horses behind them, and march on with their soldiers afoot.

We came on speedily a both sides; neither, as yet, one whit ware [*aware*] of [the] other's intent: but the Scots indeed at a rounder pace.

Between the two hillocks betwixt us and the Church, they mustered somewhat brim [*exposed*] in our eyes: at whom, as they stayed there awhile, our galley shot off, and slew the Master of Greym [*Graham*] with a five and twenty near by him: and therewith so scared the four thousand Irish archers brought by the Earl of ARGYLE; that where, as it was said, they should have been a wing to the Foreward, they could never after be made to come forward.

Hereupon, did their army hastily remove; and from thence, declining southward, took their direct way towards Fauxside Bray.

Of this, Sir RALPH VANE, Lieutenant of all our Horsemen, (as I think, he, first of all men, did note it) quickly advertised my Lord ; whose Grace thereby did readily conceive much of their meaning : which was to win of us the hill, and thereby the wind, and sun (if it had shined, as it did not; for the weather was cloudy and lowering); the gain of which three things, whither [*whichever*] party, in fight of battle, can hap to obtain, hath his force doubled against his enemy.

In all this enterprise, they used, for haste, so little the help of horses, that they plucked forth their ordnance by draught of men; which at this time began freely to shoot off towards us : whereby we were furthered warned that they meant more than a skirmish.

Herewith began every man to be smitten with the care of his office and charge ; and thereupon accordingly to apply him about it. Herewith began still riding to and fro. Herewith

a general rumour and buzzing among the soldiers ; not unlike
the noise of the sea, being heard afar off.   And herewith, my
Lord's Grace and the council, on horseback as they were,
fell straight in consultation : the sharpness of whose circumspect wisdoms, as it quickly spied out the enemy's intents,
so did it, among other things, promptly provide therein to
prevent them; as needful it was, for the time asked no leisure.

Their device was thus.   That my Lord GREY, with his
band of Boulogners, with my Lord Protector's band, and my
Lord Leiutenant's ; all to the number of an eighteen hundred
men, on the East half: and Sir RALPH VANE, with Sir
THOMAS DARCY Captain of the Pensioners, and my Lord
FITZWALTER with his band of Demi-lances ; all to the
number of a sixteen hundred, to be ready and even with my
Lord Marshal, on the West half : and thus, all these together,
afore [*before*], to encounter the enemy a front : whereby
either to break their array, and that way weaken their power by
disorder ; or, at the least, to stop them of their gate [*march*],
and force them to stay, while our Foreward might wholly
have the hill's side, and our Battle and Rereward be placed
in grounds next that in order, and best for advantage.

And after this, then that the same our horsemen should retire up the hill's side ; to come down, in order, afresh, and
infest them on both their sides; while our Battles should
occupy them in fight a front.

The policy of this device, for the state of the case, as it was,
to all that knew of it, generally allowed to be the best that
could be : even so, also, taken to be of no small danger for
my Lord Marshal, Sir RALPH VANE, and others the assailers;
the which, nevertheless, I know not whether more nobly and
wisely devised of the council, or more valiantly and willingly
executed of them.

For even there, with good courage taking their leaves of
the council, my Lord Marshal requiring only that if it went
not well with him, my Lord's Grace would be good to his wife
and children ; he said, " he would meet these Scots ! "   And
so, with their bands, these captains took their way towards
the enemy.

By this, were our Foreward and theirs with a two flight
shot asunder.   The Scots hasted with so fast a pace, that it
was thought of the most part of us, they were rather horse-

men than footmen. Our men, again, were led the more with speed.

The Master of the Ordnance, to our great advantage, then plucked up the hill certain pieces; and, soon after, planted two or three cannon of them well nigh upon the top there; whereby, having so much the help of the hill, he might shoot nighest, over our men's heads, at the enemy.

As my Lord's Grace had so circumspectly taken order for the array and station of the army, and for the execution of every man's office besides; even as it is meetest that the head should be the highest, that should well look about for the safeguard of all the other members and parts of the body; so did his Grace, first perfectly appointed in fair harness [*armour*], accompanied with no more, as I noted, than with Sir THOMAS CHALLONER Knight, one of the Clerks of the King's Majesty's Privy Council, take his way towards the height of the hill, to tarry by the ordnance, where he might both best survey us all, and succour with aid where he saw need; and also, by his presence, be a defence to the thing that stood weakest in place and most in danger. The which thereby, how much it did steed anon, shall I show.

As his Grace was half up the hill, my Lord Lieutenant, as it chanced, by him, he was ware [*aware*] the enemy were all at a sudden stay, and stood still a good while. The sight and cause hereof was marvellous to us all; but understandable of none.

My Lord's Grace thought, as indeed it most likely was, that the men had overshot themselves, and would fain have been home again; and herewith said to this effect, "These men will surely come no farther. It were best to cast where we should camp for, pain of my life! they will never fight!"

It had been hardly, I wot not how bad, but I am sure no good device, for our power to have forsaken their ground, to assail them where they stood, so far from the hill that we had wellnigh won so hardly and should keep to so much advantage. And in warfare, always, timely provision is counted great policy. Hereto his Grace was sure that we were able, better and longer to keep our hill, than they their plain.

As for fighting now, it might be more than likely to who-

ever considered it, that their courage was quite quailed, and
therefore that they had no will to come any further; but
would have been glad to have been whence they came. First,
because, at that time, besides the full muster of our footmen
(of whom they thought, we had none there; but all to have
been either shipped or a shipping): then, they saw plain that
we were sure to have the gain of the hill; and they, the
ground of disadvantage, out of their Hold, and put from
their hope.

And hereto, for that their Herald gave my Lord's Grace no
warning, the which by him, if they had meant to fight it
out, who would not have presumed that (for the estimation
of their honour) they would little stuck to have sent by him;
and he, again, and it had been but for his thousand crowns,
would have been right glad to have brought?

These be the considerations that, both then and since, did
persuade me, my Lord's Grace had good cause to say, "They
would not fight!"

Howbeit hereunto if I wist and disclosed but half as much
now, as, I am sure, of circumspection, his Grace knew then;
I do not doubt but I were able sufficiently to prove he might
well be no less certain of that he had said, than any man,
might be of an undone deed. The which, nevertheless, how
true it was, the proof of the matter soon after did declare;
which was that the Scots ran quite their way [*away*] and
would never tarry stroke with our footmen where the fight,
on both sides, should have been showed.

Notwithstanding, by this time considering, belike, the state
they stood in, that as they had left their strength too soon,
so, now to be [*it was*] too late to repent: upon a change of
countenance, they made hastily towards us again, I know
not (to say truth) whether more stoutly of courage, or more
strongly of order; methought then, I might note both in their
march.

But what after I learned, specially touching their order,
their armour, and their manner of fight, as well in going to
offend, as in standing to defend: I have thought necessary
here to utter.

Hackbutters have they few or none: and they appoint their
fight most commonly always afoot.

They came to the field, all well furnish with jack [*light iron jackets covered with white leather*] and skull [*helmet*], dagger, buckler, and swords all notably broad and thin, of exceeding good temper and universally so made to slice, that as I never saw any so good, so think I it hard to devise the better. Hereto, every man his pike; and a great kercher wrapped twice or thrice about his neck; not for cold but for [*against*] cutting.

In their array, towards the joining with the enemy, they cling and thrust so near in the fore rank, shoulder to shoulder together, with their pikes in both hands straight afore them; and their followers in that order so hard at their backs, laying their pikes over their foregoers' shoulders; that if they do assail undissevered, no force can well withstand them.

Standing at defence, they thrust shoulders likewise so nigh together; the fore rank, well nigh to kneeling, stoop low before their fellows behind holding their pikes in both hands, and therewith on their left [arm] their bucklers; the one end of the pike against their right foot, the other against the enemy breast high; their followers crossing their pike points with them foreward; and thus, each with other, so nigh as place and space will suffer, through the whole Ward so thick, that as easily shall a bare finger pierce through the skin of an angry hedgehog, as any encounter the front of their pikes.

My Lord Marshal, notwithstanding, whom no danger detracted from doing his enterprise, with the company and order afore appointed, came full in their faces from the hill's side toward them.

The countenance of war.   Herewith waxed it very hot, on both sides, with pitiful cries, horrible roar, and terrible thundering of guns besides. The day darkened above head, with smoke of shot. The sight and appearance of the enemy, even at hand, before. The danger of death on every side else. The bullets, pellets, and arrows flying each [*every*] where so thick, and so uncertainly lighting, that nowhere was there any surety of safety. Every man stricken with a dreadful fear, not so much, perchance, of death as of hurt; which things, though they were but certain to some, were yet doubted of all. Assured cruelty at the enemy's hands, without hope of mercy.   Death to fly, and danger to fight.

The whole face of the field, on both sides, upon this point of joining, both to the eye and the ear, so heavy, so deadly, lamentable, outrageous, terribly confused, and so quite against the quiet nature of man : as if, to our nobility, the regard of their honour and fame ; to the knights and captains, the estimation of their worship and honesty ; and generally to us all, the natural motion of bounden duty, our own safety, hope of victory, and the favour of GOD that we trusted we had for the equity of our quarrel ; had not been a more vehement cause of courage that the danger of death was cause of fear, the very horror of the thing had been able to make any man to forget both prowess and policy.

But my Lord Marshal and the others, with present mind and courage, warily and quickly continued their course towards them : and my Lord's Grace was then at this post, by the ordnance aloft.

The enemy were in a fallow field, whereof the furrows lay sideling towards our men.

By the side of the same furrows, next us, and a stone's cast from them, was there a cross ditch or slough, which our men must needs pass to come to them : wherein many, that could not leap over, stack fast, to no small danger of themselves, and some disorder of their fellows.

The enemy, perceiving our men's fast approach, disposed themselves to abide the brunt ; and in this order, stood still to receive them.

The Earl of ANGUS, next us, in their Foreward, as Captain of the same : with an eight thousand men ; and four or five pieces of ordnance on his right side, and a four thousand horsemen on his left.

Behind him, somewhat westward, the Governor [with the Battle] with a ten thousand Inland men, as they call them ; counted the choicest men of their country.

And the Earl HUNTLEY in the Rereward, well nigh even with the Battle on the left side, with eight thousand men also. The four thousand Irish archers, as a wing to them both, last indeed in order, and first (as they said) that ran away.

The Battle and Rereward were warded also with their ordnance, according[ly].

H   I

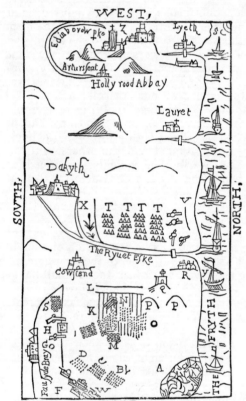

WEST,

Edinborow pko · Z · Lyeth · SC

Arthursseat

Holly rood Abbay

Lauret

Dakyth

X T T T T T V

The Ryuet Eske

Cowstand

R

y

L

S N

K P P

H O

J O

M

D C

B A

Fau syde Bray

F W

SOUTH,

NORTH,

THE FRYTH

EAST,

The First Table.

¶ The exposition of the Letters of this Table.

A. Signifieth the place we camped in, before the battle.
B. Our Rereward.
C. Our Battle.
D. Our Foreward.
E. The square Close.
F. The foot of the hillside.
G. My Lord Protector's Grace.
H. The Master of the Ordnance.
I. Our Horsemen.
K. The Slough.
L. The lane and the two turf walls.
M. Their Foreward, and horsemen by the same.
N. Their Battle.
O. Their Rereward.
P. P. The two hillocks before the church.
Q. St. Michael's of Underesk [*Inveresk*].
R. Muskelborowe [*Musselburgh*].
S. Their horsemen at the end of Fauxside Bray.
T. T. T. T. Their rows of Tents.
V. The turf wall towards the Frith.
W. Our Carriages.
X. The Marsh.
Y. Our Galley.
Z. Edinburgh Castle.

The signification of certain other notes.

• Signifieth a Footman.
o a Horseman.
⊢ a Hackbutter a foot.
⊙ a Hackbutter on horseback.
⚐ an Archer.
\ a Footmen slain.
↙ a Horsemen slain.
⦙⦙ The fallow field whereon their army stood.

EDWARD SHELLEY, Lieutenant under my Lord GREY, of his band of Boulogners, was the first on our side that was over this slough, my Lord GREY next ; and so then after, two or three ranks of the former [*leading*] bands. But badly, yet, could they make their race ; by reason, the furrows lay travers to their course. That notwithstanding, and though there were nothing likely well to be able thus a front to come within them to hurt them, as well because the Scottish men's pikes were as long or longer than their staves [*spears*], as also for that their horses were all naked without barbs [*breastplates*] whereof, though there were right many among us, yet not one put on : forasmuch as at our coming forth in the morning, we looked for nothing less than for battle that day : yet did my Lord, and SHELLEY, with the residue, so valiantly and strongly give the charge upon them, that, whether it were by their prowess or power, the left side of the enemy that his Lordship did set upon, though their order remained unbroken, was yet compelled to sway a good way back and give ground largely ; and all the residue of them besides, to stand much amazed.

Before this, as our men were well nigh at them, they stood very brave and braggart, shake their pike-points, crying, "Come here, lounds [*rascals*]! Come here, tykes [*dogs*]! Come here, heretics !" as hardly they are fair mouthed men. Though they meant but small humanity ; yet showed they hereby much civility : both of fair play, to warn ere they struck, and of formal order, to chide ere they fought.

Our captains that were behind (perceiving, at eye [*at a glance*], that both by the unevenness of the ground, by the sturdy order of the enemy, and for that their [own] fellows were so nigh and straight before them ; they were not able, to any advantage, to maintain this onset), did therefore, accord-

ing to the device in that point appointed, turned themselves,
and made a soft [*slow*] retire up towards the hill again.

Howbeit, to confess the truth, some of the number (that
knew not the prepensed [*aforethought*] policy of the council, in
this case) made, of a sober advised retire, a hasty temera-
rious flight.

Sound to any man's ear as it may, I shall never admit, for
any affection towards country or kin, to be so partial as will,
wittingly, either bolster the falsehood or bury the truth : for
honour, in my opinion, that way gotten, were unworthily won,
and a very vile gain. Howbeit hereby I cannot count any lost,
where but a few lewd soldiers ran out of array, without
standard or captain; upon no cause of need, but a mere indis-
cretion and madness. A madness, indeed !   For, first, the
Scots were not able to pursue, because they were footmen :
and, if they could, what hope by flight? so far from home
in their enemy's land ! where there was no place of refuge !

My Lord Marshal, EDWARD SHELLEY, little PRESTON,
BRAMPTON, and GERNINGHAM, Boulogners; RATCLIFFE, the
Lord FITZWALTER's brother ; Sir JOHN CLERE's son and heir ;
DIGGES of Kent; ELLERKER, a Pensioner; SEGRAVE. Of my
Lord Protector's band, my Lord EDWARD, his Grace's son,
Captain of the same band; STANLEY, WOODHOUSE, COONISBY,
HORGILL, MORRIS, DENNIS, ARTHUR, and ATKINSON ; with
others in the forerank, not being able, in this earnest
assault, both to tend [*attend*] to their fight afore, and to the
retire behind : the Scots, again (well considering hereby how
weak they remained) caught courage afresh, ran sharply forward upon them, and, without any mercy, slew every man
of our men that abode furthest in press; a six more, of
Boulogners and others, than I have here named : in all, to
the number of twenty-six, and the most part, gentlemen.

❧ The Second Table

**Showeth the placing of our footmen; the slaughter
of Edward Shelley and the others; the retire
of our band of horsemen up the hill,
and the breach of array of the
stragglers from them.**

But touching the exposition of the notes and letters; I
refer the reader to the Table before [*p.* 115].

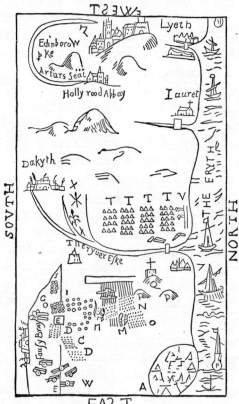

🐦 This Third Table

Showing the coming into array of our horsemen upon the hill again; the placing of the hackbutters against the enemy; the shooting of our archers: and then the coming down of our horsemen after, about the chase and slaughter of the enemy.

M. Signify the pikes and weapons let fall by the Scots, in
N.   the place where they stood.
O.   As for the other characters, I refer the Reader again to the first Table [*p.* 115].

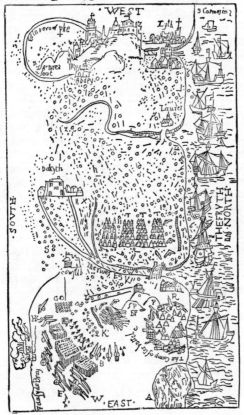

Yet my Lord GREY and my Lord EDWARD (as some grace
was) returned, but neither all in safety, nor without evident
marks they had been there : for the one, with a pike through
the mouth, was raced [*torn*] along from the tip of the tongue,
and thrust that way very dangerously, more than two inches
with the neck; and my Lord EDWARD had his horse under
him, wounded sore with swords, and I think to death.

Like as also, a little before this onset, Sir THOMAS DARCY
upon his approach to the enemy was struck glancing wise,
on the right side, with a bullet of one of their field pieces;
and thereby his body bruised with the bowing in of his
harness, his sword hilts broken, and the forefinger of his right
hand beaten flat: even so, upon the parting of this fray, was
Sir ARTHUR DARCY flashed at with swords, and so hurt upon
the wedding finger of his right hand also, as it was counted
for the first part of medicine to have it quite cut away.

About the same time, certain of the Scots ran out hastily
to the King's Majesty's Standard of the Horsemen, the
which Sir ANDREW FLAMMACK bare ; and laying fast hold of
upon the staff thereof, cried, " A King! A King!" that if
both his strength, his heart, and his horse had not been
good; and hereto, somewhat aided, at this pinch, by Sir
RALPH COPPINGER a Pensioner, both he had been slain, and
the standard lost; which the Scots, nevertheless, held so
fast that they brake and bare away the nether [*lower*] end of
the staff to the burrell [*ring*] and intended so much to the
gain of the standard, that Sir ANDREW, as hap was, 'scaped
home all safe, and else without hurt.

At this business, also, was my Lord FITZWALTER, Captain of
a number of Demi-lances, unhorsed ; but soon mounted again,
escaped, yet in great danger, and his horse all [that] he wan.

Hereat further, were CAVARLEY, the Standard Bearer of the
Men of Arms, and CLEMENT PASTON a Pensioner, each of
them thrust into the legs with pikes; and Don PHILIP, a
Spaniard, in the knee : divers others maimed and hurt ; and
many horses sore wounded beside.

❡ By this time, had our Foreward, accordingly, gotten the
full vantage of the hill's side ; and, in respect of their march,
stood sideling towards the enemy: who, nevertheless were
not able, in all parts, to stand full square in array by reason
that at the west end of them, upon their right hand and

towards the enemy, there was a square plot enclosed with turf,
as their manner of fencing [*making with walls*] in those parts
is ; one corner whereof did let the square of the same array.
Our Battle, in good order, next them, but so as in continuance of array: the former part thereof stood upon the hill's
side, the tail upon the plain.   And the Rereward wholly upon
the plain.

So that by the placing and countenance of our army in
this wise, we showed ourselves, in a manner, to compass them
in, that they should, in no way 'scape us : the which, by our
power and number, we were as well able to do, as a spinner's
web to catch a swarm of bees. Howbeit, for heart and courage,
we meant to meet with them, had they been as many more.

Those indiscreet gadlings that so fondly brake array from
the horsemen in the retire, as I said, ran so hastily through
the orders and ranks of our Foreward, as it stood, that it did
both disorder many, feared many, and was a great encouragement to the enemy.

My Lord Lieutenant, who had the guiding of the Foreward,
right valiantly had conducted them to their standing : and
there did very nobly encourage and comfort them ; bidding
them, " Pluck up their hearts ! and show themselves men ! for
there was no cause of fear.   As for victory, it was in their
own hands, if they did abide by it ! and he himself, even
there, would live and die among them ! "

And surely, as his Worthiness always right well deserveth,
so was his Honour, at that time, worthily furnished with
worthy captains.

First, Sir JOHN LUTTERELL, who had the leading of a
three hundred of his Lordship's men, that were the foremost
of this Foreward ; all with harness and weapon : and, in all
points else, so well trimmed for war that, like as, at that
time, I could well note my Lord's great cost and honour, for
their choice and perfect appointment and furniture ; so did I
then also consider Sir JOHN LUTTRELL's prowess and wisdom
for their valiant conduction, and exact observance   I mean such a
of order.   Whom (knowing, as I know) for his wit,   one as Count
                                                      BALDASSARE
manhood, good qualities, and aptness to all gentle   [CASTIGLIONE]
                                                      the Italian, in
feats besides ; I have good cause to count both a   his book of
good Captain a warfare in field, and a worthy   *The Courtier*
                                                      doth frame.
Courtier in peace at home.

Then in the same Foreward, Sir MORICE DENNIS, another Captain, who wisely first exhorting his men "to play the men, showing thereby the assurance of victory," and then to the intent they should be sure he would never shrink from them, he did with no less worship than valiance, in the hottest of this business, alighted among them, and put his horse from him.

But if I should (as cause, I confess, there was enough) make here any stay in his commendation therefore, or of the forward courage of Sir GEORGE HAWARD, who bear the King's Majesty's Standard in the Battle; or of the circumspect diligence of Sir WILLIAM PICKERING and Sir RICHARD WINGFIELD, Sergeants of the Band to the Foreward; or of the prompt forwardness of Sir CHARLES BRANDON, another captain there; or of the painful industry of Sir JAMES WILFORD, Provost Marshal, who placed himself with the foremost of this Foreward; or of the good order in march of Sir HUGH WILLOUGHBY and WILLIAM DENNIS Esquire, both captains; or of the present heart of JOHN CHALLONER, a captain also in the battle; or of the honest respect of EDWARD CHAMBERLAIN, Gentleman Harbinger [*Quartermaster*] of the Army, who willingly as then, came in order with the same Foreward; or of right many others in both these Battles (for I was not nigh the Rereward) whose behaviour and worthiness were, at that time, notable in mine eye (although I neither knew then all of them I saw; nor could since remember of them I knew) I might well be in doubt it should be too much an intrication to the matter, too great a tediousness to the reader. And therefore to say on.

The Scots were somewhat disordered with their coming out about the slaughter of our men; the which they did so earnestly then intend, they took not one to mercy. But more they were amazed at this adventurous and hardy onset. My Lord's Grace having before this, for causes aforesaid, placed himself on this Fauxside Bray, and thereby quickly perceiving the great disorder of these straggling horsemen, hemmed them in from further straying; whom Sir RALPH VANE, with great dexterity, brought in good order and array again.

And therewith, the rest of our strengths, by the policy of

my Lord's Grace, and the diligence of every captain and officer beside, were so opportunely and aptly applied, in their feat, that where this repulse by the enemy and retire of us were doubted by many, to turn to the danger of our loss: the same was wrought and advanced, according as it was devised, to our certainty of gain and victory.

For, first, at this slough, where most of our horsemen had stood, Sir PETER MEWTYS, Captain of all the Hackbutters afoot, did very valiantly conduct, and place a good number of his men, in a manner, hard at the face of the enemy. Whereunto, Sir PETER GAMBOA, a Spaniard, Captain of a two hundred Hackbutters on horseback, did readily bring his men also: who, with the hot continuance of their shot, on both parties, did so stoutly stay the enemy, that they could not well come further forward.

Then our archers that marched in array, on the right hand of our footmen, and next to the enemy, pricked them sharply with arrows, as they stood.

Therewith, the Master of the Ordnance, to their great annoyance, did gall with hail shot and other [shot] out of the great ordnance directly from the hill top; and certain other gunners, a flank, from our Rereward. Most of our artillery and missive engines then wholly thus at once, with great puissance and vehemency, occupied about them.

Herewith, the full sight of our footmen, all shadowed from them before, by our horsemen and the dust raised; whom then they were ware [aware], in such order, to be so near upon them. And to this the perfect array of our horsemen again coming courageously to set on them afresh. Miserable men! perceiving themselves, then all too late, how much too much they were misinformed, began suddenly to shrink. Their Governor, that brought them first to the bargain, like a doughty Captain, took hastily his horse that he might run foremost away. Indeed, it stood somewhat with reason that he should make first homeward that first made outward; but, as some of them said, scant [scarcely] with honour, and with shame enough. The Earl of ANGUS and other chief captains did quickly follow, as their Governor led; and with the foremost, their Irishmen.

Therewith then turned all the whole rout, kest [cast] down their weapons, ran out of their Wards, off with their jacks and with all that ever they might, betook them to the race that their Governor began.

Our men had found them at the first (as what could escape so many thousand eyes?), and sharply and quickly, with an universal outcry, "They fly! They fly!" pursued after in chase amain: and thereto so eagerly and with such fierceness, that they overtook many, and spared indeed but few; as it might then hardly have been both folly and peril to have showed any pity.

But when they were once turned; it was a wonder to see how soon, and in how sundry sorts they were scattered. The place they stood on like a wood of staves [*pikes*] strewed on the ground as rushes in a chamber; impassable they lay so thick, for either horse or man.

Here, at the first, they let fall all their pikes after that, everywhere, they scattered swords, bucklers, daggers, jacks, and all things else that either was of any weight, or might be any let to their course. Which course among them, they made specially three ways. Some along the sands by the Frith, towards Leith. Some straight towards Edinburgh, whereof part went through the park there: in the walls whereof, though they be round about of flint stone; yet were there many holes already made. And part of them by the highway that leads along by Holy Rood Abbey. And the residue, and, as we noted then, the most of them towards Dalkeith: which way, by means of the marsh, our horsemen were worst able to follow.

Sundry shifts, some shrewd, some sorry, made they in their running. Divers of them in their courses, as they were ware [*aware*] they were pursued but of one, would suddenly back, and lash at the legs of the horse or foin [*thrust*] him in the belly. And sometime did they reach at the rider also: whereby CLEMENT PASTON in the arm, and divers others otherwise, were hurt in this chase.

Some other lay flat in a furrow, as though they were dead, and thereby were passed by of our men untouched; as I heard say, the Earl of ANGUS confessed he couched till his horse happed to be brought him. Other some, to stay in the river, cowering down his body, his head under the root of a willow tree, with scant his nose above water for breath. A shift, but no succour, it was to many that had their skulls [*helmets*] on, at the stroke of the follower, to shrink their heads into their shoulders, like a tortoise into its shell. Others, again, for their more lightness, cast away shoes and doublets; and ran in their shirts. And some were also seen in this race, to fall flat down all breathless, and to have run themselves to death.

Before this, at the time of our onset, came there eastward, a five hundred of their horsemen, up along this Fauxside Bray, straight upon our ordnance and carriage. My Lord's Grace, as I said, most specially for the doubt of the same, placing himself thereby, caused a piece or two to be turned towards them; with a few shots whereof, they were soon turned also, and fled to Dalkeith. But had they kept on, they were provided for accordingly. For one parson KEBLE, a Chaplain of his Grace's, and two or three others, by and by discoverd four or five of the carts of munition, and therewith bestowed pikes, bills, bows and arrows to as many as came. So that of carters and others there were soon weaponed, there, about a thousand men; whom parson KEBLE and the others did very handsomely dispose in array, and made a pretty muster.

To return now. Soon after this notable strewing of their footmen's weapons, began a pitiful sight of the dead corpses lying dispersed abroad. Some, with their legs off; some but hought [*ham-strung*] and left lying half dead: others, with the arms cut off; divers, their necks half asunder; many, their heads cloven; of sundry, the brains pasht [*smashed*] out; some others again, their heads quite off: with a thousand other kinds of killing.

After that, and further in the chase, all, for the most part, killed either in the head or in the neck; for our horsemen could not well reach them lower with their swords.

And thus, with blood and slaughter of the enemy, this chase was continued five miles in length westward, from the place of their standing, which was in the fallow fields of Underesk [*Inveresk*], unto Edinburgh Park, and well nigh to the gates of the town itself, and unto Leith; and in breadth, nigh three miles, from the Frith sands, towards Dalkeith southward. In all which space, the dead bodies lay as thick as a man may note cattle grazing in a full replenished pasture. The river ran all red with blood: so that in the same chase were counted, as well by some of our men that

somewhat diligently did mark it, as by some of them taken
prisoners, that very much did lament it, to have been slain
above thirteen thousand. In all this compass of ground,
what with weapons, arms, hands, legs, heads, blood, and
dead bodies, their flight might have easily been tracked to
every [*each*] of their three refuges.

And for the smallness of our number, and the shortness of
the time, which was scant five hours, from one till well nigh
six, the mortality was so great, as it was thought the like
aforetime had not been seen. Indeed, it was the better
maintained with their own swords that lay each where
[*everywhere*] scattered by the way ; whereof our men, as they
brake one, still took up another. There was store enough :
and they laid it on so freely, that right many among them, at
this business, brake three or four ere they returned homeward
to the army.

I may well, perchance, confess that herein we used some
sharpness, although not as much as we might have, and little
courtesy : and yet I can safely avow, all was done by us as
rather by sundry respects driven and compelled, than either
of cruelty or of delight in slaughter. And like, some way,
to the diligent master that sharply sometimes, when warning
will not serve, doth beat his scholar : not hardly [*probably*] for
hate of the child or his own delight in beating, but for love,
he would have him amend his faults or negligence ; and beats
him once surely, because he would need to beat him no
more.

One cause of the correction we used, I may well count to
be, the tyrannous Vow that they made, which we certainly
heard of, that whensoever they fought and overcame, they
would slay so many and spare so few : a sure proof whereof
they plainly had showed at our onset before, where they
killed all, and saved not a man.

Another respect was to revenge their great and cruel
tyranny at Panyar Hough [? *Penial Heugh*], as I have said
before, where they slew the Lord EVERS, whom otherwise
they might have taken prisoner and saved ; and cruelly killed
as many else of our men as came into their hands.

We were forced yet hereto, by a further and very earnest
regard, which was the doubt of the assembling of their army
again ; whereof a cantel [*fraction*], for the number, had been

able to compare with our whole host, when it was at the greatest : and so, perchance, we should have been driven, with double labour, to beat them again, and make two works out of one; whereas we well remembered that " a thing once well done, is twice done."

To these, another, and not the meanest matter, was that their armour among them so little differed, and their apparel was so base and beggarly; wherein the Lurdein was, in a manner, all one with the Lord; and the Lound with the La[i]rde : all clad alike in jacks covered with white leather; doublets of the same or of fustian; and most commonly all white hosen. Not one! with either chain, brooch, ring, or garment of silk that I could see; unless chains of latten [*pewter*] drawn four or five times along the thighs of their hosen, and doublet sleeves for cutting: and of that sort I saw many. This vileness of port [*dress*] was the cause that so many of their great men and gentlemen were killed; and so few saved. The outward show, the semblance and sign whereby a stranger might discern a villain from a gentleman, was not to be seen among them. As for words and goodly proffer of great ransoms, they were as common and rife in the mouths of the one as the other : and therefore it came to pass that after, in the examination and counting of the prisoners, we found we had taken above twenty of their villains to one of their gentlemen : whom no man need to doubt we had rather have spared than the villains, if we could have known any difference between them in the taking.

The name of Lord the Scots take in like signification of speech as we do: but a La[i]rde with them, I take it, is as Squire [Esquire] with us.

A Lound is a name of reproach, as a Villain or such like.

And yet, notwithstanding all these our just causes and quarrels to kill them, we showed more grace, and took more to mercy, than the case on our side, for the causes aforesaid, did well deserve or require.

For, beside the Earl HUNTLEY who was appointed in good harness (likest a gentleman of any of them that I could hear of or see) who could not then escape because he lacked his horse; and therefore happed to be taken by Sir RALPH VANE; and beside the Lord of YESTER: HOBBY HAMBLETON [*HAMIL-TON*], Captain of Dunbar; the Master of Sampoole [*Semple*]: the Laird of Wimmes, taken by JOHN BREN; a brother of the Earl of CASSIL[I]S; besides one MOUTRELL. taken by

A kinsman, belike, of the Earl of ARGYLE whose proper name is CAMALL [? CAMPBELL] like as the Earl of ANGUS's is DOUGLAS, and the Earl of HUNTLEY's is GORDON.

CORNELIUS, Comptroller of the Ordnance of this army; and one of the CAMALS [? CAMPBELLS], an Irish gentleman, taken by EDWARD CHAMBERLAIN; and besides many other Scottish gentlemen more, whose names and takers I remember not well, the prisoners accounted by the Marshal's book, were numbered to above fifteen hundred.

A Scottish herald was also taken: but here not placed: because my Lord's Grace caused him forthwith freely to be released home; without ransom or loss.

Touching the slaughter, sure[ly] we killed nothing so many as, if we had minded cruelty so much, for the time and opportunity right well we might. For my Lord's Grace, of his wonted mercy, much moved with the pity of this sight, and rather glad of victory than desirous of cruelty, soon after (by guess) five o'clock, stayed his Standard of his Horsemen, at the furthest part of their camp westward; and caused the trumpets to blow a retreat.

Whereat also, Sir RALPH SADLER, Treasurer (whose great diligence at that time, and ready forwardness in the chiefest of the fray before, did worthily merit no small commendation) caused all the Footmen to stay, and then, with much travail and great pains, made them to be brought into some order again. It was a thing not yet easily to be done, by reason they all, as then, somewhat busily applied their market, the spoil of this Scottish camp: wherein were found good provision of white bread, ale, oaten cakes, mutton, butter in pots, cheese; and, in divers tents, good wine also. Good store, to say truth, of good victail, for the manner of their country.

And in some tents among them, as I heard say, were also found a dish or two, two or three goblets, or three or four chalices of silver plate: which the finders (I know not with what reverence, but hardly with some devotion) plucked out of the cold clouts and thrust into their warm bosoms.

Here now, to say somewhat of the manner of their camp. As they had no pavilions or round houses of a commendable compass: so were there few other tents with posts, as the used manner of making is; and of these few also, none of above twenty foot in length, but most far under. For the most part, they were all sumptuously beset, after their fashion, with fleur de lys, for the love of France, some of blue buckram, some of black, and some of some other colours.

These white ridges, as I called them, that, as we stood on

Fauxside Bray, did make so great a muster towards us, which I did take then to be a number of tents : when we came, we found them to be a linen drapery, of the coarser camerick [*cambric*] indeed, for it was all of canvas sheets.

They were the tenticles or rather cabins and couches of their soldiers : which (much after the common building of their country besides) they had framed of four sticks, about an ell long a piece : whereof two fastened together at one end aloft, and the two ends beneath stuck in the ground an ell asunder, standing in fashion like the bow of a sow's yoke. Over two such bows, one, as it were, at their head, the other at their feet, they stretched a sheet down on both sides whereby their cabins became roofed like a ridge, but scant shut at both ends ; and not very close beneath, on the sides, unless their sticks were the shorter, or their wives the more liberal to lend them larger napery. Howbeit within they had lined them, and stuffed them so thick with straw, that as the weather was not very cold, when they were once couched, they were as warm as [if] they had been wrapped in horsedung.

The plot of their camp was called Edminston Edge, nigh Gilberton [? *Gilmerton*], a place of the Lord of BRUNSTON[E]S, half a mile beyond Musselburgh, and a three mile on this side Edinburgh; and occupied in largeness, with divers tents and tenticles in sundry parts out of square, about a mile's compass. Wherein, as our men, upon the sound of retreat, at their retire, were somewhat assembled; we all, with a loud and entire outcry and hallowing [*holloaing*], in sign of gladness and victory, made a universal noise and shout : whereof the shrillness, as we heard after, was heard unto Edinburgh.

It was a wonder to see, but that as they say " many hands make light work " how soon the dead bodies were stripped, even from as far as the chase went, unto the place of our onset, whereby the personages of the enemies might, by the way, easily be viewed and considered : which for their tallness of stature, cleanness of skin, bigness of bone, with due proportion in all parts, I, for my part advisedly noted, to be such as but that I well saw that it was so, I would not have believed, sure[ly], so many of that sort to have been in all their country.

Among them, lay there many priests and " Kirkmen," as they call them; of whom it was bruited among us, that

I   I

there was a whole band of a three or four thousand: but we were afterwards informed that it was not altogether so.

At the place of the charge given by us, at the first, we there found our horses slain all gored and hewn, and our men so ruefully gashed and mangled, in the head especially, as not one could, by the face, be known who he was.

Little PRESTON was found there with both his hands cut off by the wreasts [wrists]; and known to be him, for that it was known he had on each arm a bracelet of gold: for the which they so chopped him.

EDWARD SHELLEY, alas, that worthy gentleman and valiant Captain! lay all pitifully disfigured and mangled among them; and nothing discernable but by his beard. Of whom, besides the properties of his person, for his wit, his good qualities, his activities in feats of war, and his perfect honesty, for the which he was, by all men of all estates, so much esteemed and so well beloved: and hereto, for that he was my so near friend, I had cause enough here, without parsimony to praise his life and lament his death, were it not that the same should be too great a digression, and too much interruption of the matter.

But touching the manner of his death, I think his merit too much, to let pass in silence: who not inferior, in fortitude of mind, either unto the Roman CURTIUS * or the two DECII: he, being in this business, foremost of all our men against the enemy: considering with himself, that as his hardy charge upon them, was sure to be their terror, and very likely to turn to the breach of their order; and herewith also that the same should be great courage to his followers that came to give the charge with him; and pondering again that his turning back at this point, should cause the contrary,

* As there fell suddenly in Rome, a great dungeon, and swallowing of ground, CURTIUS, a Roman Gentleman, for the pleasing of the gods, and that the same might cease, mounted on his horse and leapt down into the same, which then after closed up again. VALERIUS MAXIMUS, *li.* vi. *ca.* vi.

DECIUS MUS and PUBLIUS DECIUS his son, Consuls of Rome, as they should fight, the father against the Latins, and the son after that against the Samnites; and were warned, by dream, that those armies should have the victory, whose Captains were first slain in field: they both ran willingly into the hosts of their enemies. They were slain, and their armies wan the field.

PLUTARCH, *De Decio pre paral.* xxxvii. Et LIVIUS *de P. Decio li.* x. *dec.* i.

and be great danger of our confusion, was content, in his
King's and country's quarrel, in hopes the rather to leave
victory unto his countrymen, thus honourably to take death
to himself.

Whom, let no man think! no foolish hardness or weariness of life drave unto so hard an enterprise, whose sober
valiance of courage hath often otherwise, in the late wars
with France, been sufficiently approved before; and whose
state of living, I myself knew to be such as lacked nothing
that might pertain to perfect worldly wealth.

I trust it shall not be taken that I mean, hereby, to
derogate fame from any of the rest that died there, GOD
have their souls! who, I wot, bought the bargain as dear as
he: but only to do that in me may lie, to make his name
famous who, among these, in my opinion, towards his
Prince and country, did best deserve.

Nigh this place of onset, where the Scots, at their running
away, had let fall their weapons, as I said: there found we,
besides their common manner of armour, certain nice
instruments of war, as we thought. They were new boards'
ends cut off, being about a foot in breadth and half a yard in
length: having on the inside, handles made very cunningly
of two cords' ends. These, a GOD's name! were their
targets against the shot of our small artillery; for they were
not able to hold out a cannon.

And with these, found we great rattles, swelling bigger
than the belly of a pottle [*half gallon*] pot, covered with old
parchment or double paper, small stones put in them to make
a noise, and set upon the end of a staff of more than two ells
long. And this was their fine device to fray [*frighten*] our
horses, when our horsemen should come at them. Howbeit,
because the riders were no babies, nor their horses any colts;
they could neither duddle the one, nor affray the other. So
that this policy was as witless, as their power forceless.

Among these weapons, and besides divers other banners,
standards, and pennons, a banner of white sarsenet was
found, under which, it was said these "Kirkmen" came,
Whereon was painted a woman, with her hair about her
shoulders, kneeling before a crucifix; and on her right hand,
a church: after that, written along upon the banner, in great
Roman letters,

AFFLICTÆ SPONSÆ, NE OBLIVISCARIS!

which words declared that they would have this woman to signify the Church, CHRIST's Spouse, thus, in humble wise, making her petition unto CHRIST her husband that He would not now forget her, His Spouse, being scourged and persecuted; meaning, at this time, by us.

It was said it was the Abbot of Dunfermline's banner: but whether it were his, or the Bishop of DUNKELD's, the Governor's brother (they, I understand, were both in the field); and what the number of these "kirkmen" was; I could not certainly learn. But, sure[ly], it was some devout Papist's device, that not only, belike, would not endeavour to do ought for atonement and peacemaking between us; but, all contrariwise, brought forth his standard stoutly to fight in field himself against us, pretexing [*pretending*] this his great ungodliness thus bent towards the maintenance of a naughty quarrel, with colour [*pretext*] of religion, to come in aid of CHRIST's Church.

Which Church, to say truth, coming thus to battle full appointed with weapon, and guarded with such a sort [*company*] of deacons to fight; however in painting he had set her out, a man might well think that, in condition, he had rather framed her after a curst quean that would pluck her husband by the pate, except she had her will; than like a meek spouse that went about humbly by submission and prayer to desire her husband's help for redress of things amiss.

Howbeit for saving upright the subtilty of this godly man's device, it is best we take what he meant the most likely, that is, the Church malignant and Congregation of the Wicked, whereunto that ANTICHRIST, the Bishop of Rome, is *John* ca. 2. husband, whom CHRIST said, as a thief, comes never but to steal, slay, and destroy; and whose good son, this holy Prelate, in his thus coming to the field, with his AFFLICTÆ, now showed himself to be.

There was upon this Fauxside Bray (as I have before said, *p.* 99) a little Castle or Pile, which was very busy all the time of the battle, as any of our men came nigh it, to shoot at them with such artillery as they had; which was none other than hand-guns and hackbuts, and of them not a dozen either. Little hurt did they : but as they saw their fellows in the field thus driven and beaten away before their faces; they plucked in their pieces, like a dog, his tail ; and couched themselves within all mute. But, by and by, the house was set on fire : and they, for their good will, burnt and smothered within.

Thus, through the favour of GOD's bounty, by the valiance and policy of my Lord Protector's Grace, by the forward endeavour of all the nobles and council there besides; and by the willing diligence of every captain, officer, and true subject else : we, most valiantly and honourably, wan the victory over our enemies.

Of whom, thirteen thousand were slain thus in field, of which number, as we were certainly informed by sundry and the best of the prisoners then taken, beside the Earl of LOGHEN [*LOUDEN*] were the Lord FLEMING, the Master of Greym [*Graham*], the Master of Arskyn [*Erskine*], the Master Ogleby [? *Oglevy*], the Master of Avondale, the Master of Rouen[? *Rowan*]; and many others of noble birth among them.

There were slain of Lairds, Laird's sons, and other gentle-men, above twenty-six hundred : five hundred were taken prisoners, whereof many were also gentlemen ; among whom were there of name, as I have before named, the Earl HUNTLEY, Lord Chancellor of the Realm there, the Lord of YESTER, HOBBY HAMBLETON [*HAMILTON*], Captain of Dunbar ; the Master of Sampoole [*Semple*], the Laird of Wemmis, and a brother of the Earl of CASSIL[I]S.

Two thousand, by lurking and lying as though they were dead, 'scaped away in the night, all maimed and hurt.

Herewith wan we of their weapons and armour more than we would vouchsafe to give carriage for : and yet were there conveyed thence, by ship, into these parts, of jacks specially, and swords, above thirty thousand.

This night, with great gladness, and thanksgiving to GOD (as good cause we had), we pitched our camp at Edgebuckling Bray [*Brae*], beside Pynkersclough [*Pinkie Cleugh*] ; and a mile beyond the place we camped at before.

About an hour after that, in some token, as I took it, of GOD's assent and applause showed to us touching this victory ; the heavens relented and poured down a great shower of rain that lasted well nigh an hour : not unlike and

according, as after our late sovereign Lord's conquest of
Boulogne, plentiful showers did also then ensue.

And as we were then a settling, and the tents a-setting
up, among all things else commendable in our whole journey,
one thing seemed to me an intolerable disorder and abuse.
That whereas always, both in all towns of war and in all
camps of armies, quietness and stillness, without noise, is
principally in the night, after the watch is set, observed (I
need not reason why): our Northern prickers, the Borderers,
notwithstanding (with great enormity, as thought me, and
not unlike, to be plain, a masterless hound howling in a
highway, when he hath lost him he waited on) some
"hoop"-ing, some whistling, and most with crying, "A
Berwick! a Berwick!" "A Fenwick! A Fenwick!" "A
Bulmer! a Bulmer!" or so otherwise as their Captains'
name were, never ceased these troublous and dangerous
noises all the night long.

They said they did it to find out their captains and
fellows: but if the soldiers of other countries [*counties*] and
shires had used the same manner, in that case, we should
have ofttimes had the state of our camp more like the outrage
of a dissolute hunting, than the quiet of a well ordered army.
It is a feat of war, in mine opinion, that might right well be
left. I could rehearse causes (but that I take it, they are
better unspoken than uttered, unless the fault were sure to
be amended) that might show they move always more peril
to our army but in their one night's so doing, than they
show good service, as some say, in a whole voyage.

And since it is my part to be plain in my process, I will be
the bolder to show what further I noted and heard. Another
manner have they among them, of wearing handkerchers
rolled about their arms, and letters broidered upon their
caps. They said themselves, the use thereof was that each
of them might know his fellow, and thereby the sooner
assemble or in need to aid one another, and such like
respects. Howbeit there were of the army among us (some
suspicious men, perchance) that thought they used them for
collusion; and rather because they might be known to the
enemy as the enemy are known to them, for they have their
marks too: and so, in conflict, either each to spare the
other, or gently each to take the other.

Indeed men have been moved the rather to think so, because some of their crosses [*i.e., the badge of the English army, a red cross on a white ground*] were so narrow, and so singly [*slightly*] set on, that a puff of wind might have blown them from their breasts: and that they were found, right often, talking with the Scottish prickers within less than their gad's [*spear's*] length asunder; and when they perceived they had been spied, they have begun to run at one another But so apparently *perlassent* [*i.e., in a make believe manner*], as the lookers on resembled their chasing, like the running at base in an uplandish town, where the match is made for a quart of good ale: or like the play in ROBIN COOK's school; where because the punies may learn, they strike few strokes, but by assent and appointment.

I heard some men say, it did much augment their suspicion that way, because, at the battle, they saw these prickers so badly demean themselves, more intending the taking of prisoners than the surety of victory: for while other men fought, they fell to their prey; that as there were but few of them but brought home his prisoner, so were there many that had six or seven.

Many men, yet I must confess, are not disposed always to say all of the best; but are more ready, haply, to find other men's faults than to amend their own. Howbeit, I think, sure[ly], as for our prickers, if their faults had been fewer, their infamy had been less. Yet say I not this so much to dispraise them; as a means for amendment. Their captains and gentlemen again, are men, for the most part, all of right honest service and approved prowess: and such, sure[ly], as for their well-doing, would become famous, if their soldiers were as toward as they themselves be forward.

As things fell after in communication, one question among others arose, "Who killed the first man this day, in field?" The glory whereof one JERONIMO, an Italian, would fain have had: howbeit it was, after, well tried, that it was one CUTHBERT MUSGRAVE, a gentleman of my Lord of WARWICK's, who right hardily killed a gunner at his piece in the Scots' Forward, ere ever they began any whit to turn. The fact, for the forwardness, well deserving remembrance; I thought it not meet to let it slip in silence.

This night, the Scottish Governor, when he once thought

himself in some safety, with all speed, caused the Earl BOTHWELL to be let out of prison : which whether he did it for the doubt he had that we would have released him, " willed he, nilled he " ; or whether he would show himself fain to do somewhat before the people, to make some amends of his former fault, I do not know: but this, sure[ly], rather for some cause of fear than for any good will; which was well apparent to all men, in that he kept the Earl so long before in hold, without any just cause.

Sunday, the 11th of September. IN THE morning, a great sort [*company*] of us rode to the place of onset, where our men lay slain : and, what by gentlemen for their friends, and servants for their masters, all of them that were known to be ours were buried.

In the meantime, the Master and Officers of the Ordnance, did very diligently get together all the Scottish ordnance: which, because it lay in sundry places, they could not in [*bring in*] all overnight. And these were in number, a thirty pieces: whereof one culverin, three sakers, and nine smaller pieces were of brass; and of iron, seventeen pieces more, mounted on carriages.

These things thus done. Somewhat afore noon, our camp raised. We marched along the Frith side, straight towards Leith ; and approaching nigh the same about three o'clock in the afternoon, we pight [*pitched*] our field [*i.e., the camp*] a prick shot on this side the town, being on the south-east half, somewhat shadowed from Edinburgh by a hill [*Calton Hill*], but the most of it lying within the full sight and shot of the Castle there, and in distance somewhat above a quarter of a mile.

My Lord's Grace, guarded but with a small company, was come to Leith well-nigh half an hour before the army; which he found all desolate of resistance, or anybody else. There were in the haven that runneth unto the midst of the town, a thirteen vessels of divers sorts. Somewhat of oade, wines, wainscot, and salt were found in the town : but as but little of that, so nothing else of value. For how much of other things as could well be carried, the inhabitants, overnight, had packed away with them.

My Lord Marshal and most of our horsemen were bestowed and lodged in the town. My Lord's Grace, my Lord Lieutenant, and the rest of the army in the camp.

Monday,
the 12th of
September.
 HIS day, my Lord's Grace with the council and Sir RICHARD LEE, rode about the town, and to the plots and hillocks, on either side, nigh to it, to view and consider whether the same, by building, might be made tenable and defensible.

Tuesday,
the 13th of
September.
ERTAIN of our small vessels burnt Kinghorn, and a town or two more standing on the north side of the Frith, againstLeith. In the afternoon, my Lord's Grace rowed up the Frith a six or seven miles westward, as it runneth into the land ; and took in his way an island there, called Saint Colms Ins [*Inchcolm*] which standeth a four mile beyond Leith, and a good way nearer the north shore than the south: yet not within a mile, of the nearest. It is but half a mile about ; and hath in it a pretty Abbey (but the monks were gone), fresh water enough, and also conies [*rabbits*] ; and is is so naturally strong as but by one way it can be entered.

My Lord's Grace considering the plot whereof, did quickly cast to have it kept : whereby all traffic of merchandise, all commodities else coming by the Frith into their land ; and utterly the whole use of the Frith itself, with all the havens upon it, should quite be taken from them.

Wednesday,
the 14th of
September
 HIS day ; my Lord's Grace riding back again, eastward, to view divers things and places, took Dalkeith in his way ; where a house of GEORGE DOUGLAS's doth stand: and coming somewhat near it, he sent SOMERSET his Herald with a trumpet before, to know "Who kept it ; and whether the keepers would hold it, or yield it to his Grace?"

Answer was made, that " there were a sixty persons within, whom their master, lying there the Saturday at night, after the battle, did will that they, the house, and all that was in it, should be at my Lord Grace's commandment and pleasure."

Whereupon the chiefest came out ; and, in the name of

all the rest, humbled himself unto my Lord's will; proferring his Grace, in his master's name, divers fair goshawks; the which my Lord's Grace (how nobly soever he listed to show mercy upon submission, yet uttering a more majesty of honour than to base [*abase*] his generosity to the reward of his enemy) did, but not contemptuously, refuse.

So, without coming in, passed by; and rode to the place where the battle was begun to be struck: the which having a pretty while overseen, he returned by Musselburgh, and so along by the Frith; diligently marking and noting things by the way.

Many were the houses, gentlemen, and others that, as well in his return as in his going out, upon submission, his Grace received into his protection.

This day, my Lord's Grace, as well for countenance [*the appearance*] of building as though he would tarry long; as also to keep our Pioneers somewhat in exercise (whom a little rest would soon make nought), caused along the east side of Leith, a great ditch and trench to be cast towards the Frith: the work whereof continued till the morning of our departing.

Thursday, the 15th of September. Y LORD CLINTON, High Admiral, as I said, of the Fleet, taking with him the Galley, whereof one BROKE is Captain, and four or five of our smaller vessels besides, all well appointed with munition and men, rowed up the Frith a ten mile westward, to an haven town standing on the south shore, called Blackness, whereat, towards the water side, is a castle of petty strength: as nigh whereunto as the depth of water there would suffer, the Scots, for safeguard, had laid the *Mary Willoughby* and the *Anthony* of Newcastle; two tall ships which, with extreme injury, they had stolen from us beforetime, when there was no war between us. With these, lay there also another large vessel, called by them the *Bosse*, and a seven more; whereof a part were laden with merchandise.

My Lord CLINTON and his company, with right hardy approach, after a great conflict betwixt the castle and our vessels, by fine [*sheer*] force, wan from them those three ships of name; and burnt all the residue, before their faces, as they lay.

Friday,
the 16th of
September. HE Laird of BRUNSTON[E], a Scottish gentle-man who came to my Lord's Grace from their Council, for cause of communication belike, returned to them; having with him NORROY a Herald and King of Arms of ours: who found them with the old Queen [MARY of Lorraine], at Stirling, a town standing westward upon the Frith, a twenty [*or rather forty*] mile beyond Edinburgh.

Saturday,
the 17th of
September. HERE was a fellow taken in our camp, whom the Scots called "English WILLIAM." An Englishman indeed, that, before time, having done a robbery in Lincolnshire, did run away into Scotland; and, at this time, coming out of Edinburgh Castle as a spy for the Scots, was spied himself with the manner, and hanged for his meed in the best wise (because he well deserved) upon a new gibbet somewhat beside our camp, in the sight both of the town and castle. GOD have mercy on his soul!

There is no good logicioner [*logician*] but would think, I think, that a syllogism thus formed of such a thieving *major*, a runaway *minor*, and a traiterous *consequent* must needs prove, at the weakest, to such a hanging *argument*.

Sir JOHN LUTTREL Knight, having by my Lord's Grace and the council, been elected Abbot, by GOD's sufferance, of the monastery of Saint Colms In [*Inchcolm*] afore remembered; in the afternoon of this day, departed towards the island to be stalled [*installed*] in his see there accordingly: and had with him a Convent of a hundred hackbutters and fifty pioneers to keep his house and land there; and two row barks well furnished with munition, and seventy mariners for them, to keep his waters. Whereby it is thought, he shall soon become a Prelate of great power. The perfectness of his religion is not always to tarry at home; but sometimes to row out abroad on a Visitation: and when he goeth, I have heard say, he taketh always his Sumners in his bark with him; which are very open mouthed, and never talk but they are heard a mile off. So that either for love of his blessings, or fear of his cursings, he is likely to be sovereign over most of his neighbours.

My Lord's Grace, this day giving warning that our departure should be on the morrow, and minding before (with recompence somewhat according), to reward one BARTON, that had played an untrue part; commanded, over night, that his house in Leith should be set afire. And as the same was done, the same night about five o'clock, many of our soldiers that were very forward in firing, fired, with all haste, all the town besides: but so far forth, as I may think, without commission or knowledge of my Lord's Grace as that right many horses, both of his Grace's and of divers others, were in great danger ere they could be then quitted from out [got quit] of the town.

Six great ships lying in the haven there, that for age and decay were not so apt for use, were then also set afire; which all the night did burn with a great flame very solemnly.

In the time of our camping here, many Lairds and gentlemen of the country nigh there, come to my Lord to require his protection: the which his Grace did grant to whom he thought good.

This day also, came the Earl of BOTHWELL to my Lord's Grace, a gentleman of a right comely port and stature; and hereto, of right honourable and just meaning and dealing towards the King's Majesty: whom my Lord's Grace did therefore, according to his degree and demerits, very friendly welcome and entertain. Having supped, this night, with his Grace; he, after, departed.

There stood south-westward, about a quarter of a mile from our camp, a monastery they call Holy Rood Abbey. Sir WALTER BONHAM and EDWARD CHAMBERLAIN got license to suppress it. Whereupon these Commissioners making their first Visitation there, found the monks all gone: but the church and much [a great] part of the house well covered with lead. Soon after, they plucked off the lead; and had down the bells, which were but two: and, according to the statute [i.e., the English Act of Parliament for the suppression of the Monasteries], did somewhat hereby disgrace the house. As touching the monks; because they were gone, they put them to their pensions at large.

Sunday, the 18th of September. Y LORD's Grace, for considerations moving him to pity, having, all this while, spared Edinburgh from hurt; did so leave it: but, Leith and the ships still burning, soon after seven o'clock in this morning, caused the camp to dislodge. And as we were parted from where we lay, the Castle shot off a peal (with chambers hardly and all) of a twenty-four pieces.

We marched south-eastward from the Frith, into the landward.

But part of us kept the way that the chief of the chase was continued in; whereby we found most part of the dead corpses lying very ruefully, with the colour of their skins changed greenish about the place they had been smitten in, and as there too above ground unburied. Many also, we perceived to have been buried in Underesk churchyard; the graves of whom, the Scots had, very slily for sight, covered again with green turf. By divers of these dead bodies were there set up a stick with a clout, with a rag, with an old shoe, or some other mark for knowledge: the which we understood to be marks made by the friends of the dead party, when they had found him; whom then, since they durst not for fear or lack of leisure, convey away to bury while we were in those parts; they had stickt [*stuck*] up a mark to find him the sooner when we were gone.

And passing that day, all quietly, a seven mile; we camped early, for that night, at Crainston [*Cranstoun*] by a place of the Lord of ORMISTON.

This morning, his Grace making Master ANDREW DUDLEY (brother unto the Earl of WARWICK) a knight, as his valiance, sundrywhere tried, had well before deserved it, despatched my Lord Admiral and him, with ships full fraught with men and munition, towards the winning of a Hold in the east side of Scotland, called Broughty Crak [*Broughty Castle*] which standeth in such sort at the mouth of the river Tay, that being gotten, both Dundee, Saint John's Town, and many towns else (the best of the country in those parts, set upon the Tay) shall either become subject unto this Hold or else be compelled to forego their whole use of the river from having anything thereby coming inward or outward.

Monday, the 19th of September. E WENT a ten mile, and camped toward night, a little a this side a market town called Lauder: at the which, as we had indeed no friendly entertainment, so had we no envious resistance: for there was nobody at home.

Here as our tents were a pitching, a dozen or twenty of their hedge-creepers, horsemen that lay lurking thereby (like sheep-biter curs to snatch up, and it were but a sorry lamb for their prey) upon a hill, about half a mile south-east from us, ran at, and hurt one of our men.

For acquittal whereof, my Lord's Grace commanded that three or four houses, such as they were, standing also upon a hill two flight shot southward from our camp, should be burnt. THOMAS FISHER, his Grace's Secretary, rode straight thither, with a burning brand in his one hand and his gun in the other, accompanied with no more but one of his own men, and fired them all by and by [at once]. I noted it, for my part, an enterprise of a right good heart and courage: peradventure, so much the rather, because I would not gladly have taken in hand to have done it so myself; specially since part of these prickers stood then within a flight shot of him. Howbeit, as in all this journey, upon any likelihood of business, I ever saw him right well appointed, and as forward as the best; so at the skirmish which the Scots proffered at Hailes Castles on Wednesday the 7th of this month, afore written [p. 90], I saw none so near them as he. Whereby I may have good cause to be the less in doubt of his hardiness.

Here also as we were settled, our Herald NORROY returned from the Scots Council, with the Laird of BRUNSTON and Ross their Herald: who, upon their suit to my Lord's Grace, obtained that five of their Council should have his Grace's safe conduct that, at any time and place, within fifteen days, during our abode in their country or at Berwick, the same five might come and common [commune] with five of our Council touching the matters between us.

Tuesday, the 20th of September. Oss the Herald departed early with this safe conduct. Our camp raised, and we went that day a seven mile to as far as Home Castle: where we camped on the west side of a rocky hill that they call Harecra[i]g; which standeth about a mile westward from the castle [*now called Hirsil*].

The Lord HOME, as I said, lay diseased [*ill*] at Edinburgh, of his hurt in his flight, at the Friday's skirmish before the battle. The Lady his wife came straight to my Lord's Grace, making her humble suit that like as his goodness had graciously been shown to right many others, in receiving them and their houses into his Grace's protection and assurance; even so that it would please him to receive and assure her and her house, the castle.

My Lord's Grace minding never otherwise but to assure her she should be sure so to forego it, turned straight her suit of assurance into communication of rendering. For my part, I doubt not but the terror of extremity by their obstinacy, and the profit of friendship by their submission was sufficiently showed her. The which, having well, belike, considered; she left off her suit, and desire respite for consultation till the next day at noon: which having been granted her, she returned to the castle.

They say, "a match well made, is half won." We were half put in assurance of a toward answer by the promise of a prophecy among the Frenchmen, which saith

> *Chateau qui parle, et femme qui ecout*
> *L'un veut rendre, et l'autre,*

and so forth.

There were certain hackbutters that, upon appointment before, had beset the castle: who then had further commandment given them, that taking diligent heed none should pass in or out without my Lord's Grace's licence, they should also not occupy [*use*] any shot or annoyance till upon further warning.

Wednesday, the 21st of September. His lady, in this mean time, consulted with her son and heir, prisoner with us; and with other her friends, the keepers of the castle: and, at the time appointed, returned this day to my Lord's Grace, requiring first a longer respite till eight o'clock at night, and therewith safe conduct for ANDREW HOME her second son, and JOHN HOME, Lord of Coldam Knowes [? *Cowden Knowes*] a kinsman of her husband, Captains of this castle, to come and speak with his Grace in the meanwhile.

It was granted her, whereupon these Captains, about three

o'clock, came to his Lordship; and, after other covenants, with long debating, on both parts agreed upon; she and these Captains concluded to give their assent to render the castle, so far forth as the rest of the keepers would therewith be content. For two or three within, said they, were also in charge as well as they in keeping it. For knowledge of whose minds, my Lord's Grace then sent SOMERSET his Herald, with this Lady to the castle to them: who, as the Herald had made them privy of the Articles, would fain have had leisure for twenty-four hours longer to send to their Lord to Edinburgh to know his will: but being wisely and sharply called upon by the Herald, they agreed to the covenants concluded on before by their Lady and the Captains.

Whereof part were, as I saw by the sequel, that they should depart thence, the next day morning, by ten o'clock, with bag and as much baggage as they could carry; saving that all munition and victail were to be left behind them in the castle.

Howbeit forasmuch as before their nation had not been altogether so just of covenant, whereby we might have cause then firmly to credit their promise: my Lord's grace (providing each way to be ready for them) caused this night eight pieces of our ordnance fenced with baskets of earth, to be planted on the south side, towards the castle within power [range] of battery; and the hackbutters to continue their watch and ward.

Thursday, His morning, my Lord's Grace having *the 22nd of* deputed my Lord GREY to receive the ren- *September.* dering of the castle, and Sir EDWARD DUDLEY, after, to be Captain of the same; they both departed to it: and, at the time set, ANDREW HOME and four others of the chiefest there with him, came out; and yielding the castle, delivered my Lord the keys.

His Lordship causing the residue (who were in all seventy-eight in number], to come out then, saving six or seven to keep their baggage within) entered the same, with Master DUDLEY and divers other gentlemen with him. He found there indifferent good store of victual and wine: and of ordnance, two bastard culverins, one saker, and three falconets of brass; besides eight pieces of iron. The castle standeth up on a rocky crag, at a proud height over all the country about it; well nigh fenced in on every side by marshes; with thick walls, almost round in form; and which is a rare thing upon so high and stony a ground, a fair well within it.

The keeping of this castle, my Lord betaking to Master DUDLEY accordingly, returned to my Lord's Grace at the camp.

Friday, E RAISED [the camp], and came this
the 23rd of morning to Roxburgh, a three mile from
September. Home. Our camp occupied a great fallow
field between Roxburgh, and Kelsey [*Kelso*] which stood eastward a quarter of a mile off, a pretty market town, but they were all gone forth there.

My Lord's Grace, with divers of the council, and Sir RICHARD LEE (whose charge in this expedition specially was to appoint the pioneers each where in work as [*wherever*] he should think meet; and then, where my Lord's Grace assigned, to devise the form of building for fortification: whom surely the goodness of his wit and his great experience hath made right excellent in that science) went straight to Roxburgh, to cast [*plan*] what might be done there for strengthening.

The plot and site thereof hath been, in time past, a castle: and standeth [*about a mile from Kelso*] naturally very strong, upon a hill east and west, of an eight score [= 160 *yards*] in length and three score [= 60 *yards*] in breadth, drawing to narrowness at the east end: the whole ground whereof, the old walls do yet environ. Besides the height and hardness to come to, it is strongly fenced, on either side, with the course of two great rivers, Tweed on the north, and Teviot on the south: both of which joining somewhat nigh together at the west end of it. The Teviot, by a large compass about the fields we lay in, at Kelsey doth fall into this Tweed: which, with great depth and swiftness, runneth from thence eastward into the sea at Berwick; and is notable and famous for two commodities [e]specially, salmon and whetstones.

Over this, betwixt Kelsey and Roxburgh, there hath been a great stone bridge with arches, the which the Scots, in time past, have all to broken; because [*in order that*] we should not come that way to them.

Soon after my Lord's Grace's survey of the plot and determination to do as much indeed for making it defensible as the shortness of the time and the season of the year could suffer : which was that one great trench of twenty feet broad, with depth accordingly, and a wall of like breadth and height, should be made across within the castle from the one sidewall to the other, and a forty foot from the west end ; and that a like trench and wall should likewise be cast a travers, within about a quoit's cast from the east end. And hereto that the castle walls, on either side, where need was, should be mended with turf, and made with loopholes as well for shooting forward as for flanking at hand. The work of which device did make that besides the safeguard of these trenches and walls, the keepers [*garrison*] should also be much fenced by both the end walls of the castle.

The pioneers were set awork, and diligently applied in the same.

This day, the Laird of Cesforth [*Cessford*], and many other Lairds and gentlemen of Teviotdale and their Marches there, having come and communed with my Lord's Grace, made us an "assurance," which was a friendship and, as it were, a truce ; for that day, till next day at night.

This day, in the mean while their assurance lasted, these Lairds and gentlemen aforesaid, being the chiefest of the whole Marches and Teviotdale, came in again : whom my Lord's Grace, with wisdom and policy, without any fighting or bloodshed, did win into the obedience of the King's Majesty ; for the which they did willingly then also receive an oath. Whose names follow.

Lairds.

The Laird of Cesforth.
The Laird of Fernyhurst.
The Laird of Greenhead.
The Laird of Hunthill.
The Laird of Huntley.
The Laird of Markstone by Mereside.
The Laird of Browniedworth.
The Laird of Ormiston.

The Laird of Mallestaines. [*Mellerstane*].
The Laird of Walmesey.
The Laird of Linton.
The Laird of Edgerston.
The Laird of Marton [*Merton*].
The Laird of Mowe.
The Laird of Riddell.
The Laird of Beamerside.

Gentlemen.

GEORGE TROMBULL [TURNBULL].
JOHN HOLLYBURTON.
ROBERT CAR.
ROBERT CAR, of Greyden.
ADAM KIRTON.
ANDREW MEYTHER.
SAUNDERS SPURVOSE, of Erleston.
MARK CAR, of Litleden.
GEORGE CAR, of Faldenside.
ALEXANDER MACDOWELL.
CHARLES ROTHERFORD.

THOMAS CAR, of the Yare.
JOHN CAR, of Meinthorn.
WALTER HALYBURTON.
RICHARD HANGANSIDE.
ANDREW CAR.
JAMES DOUGLAS, of Cavers.
JAMES CAR, of Mersington.
GEORGE HOPPRINGLE.
WILLIAM ORMISTON, of Endmer-
den.
JOHN GRIMSLOW.

Many more there were, there, besides; whose names also for that they remain in register with these, I have thought the less necessary to write here.

My Lord's Grace did tender so much the furtherance of this work in the Castle [of Roxburgh], that, this day, as every day else during our camping there, his Grace did not stick to dig with a spade above two hours himself. Whereby, as his Estate, sure[ly] was no more embased [*lowered*] than the majesty of great Alexander, what time he set, CURTIUS *lib.* with his own hands, the poor cold soldier in his own viii. chair of Estate, to relieve him by his fire: so, by the example hereof, was every man so moved, that there were but few of the Lords, Knights, and gentlemen in the field, but with spade, shovel, or mattock, did their parts therein right willingly and uncompelled.

Sunday, the 25th of September. His day, began the Scots to bring victail to our camp; for the which they were so well entreated and paid, that, during the time we lay there, we wanted none of the commodities their country could minister.

Monday, the 26th of September. O NOTABLE thing, but the continuance of our work at the Castle. For further-ance whereof, order was taken that the Captains of footmen, each after other, should send up his hundred soldiers thither to work an hour's space.

Tuesday, the 27th of September.

THE Laird of Coldam Knowes [*Cowden Knowes*] not having so fully kept his appointment, made at Home Castle, touching his coming again to my Lord's Grace at Roxburgh; Sir RALPH VANE, with a two or three hundred horse, about three o'clock in this morning, was sent to his house for him : which was a seven mile from us. The which charge, Master VANE did so earnestly apply, as he was there, with his number, before six. But the Laird, whether he was warned thereof by privy scout or spy or not, he passed by another way; and, soon after seven, was with my Lord's Grace in the camp. Master VANE was welcomed : and having no resistence made, but all submission, and profer of good cheer (for so had the Laird charged his wife to do) ; soon after, returned to the camp.

This day, my Lord's Grace was certified by letter from my Lords CLINTON and Sir ANDREW DUDLEY, that, on the Wednesday last, being the 21st of this month, after certain of their shot discharged against the Castle of Broughty Crak, the same was yielded unto them. The which, Sir ANDREW did then enter; and, after, keep as Captain.

Wednesday, the 28th of September.

A SCOTTISH Herald, accompanied with certain Frenchmen (that were, perchance, more desirous to mark our army, than to wit [*know*] of our welfare) came, and declared from their Council, that, within a sevennight [*week*] after, their Commissioners, to whom my Lord's Grace had before granted his safe conduct, should come and commune with our Council at Berwick: Whose coming my Lord Lieutenant, Master Treasurer, and the other of our Commissioners did, so long while, there abide.

But these Scots (as men that are never so just, and in nothing so true as in breach of promise and using untruth) neither came, nor, belike, meant to come. And yet sure[ly], I take this for no fetch of a fine device: unless they mean thereby to win that they shall never need, after, to promise: *In Epigr. Mori.* using the feat of ARNUS: who with his always swearing, and his ever lying, at last, obtained that his bare word was as much in credit as his solemn oath: but his solemn oath no more than an impudent lie. However since

I am certain that sundry of them have showed themselves right honest : I would be loath here to be counted so unadvised as to arret [*impute*] the faults of many to the infamy of all.

It was said among us, they had in the meantime received letters of consolation, and many gay offers from the French King : yet had that been no cause to have broken promise with the Council of a realm.   Howbeit, as these letters were to them but an unprofitable plaster to heal their hurt then ; so are they full likely, if they trust much therein to find them a corzey [*corasive*] that will fret them a new sore.

My Lord's Grace considering that of virtue and well doing, the proper need is honour (as well therefore for reward to them that had afore done well, as for cause of encourage[ment] to others, after, to do the like), did, this day after noon, adorn many Lords, Knights, and Gentlemen, with dignities, as follow. The names and promotions of whom, I have here set in order, as they were placed in the Heralds' book.

Bannerets.

Sir RALPH SADLER, Treasurer.
Sir FRANCIS BYRAN, Captain of the Light Horsemen.
Sir RALPH VANE, Lieutenant of all the Horsemen.

These Knights were made Bannerets : a dignity above a Knight, and next to a Baron : whose acts I have partly touched in the story before.

Knights.

The Lord GREY, of Wilton ; High Marshal.

The Lord EDWARD SEYMOUR, my Lord Grace's son.

Of these, the readers shall also find before.

The Lord THOMAS HOWARD.

The Lord WALLDIKE.

Sir THOMAS DACRES.

Sir EDWARD HASTINGS.

Sir EDMUND BRIDGES.

Sir JOHN THYNNE, my Lord Grace's Steward of his Household.

Sir MILES PARTRIDGE.

Sir JOHN CONWAY.

Sir GILES POOLE.

Sir RALPH BAGNOLLE.

Sir OLIVER LAWRENCE.

Sir HENRY GATES.

Sir THOMAS CHALONER, one of the Clerks of the King's Majesty's Privy Council, and in this army, as I might call him, Chief Secretary : who, with his great pains and expedite diligence in despatch of things passing from my Lord's Grace and the council there, did make that his merit was not with the meanest.

Sir FRANCIS FLEMMING, Master of the Ordnance there. A gentleman whom long exercise and good observance hath made in that feat right perfect : whereunto, in this Voyage, he joined so much heed and diligence, as it was well found how much his service did stead.

Sir JOHN GRESHAM.
Sir WILLIAM SKIPWITH.
Sir JOHN BUTTES.
Sir GEORGE BLAGE.
Sir WILLIAM FRANCIS.
Sir FRANCIS KNOWLES.
Sir WILLIAM THORBOROW.
Sir GEORGE HAWARD.
Sir JAMES WILFORD.
Sir RALPH COPPINGER. But that I have written in the Story [*p.* 122], with what forward hardness Sir GEORGE HAWARD did bear the King's Majesty's Standard in the battle; and there also of the industrious pain of Sir JAMES WILFORD [*p.* 122]; and Sir RALPH COPPINGER did aid, not smally, in safeguard of the Standard of our Horsemen [*p.* 120]; I have been more diligent to have rehearsed it here.

Sir THOMAS WENTWORTH.
Sir JOHN MARVEN.
Sir NICHOLAS STRAUNGE.
Sir CHARLES STURTON.
Sir HUGH ASCUE.
Sir FRANCIS SALMIN.
Sir RICHARD TOWNLEY.
Sir MARMADUKE CONSTABLE.
Sir GEORGE AUDLEY.
Sir JOHN HOLCROFT.
Sir JOHN SOUTHWORTH.
Sir THOMAS DANBY.
Sir JOHN TALBOT.
Sir ROWLAND CLERK.
Sir JOHN HORSELY.
Sir JOHN FORSTER.
Sir CHRISTOPHER DIES. ⎫
Sir PETER NEGROO. ⎬ *Three Spaniards.*
Sir ALONSO DE VILLE. ⎭
Sir HENRY HUSSEY.
Sir JAMES GRANADO.
Sir WALTER BONHAM.
Sir ROBERT BRANDLING, Mayor of Newcastle, and made Knight there, at my Lord Grace's return.

As it is not to be doubted but right many more in the army, besides these, did also well and valiantly quit them (although their preferment was rather then deferred than their deserts yet to be forgotten); even so, among these were there right many, the knowledge of whose acts and demerits I could not come by: and yet would have no man any more to doubt of the worthiness of their advancement, than they are uncertain of his circumspection and wisdom, who preferred them to it. Whereupon, all men may safely thus far forth, without offence, presume; that his Grace unworthily bestowed this honour on no man.

By this day, as Roxburgh was sufficiently made tenable and defensible (the which my Lord's Grace seemed half to have vowed to see, before he would depart thence) his Grace and the council did first determine that my Lord GREY should remain upon the Borders there, as the King's Majesty's Lieutenant. And then took order for the forts, that Sir ANDREW DUDLEY, Captain of Broughty Crak, had left with him, two hundred soldiers of hackbutters and others, and a

sufficient number of pioneers for his works; Sir EDWARD
DUDLEY, Captain of Home Castle, sixty hackbutters, forty
horsemen, and a hundred pioneers; Sir RALPH BULMER,
Captain of Roxburgh, three hundred soldiers, of hackbutters
and others, and two hundred pioneers.

Thursday,
the 29th of
September, being
Michaelmas Day. A S THINGS were thus concluded: and
warning given overnight that our
camp should, this day, dissolve:
every man fell to packing apace.
My Lord's Grace, this morning, was passed over the Tweed
here, soon after seven o'clock. The best place whereof for
getting over (which was over against the west end of our
camp, and not far from the broken arches of the broken
bridge) was yet, with great stones in the bottom, so uneven
of ground; and by reason of rain that lately fell before, the
water was so deep and the stream so swift; that right many
of our horsemen and footmen were greatly in peril at their
passage, and one or two drowned. Many carriages also
were overthrown, and in great danger of being lost.

My Lord's Grace took his way straight towards Newcastle;
and thence homeward.

My Lord the Earl of WARWICK, my Lord GREY, and Sir
RALPH SADLER, with divers others, rode towards Berwick,
to abide the coming of the Scottish Commissioners.

In the mean time of tarrying there, my Lord of WARWICK
did make five knights:

Sir THOMAS NEVIL, the Lord NEVIL's brother.
Sir ANTHONY STRELLEY.
Sir — VERNEY.
Sir JOHN BARTEVILE, a Frenchman.
And another.

But the Scots (like men though slipper in covenant, yet
constant in usage, and therefore less blushing to break
promise than custom) came not at all. Whereupon my Lord
and the other of our Commissioners having tarried for them
the full time of appointment, which was until the 4th of
October; the next day after, departed thence homeward.

In part of the meantime, while my Lord's Grace was thus

doing the exploits in Scotland, as I have before written; the Earl of LINNOS [*LENNOX*], with my Lord WHARTON, Lord Warden of our West Marches against Scotland, according as his Grace had before taken order, with a number of five thousand, entered Scotland by the West Marches; and, first passing a two mile, after a day's and night's defence, they won the Church of Annan: a strong place, and very noisome always unto our men, as they passed that way. There they took seventy-two prisoners, the keepers of the same; burnt the spoil, for cumber [*encumbrance*] of carriage; and caused the Church to be blown [up] with powder.

Passing thence, a sixteen mile within the land; soon after, they won a Hold called the "Castle of Milk": the which they left well furnished with munition and men, and so returned.

Divers other notable acts they did, here left unwritten of by me, because unknown to me: but as much as I certainly heard of, I have thought meet to add hereunto; because I may well count them as part of this Expedition and Voyage.

A PERORATION
unto the gentle Reader, with a short rehearsal of the action done.

 HAVE thus absolved my book: but neither with such speed as, perchance, it had been the office of him that would take upon him to write of this matter; nor as the dignity of the argument required publication.

For it may well be thought a man that had been forth in no part of the voyage, with mean diligence might, in this space, have learned and written as much by inquiry at home. And since the power of time is, in each case, so great as things indifferently good, by choice of opportunity, are made much commendable; and again, by coming out of season may be much disgraced: right small then may I take my merit to be, that come now so intempestively [*out of time*] to tell that tale, whereof all men's ears are full of, a four months before.

Yet for excuse of my slackness (as who would not be blameless?), trusting that my plain confession may the rather move you to take things to the better, I have thought it best to render you the very cause thereof.

Which is, that after I had somewhat entered into this business, and thereby was compelled to consider the precise observance of deeds, words, and, in a manner, gestures; the diligent marking of the situation of towns, castles, and churches; of the lying of the hills, plains, and fields; of the course of rivers, of respect of winds; and of infinite such other things that ought first to have been made there while they were a doing, and while a man had been at them (the which indeed, I had not so perfectly written in my notes; therefore was driven to stress my memory the more for calling the same to mind again): and, herewith, regarding the great heed that ought to be had in rehearsal of circumstances, and in placing of things in writing, accordingly as they were done, seen, or heard—I found the enterprise a great deal more weighty than the slenderness of my wit was able quickly to pass with.

Howbeit, when, upon deeper consideration, I pondered with myself what a thing it was to make any Monument in this so prosperous a commonalty; whereof the Governors are so absolutely wise, and wherein an infinite number of men are so finely witted and so profoundedly learned beside: I

In de Art. Poet. rather regarded the counsel of the wise poet HORACE, who wills a man to keep his writings in his hands nine years (meaning a good while for correction) than to have any haste of publication, whereby at once I should lose my liberty of amendment. Which liberty, though, after, I might have never so well, yet because it is nothing so commendable to mend a fault as to make no fault; I would gladly before have had the leisure to look that the thing might have passed as faultless from me, as my diligence could have made it.

And surely, had it not been more for answering the expectation of some men of honour (who knew I was in hand with the matter; and who else, peradventure, might have doubted my diligence) than it was for mine own desire to have my doings to come soon abroad: I would have taken a better breath, ere they had come out yet.

But since the chance is cast, and the word thus uttered cannot be called again; whereby I have jeoparded [*jeopardize*]

with your three hours' reading, to make you Censor of my
three months' writing: judge ye, I pray you! as ye may with
favour! and conster my meaning to the best!

I know my need is to pray much.   For I am not so foolish
as to think myself so wise, that with a text all faultless, I
can drive forth so long a process.   But as I, for the time,
have endeavoured to say, rather as well as I can, than as
well as can be; so shall there be, for me, liberty to all men to
write what else they can utter, either further or better: which
if they do, I shall, with all my heart, become then as benign
a reader to them, as I would wish you now to be here to me.

To the intent now I would quite [*be quit*] from the cumber
of inquiry or question, such as, haply, would wit, " What a
do I had in the army? or how I had any knowledge of that
I have written?" I have thought it courtesy, not to be dangerous to show, that it pleased my very good Lord, the Earl
of WARWICK, Lieutenant of the Host (who thereby had power
to make Officers), to make me one of the Judges of the Mar-
shalsy [*i.e., in connection with the High Marshal of the Army,
Lord GREY*], as Master WILLIAM CECIL, now Master of the
Requests [*and afterwards Lord BURGHLEY*] was the other.
Whereby, we both (not being bound so straightly, in days of
travel, to the order of march; nor otherwhile, but when we
sat in Court, to any great affairs) had liberty to ride to see
the things that were done, and leisure to note occurrences that
came.   The which thing, as it chanced, we both did: but so
far from appointment between us, as neither was witing of
the other's doing till somewhat before our departure homeward.   Marry, since my coming home, indeed, his gentleness
being such as to communicate his notes to me, I have, I
confess, been thereby, both much a certained [*confirmed*] in
many things I doubted, and somewhat remembered [*put in
mind*] of that which else I might hap to have forgotten.

But now, forasmuch, as it hath pleased the most benign

goodness of GOD, so favourably to aid us in these our affairs, and so much to tender the equity of our cause, as by His Minister, and our Head in this journey, My Lord Protector's Grace, we have turned our enemy's intents for destruction of us, unto their own confusion. And, first, overturned of their Holds, Dunglas, Thornton, Anderwick, and Annan Church; overcome them, with half of their number of thirty-two thousand men; slain fifteen thousand three hundred; maimed two thousand; taken fifteen hundred; burnt Leith and Kinghorn, as we might also more of their towns, if our Chieftain had been as willing as our captains were ready; won the best part of their navy, and burnt the residue; won from them, and keep in the midst of their land, Saint Coomes Inn and Broughty Crak, and thereby, but by our leave, keep them from their whole intercourse of merchants; won also and keep the Castle of Milk and Home Castle; won of ordnance, in their forts and at the field, above eighty pieces; built Roxburgh Castle and Eymouth; and gained unto the King's Majesty's obedience, all Teviotdale and their Marches: all this, in so short a time, as within twenty-five days, with so small a loss of our side, as of under the number of sixty persons in all the whole Voyage;

And that, in this, the first year of our King's Majesty's dominion and rule: whereby, according to his singular towardness, else evident, we may well conceive an assured hope that His Highness too, shall have a most happy, and, with GOD's grace, a long reign—

I would wish and exhort that ye which were not there (for though ye were far from any danger of the loss, yet can ye not be but full partners of the winning) should effectually, with us (according as we all have cause) give and wish, first, glory and praise unto GOD, obedience and victory to our Sovereign, honour and thanks unto our Protector and Councilors [*i.e., the Privy Council*], worship to our Chivalry, commendation unto the rest that were out, and a better mind unto our enemies.

And I, trusting unto the benignity of your gentle acceptance, who[ever] shall hap to be reader of this work (with such indifferency of request touching the same, as HORACE made to his well beloved friend NUMITIUS) shall thus take my leave of you

> *Vive! Vale! si quid novisti rectius istis,*   *Epist.* 1.
> *Candidus imperti, si non, his utere mecum.*

Out of the Parsonage of Saint Mary's Hill, in London, this 28th of January, 1548.

*IMPRINTED in London, the last day of
June, in the second year of the
reign of our Sovereign Lord,
King EDWARD the VI. ;
by RICHARD GRAFTON,
Printer to his most
royal Majesty.*
M. D. X L V I I I.

¶ Cum privilegio ad imprimendum solum.

John Bon and mast Parson.

```
┌─────────────────────────┐
│                         │
│      Picture of a       │
│                         │
│  procession of Priests  │
│                         │
│   bearing the Host.     │
│                         │
└─────────────────────────┘
```

☞ Alas, poor fools ¿ so sore ye be lade ¿
No marvel is it, though your shoulders ache:
For ye bear a great god which ye yourselves made.
Make of it, what ye will ¿ it is a Wafer Cake ;
And between two irons, printed it is and bake.
And look, where idolatry is, Christ will not be there ¿
Wherefore, lay down your burden ¿ An idol, ye do bear ¿
　　　　☞ Alas, poor fools ¿

John Bon and mast Parson.

☞ The Parson.

What, JOHN BON! Good morrow to thee!

John Bon.

Now, good morrow, mast[er] Parson, so mut I thee!

Parson.

What meanest thou, JOHN! to be at work so soon?

John.

The sooner I begin, the sooner shall I have done,
For I 'tend to work no longer than none.

Parson.

Marry, JOHN, for that, GOD's blessing on thy heart!
For, surely, some there be, will go to plough and cart;
And set not by, this holy *Corpus Christi* even.

John.

They are the more to blame, I swear by Saint Stephen!
But tell me, mast[er] Parson, one thing, and you can;
What Saint is Copsi Cursty, a man, or a woman?

L   I

Parson.

Why, JOHN! knowest not that? I tell thee, it was a man.
It is CHRIST His own self, and to-morrow is His day.
We bear Him in procession, and thereby know it ye may.

John.

I know! mast[er] Parson! and nay, by my fay!
But methink it is a mad thing that ye say,
That it should be a man. How can it come to pass?
Because ye may Him bear within so small a glass.

Parson.

Why, neighbour JOHN, and art thou now there?
Now I may perceive ye love this new gear.

John.

God's forbod! master! I should be of that faction.
I question why, your masship, in way of cumlication.
A plain man, ye may see, will speak as cometh to mind:
Ye must hold us excused, for ploughmen be but blind.
I am an eld fellow, of fifter winter and more,
And yet, in all my life, I knew not this before.

Parson.

No did! Why sayest thou so? Upon thyself, thou lyest!
Thou hast ever known the sacrament to be the body of
CHRIST!

John.

Yea, sir, ye say true! All that, I know indeed;
And yet, as I remember, it is not in my *Creed*:
But as for Cropsy Cursty to be a man or no,
I knew not till this day, by the way my soul shall to!

Parson.

Why, foolish fellow! I tell thee it is so!
For it was so determined by the Church long ago;
It is both the sacrament and very CHRIST himself.

John.

No spleaser, mast[er] Parson! Then make ye CHRIST an elf;
And the maddest made man, that ever body saw!

Parson.

What! peace, mad man! Thou speakest like a daw!
It is not possible his manhood for to see.

John.

Why, sir; ye tell me it is even very He:
And if it be not His manhood, His godhead it must be.

Parson.

I tell thee, none of both! What meanest thou? Art thou
      mad?

John.

No, neither made nor drunk; but to learn I am glad:
But to displease your masship, I would be very loath,
Ye grant me here plainly, that it is none of both,
Then it is but a cake: but I pray ye, be not wroth!

Parson.

Wroth, quoth ha! By the mass! (thou makest me swear
      an oath),
I had leaver with a Doctor of Divinity to reason,
Than with a stubble cur, that eateth beans and peason.

John.

I cry ye mercy, mast[er] Parson! Patience for a season!
In all this cumlication is neither felony nor treason.

Parson.

No, by the mass! But hearest thou! It is plain heresy.

John.

I am glad it chanced so, there was no witness by ;
And if there had, I cared not ; for ye spake as ill as I.
I speak but as I heard you say, I wot not what ye thought.
Ye said "It was not God, nor man," and made it worse than
    nought.

Parson.

I meant not so.   Thou tookest me wrong !

John.

A, sir !   Ye sing another song !
I dare not reason with you long.
I see well, now, ye have a knack
To say a thing, and then go back.

Parson.

No, JOHN ! I was but a little overseen;
But thou meantest not good faith, I ween,
In all this talk that was us between.

John.

I !   No, trow, it shall not so been
That JOHN BON shall an heretic be called,
Then might he lay him so foul befald.

Parson.

But, now, if thou wilt mark me well !
From beginning to ending, I will thee tell
Of the godly service that shall be to-morrow ;
That, ere I have done, no doubt, thou wilt sorrow
To hear that such things should be foredone.
And yet, in many places, they have begun
To take away the old, and set up new.
Believe me, JOHN ! this tale is true.

John.

Go to, mast[er] Parson! Say on, and well to thrive!
Ye be the jolliest gemman [*gentleman*] that ever saw in my
    life.

Parson.

We shall first have *Matins*. Is it not a godly hearing?

John [*who is now speaking, aside*].

Fie! yes. Methink 'tis a shameful gay cheering,
For oftentimes, on my prayers, when I take no great keep,
Ye sing so arrantly well, ye make me fall asleep!

Parson.

Then have we Procession, and CHRIST about we bear.

John.

That is a poison holy thing, for GOD Himself is there.

Parson.

Then come we in, and ready us dress,
Full solemnly to go to *Mess*.

John.

Is not here a mischievous thing!
The *Mess* is vengeance holy, for all their saying!

Parson.

Then say we *Confiteor* and *Miseriatur*.

John.

JEZE LORD! 'tis abominable matter!

Parson.

And then we stand up to the altar.

John.

This gear is as good as *Our Lady's Psalter*.

Parson.

And so go forth with the other deal
Till we have read the *Pistel* and *Gospel*.

John.

That is good, mast[er] Parson, I know right well.

Parson.

Is that good! Why, what say'st thou to the other?

John.

Marry! horribly good! I say none other.

Parson.

So is all the *Mess*, I dare avow this,
As good in every point as *Pistel* or *Gospel* is.

John.

The foul evil it is! Who would think so much?
In faith, I ever thought that it had been no such.

Parson.

Then have we the *Canon*, that is holiest.

John.

A spiteful gay thing, of all that ever I wist.

Parson.

Then have we the *Memento*, even before the sacring.

John.

Ye are morenly well learned! I see by your reck'ning
That ye will not forget such an elvish thing.

Parson.

And after that, we consecrate Very God and Man;
And turn the bread to flesh, with five words we can.

John.

The devil ye do!   I trow this is pestilence business!
Ye are much bound to GOD for such a spittle holiness!
A gallows gay gift!   With five words alone,
To make both God and Man; and yet we see none!
Ye talk so unreasonably well, it maketh my heart yearn,
As eld a fellow as I am, I see well I may learn.

Parson.

Yea, JOHN! and then, with words holy and good,
Even, by and by, we turn the wine to blood.

John.

Lo!   Will ye se?   Lo! who would have thought it?
That ye could so soon from wine to blood ha brought it?
And yet, except your mouth be better tasted than mine,
I cannot feel it other but that it should be wine.
And yet I wot ne'er a cause there may be, why
Perchance, ye ha drunk blood oftner than ever did I.

Parson.

Truly, JOHN, it is blood, though it be wine in taste.
As soon as the word is spoke, the wine is gone and past

John.

A sessions on it! for me.   My wits are me benumme:
For I cannot study where the wine should become?

Parson.

Study, quoth ha!   Beware, and let such matter go!.
To meddle much with this, may bring ye soon to woe.

John.

Yea, but, mast[er] Parson! think ye it were right,
That, if I desired you to make my black ox white;
And you say, "It is done!" and still is black in sight;
Ye might me deem a fool, for to believe so light?

Parson.

I marvel much, ye will reason so far !
I fear if ye use it, it will ye mar !

John.

No, no, sir ! I trust of that I shall be 'ware,
I pray you, with your matter again forth to fare !

Parson.

And then we go forth, and CHRIST's body receive;
Even the very same that MARY did conceive.

John.

The devil it is ! Ye have a great grace
To eat GOD and Man in so short a space.

Parson.

And so we make an end, as it lieth in an order.
But now the blessed *Mess* is hated in every border,
And railed on, and reviled, with words most blasphemous:
But I trust it will be better with the help of *Catechismus.*
For though it came forth but even that other day,
Yet hath it turned many to their old way:
And where they hated *Messe,* and had it in disdain,
There have they *Messe* and *Matins* in Latin tongue again.
Yea, even in London self, JOHN, I tell the truth !
They be full glad and merry to hear of this, GOD knoweth !

John.

By my troth ! mast[er] Parson, I like full well your talk !
But mass me no more *messings* ! The right way will I walk.
For, though I have no learning, yet I know cheese from
    chalk,
And each can perceive your juggling, as crafty as ye walk !
But leave your devilish *Mass,* and the *Communion* to you take !
And then will CHRIST be with you; even for His promise
    sake !

𝔓arson.

What, art thou such a one, and kept it so close!
Well, all is not gold, that hath a fair gloss,
But, farewell, JOHN BON!   GOD bring thee in better mind!

𝔍ohn.

I thank you, sir! for that you seem very kind;
But pray not so for me! for I am well enough.
Whistle, boy! drive forth! GOD speed us and the plough!
Ha! browne done! forth, that horson crab!   [*These are cries
to the plough
horses.*]
Reecomomyne, garled! with haight, black hab!
Have a gain, bald before! hayght ree who!
Cherrily, boy, come off! that homeward we may go.

𝔉 i n i ṡ.

☞ 𝔍mprinted at 𝔏ondon, by 𝔍ohn 𝔇ay, and
𝔚illiam 𝔖eres, dwelling in 𝔖epulchres
𝔓arish, at the sign of the 𝔕esurrection,
a little above 𝔥olborn 𝔠onduite.

C U M G R A T I A E T P R I V I L E G I O A D
I M P R I M E N D U M S O L U M .

EDWARD UNDERHILL, Esq.
of the Band of Gentlemen Pensioners, surnamed, " The hot Gospeller."

Examination and Imprisonment in August 1553 ; with anecdotes of the Time.

[Harl. MS. 425.]
[*Narratives of the Days of the Reformation.* Camden Society. 1859.]

A Note of the Examination and Imprisonment of EDWARD
UNDERHILL (son and heir of THOMAS UNDERHILL of
Honingham, in the county of Warwick, Esquire) being
of the Band of the Pensioners [*see pp.* 191, 192, for a
ballet that he made against the Papists, immediately
after the Proclamation of Queen MARY at London ; she
being in Norfolk.

HE next day [4th] after the Queen was come to
the Tower [*on the* 3rd *of August,* 1553] ; the foresaid ballet [*ballad*] came into the hands of Secretary
[Sir JOHN] BOURNE ; who straightways made
inquiry for me, the said EDWARD, who dwelt at
Limehurst [*Limehouse*] ; which he having intelligence of, sent
the Sheriff of Middlesex, with a company of bills and glaives
[*lances, with a cutting blade at the end of each*] ; who came unto
my house, I being in my bed, and my wife being newly laid
in child-bed.

The High Constable, whose name was THOMAS IVE, dwelt
at the next house unto me, the said EDWARD ; whom the
Sheriff brought also with him. He, being my very friend,
desired the Sheriff and his company to stay without, for [fear
of af]frighting of my wife, being newly laid ; and he would go
and fetch me unto him. Who knocked at the door, saying,
" He must speak with me."

I, lying so near that I might hear him, called unto him,
willing him " to come unto me ! " for that he was always my
very friend, and earnest in the Gospel. Who declared unto

me that the Sheriff, with a great company with him, was
sent for me.

Whereupon I rose, made me ready, and came unto him,
demanding, " What he would with me ? "

" Sir," said he, " I have commandment from the Council
to apprehend you, and forthwith to bring you unto them."

" Why," said I, "it is now ten o'clock in the night; ye
cannot, now, carry me unto them ! "

" No, Sir," said he, " you shall go with me to my house to
London, where you shall have a bed : and to-morrow, I will
bring you unto them at the Tower."

" In the name of GOD ! [=*most certainly*]," said I : and so
went with him, requiring [*inquiring of*] him, " If I might
understand the cause."

He said, " He knew none."

" This needed not, then," said I ; " any one messenger
might have fetched me unto them " : suspecting the cause
to be, as it was indeed, the ballet.

On the morrow [*5th of August*, 1553], the Sheriff, seeing me
nothing dismayed, thinking it to be some light matter, went
not with me himself : but sent me unto the Tower with two of
his men, waiting upon me with two bills [*men with halberts*],
prisoner-like, who brought me unto the Council Chamber ;
being commanded to deliver me unto Secretary BOURNE.

Thus standing waiting at the Council Chamber door, two
or three of my fellows, the Pensioners, and my cousin-german
GILBERT WYNTER, Gentleman Usher unto the Lady ELIZA-
BETH [*see p.* 342], stood talking with me.

In the meantime, cometh Sir EDWARD HASTINGS [*see
page* 149], newly made Master of the Horse to the Queen,
and seeing me standing there prisoner, frowning earnestly
upon me, said, " Are you come ? We will talk with you or
your party, I warrant you ! " and so went into the Council.

With that, my fellows and kinsman shrank away from me,
as men greatly afraid.

I did then perceive the said Sir EDWARD bare in remembrance the controversy that was betwixt him and
me in talk and questions of religion at Calais, when the
Right Honourable the Earl of HUNTINGDON, his brother,
went over, General of 6,000 men : with whom I went the
same time, and was Controller of the Ordnance.

The Earl being visited with sickness when he came thither, for that I went over in his company, and could play and sing to the lute, therewith to pass away the time, on the nights being long, for we went over in Christmas [1552], would have me with him in his chamber; and had also a great delight to hear his brother reason with me in matters of religion. Who would be very hot, when I did overlay him with the texts of the Scripture concerning the natural presence of CHRIST in the sacrament of the altar; and would swear great oaths, specially, " by the Lord's foot ! " that after the words spoken by the priest there remained no bread, but the natural body that MARY bare.

" Nay, then, it must needs be so," would I say, " and [*if*] you prove it with such oaths ! "

Whereat the Earl would laugh heartily, saying, " Brother, give him over ! UNDERHILL is too good for you ! " Wherewith he would be very angry.

The greatest hold that he took of, was of the 3rd of JOHN, upon those words, "And no man ascendeth up to heaven, but He that came down from heaven, that is to say, the Son of Man which is in heaven." I drove him from the 6th of JOHN and all other places that he could allege; but from this, he would not be removed, but that those words proved his natural body to be in heaven and in the sacrament also. I told him he as grossly understood CHRIST, as NICODEMUS did in the same place, of " being born anew."

In my opinion, any man that is not given up of GOD, may be satisfied concerning the natural presence in the Supper of the Lord, by the Gospel of Saint JOHN, reading from the first chapter to the end of the seventeenth; with the witness of the first of the *Acts of the Apostles* of CHRIST's ascension and coming again; if ever he will be satisfied, without the help of any Doctors.

Undoubtedly, the apprehending of me was for this matter: but the great mercy of GOD so provided for me, that Master HASTINGS was not at my examination. For tarrying thus at the Chamber door, Doctor Cox [*afterwards Bishop of ELY*] was within; who came forth, and was sent to the Marshalsea. Then came forth the Lord FERRERS, [Viscount HEREFORD], and was committed to the Tower. Then it was dinner time, and all were commanded to depart until after dinner.

My two waiting men and I went to an alehouse to dinner; and, longing to know my pain [*punishment*], I made haste to get to the Council Chamber door, that I might be the first.

Immediately, as they had dined, Secretary BOURNE came to the door, looking as a wolf doth for a lamb; unto whom my two keepers delivered me, standing next unto the door: for there were more behind me.

He took me in greedily, and shut to the door; leaving me at the nether [*lower*] end of the Chamber, he went unto the Council showing them of me: and then beckoned me to come near.

Then they began the table, and sat them down. The Earl of BEDFORD sat as chief, uppermost upon the bench. Next unto him, the Earl of SUSSEX; next him, Sir RICHARD SOUTHWELL.

On the side next me, sat the Earl of ARUNDEL; next him, the Lord PAGET. By them, stood Sir JOHN GAGE, then Constable of the Tower; the Earl of BATH, and Master [*afterwards Sir JOHN*] MASON.

At the board's end, stood Serjeant MORGAN [*who, later on, condemned Lady JANE GREY*] that afterwards died mad; and Secretary [Sir JOHN] BOURNE.

The Lord WENTWORTH [*the Lord Deputy of Calais, when lost; see p.* 292] stood in the bay window, talking with one, all the while of my examination, whom I knew not.

My Lord of BEDFORD being my very friend, (for that my chance was to be at the recovering of his son, my Lord RUSSELL, when he was cast into the Thames against the Limehurst, whom I carried to my house and got him to bed; who was in great peril of his life, the weather being very cold) would not seem to be familiar with me, nor called me not by my name, but said, "Come hither, sirrah! did not you set forth a ballet of late, in print?"

I kneeled down, saying, "Yes, truly, my Lord! Is that the cause I am called before your Honours?"

"Ay, marry," said Secretary BOURNE, "you have one of them about you, I am sure."

"Nay, truly, have I not," said I.

Then he took one out of his bosom, and read it over distinctly; the Council giving diligent ear.

When he had ended, "I trust, my Lords," said I, "I have not offended the Queen's Majesty in this ballet; nor spoken against her title, but maintained it."

"You have, sir," said Morgan, "yes, I can divide your ballet, and make a distinction in it; and so prove at the least sedition in it."

"Ay, sir," said I, "you men of law will make of a matter what ye list!"

"Lo," said Sir RICHARD SOUTHWELL, "how he can give a taunt! You maintain the Queen's title, with the help of an arrant heretic, TYNDALE."

"You speak of Papists there, sir," said Master MASON, "I pray you, how define you a Papist?"

I look upon him, turning towards him; for he stood on the side of me, "Why, sir," said I, "it is not long since you could define a Papist better than I" [*meaning that he had turned with the new change of religion*]. With that some of them secretly smiled; as the Lords of BEDFORD, ARUNDEL, SUSSEX, and PAGET.

In great haste, Sir JOHN GAGE took the matter in hand, "Thou callest men Papists there," said he, "who be they that thou judgest to be Papists?"

I said, "Sir, I do name no man, and I came not hither to accuse any, nor none will I accuse; but your Honours do know that in this Controversy that hath been, some be called Papists, and some Protestants."

"But we must know whom thou judgest to be Papists, and that we command thee, upon thine allegiance to declare!"

"Sir," said I, "I think if you look among the priests in Paul's, ye shall find some old *Mumpsimuses* there."

"*Mumpsimuses*, knave!" said he, "*Mumpsimuses*! Thou art an heretic knave, by God's blood!"

"Ay, by the mass!" says the Earl of BATH, "I warrant him an heretic knave indeed."

"I beseech your Honours!" said I, speaking to the Lords that sat at table; for those other stood by, and were not then of the Council, "be my good Lords! I have offended no laws, and I have served the Queen's Majesty's father and brother a long time; and in their service have spent and con-

sumed part of my living, never having, as yet, any preferment
or recompense ; and the rest of my fellows likewise, to our
utter undoings, unless the Queen's Highness be good unto
us. And for my part, I went not forth against Her Majesty;
notwithstanding that I was commanded, nor liked those
doings."

" No, but with your writings, you would set us together by
the ears ! " said the Earl of ARUNDEL.

" He hath spent his living wantonly," saith BOURNE, " and
now saith he has spent it in the King's service; which I am
sorry for. He is come of a worshipful house in Worcestershire."

" It is untruly said of you," said I, " that I have spent my
living wantonly : for I never consumed any part thereof until
I came into the King's service ; which I do not repent, nor
doubted of recompense, if either of my two masters had lived.
I perceive you [to be] BOURNE's son of Worcester; who was
beholden unto my uncle WYNTER, and therefore you have no
cause to be my enemy : nor you never knew me, nor I you
before now, which is too soon."

" I have heard enough of you," said he.

" So have I of you," said I, " how that Master SHELDON
drave you out of Worcestershire, for your behaviour."

With that, came Sir EDWARD HASTINGS from the Queen,
in great haste, saying, " My Lords! you must set all things
apart, and come forthwith to the Queen."

Then said the Earl of SUSSEX, " Have this gentleman unto
the Fleet until we may talk further with him ! " though I
was " knave," before, of Master GAGE.

" To the Fleet ! " said Master SOUTHWELL, " have him to
the Marshalsea ! "

" Have the gentleman to Newgate ! " saith Master GAGE
again, " Call a couple of the Guard here."

" Ay," saith BOURNE, " and there shall be a letter sent to
the keeper how he shall use him ; for we have other manner
of matters to him than these."

" So had ye need," said I, " or else I care not for you ! "

" Deliver him to Master [after Sir WILLIAM] GARRARD,
the Sheriff [of London]," said he, " and bid him send him to
Newgate."

" My Lord," said I, unto my Lord of ARUNDEL, (for that he

was next to me) as they were rising, " I trust you will not see me thus used, to be sent to Newgate. I am neither thief nor traitor."

" You are a naughty fellow ! " said he, " you were always tutting in the Duke of NORTHUMBERLAND's ear, that you were ! "

" I would he had given better ear unto me," said I ; " it had not been with him then, as it is now" [*waiting his trial in the Tower*].

Master HASTINGS passing by me, I thought good to prove him ; although he threatened me, before noon.

" Sir," said I, " I pray you speak for me, that I be not sent to Newgate ; but rather unto the Fleet, which was first named. I have not offended. I am a Gentleman, as you know ; and one of your fellows, when you were of that Band of the Pensioners."

Very quietly, he said unto me, " I was not at the talk, Master UNDERHILL ; and therefore I can say nothing to it." But I think he was well content with the place I was appointed to.

So went I forth with my two fellows of the Guard, who were glad they had the leading of me, for they were great Papists.

" Where is that knave, the printer [*of the ballad*] ? " said Master GAGE.

" I know not," said I.

When we came to the Tower gate, where Sir JOHN BRYDGES [*afterwards Lord CHANDOS of Sudeley, see p.* 345] had the charge, [who was there] with his brother Master THOMAS ; with whom I was well acquainted, (but not with Sir JOHN) who, seeing the two of the Guard leading me, without their halberts, rebuked them ; and stayed me while they went for their halberts.

His brother said unto me, " I am sorry you should be an offender, Master UNDERHILL."

" I am none, Sir ! " said I, " nor went I against the Queen."

" I am glad of that," said he.

And so forth we went at the gate, where was a great throng of people to hear and see what prisoners were committed : and

amongst whom stood, my friend Master IVE, the High Constable, my next neighbour.

One of the Guard went forth at the wicket before me, to
take me by the arm, the other held me by the other arm ;
fearing, belike, I would have shifted [*escaped*] from them
amongst the people.

When my friend, who had watched at the gate all the forenoon saw me thus led ; he followed afar off, as PETER did
CHRIST, to see what should become of me. Many also followed, some that knew me : some to learn who I was ; for
that I was in a gown of satin.

Thus passed we through the streets, well accompanied,
unto Master GARRARD, the Sheriff's house, in the Stocks
Market. My friend Master IVE tarried at the gate.

These two of the Guard declared unto Master Sheriff, that
they were commanded by the Council to deliver me unto him,
and he to send me unto Newgate : saying, " Sir, if it please
you, we will carry him thither."

With that, I stepped unto Master Sheriff, and, taking him
a little aside, requested him that, forasmuch as their commission was but to deliver me unto him, and *he* to send me into
Newgate, that he would send me by his officers : for the
request was of mere malice.

" With a good-will !" said Master Sheriff.

" Masters !" said he, " you may depart ! I will send my
officers with this gentleman anon ; when they be come in."

" We will see him carried, Sir !" said they, " for our discharge."

Then the Sheriff said sharply unto them, " What ! do you
think that I will not do the Council's commandment ? You
are discharged by delivering him unto me ! "

With that, they departed.

My friend, Master IVE, seeing them depart and leave me
behind, was very glad thereof : and tarried still at the gate
to see farther.

All this talk in the Sheriff's hall, did my Lord RUSSELL,
son and heir to the Earl of BEDFORD, hear and see ; who was
at commandment [*under arrest*] in the Sheriff's house, and his
chamber joining into the hall, wherein he might look : who
was very sorry for me, for that I had been familiar with him
in matters of religion, as well on the other side the seas as

M   I

at home. He sent me on the morrow, 20s. [=*about £10 now*] ; and every week as much, while I was in Newgate.

When these two companions of the Guard were gone, the Sheriff sent two of his officers with me, who took no bills with them, nor lead me; but followed a pretty way behind me : for as I said unto Master Sheriff, "But for order's sake and to save him blameless, I would have gone unto Newgate myself, at the Council's commandment, or his either."

When I came into the street, my friend Master IVE, seeing me have such liberty, and such distance betwixt me and the officers, he stepped before them, and so went talking with me through Cheapside : so that it was not well perceived that I was apprehended, but by the great company that followed.

The officers delivered me unto the Keeper of Newgate, as they were commanded : who unlocked a door, and willed me to go up the stairs into the Hall. My friend IVE went up with me; where we found three or four prisoners that had the liberty of the house.

After a little talk with my friend, I required him not to let my wife know that I was sent to Newgate, but [to say] to the Counter, until such time that she were near her *churching* : and that she should send me my night-gown, my *Bible*, and my Lute. And so he departed.

In a while after, it was supper time [*i.e., about* 5 *p.m.*]. The board was covered in the same hall. The Keeper, whose name was ALEXANDER, and his wife came to supper; and half a dozen prisoners that were there for felonies : for I was the first, for religion, that was sent unto that prison; but the cause why, the Keeper knew not.

One of those prisoners took acquaintance of [*recognised*] me, and said, "He was a soldier under Sir RICHARD CROM-WELL in the journey [*in July*, 1543] to Landreci [in Hain-ault], where he did know me and whose servant I was, at the same time; and who, the next year following [1544], when the famous King HENRY VIII. went unto Boulogne, did put me unto his Majesty into the room of a man-at-arms. Of the which Band, there were 200 of us, upon barded horses, all in one suit of red and yellow damask, the bards of our horses and plumes of feathers of the same colours, to attend upon his Majesty for the defence of his person."

After supper, this good fellow whose name was BRYSTOW
procured me to have a bed in his chamber. He could play well
upon the rebeck [*violin*]. He was a tall man, and afterwards
of the Queen MARY's Guard, and yet a Protestant, which he
kept secret : " For else," he said, " he should not have found
such favour as he did at the Keeper's hands, and his wife's ;
for to such as love the Gospel, they were very cruel."

" Well," said I, " I have sent for my *Bible* ; and by GOD's
grace, therein shall be my daily exercise. I will no hide it
from them."

" Sir ! " said he, " I am poor ; but they will bear with you,
for that they see your estate is to pay well ; and I will shew
you the nature and manner of them : for I have be n here a
a good while. They both do love music very well ; wherefore you with your lute, and I to play with you on my rebeck,
will please them greatly. He loveth to be merry, and to
drink wine ; and she also. If you will bestow upon them
every dinner and supper a quart of wine, and some music :
you shall be their white son, and have all the favour that
they can shew you ! " And so it came to pass.

And now I think it good a little to digress from my
matter concerning my imprisonment and my deliverance ;
and to note the great mercy of GOD shewed unto his
servants in that great Persecution in Queen MARY's
time : how mightily and how many ways he preserved
such as did fear Him, even as He preserved DANIEL,
JEREMY, PAUL, and many in the old time.

Some were moved by His Spirit to flee over the seas.
Some were preserved still in London, that, in all the
time of persecution, never bowed their knees unto Baal :
for there was no such place to shift [*hide*] in, in this
realm, as London, notwithstanding their great spiall and
search ; nor no better place to shift the Easter time
[*to avoid being houselled, i.e., taking the sacrament*] than in
Queen MARY's Court, serving in the room I did, as shall
be shewed hereafter.

A great number, God did strengthen constantly to
stand to His Word, to glorify His name, which be
praised for ever and ever, world without end ! And some
be preserved for these days.

And now again to prosecute the matter of my trouble and

wonderful deliverance out of that loathsome gaol of New-gate.

When that I had been there about two weeks [5th–18th August, 1553], through the evil savours, and great unquietness of the lodgings, as also by occasion of drinking of a draught of strong Hollock [a sweet] wine, as I was going to bed, which my chamber fellow would needs have me to pledge him in, I was cast into an extreme burning ague, that I could take no rest, and desiring to change my lodging. And so did, from one to another, but none could I abide; there was so many evil savours, and so much noise of prisoners.

The Keeper and his wife offered me his own parlour, where he himself lay: which was furthest from noise; but it was near the kitchen, the savour of which I could not abide. Then did she lay me in a chamber, where she said never a prisoner lay, which was her store chamber, where all her plate and money lay; which was much.

So much friendship I found at their hands, notwithstanding that they were spoken unto, by several Papists. And the Woodmongers of London, with whom I had had a great conflict for presenting them for false marking of billets; they required the Keeper to show me no favour, and to lay irons upon me, declaring that "I was the greatest heretic in London."

My very friend Master RECORDE, Doctor of Physic, singularly seen in all the seven sciences, and a great Divine, visited me in the prison (to his great peril if it had been known, who long time was at charges and pains with me, gratis), and also after I was delivered. By means whereof, and the Providence of GOD, I received my health.

My wife then was churched before her time, to be a suitor for my deliverance; who put up a Supplication unto the Council declaring my extreme sickness and small cause to be committed unto so loathsome a gaol; requiring that I might be delivered, putting in sureties to be forthcoming to answer farther when I should be called. Which she obtained by the help of Master [afterwards Sir] JOHN THROGMORTON, being the Master of the Requests, and my countryman [i.e., of Worcestershire] and my kinsman. He, understanding who were my enemies, took a time in their absence, and obtained

[*on 21st August,* 1553] a letter to the Keeper, subscribed by the
Earl of BEDFORD, the Earl of SUSSEX, [STEPHEN GARDINER
the Bishop of] WINCHESTER, [Sir ROBERT] ROCHESTER
[Comptroller of the Household], and [Sir EDWARD] WALDE-
GRAVE, to be delivered; putting in surety, according to the
request of my wife's Supplication.

With whom WINCHESTER talked, concerning the
christening of her child at the church at the Tower Hill;
and the gossips [*sponsors*], which were the Duke of
SUFFOLK, the Earl of PEMBROKE, and the Lady JANE,
then being Queen: with the which, he [*GARDINER*] was
much offended.

My Lady THROGMORTON, wife unto Sir NICHOLAS
THROGMORTON, was the Queen's deputy; who named
my son GUILDFORD after her [*the Queen's*] husband.

Immediately after the christening was done [*on the
19th of July,* 1553], Queen MARY was proclaimed in
Cheapside; and when my Lady THROGMORTON came
into the Tower, the Cloth of Estate was taken down,
and all things defaced. A sudden change! She would
have gone forth again; but could not be suffered.

But now again to my matter.

When my wife had obtained the letter, joyful she was; and
brought her brother, JOHN SPERYNE of London, merchant,
with her; a very friendly man, and zealous in the LORD:
who was bound with me, according to the Council's letters
before Master CHEDELY, Justice of the Peace: who came
into the prison unto me; for I was so sick and weak that I
was constrained to tarry a while longer, and my wife with me
day and night.

During all the time of my sickness, I was constrained to
pay 8*d.* [*=about* 6*s.* 8*d. now*] every meal; and as much for
my wife, and for every friend that came to see me, if they
were alone with me at dinner or supper time, whether they
came to the table or not; and paid also 40*s.* for a fine for
irons [*i.e., for not being chained*] which they said, "They
shewed me great favour in; I should have else paid £4 or £5."

Thus, when they perceived I did not amend, but rather
[grew] worse and worse; they thought it best to venture the
the matter and provided a horse litter to carry me home to
Limehurst. I was so weak that I was not able to get down

the stairs ; wherefore one that was servant to the gaoler, who, beforetime, had been my man, who was also very diligently and friendly unto me, took me in his arms, and carried me down the stairs to the horse-litter, which stood ready at the prison door ; and went with me to my house.

Many people were gathered to see my coming forth, who praised GOD for my deliverance, being very sorry to see my state, and the lamentation of my wife and her friends, who judged I would not live until I came home.

I was not able to endure the going of the horse-litter, wherefore they were fain to go very softly, and oftentimes to stay ; at which times, many of my acquaintances and friends and others resorted to see me : so that it was two hours ere we could pass from Newgate to Aldgate ; and so within night, before I could get to my house. Where many of my neighbours resorted to see me taken out of the horse-litter ; who lamented and prayed for me, thinking it not possible for me to escape death, but by the great mercy of GOD.

Thus I continued for the space of eight or ten days, without any likelihood or hope of amendment.

I was sent to Newgate, the 5th day of August ; and was delivered the 5th day of September.

The 1st day of October, was Queen MARY crowned ; by which time I was able to walk up and down my chamber. Being very desirous to see the Queen pass through the City, I got up on horseback, being scant able to sit, girded in a long night-gown ; with double kerchiefs about my head, a great hat upon them ; my beard dubbed [clotted] hard too. My face so lean and pale that I was the very Image of Death ; wondered at of all that did behold me ; and unknown to any. My wife and neighbours were too too sorry that I would needs go forth ; thinking I would not return alive.

Thus went I forth, having on either side of me a man to stay [uphold] me ; and so went to the West end of Paul's ; and there placed myself amongst others that sat on horseback to see the Queen pass by.

Before her coming, I beheld Paul's steeple bearing top and top-gallant [yards] like a royal ship, with many flags and banners : and a man [PETER, a Dutchman] triumphing and dancing in the top.

I said unto one that sat on horseback by me, who had not seen any coronation, " At the coronation of King EDWARD, I saw Paul's steeple lie at anchor, and now she weareth top and top-gallant. Surely, the next will be shipwreck, ere it be long!" which chanceth sometimes by tempestuous winds, sometimes by lightnings and fire from heaven.

But I thought that it should rather perish with some horrible wind, than with lightning or thunderbolt [*evidently alluding to the destruction by lightning of the Steeple, on the 4th June*, 1561]; but such are the wonderful works of GOD, whose gunners will not miss the mark that He doth appoint, be it never so little.

When the Queen passed by, many beheld me, for they might almost touch me, the room [*space*] was so narrow; marvelling, belike, that one in such a state would venture forth. Many of my fellows the Pensioners, and others, and divers of the Council beheld me: and none of them all knew me.

I might hear them say one to another, " There is one that loveth the Queen well, belike; for he ventureth greatly to see her. He is very like never to see her more." Thus my men whose hearing was quicker than mine, that stood by me, heard many of them say.

The Queen herself, when she passed by, beheld me. Thus much I thought good to write, to shew how GOD doth preserve that which seemeth to man impossible; as many that day did judge of me. Thus returned I home.

And about two months after [*i.e., in December*], I was able to walk to London at an easy pace; but still with my kerchiefs and pale lean face. I muffled me with a sarsenet, which the rude people in the streets would murmur at, saying, " What is he? Dare he not show his face?"

I did repair to my old familiar acquaintance, as drapers, mercers, and others: and stood talking with them, and cheapened their wares; and there was not one of them that knew me.

Then would I say unto them, " Do you not know me? Look better upon me! Do you not know my voice?" For that also was altered.

"Truly," would they say, "you must pardon me! I cannot call you to remembrance."

Then would I declare my name unto them; whereat they so marvelled, that they could scarcely credit me, but for the familiar acquaintance that I put them in remembrance of.

Thus passed I forth the time at Limehurst until Christmas [1553] was passed, then I waxed something strong. I then thought it best to shift from thence; for that I had there fierce enemies; especially [HENRY MORE] the Vicar of Stepney, Abbot *quondam* of [St. Mary de Grace on] Tower Hill. [*He died in November*, 1554.]

Whom I apprehended in King EDWARD's time, and carried him to Croydon to CRANMER, Bishop of CANTERBURY, for that he disturbed the Preachers in his Church [*at Stepney*] causing the bells to be rung when they were at the Sermon; and sometimes begin to sing in the Choir before the sermon were half done, and sometimes challenge the Preacher in the Pulpit. For he was a strong stout Popish prelate: whom the godly men of the parish were weary of; specially my neighbours of the Limehurst, as Master DRIVER, Master IVE, Master POINTER, Master MARCHE, and others.

Yet durst they not meddle with him, until it was my hap to come and dwell amongst them: and for that I was the King's Servant, I took it upon me; and they went with me to the Bishop to witness those things against him. Who was too full of lenity. A little he rebuked him, and bad him do no more so.

"My Lord," said I, "methinks, you are too gentle unto so stout a Papist!"

"Well," said he, "we have no law to punish them by."

"We have, my Lord!" said I. "If I had your authority, I would be so bold to un-Vicar him; or minister some sharp punishment unto him, and such other. If ever it come to their turn; they will show you no such favour."

"Well," said he, "if GOD so provide, we must abide it."

"Surely," said I, "GOD will never cone you thank for this; but rather take the sword from such as will not use it upon His enemies." And thus we departed.

The like favour is shewed now [*i.e., in ELIZABETH's reign*]; and therefore the like plague will follow.

There was also another spiteful enemy at Stepney, called BANBERY, a shifter, a dicer, &c., like unto DAPERS the dicer, MORGAN of Salisbury Court, busking [Sir THOMAS, *also called* Long] PALMER, lusty YOUNG, [Sir] RALPH BAGNALL [*see* page 149], [Sir] MILES PARTRIDGE [*idem*], and such others. With which companions, I was conversant a while; until I fell to reading the Scriptures, and following the Preachers.

Then, against the wickedness of those men, which I had seen among them; I put forth a ballet, uttering the falsehood and knavery that I was made privy unto. For the which, they so hated me that they raised false slanders and bruits of me, saying that "I was a spy for the Duke of NORTHUMBERLAND": and calling me [Bishop] "HOOPER's companion," for a bill that I set up upon Paul's gate, in defence of HOOPER; and another at St. Magnus's Church, where he was too much abused, with railing bills cast into the pulpit and other ways.

Thus became I odious unto most men, and many times in danger of my life, even in King EDWARD's days. As also for apprehending one ALLEN, a false prophesier [*of whom UNDERHILL says elsewhere*, This ROBERT ALLEN was called the God of Norfolk, before they received the light of the Gospel]; who bruited [*in January*, 1551] that King EDWARD was dead, two years before it came to pass; who was a great calculator for the same. But these jugglers and wicked dicers were still in favour among the magistrates, and were advanced; who were the sowers of sedition, and the destroyers of the two Dukes.

I pray God the like be not practised by such flatterers in these days [*i.e., in ELIZABETH's reign*], according to the old proverb, "He that will in Court dwell, must curry Fauvell." And

> *He that will in Court abide,*
> *Must curry Fauvell back and side,*

[*i.e.,* he must curry or groom a horse, of Fauvell (a bright yellow or tawny) colour (opposed to Sorell, a dark colour), back and side.]

for such get most gain.

I was also called "the hot Gospeller!" jesting and mocking me, saying, "He is all of the Spirit!"

This was their common custom, at their tables, to jest and mock the Preachers and earnest followers of the Gospel; even among the magistrates: or else [speak] in wanton and ribald talk; which when they fell into, one or other would look through [along] the board, saying, "Take heed that UNDERHILL be not here!"

At Stratford on the Bow [now Stratford at Bow], I took the pix of the altar; being of copper, stored with copper gods: the Curate being present, and a Popish Justice dwelling in the town, called Justice TAWE.

There was commandment it should not hang in a string over the altar; and then, they set it upon the altar.

For this act, the Justice's wife with the women of the town, conspired to have murdered me; which one of them gave me warning of, whose good will to the Gospel was not unknown unto the rest. Thus the Lord preserved me from them, and many other dangers more; but specially from hell fire, but that, of His mercy, He called me from the company of the wicked.

This BANBERY, aforesaid, was the spy for Stepney parish; as JOHN AVALES, BEARD, and such others were for London : who [i.e., BANBERY] caused my friend and neighbour Master IVE to be sent unto the Marshalsea, but the LORD shortly delivered him. Wherefore I thought it best to avoid [leave]; because my not coming to the church there, should by him be marked and presented.

Then took I a little house in a secret corner, at the nether [lower] end of Wood Street; where I might better shift the matter.

Sir HUMPHREY RATCLIFFE was the Lieutenant of the Pensioners, and always favoured the Gospel; by whose means I had my wages still paid me [70 marks a year = £46 13s. 4d. = about £500 now; besides a free diet].

When [Sir THOMAS] WYATT was come to Southwark [6th February, 1554] the Pensioners were commanded to watch in armour that night. at the Court : which I hearing of, thought it best, in like sort, to be there; lest by my absence I might have some quarrel piked unto [*picked with*] me; or, at the least, be stricken out off the book for receiving any more wages.

After supper, I put on my armour as the rest did; for we were appointed to watch all the night.

So, being all armed, we came up into the Chamber of Presence, with our poleaxes in our hands. Wherewith the Ladies were very fearful. Some lamenting, crying, and wringing their hands, said, "Alas, there is some great mischief toward! We shall all be destroyed this night! What a sight is this! to see the Queen's Chamber full of armed men. The like was never seen, nor heard of!"

The Master [JOHN] NORRIS, who was a Gentleman Usher of the Utter [*Outer*] Chamber in King HENRY VIII.'s time, and all King EDWARD's time; always a rank Papist, and therefore was now Chief Usher of Queen MARY's Privy Chamber: he was appointed to call the Watch, and see if any were lacking. Unto whom, MOORE, the Clerk of our Cheque, delivered the book of our names; which he perused before he would call them at the cupboard. And when he came to my name, "What!" said he, "what doth he here?"

"Sir," said the Clerk, "he is here ready to serve as the rest be."

"Nay, by God's body!" said he, "that heretic shall not be called to watch here! Give me a pen!" So he struck out my name out of the book.

The Clerk of the Cheque sought me out, and said unto me, "Master UNDERHILL, you need not to watch! you may depart to your lodging!"

"May I?" said I, "I would be glad of that," thinking I had been favoured, because I was not recovered from my sickness: but I did not well trust him, because he was also a Papist. "May I depart indeed?" said I, "will you be my discharge?"

"I tell you true," said he, "Master NORRIS hath stricken you out of the book, saying these words, 'That heretic shall not watch here!' I tell you true what he said."

"Marry, I thank him!" said I, "and you also! You could not do me a greater pleasure!"

"Nay, burden not me withal!" said he, "it is not my doing."

So departed I into the Hall, where our men were appointed to watch. I took my men with me, and a link; and went my ways.

When I came to the Court gate, there I met with Master CLEMENT THROGMORTON [*father of JOB THROGMORTON, the Martinist of* 1589], and GEORGE FERRERS [*the Poet and Historian; see p.* 289], tending their links, to go to London. Master THROGMORTON was come post from Coventry; and had been with the Queen to declare unto her the taking of the Duke of SUFFOLK. Master FERRERS was sent from the Council unto the Lord WILLIAM HOWARD, who had the charge of the watch at London Bridge.

As we went, for that they were both my friends and Protestants, I told them of my good hap, and manner of discharge of the Watch at the Court.

When we came to Ludgate, it was past eleven o'clock. The gate was fast locked; and a great watch within the gate of Londoners, but none without: whereof HENRY PECKHAM had the charge, under his father; who, belike, was gone to his father, or to look to the water side.

Master THROGMORTON knocked hard, and called to them, saying, "Here are three or four gentlemen come from the Court that must come in; and therefore open the gate!"

"Who?" quoth one, "What?" quoth another; and much laughing they made.

"Can ye tell what you do, sirs?" said Master THROGMORTON, declaring his name, and that he had been with the Queen to shew her Grace of the taking of the Duke of SUFFOLK, "and my lodging is within, as I am sure, some of you do know!"

"And," said FERRERS, "I am FERRERS, that was Lord of Misrule with King EDWARD; and am sent from the Council unto my Lord WILLIAM, who hath charge of the Bridge as you know, upon weighty affairs: and therefore let us in, or else ye be not the Queen's friends!"

Still there was much laughing amongst them.

Then said two or three of them, "We have not the keys. We are not trusted with them. The keys be carried away for this night."

"What shall I do?" said Master THROGMORTON, "I am

weary and faint, and I now wax cold. I am not acquainted hereabout; nor no man dare open his doors at this dangerous time; nor am I able to go back again to the Court. I shall perish this night!"

"Well," said I, "Let us go to Newgate! I think I shall get in there."

"Tush!" said he, "it is but in vain. We shall be answered there as we are here."

"Well," said I, "and [if] the worst fall, I can lodge ye in Newgate. Ye know what acquaintance I have there! and the Keeper's door is without the gate."

"That were a bad shift!" said he, "I had almost as leave die in the streets; yet I will, rather than wander again to the Court."

"Well," said I, "let us go and prove! I believe the Keeper will help us in at the gate, or else let us in through his wards, for he hath a door on the inside also. If all this fail, I have a friend at the gate, NEWMAN the ironmonger; in whose house I have been lodged: where, I dare warrant you, we shall have lodging, or at the least, house-room and fire."

"Marry, this is well said!" saith FERRERS.

So to Newgate, we went: where was a great Watch without the gate, which my friend NEWMAN had the charge of; for that he was the Constable. They marvelled to see there, torches coming at that time of the night.

When we came to them, "Master UNDERHILL," said NEWMAN, "what news, that you walk so late?"

"None but good!" said I, "We come from the Court, and would have gone in at Ludgate, and cannot be let in: wherefore, I pray you, if you cannot help us in here, let us have lodging with you!"

"Marry, that ye shall!" said he, "or go in at the gate whether ye will!"

"Godamercy, gentle friend!" said Master THROGMORTON; "I pray you let us go in, if it may be!"

He called to the Constable within the gate, who opened the gate forthwith. "How happy was I!" said Master THROGMORTON, "that I met with you. I had been lost else."

When WYATT was come about [i.e., *from Southwark, through*

Kingston, to Westminster on 7th February 1554], notwith-standing my discharge of the watch by Master NORRIS, I put on my armour, and went to the Court [*at Whitehall Palace*]: where I found all my fellows in the Hall, which they were appointed to keep that day.

Old Sir JOHN GAGE was appointed without the utter [*outer*] gate, with some of his Guard, and his servants and others with him. The rest of the Guard were in the Great Court, the gates standing open. Sir RICHARD SOUTHWELL had charge of the back sides, as the Wood Yard and that way, with 500 men.

The Queen was in the Gallery by the Gatehouse.

Then came KNEVETT and THOMAS COBHAM with a com-pany of the rebels with them, through the Gatehouse from Westminster: wherewith Sir JOHN GAGE and three of the Judges [of the Common Pleas] that were meanly armed in old brigantines [*jackets of quilted leather, covered with iron plates*] were so frighted, that they fled in at the gates in such haste, that old GAGE fell down in the dirt and was foul arrayed: and so shut the gates, whereat the rebels shot many arrows.

By means of this great hurly burly in shutting of the gates, the Guard that were in the Court made as great haste in at the Hall door; and would have come into the Hall amongst us, which we would not suffer. Then they went thronging towards the Water Gate, the kitchens, and those ways.

Master GAGE came in amongst us, all dirt; and so frighted that he could not speak to us. Then came the three Judges; so frighted that we could not keep them out, except we should beat them down.

With that we issued out of the Hall into the Court, to see what the matter was; where there were none left but the porters, the gates being fast shut. As we went towards the gate, meaning to go forth, Sir RICHARD SOUTHWELL came forth of the back yards into the Court.

"Sir!" said we, "command the gates to be opened that we may go to the Queen's enemies! We will else break them open! It is too much shame that the gates should thus be shut for a few rebels! The Queen shall see us fell down her enemies this day, before her face!"

"Masters!" said he, and put his morion off his head, "I shall desire you all, as you be Gentlemen, to stay yourselves here; that I may go up to the Queen to know her pleasure; and you shall have the gates opened. And, as I am a Gentleman! I will make speed!"

Upon this, we stayed; and he made a speedy return: and brought us word, the Queen was content that we should have the gates opened: "But her request is," said he, "that you will not go forth of her sight; for her only trust is in you, for the defence of her person this day."

So the gate was opened, and we marched before the Gallery window: where she spake unto us; requiring us, "As we were Gentlemen, in whom she only trusted, that we would not go from that place."

There we marched up and down the space of an hour; and then came a herald posting, to bring the news that WYATT was taken.

Immediately came Sir MAURICE BERKELEY and WYATT behind him; unto whom he did yield at the Temple Gate: and THOMAS COBHAM behind another gentleman.

Anon after, we [*the Gentlemen Pensioners*] were all brought unto the Queen's presence, and every one kissed her hand; of whom we had great thanks and large promises how good she would be unto us: but few or none of us got anything, although she was very liberal to many others, that were enemies unto GOD's Word, as few of us were.

Thus went I home to my house, where[in] I kept, and came little abroad, until the marriage was concluded with King PHILIP.

Then was there [the] preparing [*in July*, 1555] to go with the Queen, unto Winchester; and all the Books of the Ordinaries were perused by [STEPHEN GARDINER] the Bishop of WINCHESTER and the Earl of ARUNDEL, to consider of every man.

Sir HUMPHREY RATCLIFFE, our Lieutenant, brought unto him the Book of the Pensioners; which when they overlooked, they came unto my name.

"What doth he here?" said the Earl of ARUNDEL.

"I know no cause why he should not be here," said Master RATCLIFFE, "he is an honest man. He hath served from the beginning of the Band [*founded in December*, 1539, *as the*

Band of Spears.   It consisted of a Captain, Lieutenant, Standard bearer, Clerk of the Cheque, and Gentleman Harbinger, and fifty Gentlemen ; chosen out of the best and most ancient families of England.   Some of them sons to Earls, Barons, Knights, and Esquires : men thereunto specially recommended for their worthiness and sufficiency ; without any stain or taint of dishonour, or disparagement in blood], and was as forward as any to serve the Queen, in the time of WYATT's rebellion."

"Let him pass then ! " said the Bishop.

"Well," said the Earl, "you may do so ; but I assure you, my Lord ! he is an arch-heretic ! "

Thus I passed once again.

When we came to Winchester, being in the Chamber of Presence, with my fellows, Master NORRIS came forth of the Queen's Privy Chamber ; unto whom we did reverence, as his place required.

"What ! " saith he unto me ; " what do you here ? "

"Marry, sir ! " said I, " what do you here ? "

"Eh ! " said he, " are you so short with me ? "

"Sir ! " said I, " I must and will forbear, for the place you be in ; but if you were in the place you were in, of the Outer Chamber, I would be shorter with you !   You were then the doorkeeper ; when we waited at the table.   Your office is not to find fault at my being here.   I am at this time appointed to serve here, by those that be in authority ; who know me, as well as you do ! "

"They shall know you better ! " said he, " and the Queen also."

With that, said Master JOHN CALVELEY, one of my fellows (brother unto Sir HUGH CALVELEY, of Cheshire), who served at the journey to Laundercei in the same Band that I did, " In good faith ! Master NORRIS, methinks you do not well ! This gentleman, our fellow, hath served of long time, and was ready to venture his life in defence of the Queen's Majesty at the last service, and as forward as any was there ; and also being appointed and ready to serve here again now, to his great charges, as it is unto us all, methinks you do not the part of a Gentleman thus to seek him ! "

"What ! " said he, " I perceive you will hold together ! "

"Else we were worse than beasts," said my fellow ; " if we

would not, in all lawful cases, so hold together; he that toucheth one of us, shall touch all."

So went he from us, into the Privy Chamber; and from that time never meddled more with me.

On the marriage day [25th July, 1555, at Winchester], the King and the Queen dined in the hall in the Bishop's Palace; sitting under the Cloth of Estate, and none else at that table. The Nobility sat at the side tables. We were the chief servitors, to carry the meat; and the Earl of SUSSEX, our Captain, was the Sewer.

The second course at the marriage of a King is given unto the bearers; I mean the meat, but not the dishes, for they were of gold.

It was my chance to carry a great pasty of a red deer in a great charger, very delicately baked; which, for the weight thereof, divers refused [i.e., to carry]. The which pasty I sent unto London, to my wife and her brother; who cheered therewith many of their friends.

I will not take upon me, to write the manner of the marriage, of the feast, nor of the dancing of the Spaniards, that day; who were greatly out of countenance, specially King PHILIP dancing with the Queen, when they did see my Lord BRAY, Master CAREW, and others so far exceed them; but will leave it unto the learned, as it behoveth him to be, that shall write a Story of so great a Triumph.

Which being ended, their repair was to London. Where, shortly after, began the cruel persecution of the Preachers and earnest professors and followers of the Gospel; and searching of men's houses for their books. Wherefore I got old HENRY DAUNCE, the bricklayer of Whitechapel; who used to preach the Gospel in his garden, every holiday, where I have seen a thousand people: he did inclose my books in a brick wall by the chimney's side in my chamber; where they were preserved from moulding or mice, until the first year of our most gracious Queen ELIZABETH, &c.

Notwithstanding that, I removed from thence, and went unto Coventry; and got me a house a mile out of that city in a wood side. But before I removed from the said house [in Wood Street] in London; I had two children born there, a

N   I

wench [*i.e., a girl, his fifth daughter, ANNE, born 4th January,
1554*], and a boy [*his second son, EDWARD, born 10th February
1555*].

It was a great grief to me, to see so much innocent blood
shed for the Verity. I was also threatened by JOHN AVALES
and BEARD: which I understood by Master LUKE [SHEPHERD],
my very friend, of Coleman Street, physician; who was great
with some that kept them company, and yet were honest
men. Whom I caused to let them understand, that "If they
did attempt to take me, except they had a warrant signed
with four or five of the Council's hands, I would go further
with them than PETER did, who strake off but the ear of
MALCHUS; but I would surely strike off head and all."
Which was declared unto them; so that I oftentimes met
them, but they would not meddle with me. So mightily the
merciful LORD defended me; as also from being present at
that blasphemous *Mass*, in all the time of Queen MARY.

This LUKE [SHEPHERD] wrote many proper books
against the Papists, for the which he was imprisoned
in the Fleet; especially a book called *JOHN BON and
mast. Person*, who reasoned together of the natural presence in the Sacrament [*see pp.* 161-9]. Which book he
wrote in the time of King EDWARD; wherewith the
Papists were sore grieved, specially SIR JOHN GRESHAM,
then being Mayor [*i.e., October* 1547-*October* 1548; *but on
p.* 185 *UNDERHILL dates in* 1551 *ALLEN'S prophecy, which
he here represents as made at the time of the publication of
JOHN BON, i.e.* 1548].

JOHN DAY did print the same book [*in* 1548]; whom the
Mayor sent for, to know the maker [*author*] thereof saying
"He should also go to prison, for printing the same."

It was my chance to come in the same time; for that
I had found out where [ROBERT] ALLEN the Prophesier,
had a chamber; through whom there was a bruit in the
city, that the King was dead: which I declared to the
Mayor, requiring him to have an Officer to apprehend
him.

"Marry," said the Mayor, "I have received letters to
make search for such this night at midnight."

He was going unto dinner; who willed me to take part
of the same.

As we were at dinner, he said " There was a book put forth, called *JOHN BON*; the maker whereof, he would gladly search for."

" Why so ? " said I, " that book is a good book. I have one of them here, and there are many of them in the Court."

" Have you so ? " said he, " I pray you, let me see it ; for I have not seen any of them."

So he took it, and read a little of it, and laughed thereat, as it was both pithy and merry. By means whereof, JOHN DAY, sitting at a sideboard after dinner, was bidden [to] go home ; who had, else, gone to prison.

When we had dined, the Mayor sent two of his Officers with me to seek ALLEN ; whom we met withal in Paul's [Church], and took him with us unto his chamber ; where we found figures set to calculate the nativity of the King, and a judgement given of his death ; whereof this foolish wretch thought himself so sure, that he, and his counsellors the Papists, bruited it all over.

The King lay at Hampton Court, the same time ; and my Lord Protector [*the Duke of SOMERSET*] at the Sion [*Sion House, near Isleworth*]; unto whom I carried this ALLEN, with his books of conjurations, calculations, and many things belonging to that devilish art : which he affirmed before my Lord, "was a lawful science, for the statute [33 *Hen. VIII. c.* 8.] against such was repealed [by 1 *Edw. VI. c.* 12]."

" Thou foolish knave ! " said my Lord, "if thou, and all that be of thy science tell me what I shall do to-morrow, I will give thee all that I have ! " Commanding me to carry him unto the Tower : and wrote a letter to Sir JOHN MARKHAM, then being Lieutenant, to cause him to be examined by such as were learned.

Master MARKHAM, as he was both wise and zealous in the LORD, talked with him. Unto whom he did affirm that " He knew more of the science of Astronomy than all the Universities of Oxford and Cambridge." Whereupon he sent for my friend, before spoken of, Doctor RECORDE ; who examined him : and he knew not the rules of Astronomy ; but " Was a very unlearned ass; and a sorcerer, for the which he was worthy hanging," said Master RECORDE.

To have further matters unto [*in reference to*] him, we sent for THOMAS ROBYNS *alias* MORGAN, commonly called Little MORGAN or TOM MORGAN (brother unto great [*big*] MORGAN, of Salisbury Court, the great dicer); who, when I was a companion with him, told me many stories of this ALLEN: what a cunning man he was! and what things he could do! as, to make a woman love a man, to teach men how to win at the dice, what should become of this realm; [there was] nothing, but he knew it! So he had his chambers in divers places of the city, whither resorted many women, for things stolen or lost, to know their fortunes, and their children's fortunes; where the ruffling roister[er]s and dicers made their ma[t]ches.

When this MORGAN and ALLEN were brought together; MORGAN utterly denied that ever he had seen him, or known him.

"Yes," said ALLEN, "you know me! and I know you!" For he had confessed that, before his coming.

Upon this, Master Lieutenant stayed Little MORGAN also a prisoner in the Tower.

I caused also Master GASTON the lawyer [*not to be confounded with GASCOIGNE the Poet, of Gray's Inn; who did not marry Widow BRETON till after 13th June, 1559*], who was also a great dicer, to be apprehended. In whose house, ALLEN was much; and had a chamber there, where many things were practised.

GASTON had an old wife, who was laid under the board all night, for dead; and when the women, in the morning, came to wind her, they found that there was life in her; and so recovered her: and she lived about two years after.

By the resort of such as came to seek for things stolen and lost, which they would hide for the nonce, to blear their husband's eyes withal, [afterwards] saying, "the wise man told them"; of such, GASTON had choice for himself and his friends, young lawyers of the Temple.

Thus became I so despised and odious unto the lawyers, Lords and ladies, gentlemen, merchants, knaves, and thieves; that I walked as dangerously as DANIEL amongst the lions. Yet from them all, the LORD delivered me: notwithstanding their often devices and conspiracies by violence to have shed my blood, or with sorcery [to have] destroyed me.

These aforesaid were in the Tower about the space of a year; and then by friendship delivered. So 'scapeth always the wicked, and such as GOD commandeth should not live among the people.

Yea, even now in these days also; so that, methinks, I see the ruin of London and this whole realm to be even at hand; for GOD will not suffer any longer. Love is clean banished. No man is sorry for JOSEPH's hurt.

*A Prayer, taken out of the Psalms of DAVID,
daily and nightly, to be said of
EDWARD UNDERHILL.*

ORD! teach me the understanding of Thy commandments! that I may apply myself for the keeping of the same, as long as I live! Give me such wisdom that I may understand, and so to fulfil the thing that Thy law deviseth! to keep it also with my whole heart, that I do nothing against it! Guide me after the true understanding of Thy commandments! for that hath been always my special desire. Incline mine heart unto the love of Thy statutes, and cause me utterly to abhor covetousness! Turn mine eyes aside! lest they be 'tangled with the love of most vain things; but lead me, rather, unto life through Thy warnings! Set such a Word before Thy servant, as may most chiefly further him to worship Thee! Take away the shame that I am afraid of! for Thy judgements are greatly mixed with mercy. As for me, verily, I have loved Thy commandments; wherefore keep me alive according to Thy righteousness!

Love GOD, above all things! and thy neighbour as thyself!
  That this is CHRIST's doctrine, no man can it deny,
Which little is regarded in England's commonwealth,
  Wherefore great plagues at hand be, the realm for to
    destroy.

Do as thou wouldst be done unto! No place here he can have.
  Of all he is refused. No man will him receive.
But Private Wealth, that cursed wretch, and most vile
    slave!
  Over all, he is embraced; and fast to him, they cleave.

He that hath this world's goods, and seeth his neighbour lack;
  And of him hath no compassion, nor sheweth him no love,
Nor relieveth his necessity, but suffers him to go to wrack;
  GOD dwelleth not in that man, the Scriptures plainly prove.

Example we have by DIVES, that daintily did fare,
  In worldly wealth and riches therein he did excel;
Of poor LAZARUS's misery he had thereof no care:
  Therefore was suddenly taken, and tormented in hell.

E D W A R D   U N D E R H I L L.

The History of Wyat's Rebellion :

With the order and manner of resisting the same.

WHEREUNTO, IN THE END, IS ADDED

An earnest Conference with the degenerate and seditious rebels for the search of the Cause of their daily disorder.

Made and compiled by
JOHN PROCTOR.

[SECOND EDITION.]
Mense Januarii, anno 1555.

To the most excellent and most virtuous Lady, our most
gracious Sovereign, MARY, by the grace of GOD,
Queen of England, France, Naples, Hierusalem, and
Ireland; Defender of the Faith; Princess of Spain,
and Sicily; Archduchess of Austria; Duchess of
Milan, Burgundy, and Brabant; Countess of Hapsburg, Flanders, and Tyrol;
your Majesty's most faithful, loving, and
obedient subject, JOHN PROCTOR, wisheth
all grace, long peace, quiet reign,
from GOD the Father,
the Son, and the
HOLY GHOST.

T hath been allowed, most gracious Sovereign,
for a necessary policy in all Ages, as stories
do witness, that the flagitious enterprises of
the wicked, which have at any time attempted
with traitorous force to subvert or alter the Public
State of their countries, as also the wise and virtuous
policies of the good practised to preserve the Common
Weal and to repel the enemies of the same, should by

writing be committed to eternal memory. Partly that they of that Age in whose time such things happened might by the oft reading conceive a certain gladness in considering with themselves, and beholding as it were in a glass, from what calamity and extreme ruin, by what policy and wisdom, their native countries were delivered ; besides the great misery and peril they themselves have escaped : partly for a doctrine and a monition serving both for the present and future time. But chiefly and principally that the traitors themselves (who, through hatred to their Prince or country, shall, either of their own malicious disposition be stirred ; or else by other perverse counsel thereunto induced) may always have before their eyes the miserable end that happeneth as just reward to all such caytives [*caitiffs*] as, either of ambition not satisfied with their own state will seek preposterously to aspire to honour ; or of malice to their Prince, will enter into that horrible crime of Privy Conspiracy or Open Rebellion.

The industry of Writers doth sufficiently declare in a number of stories that conspiracy and treason hath always turned to the authors a wretched and miserable end : and if their persons happen at any time to escape temporal punishment, as rarely they have done ; yet their names, specially of the notorious and principal offenders, have been always had in such vile and odible detestation in all Ages and among all nations as, for the same, they have been ever after abhorred of all good men.

These general considerations, moving others to indict [*endite*] and pen stories, moved me also to gather together and to register for memory the marvellous practice of WYAT his detestable Rebellion ; little inferior to the most dangerous reported in any history, either for desperate courage in the author, or for the monstrous end purposed by his Rebellion.

Yet I thought nothing less at the beginning than to publish the same at this time, or at this Age: minding only to gather notes thereof, where the truth might be best known, for the which I made earnest and diligent investigation; and to leave them to be published by others hereafter, to the behoof of our posterity.

But hearing the sundry tales thereof, far dissonant in the utterance, and many of them as far wide from truth, fashioned from the speakers to advance, or deprave, as they fantased [*favoured*] the parties; and understanding besides what notable infamy sprang of this Rebellion to the whole country of Kent, and to every member of the same, where sundry and many of them, to mine own knowledge, shewed themselves most faithful and worthy subjects, as by the story [it]self shall evidently appear, which either of haste or of purpose were omitted in a printed book late[ly] set forth at Canterbury. I thought these to be special considerations whereby I ought, of duty to my country [*County*], to compile and digest such notes as I had gathered concerning that Rebellion, in some form or fashion of History; and to publish the same in this Age, and at this present, contrary to my first intent: as well that the very truth of that rebellious enterprise might be thoroughly known, as that also the Shire where that vile Rebellion was practised might, by opening the full truth in some part, be delivered from the infamy which, as by report I hear, is made so general in other Shires as though very few of Kent were free from WYAT's conspiracy.

Most humbly beseeching your Highness to take this my travail in so good and gracious part ; as of your Grace's benign and gentle nature it hath pleased you to accept my former books dedicated unto your Highness. Whereby I mind nothing less than to excuse, or accuse, any affectionately [*partially*] ; but to set forth each man's doings truly according to their demerits : that by the contemplation hereof both the good may be encouraged in the execution of perfect obedience and unspotted loyalty ; and the wicked restrained from the hateful practice of such detestable purposes.

The Blessed Trinity preserve your Highness !

To the Loving Reader.

HE safe and sure recordation of pains and perils past hath present delectation, saith TULLY. For things, were they never so bitter and unpleasant in the execution, being after in peace and security renewed by report or chronicle, are both plausible [*praiseworthy*] and profitable, whether they touched ourselves or others.

Being thus in this point persuaded, loving Reader, I thought it a travail neither unpleasant for thee, nor unthankful for me, to contrive the late Rebellion practised by WYAT in form of a Chronicle, as thou seest. Whereby as I mean not to please the evil, nor displease the good ; so I much desire to amend the one by setting before his eye the lamentable Image of hateful Rebellion, for the increase of obedience ; and to help the other by setting forth the unspotted loyalty of such as adventurously and faithfully served in this dangerous time, for the increase of knowledge and policy the better to repress the like dangers, if any hereafter happen.

And further, although hereby I covet not to renew a fear of a danger past, yet would I gladly increase a care and study in every good man's heart to avoid a like danger that may happen, and most times happeneth ; when a danger with much difficulty avoided is not sufficient warning to beware of the next.

I have forborne to touch any man by name, WYAT only except ; and a few others which the story would not permit to be left out. Yet take me not that I mean to excuse any man's fault thereby. For what, should I shew myself so ungrate or unnatural unto my natural countrymen ; as namely to blaze them to the World whom, either their own good hap or the Queen's surpassing mercy, would to be covered at this time?

And although I touch some by name, terming them in certain places "traitors and rebels," just titles of their deserts : yet, GOD is my witness!, I do it not of malice or envy to any of their persons. I never hated any of them ; no, not WYAT himself! whom, although he was utterly unknown unto me, yet for the sundry and singular gifts wherewith he was largely endued, I had him in great admiration. And now I rather pity his unhappy case than malice his person : and do much lament that so many good and commendable qualities were abused in the service of cursed Heresy ; whose reward was never other than shameful confusion, by one way or other, to all that followed her ways.

Finally, if thou suppose I have not fully set forth the whole case, all as it was, I shall not againsay it ; neither thought I it necessary so to do ; but rather so much as for this time might be both plausible [*praiseworthy*] and profitable, and should satisfy such points as in the *Dedicatory Epistle* to the Queen's Majesty are expressed.

Hereafter it may be that further be said touching this matter. In mean time thou hast no just cause, I trust, to be offended with this my present enterprise, either for the manner of handling or for the matter herein handled : the one having sufficient perspicuity and plainness, the other full truth ; for which I have made such diligent investigation, as I have found it and have herein expressed the same, especially so much as concerneth Kent.

Vale !

Wyat's Rebellion:
with the order and manner of
resisting the same.

HAT a restless evil Heresy is! ever travailing to bring forth mischief! The dangerous nature of Heresy. never ceasing to protrude all those in whose hearts she is received to confusion! By what plausible allurements at her entry, she catcheth favourable entertainment! With what ways of craft and subtilty she dilateth her dominion! and finally how, of course, she toileth to be supported by Faction, Sedition, and Rebellion! to the great peril of subversion of that State where, as a plague, she happeneth to find habitation : as well the lamentable history of the Bohemians and Germans, with all others treating of like enterprises by heretics, as also WYAT's late conspiracy practised with open force, doth plenteously declare. Who, as it should evidently seem by the trade of his life Heresy the special ground of WYAT's Rebellion. and the late disclosing of himself, was so fervently affected to heresy, although he laboured by false persuasion otherwise to have coloured it; that, burning inwardly with a prepensed treason in his breast for the continuance of the same within the realm, he persuaded to himself such an impossibility therein (the Queen's Highness prospering and bearing the sceptre of high governance) as could by no means be brought about without rebellion : the

Rebellion, the only refuge of heretics.

only refuge, as I said, that indurate heretics have always sought, for maintenance of their heresy ; living under a Catholic Prince.

He therefore, being thus inflamed, could no longer contain,

WYAT persuaded that the Queen and Heresy could not reign together.

but immediately upon the beginning of the Queen's most happy reign, forsaking his habitation in the country, went to London of purpose to stir [HENRY GREY,] the Duke of SUFFOLK and his brethren, with others of power in further countries [*Counties*],

WYAT's repair to London to stir others to his Rebellion.

whom he knew to be like affected to heresies and consequently to burn in sembable desire for continuance of the same : leaving nevertheless such behind him in Kent, to solicit his and their unhappy case ; whom he knew so much addicted thereunto as, in his absence, for their diligence in such a ministry needed no overseer.

He remained in London till he thought himself thoroughly furnished every way, and everywhere within the realm, to attempt his determined enterprise ; when apt time should

WYAT's return into Kent.

serve. Which done, he returned into Kent : not of purpose then to proceed ; but, understanding his strength, practised there by his agents to set things in order, and so to return to London ; abiding the time appointed therefore by him and his complices.

But, so it befell, in the mean time, that, at his being in the country, the [Privy] Council committed a Gentleman of that Shire to ward, one to WYAT above all others most dear : whereby the common bruit grew that he, (suspecting his secrets to be revealed, and upon that occasion to be sent for by the Council) felt himself, as it were for his own surety,

WYAT preventeth the time.

compelled to anticipate his time. But whether that were the cause or no, doubtful it is.

But certain it was that WYAT, then proceeding in his detestable purpose, armed himself and as many as he could : and, giving intelligence of his determination to his com-

The first day of WYAT's stir, at Maidstone.

plices, as well at London as elsewhere, the Thursday after, at Maidstone, in the market time, being the 25th day of January [1554], in the first year of the Queen's reign, by Proclamation in writing, published his devilish pretence.

And considering with himself that to make the pretence of his Rebellion to be the restoring or continuance of the new and newly-forged Religion was neither agreeable to the nature of Heresy (which always defendeth itself by the name and countenance of other matter more plausible); neither so apt to further his wicked purpose, being not a case so general to allure all sorts to take part with him: he determined to speak no word of Religion, but to make the only colour [*pretence*] of his commotion, only to withstand Strangers [*i.e. the Spaniards*], and to advance Liberty. *The cause why* WYAT *made not Religion the outward pretence of his Rebellion.* *The colour of* WYAT's *Rebellion.*

For as he made his full reckoning that such as accorded with him in religion would wholly join with him in that rebellion; so he trusted that the Catholics for the most part would gladly embrace that quarrel against the Strangers; whose name he took to become odible to all sorts by the seditious and malicious report which he and his had maliciously imagined and blown abroad against that nation, as a preparative to their abominable treason. WYAT's *preparative to his Rebellion.*

His Proclamation therefore published at Maidstone, and so in other places, persuaded that quarrel to be taken in hand in the defence of the realm from overrunning by Strangers and for the advancement of Liberty: where, in very deed, his only and very matter was the continuance of heresy: as by his own words at sundry times shall hereafter appear.

And to the end the people should not think that he alone, with a few other mean Gentlemen, had taken that traitorous enterprise in hand without comfort or aid of higher powers, he untruly and maliciously added further to his Proclamation, by persuasion to the people: WYAT's *untrue persuasions to further his Rebellion.*

That all the Nobility of the realm and the whole [Privy] Council (one or two only except) were agreeable to his pretensed treason, and would with all their power and strength further the same; (which he found most untrue, to his subversion): and That the Lord ABERGAVENNY, [Sir THOMAS CHEYNEY,] the Lord Warden [of the Cinque Ports], Sir ROBERT SOUTHWELL, High Sheriff, with all other Gentlemen would join with him in this enterprise, and set their foot by his, to repel the Strangers.

O   I

This Proclamation and such annexed persuasions made at

How WYAT's untrne persuasions abused the people. Maidstone on the market day, and in other parts of the Shire, had so wrought in the hearts of the people that divers (which before hated him, and he them) were now, as it seemed, upon this occasion, mutually reconciled; and said unto him, "Sir, is your quarrel only to defend us from overrunning by Strangers and to advance Liberty; and not against the Queen?"

The nature of a heretic is to say one thing and think another. "No," quod WYAT, "we mind nothing less than any wise to touch her Grace; but to serve her and honour her, according to our duties."

"Well," quod they, "give us then your hand. We will stick to you to death in this quarrel!"

That done, there came to him one other, of good wealth, saying, "Sir," quod he, "they say I love potage well. I will sell all my spoons, and all the plate in my house rather than your purpose shall quail; and sup my potage with my mouth [see p. 234]. I trust," quod he, "you will restore the right religion again."

"Whist!" quod WYAT, "you may not so much as name

WYAT's own words to prove Heresy to be the ground of his Rebellion. religion, for that will withdraw from us the hearts of many. You must only make your quarrel for overrunning by Strangers. And yet to thee, be it said in counsel, as unto my friend, we mind *only* the restitution of GOD's Word. But no words!"

By these his words it appeared that his principal intent was not to keep out Strangers, which commonly do not invade to our hindrance but by rebellion amongst ourselves; nor to advance Liberty, which ever decayeth through treason: but to advance Heresy, the Lady Regent of his life and doings.

This same Thursday [25th January 1554] as WYAT, THOMAS ISLEY, and others were occupied at Maidstone with Proclamations to stir the people and such like; so were others his confederates occupied in like manner by Proclamations at Milton, Ashford, and other towns in the east parts of the Shire. Through whose allurements, the multitude were grown so earnestly affected to WYAT's purpose that they suffered Master CHRISTOPHER ROPER, a man of good worship and so esteemed of them, to be taken of

WYAT's ministers, and carried out of the market place, without any manner of rescue: for that he, The apprehension of Master CHRISTOPHER ROPER by the rebels. having his heart and eye full fixed upon the Queen, not only withstood the reading of WYAT's traitorous Proclamation at Milton; but also in the same place proclaimed him and all his, traitors. And being roughly charged therewith by WYAT and others his gallants, Master CHRISTOPHER ROPER's words to WYAT. when he was brought to Rochester, he answered, "This tongue spake it, and doth now avow it."

They suffered Master TUCKE also, and Master DORREL of Calehill, being Gentlemen of good worship and The apprehension of Master TUCKE and Master DORREL. Justices of Peace, to be taken out of their houses by the rebels; and conveyed, without any manner of rescue, in the day time, to Rochester, being twenty miles distant: where they, with Master ROPER, were kept as prisoners in great danger of life.

In like manner, Sir HENRY ISLEY, ANTHONY KNEVET, WILLIAM KNEVET, with others, were at Tonbridge, Sevenoaks, and other towns in the west parts of the Shire, stirring the people by alarms, drums, and Proclamations.

Now ye shall understand that the evening afore [24th January 1554] the publishing his pretence at How WYAT wrote to the Sheriff of his intent to stir. Maidstone, WYAT sent a letter, by one THOMAS MONDE, a man of much honesty, to Sir ROBERT SOUTHWELL, being Sheriff of the Shire: unto_whom long before, as I can understand, he had neither spoken nor written other than in defiance; they being in contention for matters of religion as it was said. Nevertheless to serve his purpose, dissembling his great malice and haughty courage, he wrote a letter to him of such effect as followeth:

The effect of WYAT's letter to Sir ROBERT SOUTHWELL, Sheriff of Kent.

FTER hearty commendations. There hath been between you and me many quarrels and grudges, and I ever the sufferer; and yet have you sought the end which is now friendly offered unto you, if you be willing to receive it.

But whatsoever private quarrel you have to me, I doubt not but your wisdom is too much, seeing so many perils at hand to us both (this pretensed Marriage [*of King Philip to Queen Mary*] taking effect), to dissent from us in so necessary a purpose as wherein we now determine to enter for the common wealth of the whole realm. And that you may the better understand our pretence, I send you the copy of our Proclamation comprehending the sum and effect of our meaning : whereunto if the common wealth shall find you an enemy, say not hereafter but that you were friendly warned.

We forbear to write to the Lord Abergavenny ; for what you may do with him, if you list, we know.

The style of Wyat's Proclamation.

A Proclamation agreed unto by Thomas Wyat, George Harper, Henry Isley,

Wyat's false presumption of *the best of the* Shire.

Knights ; and by divers of the best of the Shire ; sent unto the commons of the same.

ORASMUCH as it is now spread abroad, and certainly pronounced by [Stephen Gardiner, Bishop of Winchester] the Lord Chancellor and others of the [Privy] Council, of the Queen's determinate pleasure to marry with a Stranger, &c. We there-

Because. fore write unto you, because you be our friends, and because you be Englishmen, that you will join with us, as we will with you unto death, in this behalf ; protesting unto you before GOD, that no earthly cause could move us unto this enterprise but this alone : wherein we seek no

Such Councillors, he meaneth, as would favour heresy, &c. harm to the Queen, but better counsel and Councillors ; which also we would have foreborne in all other matters, saving only in this. For herein lieth the health and wealth of us all.

For trial hereof and manifest proof of this intended pur-

Lo, loud lie! pose, lo now, even at hand, Spaniards be now already arrived at Dover, at one passage, to the number of a

hundred, passing upward to London in companies of ten,
four, and six, with harness [*armour*] harquebusses and
morians [*helmets*] with match light[ed]; the foremost company whereof be already at Rochester.

We shall require you therefore to repair to such places as
the bearers hereof shall pronounce unto you, there to
assemble and determine what may be best for the advancement of Liberty and common wealth in this behalf, and to
bring with you such aid as you may.

The end of WYAT's Proclamation.

The messenger that brought the letter, with the Proclamation, from WYAT to the Sheriff, being not privy to the contents thereof and having charge, upon his life, to return an
answer with all speed, importuned the Sheriff so much therefore (although he saw him greatly busied in giving advertisement throughout the Shire of WYAT's traitorous determination) as he nevertheless (to satisfy the messenger, whom he
knew to be a right honest man; notwithstanding his diligence
was abused in so lewd a message), made him answer out of
hand as followeth:

The Sheriff's answer to the Messenger that brought WYAT's letter.

 " NEIGHBOUR MONDE, rather to satisfy your im-
portunity than to answer WYAT's letter, whom
in this case I disdain to answer, or to speak with
you apart coming from a traitor, you may say
unto him, That as indeed I have been desirous of
his friendship for neighbourhood's sake, so have I much more
desired his reformation in divers points of great disorder:
whereby he certainly knew, as well by my speech to himself
as other means coming to his knowledge, that I have sithens
the beginning of the Queen's reign holden him and some of
his colleges [*colleagues*] in this conspiracy vehemently suspected for like matters as now they have attempted.

"Wherein seeing he hath not deceived me, but by opening himself hath manifestly verified mine opinion conceived of him ; I purpose not to purchase his friendship so dear[ly] as for the game of him to lose myself and my posterity in perpetual infamy. And if such things which his fond [*foolish*] head hath weighed for perils, to the condemnation of the whole wisdom of the realm (they allowing the same for good), had been indeed as perilous as he with others, for want of due consideration, deemeth them : his duty had been to have opened his opinion therein as a humble and reverent petitioner to the Queen's Highness, or to some of her Grace's Council. But to press his Sovereign, in any suit or upon any occasion, with weapon and armour, by stirring her subjects to rebellion ; that is, and always hath been, account-ed the part of the most arrogant and presumptuous traitors : and so do I note him and his mates, as you may tell them ; and shall, GOD willing, provide for them accordingly.

"Now good man MONDE, it shall be in your choice whether you will carry this message or no. But, as your friend, I shall advise you to seek out better company."

The messenger excusing himself by ignorance, departed to WYAT with answer : and, soon after, returned to the Sheriff ; under whom he served the Queen very faithfully.

The Sheriff being made privy, as ye have heard, by WYAT to his traitorous pretence the night before he stirred ; and wanting no good will, as it should seem, with the help of the Lord ABERGAVENNY who was as forward as he, to have resisted the reading of WYAT's Proclamation at Maidstone the day following and to disperse his force, sent for Gentle-men and yeomen in all haste to that end.

But before he could gather Power meet to attempt the repressing of such a force (sundry of his neighbours of greatest possessions, and towns most populous, which should have been his chief aid, being contrary bent), WYAT accom-panied with a force well armed and weaponed marched to Rochester the same Thursday [25th January 1554]; HARPER and others meeting him in the way. Where fortifying the east parts of the town, and breaking up the bridge towards the west ; he abode the coming of his appointed strength : suffering all passengers to pass quietly through the town, to

London, or to the sea; taking nothing from them but only
their weapons.

And being the Friday [26th January] all day at Rochester,
and not hearing from ISLEY, the town of Tonbridge, and
other his conjurates of the west part of the Shire; he
addressed an earnest letter the Saturday morning [27th
January] to ISLEY, the KNEVETS, and others, with the town of
Tonbridge, requiring them to accelerate their coming unto him.

According whereunto ISLEY, the KNEVETS, with others,
being newly returned from Penshurst (where they rifled Sir
HENRY SIDNEY [of] his armour;   he being   The rifling of
attendant upon the Queen's Highness as a faithful   Sir HENRY
SIDNEY his
subject), perceiving WYAT to long for their com-   armour.
ing, resolved to observe their promise and march forwards
that night towards WYAT.

But understanding that the Lord ABERGAVENNY, the
Sheriff, and GEORGE CLARKE had now gathered a force, and
were prest to encounter them: first ere they departed out of
the town, they thought it good by some kind of Proclamation,
to alienate the people's hearts from them; as they did in the
manner following:

The copy of the Proclamation made at Tonbridge,
by Sir HENRY ISLEY, ANTONY KNEVET
and his brother, with others.

OU shall understand that HENRY [NEVILLE]
Lord ABERGAVENNY, ROBERT SOUTHWELL
Knight, GEORGE CLARKE Gentleman, have most
traitorously, to the disturbance of the common
wealth, stirred and raised up the Queen's most
loving subjects of this realm to defend the most wicked and
devilish enterprise of certain of the wicked and perverse
Councillors, to the utter confusion of this her Grace's realm,
and the perpetual servitude of all the Queen's most loving
subjects.   In consideration whereof, we Sir THOMAS WYAT
Knight, Sir GEORGE HARPER Knight, Sir HENRY ISLEY
Knight, ANTONY KNEVET Esquire, with all the faithful
Gentlemen of Kent and trusty commons of the same, do

pronounce the said HENRY Lord ABERGAVENNY, ROBERT SOUTHWELL and GEORGE CLARKE Gentleman, to be traitors to GOD, the Crown, and the common wealth.

This done, with all speed calling their company together by noise of drums, and leaving their direct way to Rochester, for that they would not come under the wing of the Lord ABERGAVENNY and the Sheriff, they marched that night [27th January] to Sevenoaks. Taking order with such as were left behind in the town [of Tonbridge], that they should be in a readiness to come whensoever they should be sent for by WYAT; and that by no ways they should believe any tales. "For," quod they, "the Council will now send abroad flying lies and tales to discredit us and discomfort you: for it is their policy."

ANTONY KNEVET, after he was lept to his horse, took one by the hand, and said, "Fare you well. And if you hap to hear that I am taken, never believe it: for undoubtedly I will either die in the field or achieve my purpose." But within four and twenty hours he brake his promise, and ran away no faster than his legs could carry him.

Well, I shall now leave them marching to Sevenoaks; and The Herald's coming to Rochester. return to WYAT at Rochester. This present Saturday [27th January] came unto him from the Queen's Highness a Herald and a trumpeter.

WYAT, at the sound of the trumpet, came to the bridge, where the Herald was with his coat armour carrying the Arms of England on his back. But WYAT, without using any reverence to him either for his coat or office, would not suffer him to come into the town to declare his message; and [the Herald] pressing to come in, he offered to strike him: whereupon the Herald stayed and did his message there, so that only WYAT with a few with him heard it. Which, as men could gather by the report of them that heard it, was promise of pardon to as many as would retire to their houses within four and twenty hours after the Proclamation, and become good subjects. But WYAT would not suffer his soldiers in anywise to hear it, nor any other Proclamation coming from the Queen.

In the mean time also, Sir THOMAS CHEYNEY, Lord

Warden, being a most faithful and noble subject, had sent
him such salutations as of honour ought to be used The Lord
to a traitor.   And being very desirous to be doing Warden's
greeting to
with him, and to prove on his body what in WYAT.
words of greeting he had affirmed, felt yet by his discretion
and long experience great causes of stay.   For WYAT
desired nothing more than his coming forth; persuading
[himself] that he wanted no friends about him, nor any
others that would take in hand to repress him with force
gathered in that Shire.   And, undoubtedly, doubtful were
the hearts of the people, and marvellously bent to favour
WYAT and his purpose; as by daily events appeared.

The Lord ABERGAVENNY and the Sheriff who, the
Saturday [27th January] next after WYAT's stir, were at
Malling in the way towards Rochester (where WYAT lay);
having with them a company of well appointed subjects.
In whom notwithstanding for the more part they had good
opinion of trustiness and honesty: yet having the general
case of the people's disposition in their eye; and not without
cause suspecting in their Band, amongst so many faithful
and good, some such to be, upon trust of whose trustless
and brittle aid it were no good policy to adventure far—
pondering therewith that this illusion of the people, whereby
they were so far drawn from their right course and duty,
grew chiefly by such crafty and false persuasions as WYAT
and his mates had set forth in sundry parts of the Shire,
by way of Proclamation in writing: wherein, amongst other
gross lies they had set forth also matters of untruth to
discredit the Lord ABERGAVENNY and the Sheriff; as
WYAT, in his persuasions, that they would join with him;
and ISLEY, in his Proclamation that they had traitorously
assembled the Queen's loving subjects against her Grace
and the realm.

It seemed unto them very good and necessary to spend
some time at Malling in advising and lessening [*lessoning*]
the multitude; and by way of exhortation to impugn those
traitorous Proclamations, and refell such gross and false
lies therein contained; and finally to dissuade the people,
which, that day being market day, were assembled to a great
number of all sorts, from the traitors and their attempts.

And accordingly the Sheriff had penned an Exhortation
to that purpose, which was pronounced out of writing in
Malling; and sent after by him into other parts. The
hearing whereof did undoubtedly much move the people,
as after shall appear.

I shall report the same in substance truly; howbeit not
fully in the same form and manner as I found it, and as
it was penned and pronounced by the Sheriff: who, in
the utterance and setting forth thereof, spared not to speak
plainly and touch sharply, as then the present time and
case employed vehement occasion.

An Exhortation made by Sir ROBERT SOUTHWELL
Knight, Sheriff of Kent, at Malling, the Satur-
day being the 27th day of January, and
market day there, to a great assembly
of people; refelling and confuting
WYAT and his complices'
traitorous Proclama-
tions. WYAT being
at Rochester,
four miles
distant.

OVING neighbours and friends. Where of late
there hath been most pestilent and traitorous
Proclamations, as ye have heard, set forth by
THOMAS WYAT, GEORGE HARPER, HENRY
ISLEY, and others, as most arrant traitors to the
Queen and the realm; some of them the Queen's ancient
enemies aforetime, and double traitors: yet notwithstanding
accounting themselves to be the best of the Shire in their
Proclamations; and in the same reputing and pronouncing
others as traitors whom ye can witness to have been, from
time to time, true and faithful subjects to the Queen and
this our common weal, as the Lord ABERGAVENNY here

present, myself, and other Gentlemen now prest and
ready with you, according to our duty, to serve our noble
Queen. I shall need to spend the less time to declare
unto you how evil they be, or how evil their enterprise
is that they have taken in hand : forasmuch as this their
arrogant presumption and presumptuous pride in advancing
themselves so far from all truth, and in depraving of others
so maliciously for executing their bounden duty, ought
abundantly to persuade what they be, to all of consideration,
without further circumstance.

"But forasmuch as in their Proclamations they fill the
ears of the Queen's liege people with gross and manifest
lies to stir them against her Grace, in the utterance whereof
they use this demonstration, "Lo!" signifying some notable
thing near at hand, for credit worthy impression in their
memory, as :—

> 'Lo, a great number of Strangers be now arrived
> at Dover in harness [*armour*] with harquebusses
> morians and matchlight.'

"I say unto you, neighbours and friends, upon pain to
be torn in pieces with your hands, that it is untrue ; and
a manifest lie invented by them to provoke and irritate
the Queen's simple people to join with them in their traitorous
enterprise. And therefore I have perfect hope that you,
being afore time abused with their crafty and deceitful
treason, will not now once again (having experience of
their former evil) be trapped, for any persuasion, in so
heinous a snare as this most vile and horrible crime of
treason.

"Do you not see and note that, as in the beginning
of the Queen's most gracious reign, some of them sought
to deprive her Grace of her princely estate and rightful
dignity, minding to advance thereunto the Lady JANE,
daughter to the Duke of SUFFOLK ; so are they and others
newly confedered [*confederated*] with the Duke and his
brethren, being in arms at this present for the same purpose,
and daily looking for aid of these traitors and others of
their conspiracy : as by the Queen's most gracious letters,
signed with her own hand, and ready to be read here, may
plainly appear unto you? And will you now nevertheless
aid them any ways, or sit still whilst they go about thus

wrongfully and traitorously to depose their, and our, most gracious Sovereign Lady and Queen! the comfort of us all! the stay of us all! the only safeguard of us all! to whom can no displeasure or danger chance, but the same must double [*doubly*] redound to all and every of us!

"No, friends and neighbours, I trust never to live to see you so far abused. They go about to blear you with matters of Strangers, as though they should come to overrun you and us also. He seemeth very blind, and willingly blinded, that will have his sight dimmed with such a fond [*foolish*] mist! For if they meant to resist Strangers, as they mind nothing less: they would then prepare to go to the sea coasts; and not to the Queen's most royal person, with such a company in arms and weapon[s].

"Ye can consider, I trust, this noble Gentleman, the Lord ABERGAVENNY here present, being of an ancient and great parentage, born among you; and such other Gentlemen as you see here, which be no strangers unto you; myself also, although a poor Gentleman (who I trust at no time hath abused you), hath somewhat to lose as well as they; and would be as loth to be overrun with Strangers as they; if any such thing were meant. But for that we know most certainly that there is meant no manner of evil to us by those Strangers; but rather aid profit and comfort against other strangers, our ancient enemies [*the French*]; with whom they, as most arrant and degenerate traitors, do indeed unkindly and unnaturally join : we, in her Grace's defence, will spend both life and what we have beside, to the uttermost penny, against them.

"Well, I can no more now say unto you, but (understanding the Queen's Highness, as a most merciful Princess, to be once again determined to pardon as many as, by their traitorous and deceitful Proclamations and other illusions, were allured to this last treason; so they repair to their habitations within four and twenty hours after her Grace's Proclamation read, and become true subjects to her Grace) to advise such as hath taken part with those traitors, or have withdrawn themselves (contrary to their allegiance) from aiding and serving of their Sovereign, according to their duties, against her enemies, thankfully to accept and embrace her most gracious pardon ; and use means of themselves to apprehend those arrant and principal traitors, and make a present of them to the Queen's Highness; or leave them to themselves, as most detestable traitors: who being once so graciously and mercifully forgiven could not but carry the clemency of the same in their hearts to the furtherance of all obedience whiles they lived, if there had been any spark of grace in them.

"And further I have to say unto you that as these traitors, by their Proclamations without authority, have moved you to stir against the Queen your Sovereign; and appointed you places where to meet and consult for the furtherance of their traitorous purpose and to bring with you such aid as you can: so shall I require you, and in her Grace's name charge you that be here present, not to come there; but that you, and such as be absent, taking knowledge hereby, repair to such places as I, the Queen's Sheriff and Officer, shall appoint you, with such aid as you can bring for the better service of the Queen and the Shire: where you shall be assured to receive comfort, thanks, and honesty to the end of your lives and your posterity. And the other way but endless shame and utter undoing to you and yours; which shall be worst to yourselves, and yet a great grief to us your neighbours: whose advice in all other your private causes you have been content to follow; and now in this weightiest that hath, or may, happen to you will refuse us, and follow them that hath ever abused you to your and their utter confusion.

At Malling, the 27th of January [1554], *anno Mariæ primo.* GOD save Queen MARY and all her well willers!"

The Sheriff reading this Exhortation, caused one BARRAM, a Gentleman and servant to the Lord ABERGAVENNY, to pronounce it, as he read it, so loud and so distinctly as the people assembled round about him, to a very great number, in manner of a ring, might easily hear and understand every word proceeding from BARRAM: who of his own head cried out unto them, "You may not so much as lift up your finger against your King or Queen!"

And after the people had heard the Sheriff's Exhortation;

and cried "GOD save Queen MARY!" which they did most heartily, spending therein a convenient time; the Sheriff used these words unto them:

"Masters," quod he, "although I alone did speak unto you; yet what words were spoken to you by me were also spoken to you by the Lord ABER-GAVENNY and all the Gentlemen here present: in whose persons I then spake; and now require at your hands a plain and resolute answer. Will you now therefore join with such as you see evidently to be arrant traitors; or else with the Lord ABERGAVENNY and such Gentlemen as you see here present, that will live and die with you in defence of our rightful Queen against these traitors?"

The Sheriff's speech to the multitude.

The people with one voice defied WYAT and his complices as arrant traitors, and said that they now well espied they had but abused them. Wherefore in defence of Queen MARY, they would die upon them: expressing their minds with such earnest shouts and cries as shewed to proceed unfeignedly from their hearts; which after was confirmed by a better experience the day following, as ye shall anon hear.

The people's answer to the Sheriff.

But by the way ye shall understand that WYAT hearing of this Proclamation, said, "I know that BARRAM well; but yet I never took him to have so wide a throat. If I live, I may happen to make him crow a higher note in another place." What trow you should then have become of the author?

Wyat's promise of Barram's reward.

In the Sunday following [28th January 1554], the Lord ABERGAVENNY, the Sheriff, and the rest of the Gentlemen were determined to have marched in the morning early towards Rochester, to have aided the Duke of NORFOLK and Sir HENRY JERNINGHAM Captain of the Guard, then being at Gravesend, towards WYAT; with a certain Band [*Regiment*] of White Coats, to the number of 600, sent unto them from London; whereof BRET and others were their Captains.

The Duke of NORFOLK and Sir HENRY JERNING-HAM's coming to Gravesend.

ROGER APPULTON Gentleman was also at Gravesend with the Duke, attendant to serve: wherein likewise was THOMAS SWAN Gentleman.

ROGER APPULTON and THOMAS SWAN trusty Gentlemen.

This Saturday [27th January] at night, the Lord ABER-
GAVENNY suspecting WYAT and his complices (living within
four miles of them; and being so much provoked in that
they were, in the day, so rightly set forth in their colours
[*illusions*] at Malling) would, for revenge, work some
annoyance to them or his Band that night, either by a
camasado [*night attack*] or by some other means; did
therefore, to prevent the same, set a strong watch in the
market place at Malling and other parts of entry The Lord
into the town: and gave the watchword himself ABERGAVENNY
before he would take any rest. sets the watch
in person.

But between one and two of the clock in the night, when
everybody was taken to rest save the watch, there A larom at
happened a larom [*an alarm*], sundry crying, Malling.
"Treason! Treason! We are all betrayed!" in such sort
that such as were in their beds or newly risen thought
verily that, either WYAT with his Band had been in the
town, or very near.

The thing was so sudden and happened in such a time as
men not acquainted with like matters were so amazed
that some of them knew not well what to do: and yet
in the end it proved to [be] nothing.

For it grew by a messenger that came, very late in the
night, desiring to speak with the Lord ABERGAVENNY or
Master Sheriff, to give them certain advertisement, That
Sir HENRY ISLEY, the two KNEVETS, and certain others,
with 500 Wealdish men [*i.e., from the Weald of Kent*] were
at Sevenoaks; and would march in the morning early from
thence towards Rochester, for the aid of WYAT A meaning of
against the Duke of NORFOLK: and in their way, the rebels to
burn and destroy the house of GEORGE CLARKE GEORGE
aforesaid. CLARKE'S
house.

Whereupon the Lord ABERGAVENNY and the Sheriff,
by the advice of the Gentlemen before named, for that
the said CLARKE had been a painful [*painstaking*] and
serviceable Gentleman, changed their purposed journey from
Rochester, to encounter with ISLEY and his Band, to cut
them [off] from WYAT and save CLARKE from spoil.

And so, in the morning early, being Sunday [28th January 1554], the Lord ABERGAVENNY; the Sheriff; WAR-

Ram Sentleger, Richard Covert, Thomas Roydon,
The marching of the Lord Abergavenny and the Sheriff to encounter Isley. Antony Weldon, Henry Barney, George Clarke, John Dodge, Thomas Watton, Hugh Catlyn, Thomas Henley, Christopher Dorrel, Hugh Cartwright, John Sybil, Esquires; John Clarke, Darsie of Wrotham, Thomas Chapman, James Barram, Jasper Iden, John Lambe, Walter Heronden, Walter Taylor, John Raynoldes, Thomas Tuttesham, John Allen, and Thomas Holdiche, Gentlemen; with yeomen to the number of 600 or thereabouts; marched out of Malling in order till Wrotham Heath. they came to Wrotham Heath: where they might easily hear the sound of the traitor's drums; and so, making haste, pursued them till they came to a place Barrow Green. called Barrow Green [*Borough Green*] through which lay their right and ready way that the traitors should take, marching from Sevenoaks towards Master Clarke.

The Lord Abergavenny, being **very** glad that he had prevented [*anticipated*] them in winning the Green, sent out spials [*spies*] to understand their nearness, and to discrive [*ascertain*] their number: reposing themselves there till the return of his spials: who at their coming said, That he needed not to take further pains to pursue them, for they were at hand, coming towards him as fast as they could march. Which was glad tidings to the Lord Abergavenny and his Band. And taking order forthwith to set his men in array; he determined to abide their coming, and there to take or give the overthrow.

Which the traitors understanding, Whether it was for that they misliked the match, or the place to fight; whiles The shrinking of the rebels. the Lord Abergavenny and his Band were busy in placing themselves; they shrank as secretly as they could by a bye-way. And were so far gone before the Lord Abergavenny understood thereof by his spials; as for doubt [*fear*] of overtaking them afore their coming to Rochester, he was driven to make such haste for the overtaking of them as divers of his footmen were far behind at the onset giving.

The first sight that the Lord Abergavenny could have of them, after they forsook their purposed way, was as they ascended Wrotham Hill, directly over [against] Yaldam, Master PECKHAM's house. Where they, thinking to have great advantage by the winning of the Hill, dis- The displaying played their Ensigns bravely: seeming to be in great ruff. But it was not long after ere their courage was abated. For the Lord ABERGAVENNY, the Sheriff, and the rest of the Gentlemen, with such other of the Queen's true and faithful subjects, as with great pains taking to climb the Hill and to hold way with The rebel's the Horsemen, overtook the rebels at a field called Blacksoll Field in the parish of Wrotham, Blacksoll a mile distant from the very top of the Hill; where the Lord ABERGAVENNY, the Sheriff, the Gentlemen afore-named, and others the Queen's true and faithful subjects, handled them so hot and so fiercely that, after a The Skirmish. small shot with long bows by the traitors, and a fierce brag shewed by some of the Horsemen, they took their flight away as fast as they could. Yet of them were taken prisoners above three score.

In this conflict WARRAM SENTLEGER, who brought with him a good company of soldiers and [was] always a ser-viceable Gentleman, also GEORGE CLARKE, ANTONY WELDON, and RICHARD CLARKE did very honestly behave themselves. WILLIAM SENTLEGER, hearing of a fray towards between the Queen's true subjects and the traitors, came to the Lord ABERGAVENNY into the field, with all haste, not an hour before the Skirmish; who with the rest of the Gentlemen, with certain of the Lord ABERGAVENNY's and [the] Sheriff's servants, being all well horsed, served faithfully: and from thence chased the Horsemen till they came to a wood called The chase of Hartley Wood, four miles distant from the place the Horsemen. where the onset began.

The Queen's true subjects did so much abhor their treason, and had the traitors in such detestation, as with great difficulty any escaped with life that were taken prisoners; and yet were they all very well armed and weaponed, and had also great advantage by the place of fight. Sir HENRY ISLEY lay all that night in the Wood, and fled after into Hampshire. The two KNEVETS, being well horsed, were so hastily pursued as they were driven

P   I

to leave their horses, and creep into the Wood; and for haste to rip their boots from their legs and run away in the vampage of their hose. The chase continued so long as night came on before it was full finished.

Thus were ISLEY, the KNEVETS, and their Band overthrown by the faithful service of divers Gentlemen and yeomen serving under the Lord ABERGAVENNY and the Sheriff; whose forwardness courage and wisdom in this traitorous broil no doubt was very much praiseworthy; as well for their speedy acceleration of their strength which (considering how they were every way [en]compassed with the traitors) was no small matter in so little space; and for their wise and politic handling also in keeping them together from WYAT, who marvellously and by sundry ways sought to allure them away. For had not they, in their own persons, to the encouraging of their company adventured far; and by their wisdom, discretion and great charge, politically handled the matter: some think that WYAT had been at London before he was looked for by any good man, with no small train; whose journey was greatly hindered, and his company very much discomfited by this repulse given to ISLEY and his Band. Where, amongst other things, GOD's secret hand was greatly felt, to the great comfort and present aid of true subjects against the traitors: who having such advantage of the place, as indeed they had, were like rather to give, than receive, so foul an overthrow. But this it is, you see, to serve in a true cause; and her whom GOD so favoureth that he will not suffer the malice and rage of her enemies at any time to prevail against her: to whom he hath given so many notable victories and so miraculous that her enemies might seem rather to have been overthrown *Spiritu DEI* than vanquished *humano robore*.

The Lord ABERGAVENNY, the Sheriff, and the Gentle-
_{Thanksgiving} men with them, after they had given humble
_{to GOD for}
_{victory.} thanks to GOD for the victory, which they did
very reverently in the Field, and taken order for the prisoners, were driven to divide themselves for want of harborough [*lodging*] and vittaile [*victuals*] for the soldiers, that had well deserved both. The Lord ABERGAVENNY and certain

with him went to Wrotham. The Sheriff and certain with him to Otford, where they had much to do to get vittaile for their soldiers.

The Lord ABERGAVENNY and the Sheriff (suspecting that some of those Gentlemen lately discomfited in this Skirmish would not long tarry in the realm, but make shift to pass the seas ; yea, by spial [*spies*], understanding that WYAT himself with some of his company thereunto bent) devised to lay [*warn*] the country [round] about, that they might not escape. And considering that they would not do it at Dover, nor in that coast [*district*] ; they knowing [Sir THOMAS CHEYNEY] the Lord Warden to have such watch unto them : but rather, for sundry respects, at Rye, or more southward. And having great proof of THOMAS DORRELL the younger his fidelity ; he returned the same DORRELL, being THOMAS DORRELL of Scotney the younger. newly come unto him with 80 men well appointed, into Sussex : giving him strait charge that, consulting with Sir JOHN GUILDFORD, they should, both day and night, set a sure watch for the passing of any that way to the seacoast ; and further to take such order as no munition, fish, wine, or other vittaile coming out of these parts, should pass to the relief of the traitors.

ANTONY KNEVET, notwithstanding great and strait watch laid round about the country by the Sheriff for the apprehension of him and others that fled, arrived that Sunday [28th January 1554] at night late at Rochester : where his news was so joyful that HARPER forthwith found the mean[s] to rid himself out of their HARPER's running away from WYAT. company, without any leave taking ; and ran to the Duke of NORFOLK. To whom he seemed so greatly to lament his treason, that the Duke, pitying his case, the rather for the long acquaintance between them in times past, received him to grace. But, within a day after, he ran from the Duke and returned to his old mate ; as hereafter shall appear.

WYAT hearing of ISLEY his overthrow, and understanding by the proceeding at Malling the day before, that those things set forth in his Proclamations whereby he thought his strength at home to be most surely knit unto him, were now become rather a weakening than otherwise ;

the people there being ready to fall from him for his so abusing of them : he fell into so great extreme anguish and sorrow, as writing a letter of expostulation to some of his familiars abroad, in reprehension of their infidelity in that WYAT bewail-they sticked not to him so fast as they promised, ing his case with tears. he bedewed the paper whereupon he wrote with tears issuing so abundantly from his eyes as it would bear WYAT's coat of no ink. And so leaving to write, calling for a fence quilted with angels. privy coat [of armour] that he had quilted with angels [*a gold coin of the value of* 10s.] not long afore ; which might serve both for his defence, and [also be] a refuge for his necessity being in another country : he WYAT's prac practised with such as were near unto him, where tice to fly by sea. they might have ready passage, and most for their surety to take the sea. " For England," said he, " is no place for us to rest in."

His company also shrank from him as fast as they could devise means to escape : whereunto THOMAS ISLEY and others had a greater respect than himself ; he seeming to take care for nothing but how he might safely convey himself [away] ; being well friended, it was thought, with some of the ship-masters.

Thus was WYAT so mated by the Lord ABERGAVENNY, WYAT mated. the Sheriff, and their Band as he was at his wits' end, as ye have heard : and chiefly by keeping him from that, which by spial about him they afterwards understood him specially to desire ; which was offer of battle. He and his being fully persuaded that there could be no great force raised against him in the Shire ; whereof the most part should not be his when it should come to the shew. Wherein although he might be deceived, as indeed he was ; yet his quarrel, with the disposition of the people thereunto well considered, with the end of his travail which could be but spoil and ravin (ready means and lures to draw the careless multitude unto him): it seemed to the Lord ABERGAVENNY and such as served with him, better policy for to weary WYAT, and weaken him by the cutting away of his strength from him ; than to offer him battle till the Duke of NORFOLK's coming : whom the Lord ABERGAVENNY and the Sheriff knew to be at hand towards WYAT ; unto whom they and all the Gentlemen of their Band, after their Skirmish with ISLEY, made the haste possible they might.

But before their coming, the case was wonderfully changed, to the great discomfort of all the Queen's true subjects: and that came to pass that [*which*] of all men was least feared. For who was it that suspected such cruel and malicious disposition to remain in any English heart towards his country, in any subject's thought towards his Sovereign, that, receiving her Grace's armour weapons and money, would have played so traitorous a part as these Captains did with their Band? It is so strange a case as the world never saw. It is so malicious a part as the Jew would not have done the like, having received his hire to serve.

So it was that the noble Duke, being an ancient and worthy Captain (and yet, by long imprisonment, so dis-wonted from the knowlege of our malicious World and the iniquity of our Time, as he suspecting nothing less than that which followed; but judging every man to accord with him in desire to serve truly) marched forth the Monday [29th January 1554], about ten of the clock in the morning, from Gravesend to Stroud towards Rochester; and about four of the clock in the afternoon of the same day, he arrived at Stroud, near unto Rochester: having with him the Captain of the Guard; MAURICE GRIFFITH, now Bishop of Rochester; Sir EDWARD BRAYE, Sir JOHN FOGGE, Knights; JOHN COVERTE, ROGER APPULTON, Esquires; and THOMAS SWAN, Gentleman: with certain of the Guard, and others, to the number of 200 or thereabout.

The Duke's marching from Stroud to Rochester.

The names of the Gentlemen serving under the Duke.

Besides BRET and other five Captains: who, with their Band, being 600, all in white coats, tarried behind at a hill called Spittle [*Hospital*] Hill, near unto Stroud; whiles the Duke went to Stroud to see the planting of the ordnance. Which being ready charged and bent upon the town of Rochester; and perceiving WYAT and the other traitors, by hanging out their flags upon the bridge wall, to be in great bravery; which considering the miserable state they were in the night before, could not be, had they not received some new comfort

BRET, Chief Captain of the White Coats.

by some traitorous mean[s]: the Duke commanded one of the pieces to be fired for shot into Rochester.

And, as the gunner was firing the piece, Sir EDWARD BRAY's eldest son came in all haste to the Duke saying, "Sir, did I not tell your Grace, this morning, that yonder false wretches would deceive you?"

"How know you that?" quod the Duke.

"Why, Sir," quod BRAVE, "you may see them, as false traitors [ready] bent against you,"

And immediately BRET and other Captains of the White Coats with their Band, being upon the Hill and at the back of the Duke, made great and loud shouts sundry times, crying "We are all Englishmen! We are all Englishmen!": fashioning themselves in array, ready bent with their weapons to set upon the Duke, if he had made any resistance.

The revolt of the Captains of the White Coats and their Band.

Whereupon the Duke and the Captain of the Guard commanded the pieces that were bent upon the town, to be turned upon BRET and his Band. But, upon further consideration, the shot was spared: and the Duke's Grace with the Captain of the Guard Sir HENRY JERNINGHAM, considering (not without bleeding hearts) their chief strength thus turned upon them, so that they were now environed both behind and before with traitorous enemies, shifted themselves away; as did also their company.

After whose departure, WYAT, accompanied with two or three and not many more, came out of Rochester half a mile from the town at the least, to meet the six Captains of the White Coats. Amongst whom was HARPER, notwithstanding his crouching and kneeling before the Duke; and fair promises that he would undertake that WYAT should have yielded. Who, footing afore the other Captains, with his sword drawn, said to WYAT, "I promised you a good turn, and say not now but I have paid it."

HARPER returned to his old mate.

Who had seen the embracing, clipping, and congratulation used at this meeting from traitor to traitor, might justly wonder thereat. Shortly after they had well clawed one another, they went together like themselves into Rochester.

When this, of all other most infortunate chance[s], came to

the knowledge of the Lord ABERGAVENNY, the Sheriff, and their friends; they were not a little troubled with the strangeness of the case: much doubting that the people, which before seemed brought to good frame, would be impaired by this alteration; and such as were afore evil disposed would not be greatly amended thereby.

The Sheriff, being the same night at Maidstone, that had come the same day from Otford, fourteen miles distant, to meet THOMAS GUILDFORD, STEVEN DORRELL, EDWARD HORDEN, JOHN ROBARTES, and JOHN FINCH, Esquires, to march towards the Duke. *The Sheriff's being at Maidstone.* And in the morning, so far from any mistrust of that which followed the same day [Monday, 29th January 1554], as having no sure place to convey the prisoners, taken the day before in the Skirmish with ISLEY, he left the chiefest and trustiest of his servants and friends, both Gentlemen and yeomen, of all his Band at Malling, for the safeguard of the prisoners; where also lay the Lord ABERGAVENNY and his Band: doubting [*fearing*] that ISLEY and the rest that escaped would have made some means that night to have recovered the prisoners; sundry of whom, being men of good wealth and well friended, and [at that moment] living within four miles of WYAT.

Upon these news, whether it were for the absence [from Maidstone] of the Lord ABERGAVENNY and his strength, or mistrusting false measure in the town [of Maidstone], or moved with example of the *The Sheriff's secret return to Malling.* revolt of the White Coats: he thought, it should seem, Maidstone no meet place for him to make any abode; nor yet good policy, all parts considered, to disclose the time of his removing. But judging plainly himself the only mark of these parts whereat the traitors shot; or falling any ways into their hands, so newly after the case of the Duke, one part of the tragedy to be then ended: he returned to his strength; giving knowledge to the Gentlemen remaining in Maidstone to repair to his house for consultation, What was to be done for the redubbing of that unhappy chance?

In which consultation there did rise so many different opinions; some saying, They would to the Queen; and some, to the Earl of PEMBROKE being her Grace's Lieutenant: that the Sheriff, without further debating, intreating the Lord ABERGAVENNY and certain Gentlemen to remain and entertain such of their Bands as they could hold till his return, which he promised should be without delay, [and then] went to the [Privy] Council for knowledge of their pleasure; where he tarried uneth [*scarcely*] two hours, but returned in post the same night [to Malling]. And at his coming, the Lord ABERGAVENNY and he assembled as many of their force as they could call together.

The traitors and their friends were grown as men revived from death to life, flattering themselves that a thing so far above men's expectation could not have happened to them so fortunately but by GOD'S miraculous provision, as favouring greatly their case: and so it blew abroad, as well by wind as by writing; the more part of the people being ready to believe it, as the case, in the heads of the multitude, was wonderfully changed both for strength and opinion.

WYAT advertised by his letter the Duke of SUFFOLK WYAT of his victory "by GOD'S provision" as he termed advertisement it: whose letter was intercepted in Essex, as to the Duke of Suffolk. the messenger passed the ferry, by a servant of Sir ROBERT SOUTHWELL'S; and brought to the Council.

He wrote also to the Duke of NORFOLK, but in another style; his letters being open and importing such matter as followeth:

"Be it known to all men, and especially to the Duke of WYAT's letter NORFOLK, that I have taken nothing in hand to the Duke of Norfolk. but what I will maintain with the expense of my life; which, before it depart out of my body, shall be sold full dear, &c."

Such of those parts as hung in the wind, as Neuters, (whereof were no small number that had lurked in caves An Invective all the tempest, watching but where should come against the the victory, that for example of the evil were Neuters. nothing inferior to the arrantest traitors but rather for a number of respects much worse), began to appear very cheerful, giving themselves great thanks for handling the matter so finely, that conveying themselves out of the way by their policy could avoid charge and peril so wittily.

And as they met with such as had served faithfully, with whom they durst be frank, they spared not to open their mouths largely, pouring out such language as could be but lamentable, or rather odible, to every true ear, to understand any subject so far perverted from his allegiance and duty that, for gain or security of their own persons, would rejoice in sitting still as indifferent where the Crown is a party; or to persuade security to themselves, be they never in so strong a hold, where their Sovereign is in peril. Which, all things rightly weighed, seemed a strange persuasion to account either gain or saving in sparing some part of the accidents by sitting still to adventure the loss of the principal whereupon life and the whole dependeth; or by affecting a little corruption inordinately, to lose both honest fame and good opinion of his country [*County*]; which every honest man ought to seek to preserve as tenderly as the well-doing of himself and his whole posterity.

Thus may we evidently see the divers effects of divers inclinations according to truth and untruth of perfect obedience prevailing in men's hearts. These Neuters, or counterfeits (that would be neither open foes nor adventurous friends; but as wily vultures, hovering in the wind to catch and gripe some part of the prey, although they would no part of the fray) persuaded themselves to save that which in their opinion the true hearty subject should lose by giving such adventure; that was security of body and goods. Which grant they saved; yet, in the just judgment of the honest, they deserved thereby the same blot of infamy that is due to the open enemies.

On the other side, the true and faithful, whose hearts and hands such dim colour [*illusion*] of unthankful policy could not withhold from the utterance of needful service in such general case of danger, thought it rather a gain to adventure body and goods; whereby either to preserve the head and the whole, which was cruelly pursued; or at least by defence of the same to purchase unto them and their names the honest opinion of unspotted members, and the immortality of good fame wherewith truth always rewardeth unfeigned service. For such an incomparable virtue is faithful loyalty, so much abhorring all corruptible allurements, that whose hearts she hath in governance; with such, neither savour of gain nor hope of security, neither persuasion of friendship ne other enticement, can so much prevail as, for any respect, they will digress from the right course of true service. Where the contrary, wanting that perfection (to taste of Fortune's corruptible members, whereafter they gape; to obtain quiet to the restive carcase, and lucre to themselves, the thing they only seek), are easily drawn to run a clean contrary race.

The naughty [*worthless*] brood therefore of Counterfeits, of all others not tolerable in a common weal, are specially to be looked to in their beginning; lest their evil example by long sufferance grow to such a precedent at the last, that the common. saying "Good to sleep in a whole skin," being espied to escape without danger of reprehension, be taken for a policy; and thereby outweigh the just peize [*weight*] of bounden duty.

After this most unhappy chance, the traitors with their new adjuncts fell to a great and solemn council that same night at Rochester for their proceeding in their pretensed [*intended*] treason. In discourse whereof proceeded such unfitting talk, as well towards the Queen's Highness as her honourable Council, tending to the alteration of the whole State, as abhorred the ears of some of the self traitors; that, understanding by that talk the end of their purpose, whereof before they were ignorant, wished themselves under the earth for being so unhappy as to be so much as acquainted with so damnable an enterprise. Such an opinion had they, as they deemed very few Councillors, or Officers of authority or of Nobility, within the realm worthy the places whereunto they were called: and persuading great choice to be amongst themselves for the supplying of that want, such overweening had they of themselves and made so sure a reckoning of the victory, as they disposed the honourable Offices of the Realm among themselves.

A consultation of the rebels after the revolt of the White Coats.

WYAT thought himself now so sure of the victory as seeing him that offered "to sell his spoons and all the plate that he had rather than his purpose should quail, and sup his pottage with his mouth" [*p. 210*], warranted him, That he should eat his pottage with silver, as he did.

England, when good counsel should stand it in most available steed, needed no better counsellors than such as they were, if they had half the wit they thought themselves to have, coupled with grace and honesty. But what they had indeed, their acts declare plainly to their own confusion ; as it hath always, and ever hereafter shall, to as many as be of like disposition.

One of them, that had some wit indeed, although he wanted grace, perceiving by their talk in what fond [*foolish*] frenzy they were entered ; to interrupt them therein, he said, That such matters were good to be treated of at further opportunity : but for the present it were meet to devise upon their next journey [*expedition*] ; and whether it should be good policy in them, minding to march towards London, to leave the Lord ABERGAVENNY and the Sheriff at liberty (that annoyed their friends, and by all likelihood would not so cease as they may or dare) at their back, being left at large.

One of them, taking upon him first to answer, thought nothing more necessary than their sequestration : and if his advice might have been heard in the beginning [of the Rebellion], the Sheriff should have been in hold, as I have heard, before anything should have been attempted.

A device to apprehend the Sheriff.

But the Captains to the White Coats (meet counsellors for such an enterprise !), having the spoil of London in their eyes, would not dispute that was past : but for the present they persuaded clean contrary to the former opinion ; saying That their going about the apprehension of the Sheriff should be but a loss of time. "For London," said they, "longed sore[ly] for their coming ; which they could by no means protract without breeding great peril and weakness to themselves." And having London at their commandment, whereof they were in no manner of doubt, if it were not lost by their sloth ; their revenge to the Lord ABERGAVENNY, the Sheriff, with others [of] their enemies, would easily follow.

The mis-reckoning of the rebels upon London.

WYAT, savouring full well their disposition, and understanding their meaning by their arguments, and knowing also that without his assenting thereto he could not long have their company, yielded to their counsel.

And so, being out of measure exalted into haughty courage and pride by the revolt of the White Coats, he marched the day after, being Tuesday [30th January 1554], in great pomp and glory, carrying with him six pieces of ordnance which they had gotten of the Queen's, besides their own, to Cowling Castle, a hold of the Lord COBHAM's, four miles distant from Rochester ; and not much out of their way towards London : where the Lord COBHAM was.

WYAT at his coming to Cowling Castle, bent his ordnance against the gate ; and with great and sundry shots and fire brake and burned up a way through the gate. The Lord COBHAM defended his Castle as stoutly as any man might do, having so few against so great a number ; and so little munition ; [he] himself discharging his gun at such as approached the gate right hardily. And in that assault two of his own men were slain.

The assault of Cowling Castle.

After this assault, and talk with the Lord COBHAM, WYAT marched to Gravesend ; where he reposed that night.

From Gravesend, he and his Band marched, the Wednesday next after [31st January 1554], to Dartford, where he reposed that night.

WYAT's marching to Dartford.

Whither came Sir EDWARD HASTINGS, Master of the Queen's Horse, and Sir THOMAS CORNWALLIS Knights, both of her Grace's honourable Privy Council, sent from the Queen to WYAT to understand the cause of his commotion ; and also, as it was said, finding any repentant submission in him, to promise pardon, or at the least great hope thereof.

The coming of the Master of the Horse and Sir THOMAS CORNWALLIS to WYAT.

WYAT, understanding [of] their coming and taking with him certain of his Band, went to the west end of the town, where he had planted his ordnance ; and at the [a]lighting of Master HASTINGS and Sir THOMAS CORNWALLIS from their horses, WYAT, having a partisan [*halberd*] in his hand, advanced himself somewhat afore such Gentlemen as were with him ; and, using but little reverence due from a subject to [Privy] Councillors, traced near them.

Pride.

To whom, the Master of the Horse spake in substance as followeth :

"The Queen's Majesty requireth to understand the very cause wherefore you have thus gathered together in arms her liege people, which is the part of a traitor ; and yet, in your Proclamations and persuasions, you call yourself a true subject : which cannot stand together."

"I am no traitor," quod WYAT, "and the cause whereof I have gathered the people is to defend the realm from our overrunnning by Strangers ; which follows, this Marriage taking place."

"Why," quod the Queen's Agents, "there be no Strangers yet come whom either for power or number ye need to suspect. But if this be your only quarrel, because, ye mislike the Marriage : will ye come to communication touching that case ? and the Queen, of her gracious goodness, is content ye shall be heard."

To whom WYAT shaped such answer as clearly might declare his malicious intent and traitorous heart WYAT's arrogant answer. to the Queen's own person and royal estate. "I yield thereto," quod WYAT, "but for my surety I will rather be trusted than trust. And therefore I demand the custody of the Tower, and [of] her Grace in the Tower ; the displacing of certain Councillors, and placing others in their rooms as to me shall seem best."

Upon this lewd answer, long and stout conference was between them : insomuch that the Master of the Horse said unto him, with a stout courage, "WYAT, before thou shalt have that thy traitorous demand granted, thou shalt die and 20,000 with thee ! "

Shortly after, the Master of the Horse with Master CORNWALLIS, finding him an arrant traitor and desperately set to all mischief, returned to the Queen's Majesty.

The common people being with him, and calling to their remembrance how WYAT, in all appearance, made his whole matter of stir for Strangers, and no ways against the Queen ; and perceiving how unreverently he used himself as well to the Queen's Herald at Rochester as to the Privy Council[lors] at Dartford ; and considering within themselves also that he would suffer none of the Queen's Proclamations to be read among them : their hearts began to rise against him. And among themselves sundry of them much murmured, wishing with the loss of all they had they had never been acquainted with WYAT nor his doings ; and indeed sought as many ways as they could to be rid of him

Which perceived by WYAT and his mates, they devised a
A crafty bruit [*rumour*] to be sounded in his Band, that the
policy. Lord ABERGAVENNY and the Sheriff did cause to
be hanged as many as they could take, coming from WYAT's
Band : wherewith the people, standing in a great maze what
to do, were wonderfully perplexed.

The Queen understanding by the Master of the Horse and
Sir THOMAS CORNWALLIS the arrogancy of WYAT, and notwithstanding that she perceived her merciful inclination
rather to provoke him than otherwise : yet seemed she
nothing willing, even then, by violence and force, as she
easily might, to suppress him : but yet a longer time to
suffer and abide, if by delay and mercy her enemy might be
won to reconciliation.

The Nobility (which were at that time with her Grace,
The suit of the perceiving such surmounting mercy rather to
Nobles to the
Queen. increase than any ways to abate courage and
malice in the insolent and proud heart of the traitors ;
and further understanding that the traitors deemed the
contation or forbearing to proceed rather of debility or fear
than of mercy and clemency) counselled with her Grace that,
with her gracious leave and licence, they might set upon him
and his Band before he should pass Blackheath : declaring
that to suffer such an arrogant traitor, being but a mean
member, to approach thus contemptuously so near her royal
person, as it were in defiance of her Grace and her true
subjects, should greatly redound to their dishonours in the
opinion of all faithful men throughout the world.

The Queen gave them all most hearty and loving thanks
The Queen's saying That she nothing doubted of their true hearts
answer to the
Nobles. towards her : yet was she loth to make any proof
or trial thereof in such quarrel as should be with loss of blood.
" For to repress them with violence, and subdue them by the
sword could not have so happy success but many of my
poor subjects" quod she, "should dearly bye [*abide*] it with the
loss of their lives." Wherefore she determined to suffer as
long as she might ; and to forbear that practice till there
were no other hope ne remedy. For albeit in the capital
traitors there could be but great default : yet in the multitude
she was persuaded to be no malice, but only misled by their

Captains; and rather seduced by ignorance than upon any evil purpose meant to her Grace. Wherefore she desired them to be contented: for she was fully determined to continue her merciful sufferance and other her gentle means so long as she might; and [to] vanquish her enemies without the sword, if any sparkle of obedience or natural zeal remain in their hearts. Notwithstanding, she required them to prepare and retain their force in a readiness, if their [*the rebels'*] stony hearts should drive her to use extremity.

But her Highness doubting [*fearing*] that London, being her Chamber and a city holden of dear price in her princely heart, might, by WYAT and such ruffens [*ruffians*] as were with him, be in danger of spoil, to the utter ruin of the same: her Highness therefore, as a most tender and loving Governess, went the same day [31st January 1554] in her royal person to the Guild Hall to foresee those perils.

Where, among other matter proceeding from her incomparable wisdom, her Grace declared how she had *The Queen's* sent that day two of her Privy Council to the *speech in the Guild Hall* traitor WYAT: desirous rather to quiet their tumult *in London.* by mercy than by the justice of the sword to vanquish: whose most godly heart fraight[ed] with all mercy and clemency, abhorred from all effusion of blood.

Her Highness also there shewed the insolent and proud answer returned from WYAT: whereat the faithful citizens were much offended; and in plain terms defied him as a most rank traitor, with all his conjurates.

And touching the Marriage, her Highness affirmed that nothing was done herein by herself alone, but with consent and advisement of the whole Council, upon deliberate consultation, that this conjunction and Second Marriage should greatly advance this realm (whereunto she was first married) to much honour, quiet, and gain.

"For," quod her Grace, "I am already married to this Common Weal and the faithful members of the same; the spousal ring whereof I have on my finger: which never hitherto was, nor hereafter shall be, left off. Protesting unto you nothing to be more acceptable to my heart, nor more answerable to my will, than your advancement in wealth and welfare, with the furtherance of GOD's glory." And to declare her tender and princely heart towards them, she promised constantly not to depart from them, although by her Council she had been much moved to the contrary : but would remain near and prest to adventure the spense [*shedding*] of her royal blood in defence of them.

Such matter passed from her besides as did so wonderfully enamour the hearts of the hearers as it was a world to hear with what shouts they exalted the honour and magnanimity of Queen MARY.

This done her Grace returned towards Whitehall, and passing through the streets, being full of people pressing to behold her Grace wherein they had singular delight and pleasure, one amongst all, most impudent of all others,

A malepert Artificer.

stepped forward saying, "Your Grace may do well to make your Foreward [*Vanguard*] in battle, of your Bishops and Priests : for they be trusty, and will not deceive you ! "

For which words, he was commanded to Newgate : who deserved to be hanged at the next bough, for example to all others, so impudently and arrogantly to assault his Sovereign and Queen with such seditious and traitorous language. The voice went that he was a Hosier. Out of all doubt, he was a traitor and a heretic ; whose heart was wholly in WYAT'S bosom, although his body were absent. For it was not possible any faithful subject, or true Christian, to utter such shameless speech to his liege Lady and Princess as he did then. But such is the fruit of heresy, Contempt of GOD and man ; as by daily experience is seen.

The Thursday next after [1st February 1554], WYAT hav-

WYAT's marching to Deptford strand.

ing fourteen Ensigns in his Band and not past four thousand men, although they were accounted of a far greater number, marched to Deptford strand, eight miles from Dartford and within four miles of London. Where, upon such advertisement as he received by espial of the Queen's being in the Guild Hall and the order of the people to her, he remained that night and the next whole day : divers of his own company doubting [*suspecting*] by his longer tarrying there than he did in other places, with other presumptions, that he would have passed the water [*i.e. the Thames*] into Essex.

His prisoners, as Master CHRISTOPHER ROPER, GEORGE

DORREL of Calehill [and] JOHN TUCKE Esquires, who were kept very straitly, being sickly and having within the town no convenient harborough or attendance, were licensed by WYAT, upon promise of their worship to be true prisoners, to provide for themselves out from the town, where they best might. But they, thinking no part of their worship stained in breaking promise with a traitor, sought ways to escape; and came no more at him.

The departure of Master CHRISTOPHER ROPER and Master DORREL from WYAT.

On the Saturday following [3rd February 1554], very early, WYAT marched to Southwark: where approaching the Gate at London Bridge foot, [he] called for the opening of the same; which he found not so ready as he looked for.

WYAT's marching to Southwark.

After he had been a little while in Southwark, divers of the soldiers went to Winchester Place [*the town residence of the Bishop of WINCHESTER*]. Where one of them, being a Gentleman, began to shew his game before all the cards were full[y] dealed; I mean, to rifle and spoil: which indeed was the determinate end of their purpose; but the time was not yet come, nor they come to the place, where they should begin it.

Whereunto WYAT, having further respect than the young Gentleman had, shewed himself, with stern and fiery visage, so much to be offended with his doings that he made divers believe that he would have hanged him upon the wharf. Which whereof it grew, either of hatred to the evil, or of policy to purchase credit for a further mischief, as well the nature and course of rebellion, as also WYAT's own words, may easily let us understand.

Who, the Monday [22nd January 1554] next afore this stir, devising with two of his friends for the execution of his pretensed [*intended*] purpose; one of them at length said unto him, " I have no doubt but you shall be able to assemble a great force: but how you shall be able to continue the same with you, having not sufficient treasure and money, the only bait wherewith the multitude is holden, I stand much in doubt."

" What then ? " quod WYAT.

" Marry," said the other, " methinketh a good way for your provision thereof, after your force is once gathered, that ye apprehend [Sir THOMAS CHEYNEY] the Lord Warden, the Lord ABERGAVENNY, Sir ROBERT SOUTHWELL, Sir THOMAS MOYLE, with others; of whose hearts and affections towards you and your case you stand in doubt: whereby ye shall not only have them in safety which are most like[ly] within the Shire to withstand your enterprise; but also provide you both treasure and money, which they want not, for the relief of your Band."

"Ah," quod WYAT, "is this the best counsel ye can give? If we pretend to keep out Strangers, and begin our quarrel with the spoil of our own country [*County*] men; what will the whole realm, trow ye, then deem of us? Nay, your advice is naught; and your way, the next way to accelerate our confusion. For if we will go forwards in our matter and make the best of it to our purpose, Spoil and Tyranny may not be our guides. We must, by all means, devise, and all little enough, to continue good opinion in the heads of the multitude of some plausible [*praiseworthy*] end to succeed by our stir: otherwise we undo ourselves. For perceiving at our entry that our minds run of spoil: who will not rather resist us, and abide the adventure of that whereof we bear them in hand; than to be in certain to be spoiled by us? And I see no cause why you should doubt of money; seeing ye know that such Gentlemen as are confedered with us, keeping appointment; their soldiers shall come ready furnished to bear their own charges for nine days: and our hap shall be very hard if we be not at London shortly after we stir; and that with so great a company as shall be out of danger to be stopped by any of the Shire upon such a sudden, or letted [*hindered*] of entry into London finding half the friends there as we think to have. And being once in London, and having the Tower in our hands; I trust you think we shall not lack money long after, if any be to be had there, or in the Aldermen's coffers."

WYAT'S reckoning of the spoil of the Tower and London.

To that said another, that had spoken as yet never a word, "I know Commoners in London that have more ready money than some of the Aldermen."

"Soft," quod WYAT, "I pray you in any wise forbear all such talk till we come to the place where we would be. In mean time let us work secretly; and by all tokens and signs shew ourselves to favour and maintain our pretence of Strangers only."

Such and the like communication was betweeen WYAT and two others the Monday [22nd January] before his rising. Whereby it is evident that their final intent was to advance themselves by spoil of other men's goods: although they pretended otherwise.

And to colour [*make pretence of*] the same, WYAT so fell out with this Gentleman for rifling the Lord Chancellor's House [*i.e., the House in Southwark of STEPHEN GARDINER, Bishop of WINCHESTER,*] that he made a number believe he would have hanged him out of hand: had not BRET and others entreated for him.

When they had lien in Southwark a day or two, and found themselves deceived in London: which (by *The Lord* the great diligence and politic handling of that *WILLIAM* worthy and faithful Knight, the Lord WILLIAM *HOWARD,* HOWARD, Admiral of England, that had the *Admiral of* *England.* special charge thereof; with the aid of Sir THOMAS WIGHT, Knight, Mayor of London, his brethren [the Aldermen] and citizens) was so well preserved as the traitors thereby were disappointed of that they looked most certainly for— WYAT, as a man desperate and setting all at sixe[s] and seven, adventuring the breaking down of a wall out of a house joining to the Gate at the Bridge foot, *WYAT's com-* whereby he might enter into the leads over the *ing into the* *Porter's Lodge* Gate, came down into the Lodge about eleven *at the Bridge* *foot.* of the clock in the night: where he found the Porter in a slumber; [and] his wife with others *Care away.* waking, watching a coal.

But seeing WYAT, they began suddenly to start as greatly amazed.

"Whist!" quod WYAT, "as you love your lives, sit you still! You shall have no hurt!"

Glad were they of that warranty, pardye! What should they do, people better accustomed with the tankard of beer to pass forth the night, than acquainted with target and spear to endure the fight.

WYAT and a few with him went forth as far as the Drawbridge [in the middle of London Bridge]: on the further side whereof he saw the Lord Admiral, the Lord Mayor, Sir ANDREW JUDD, and one or two others in consultation for ordering of the Bridge : whereunto he gave diligent ear a good time, and [was] not seen. At length [he] conceived by their talk more than he could digest ; and, perceiving the great ordnance there bent, returned, saying to his mates, " This place is too hot for us."

And when he was come to his colleges [*colleagues*], and declared upon his exploit what he had heard and seen ; they then all together fell to a new council what was to be done.

Some would then return to Greenwich, and so pass the water into Essex (whereby their company as they thought should increase), and enter into London by Ald Gate.

The rebels at their wits' end.

And some would to Kingston-upon-Thames, and so further west[ward].

And some, of the which WYAT himself was chief, would return into Kent to meet with the Lord ABERGAVENNY, the Sheriff, Sir THOMAS MOYLE, Sir THOMAS KEMP, Sir THOMAS FINCH, that were at Rochester, coming on WYAT's back with a great company well appointed : falsely persuading himself that he should find among them more friends than enemies. But whether his desire to return into Kent grew upon hope he had to find aid there ; or whether it was to shift himself away ; it was much doubted of his own company. And some of them that knew him well, except they were much deceived, reported not long before their execution, that his desire to retire into Kent was only to shift himself over the sea.

The Lord Warden [SIR THOMAS CHEYNEY] being now come to Rochester, as ye heard, and very honourably furnished with horse and men well appointed, to no small number, entering into consultation with such Gentlemen as were there, for the better proceeding in their service, shewed a great desire to accelerate the onset upon the traitors : lest malice should impute both his former and present stay rather to want of forwardness than to good policy. Wherefore he desired to pursue after them with all expedition.

The Lord Warden's being at Rochester towards WYAT.

Whereunto the Gentlemen, being then in arms with him, said, "As for your Lordship's contation [*delay*] hitherto, it shall be weighed not as fools by fancy and malice deem; but as wise men shall measure it by their discretion of wisdom. We see not but unadvised hardiness [*rashness*] and preproperous [? *preposterous*] haste in most matters have these two companions: Error in the beginning, and Repentance in the end. And for this our case, whoso understandeth the same cannot but confess your Lordship's deliberate forbearing to have proceeded of great wisdom, as wherein haste could little prevail. And whereas your Lordship is so desirous to pursue after WYAT and his Band, you see how they have lien in Southwark and within four miles of London these four days [Thursday 1st, to Sunday 4th February 1554]; and yet not meddled with by the Queen's army, being so near: which is neither for want of men, nor of forwardness in that noble Gen- The Earl of tleman, the Earl of PEMBROKE, the Queen's PEMBROKE, the Queen's Lieutenant; but upon great policy and further Lieutenant. respect no doubt than we seem to conceive.

"Wherefore your Lordship may do better to pause, and first to advertise the Queen's Majesty and the Lord Lieutenant [the Earl of PEMBROKE] both what your Lordship, upon grave and deep consideration, hath conceived in this doubtful time, and also in what readiness your Lordship is, and other Gentlemen with you: whose pleasures known, we may then happily proceed in service; both with good contentation to them above [us], and best surety for ourselves. Otherwise if fortune should not favour our journey [*expedition*], there may be thought in us more impotent will to haste than provident policy to speed. And danger hereby can none follow, our enemies lying between her Grace's army and us: considering withal that London is so well furnished, and so willing to resist their entry."

Whereupon the Lord Warden went in post to the Queen; leaving the Lord ABERGAVENNY and the rest of the Gentlemen with his and their Bands until his return: which was very shortly after.

Who, according to his first purpose, with the rest of the Gentlemen, marched forth towards WYAT. Which who had seen so well appointed, and with what willing hearts they went ; and had known withal the faithful dealing of sundry Gentlemen besides in other parts of the Shire, ought to say, That notwithstanding there were many evil; yet were there many worthy, Gentlemen and honest faithful yeomen in Kent, free from WYAT's conspiracy : and that the same [would] receive some injury at his hand that, taking upon him to set forth any Chronicle, should name only four Gentlemen of this Shire to be workers against WYAT. For though every man pursued him not in the beginning, many of them dwelling far from him : yet were they as well occupied where they were, and as much towards WYAT's confusion, by staying and withholding [a] great force, through their earnest persuasions and labour, that else would have been with WYAT.

Now to return to WYAT : whom in this meantime BRET and the other Captains espying to have a desire to be gone, dissembling the knowledge thereof, [they] wrought all the secret means they could devise to stay his going ; as having the weight of their lives depending upon this enter-prise as well as he.

One of them, by agreement in their consultation, said to him : " You see," quod he, " with what difficulty you keep your soldiers here : notwithstanding they be in a town where they are in a manner as pent in, and thereby the more uneasy to get away ; being so narrowly looked to. And now if you shall leave the town and retire into Kent, as some of your company suspect you will, whereby they and all others shall judge you to be in despair of the aid of London ; the hope whereof hath been hitherto the greatest occasion of stay of such as be already here, and the comfort for the coming of others to the increase of your power : you may assure yourself that such as be here will not tarry long after with you, finding time to escape as they shall easily enough, being at large ; nor such as be absent will have haste to repair unto you, when they shall perceive you to be in despair of London. And so you shall weaken yourself, to the comfort of your enemies and discomfort of your friends."

BRET, under colour [*pretence*] of singular affection to WYAT, devising an apt occasion to avoid suspicion (which

wanted not among them), required to speak with him
apart ; and having him alone, said :

" It shall not be amiss that, for your own surety, you have
in remembrance the effect of the several Proclama- BRET's words
tions made at Dartford : the one by Master WIL- to WYAT.
LIAM ROPER, wherein you were betraitored ; the other by
Master APPULTON, which, as I hear, was also made at London
and in other parts of the realm, wherein is promised the
inheritance of One Hundred Pounds [in] land to such as
can apprehend and present you to the Queen.

" Now what fantasies may grow into the heads of your
own fellows, for the safeguard of themselves ; of whom you
have had already some experience, it is to be doubted : or
what may grow in the heads of your soldiers when, failing
of the aid of London, they shall be in despair of your
enterprise, it is also to be doubted. On the other part,
when such of Kent, on whom it seemeth you repose some
trust, shall hear of your retire : their disposition perhaps
will be much changed. And therefore it standeth you in
hand to look to the matter substantially."

WYAT (having the same confidence in BRET, that BRET
would WYAT to have had in others ; remem- Trustless
bering his most deceitful treason to the Queen, traitors !
contrary to the trust reposed in him for the conduct of the
White Coats ; and feeling his grief doubled, and his desire
to convey himself away so much the more increased, by
BRET's secret talk with him) ; as a stricken deer, wandereth
aside, all alone complaining with himself [of] his most
unhappy fate.

And soon after calling THOMAS ISLEY unto him, said,
" Ah, cousin ISLEY, in what extreme misery are we ?
The revolt of these Captains with the White Coats seemed
a benefit in the beginning ; and as a thing sent by GOD
for our good, and to comfort us forward in our enterprise :
which I now feel to our confusion. Ah, cousin, this it is
to enter such a quarrel, which notwithstanding we now see
must have a ruthful end ; yet of necessity we must prosecute
the same."

WYAT as desperate (finding others to accord with BRET's
opinion, upon his conference with them : by whom for
direction of his traitorous journey [expedition] he was chiefly

advised; although for this shifting away there were others whom he better trusted) marched, the Tuesday being Shrove

WYAT's marching to Kingston. Tuesday [6th February 1554], out of Southwark to Kingston upon Thames, ten miles distant; where they arrived about four of the clock in the afternoon.

And finding thirty feet or thereabouts of the bridge taken away, saving the posts that were left standing; WYAT practiced [*bargained*] with two mariners to swim over to convey a barge unto him. Which the mariners, tempted with great promises of preferment, did. Wherein WYAT and certain

WYAT's passage at Kingston. with him were conveyed over: who, in the time that the number of the soldiers baited [*lunched*] in the town, caused the bridge to be trimmed with ladders planks and beams, the same tied together with ropes and boards as, by ten of the clock in the night, [it] was in such plight that both his ordnance and Band of men might pass over without peril.

And so, about eleven of the clock in the same night, WYAT with his Band, without either resistance or peril, marched over the bridge towards London; having such a loving heart in his body to the Queen as before day he meant to have been at the Court Gate [of Whitehall]. Which he could never have attempted, having any sparkle of that good zeal in his breast to the Queen's surety as, to further his treason, he outwardly pretended to the World; considering the danger that might have grown, by the fear thereof, to her Grace.

But, as GOD would, partly by weariness of his soldiers, and partly by the breach [*break down*] of the wheels that carried his ordnance; it was nine of the clock of the day following, being Ash Wednesday [7th February 1554], before he came so far as Hyde Park: where his courage, being tofore as ye have heard not very lusty, began now utterly to die; beholding as it were before his face the present bane and confusion whereunto his malicious intent was shaped.

Yet desperation being his lewd guide, he marcheth forward; and cometh within the power of Sir WILLIAM HERBERT, Earl of PEMBROKE; being, that day, the Queen's Lieutenant General in the field. Who yet (with divers other Noblemen and faithful subjects, being then in arms with him prest and ready to receive so impudent a race of traitorous rebels to their deserved breakfast) understanding, partly by sure spial, partly by their own view, that the rebels exceeded not the number of four thousand, and most of them naked [*unarmed*], void of all policy and skill; considering withal that they could not set upon WYAT and his whole Band but great effusion of blood should follow, the Queen's army being so greedy to be revenged and the other so impotent to resist, determined rather by policy to achieve the victory than by bloodshed to confound the rebels. Wherein they should please GOD, answer the Queen's merciful expectation, and purchase unto themselves most renown and honour of that day's service.

Upon these resolutions, they permitted WYAT with the fore part of his Band to pass quietly along; and through between the Queen's Majesty's Horsemen: the Lord CLINTON being Marshal of the Field and Captain of the barbed horses and Demi-lances on the south side; JACK of MUSGRAVE being Captain of the Light Horsemen on the north side. The great ordnance being charged to shoot full upon the breast of the rebels coming eastward: the Earl of PEMBROKE with the Main Battle of footmen as well for handguns, morishpikes, bows, and bills, standing in goodly array on the north-east side, behind the said great ordnance, ready to set upon the rebels in the face coming towards Holborn.

WYAT, coming in the forefront of his Band, perceiving that he was thus beset with horsemen on both sides, the great ordnance and the footmen before his face north-eastward; so that he could no ways escape, but necessarily must fall into their hands, although for policy he was suffered and a great part of his men to pass so far quietly and without resistance through the Horsemen—he suddenly forsook his way intended through Holborn; and, with might and main, as fast as they could, he and his mates ran down underneath the Park Wall of brick adjoining to the Queen's Manor House, called St. James's.

The Lord CLINTON, observing his time; first with his Demi-lances brake their array, and divided WYAT's Band in two parts. Then came the Light Horsemen, who so hardly pursued the tail of his Band, that they slew many, hurt more, and took most of them.

Whilst the said Horsemen were thus in fight with the tail of his Band; Wyat himself and 500-men or thereabouts peked [*pushed*] on still all along under St. James's Park Wall until he came to Charing Cross: where divers of the Queen's Household servants and others fought with them, and in the end killed 16 of the rebels.

Nevertheless Wyat, having escaped with a part of his company, marching along in battle [ar]ray, entered into Fleet street, and came over Fleet Bridge towards Lud Gate.

And although no man resisted his passage through the streets thus far: yet, when at length he perceived that he had no help of friends at London and the suburbs as he looked for, [he] left his men standing still in battle array; and rode back as far as the Temple Bar Gate, with a naked [*drawn*] sword in his hands the hilts upward, as some report.

At which Gate, he would have gone through towards Charing Cross, to the residue of his men: but he was then stopped by force, of the Queen's true subjects; who would not suffer him to pass without Temple Bar.

At length came one Sir Maurice Berkeley Knight unto him, and required him to consider that he could not prevail in this wicked purpose ; and that his men were all taken and slain in the Field: and therefore willed him to cease off from any further occasion of bloodshed ; exhorting him to yield himself prisoner, and to stand to the Queen's mercy.

Which to do, Wyat refused; and said That he would rather be slain than yield to any man.

And yet, nevertheless, as it chanced, there came a Herald of Arms immediately, riding in the Queen's Coat Armour to this place: to his Coat shortly after Wyat submitted himself prisoner ; and so went to the Court at Westminster, and there was brought before the Privy Council ; and shortly after, within one hour, sent from thence to the Tower of London [a] prisoner.

Amongst other things this is to be remembered, that whiles the said Wyat and certain of his men, as aforesaid,

were coming thus towards Fleet street; a certain Captain of
the said rebels, with divers of his soldiers, returned from
Charing Cross down to the Court Gate at Whitehall, and
gave a larum [*an alarm*] before the Gate: and shot divers
arrows into the said Court, the Gate being open. Insomuch
that one Master NICHOLAS ROCKEWOOD, being a Gentleman
of Lincoln's Inn and in armour at the said Court Gate, was
shot through his nose with an arrow by the rebels. [*See
EDWARD UNDERHILL'S account of this fright in this* Vol.,
p. 190.]

For the coming of the said rebels was not looked for that
way: but [it was] thought that the Queen's army should
have joined battle with them in the Field; according to
promise made by the said WYAT on his behalf: who promised that he would come to the Queen's Foot Battle
[*Infantry*], and fight with them pike against pike and man
to man. Which, when it came to the very point, he
refused; and shrank [by] a bye way by Saint James's Park
Wall for his refuge, as you have heard before: where many
of them were slain by Horsemen, so that they came not nigh
the Queen's power of the Foot Battle. Which increased
some desperate boldness in the despairing rebels: not
without great discomfiture to all the Court and the city
of London; perceiving that he was himself, and so many
rebels with him, come through the Queen's army thus
far.

Whereupon grew great admiration [*wonderment*] amongst
them that knew not their doings in the Field: how for policy,
and to avoid much manslaughter, WYAT was suffered purposely to pass along. Insomuch divers timorous and cold
hearted soldiers came to the Queen, crying, "All is lost!
Away! Away! A barge! A barge!"

Yet her Grace never changed her cheer, nor removed
one foot out of the House: but asked for the Lord of
PEMBROKE, in whom her Grace had worthily reposed great
confidence.

Answer being made, That he was in the Field.

"Well then," quod her Grace, "fall to prayer! and I
warrant you, we shall hear better news anon. For my Lord
will not deceive me, I know well. If he would, GOD will
not: in whom my chief trust is, who will not deceive me."

And indeed, shortly after, news came all of victory, [and] how that WYAT was taken.

This day [7th February 1554], the Judges in the Common Place [*Common Pleas*] at Westminster sat in armour. The Mayor, Aldermen, and the householders of the city, by four of the clock in the morning, were in armour: the Lord WILLIAM HOWARD, High Admiral, being amongst them. Who, as I have tofore said, was by the Queen's Majesty appointed Captain General and Lieutenant for the time, to confer in counsel and join in execution with the Lord Mayor and his Brethren [the Aldermen] for the sure and speedy guarding and warding of the city: to the preservation whereof the Queen's Grace had special regard. The Gates were diligently watched; every Gate with 100 men: Moor Gate being closed up and rampired.

Thus was this wily heretic and open traitor WYAT, and his complices, brought to their confusion; and to the end which never missed all such malicious[ly] disposed wretches. Partly by the wisdom and policy of him that was armed in the Field, the worthy Earl of PEMBROKE; but chiefly by the mighty hand of GOD, at the contemplation of her high merits and virtues; who remaining in the closet of stedfast hope and confidence, being appointed with the armour of faith, fought with ardent and continual prayer, in perfect devotion, under the banner and ensign of GOD: who indeed alone gave this victory, and alone without policy or might of man overthrew her enemies; yet so that he therewith declared his special favour and pleasure towards his servant, that noble Knight, the Earl of PEMBROKE, in appointing him chief champion this day to defend his chosen and elect Virgin; whose faith hath not been wavering in his Catholic religion nor his truth and service doubtful at any time towards his Prince.

WYAT, as is said, was committed to the Tower. So were divers other Gentlemen: as, soon after, was HENRY GREY Duke of SUFFOLK and his two brethren.

The Duke, being so hardly pursued by the Lord

HASTINGS, Earl of HUNTINGDON, was by him appre- The Duke of
hended in Leicestershire. Whereby he declared SUFFOLK's
himself, as well in honour and unspotted loyalty apprehension
as in parentage and patrimony, to succeed his great by the Earl of
grandfather the Lord HASTINGS; whose fidelity HASTINGS.
and stedfast truth towards King EDWARD IV. and his
children, the Chronicles report to his immortal honour.

Of the common people there was such a number taken in
the chase by the Earl of PEMBROKE that besides the usual
gaols, sundry churches in London were made places for their
safeguard, till order was taken for their enlargement.

The Duke [of SUFFOLK] was arraigned by his Peers, and
by verdict found guilty of Treason, before the Duke of
NORFOLK, being Lord Constable, and that day his Judge.
Both he, and his brother THOMAS, at several days, made
their end at Tower Hill, by loss of their heads.

Sundry others of WYAT's complices, being arraigned, and
condemned upon their confession of treason, suffered in
divers parts of the Shire, as:
HENRY ISLEY Knight, THOMAS ISLEY his brother, and
WALTER MANTEL, at Maidstone; where WYAT first
displayed his standard.
ANTHONY KNEVET, WILLIAM his brother, with another
of the MANTELS, at Sevenoaks.
BRET, at Rochester, hanging in chains.
And of the common sort very few were executed, save
only of the White Coats; that, to say truth, deserved it
trebly.
WYAT himself, last of all, was arraigned at Westminster;
the Earl of SUSSEX, Sir EDWARD HASTINGS, and Sir
THOMAS CORNWALLIS being his Judges: where and before
whom, he most earnestly craved life; not by plea of his
matter or justifying of himself, but by earnest suit, in
humble submission, for the Queen's mercy.

It seemeth not amiss here to make report of such special
words as by him were uttered at his arraignment: WYAT's words
which I myself heard, standing not ten feet from at his arraignment.

him at that time. By the which words may appear both what he himself thought of his doings, how much he misliked the same, and also how penitent and sorrowful he was therefor.

Certain words proceeding from WYAT, at his arraignment.

Y Lords, I must confess myself guilty; as, in the end, truth must enforce me to say: and that I am justly plagued for my sins, which most grievously I have committed against GOD; who hath suffered me to fall into this beastly brutishness and horrible offence of treason. And lo, in me the like end; as all such that have attempted like enterprizes, from the beginning have had. For peruse the Chronicles throughout, and you shall find that rebellion never from the beginning prospered. For the love of GOD, all you Gentlemen that be here present remember! and be here taught by the examples past, and also by this my present infelicity and heinous offence!

"O most miserable, mischievous, brutish, and beastly furious imagination of mine! For I thought that by the marriage of the Prince of Spain, this realm should have been in danger: and that I, that have lived a free born man, should, with my country, have been brought to bondage and servitude by aliens and Strangers. Which brutish beastliness then seemed reason; and wrought so far and to such effect as it led me to the practice and use of this committed treason: that now understanding the great commodity honour and surety which this realm shall receive by this marriage; if it shall please the Queen to be merciful to me there is no man living that shall be more trusty and faithful to serve her Grace; no, nor more ready to die at her Highness's foot, whatsoever the quarrel be."

Thus far touching WYAT's words at his arraignment, I thought not superfluous here to report, to the end that all others blindly fallen into the same error, would by the example of WYAT rise also to repentance; as well confessing to the World with open voice their detestable mischief, as also from the very heart with tears detesting the same; as, in utterance of the former words, he plentifully did.

He lost his head at Tower Hill; and his body, divided, was set up in divers parts about London.

Other poor men, being taken in WYAT's Band, and kept a time in divers churches and prisons without the city [of London], kneeling all, with halters about their necks, before the Queen's Highness at Whitehall; her Grace mercifully pardoned, to the number of 600: who immediatey thereupon, with great shouts, casting their halters up into the air, cried "GOD save your Grace! GOD save your Grace!" *Of such as did penance by wearing halters before the Queen.*

Howbeit sundry of them that did wear halters afore the Queen's Highness were afterwards, by means, called before the Justices in the country to be arraigned: but her Grace, being moved thereof by the Sheriff, would them to be no further vexed.

Thus have ye heard of WYAT's end, and [of] some of his complices: by whose lamentable tragedy, and others of like sort that happened in our Age, not only we, but such as shall succeed us, may be abundantly taught to foresee what it is to enter into rebellion. For neither could WYAT with his stoutness, nor yet with the pretence of his quarrel coloured with a meaning to defend his country from over-running by Strangers, nor yet through the aid of sundry conspirators of great power, ne by any other policy, prevail.

Six of the Gentlemen that were offenders were pardoned, going to their execution, by the Queen's clemency, at Rochester: as were also all the others of the whole Kentish Gentlemen remitted; a few of the rankest excepted, that, only for example, suffered.

The Queen's Highness, not long after, sent out her Commission to Sir THOMAS MOYLE, Sir JOHN GUILDFORD,

Sir THOMAS KEMP; WARRAM SENTLEGER, THOMAS ROYDON, CHRISTOPHER ROPER, GEORGE DORRELL of Calehill, GEORGE FANE, JOHN TUCKE, JOHN ROBARTS, THOMAS LOVELACE, JOHN LEONARD, Esquires; with others: not only to bail and set at large such as were in prison in the country [*County of Kent*] for that offence, being of no small number; but also to compound [*fine*] with the offenders, according to the quality of their offences. Which manner of order, being not heard of in the like case, or at the least very rarely, declared a singular clemency and benignity in the Queen: that, being followed so cruelly, would yet be so moved with pity as to vouchsafe to answer them with so much lenity, in the executing of so few, in comparison to so great a number and so large a cause; being all in her Grace's mercy to dispose at her pleasure. And besides [to] suffer the rest to escape with so small abashment of their countenance [*small amount of fine*] after so heinous [an] offence.

He that shall peruse this Story diligently, and consider all parts thereof exactly, with remembrance of things past since the beginning of the Queen's most happy reign, must of force recognize, of what condition soever he be, the magnificence mercy and fortitude of this most noble Princess, as from time to time with such patience to endure so great malice of her own subjects, with such lenity to forbear the revenge of so intolerable outrage, with such mercy in the end to pardon and remit so heinous and great offenders. Happy was it with those heinous offenders that her Grace's most worthy and honourable Council were so agreeable to her virtuous inclination! as inclined rather to pursue merciful pardon for continuance of life than to prosecute revenge by execution of death.

It is to be wished by all good men with one assent that, provoked with so great clemency, these degenerates reform themselves! and forbear thus to attempt so gracious a Princess! unto whom, by GOD's authority, the sword is not vainly committed; lest thereby they procure to themselves damnation in seeking by such outrage their own death and confusion. From the desire whereof we see, by a number of

evident arguments, the Queen's Highness and her honourable Council to be so far as, by all means they can imagine,
they seek to eschew that they by most wilful
and malicious means follow to
their subversion.

[The following are omitted for want of space.]
An earnest Conference with the Degenerates
and Seditious, for the search of the cause
of their great disorder.

A Table [*or Index*].

Imprinted at London by ROBERT CALEY within the
Precinct of the late dissolved House of the
Grey Friars, now converted to a Hospi-
tal called Christ's Hospital
The 10th day of January 1555.

Cum privilegio ad imprimendum solum.

R   I

¶ A compendious Register in metre, containing the names and patient sufferings of the members of Jesus Christ, and the tormented, and cruelly burned within England; since the death of our famous King, of immortal memory, E D W A R D the Sixth, to the entrance and beginning of the reign of our Sovereign and dearest Lady E L I Z A B E T H, of England, France, and Ireland, Queen; Defender of the Faith; to whose Highness truly and properly appertaineth, next and immediately under GOD, the supreme power and authority of the Churches of England and Ireland.

So be it.

❦

Anno. 1559.

Apocalypse 7.

AND one of the angels (saith Saint John) spake, saying unto me, " What are they, which are arrayed in long white garments; and whence come they ? " (before the people, before sealed by the angel). And I said unto him, " Lord, thou wottest ! " And he said unto me, " These are they which came out of great tribulation; and washed their garments, and made them white in the blood of the Lamb. Therefore are they in the presence of the Throne of GOD, and serve Him, day and night, in His Temple :
and He that sitteth
in the Throne
will
dwell among
them."

To the Right Honourable
Lord Parr, Marquis of Northampton;
Thomas Brice, your Lordship's daily Orator,
wisheth continual increase of grace,
concord, and consolation in Him
that is, was, and is to come,
even the First and
the Last.
Amen.

IT MAY please your goodness, Honourable Lord! to receive in good part, the little labour of my pen : which, albeit the rudeness and quantity thereof procureth not to be dedicate[d] to so honourable a Personage ; yet the matter itself is of such worthiness, as duly deserveth to be graven in gold. But who goeth about so finely to depict with APELLES's instrument, this said *Register*, thinking to exceed the rest ? Not I ! poor wretch ! because I am assured that such a worthy work as thereof may be written, cannot, neither shall pass untouched among so many godly learned. But were it, that no man hereafter should, in more ample and learned manner, set forth the same ; yet should my presumption (if I so meant) be turned to reproach : for this I believe, that they be in such sort registered in the Book of the Living, as passeth either pen, ink, or memory to declare.

This my simplicity and too bold attempt might move your Honour to conjecture in me much rudeness, or, at the least, might persuade me so to think : but that experience hath showed me the humility and gentleness of your long tried patience ; the certain knowledge whereof hath pricked me forward in this my pretence. And being thereunto requested of a faithful brother and friend ; I have, with more industry than learning, GOD knoweth ! finished the same.

Which being, as I thought, brought to good end; I desired, according to the accustomed manner, to dedicate the same unto such [an] one, as would not contemn so simple a gift. And calling you to mind, Right Honourable Lord ! I knew none more meet. First, because your knowledge in CHRIST teacheth you the same godly and virtuous life ; which not only your Lordship, but all other Honourable, &c., ought to ensue. Secondly, because these late years, you have had good experience of the troubles and miseries of the faithful, which have patiently embraced in their arms, the comfortable, although painful, cross of CHRIST ; which, in so great a number, is commonly not so plenteous as commendable. But what stand I praising this patience in them (which yet deserveth the same)? seeing the mighty GOD and His CHRIST hath prepared, from everlasting, for such, a glorious, rich and incomprehensible Crown of Felicity and continual comforts.

This my short and simple work, I commend and dedicate unto your Lordship ! craving pardon at your hands, for this my too homely and rude enterprise : considering that albeit golden fruit were offered in pewter and by the hands of a simple man ; yet is the fruit notwithstanding still precious, and neither abased by the pewter, nor the giver. Even so, Honourable Lord ! though the verses be simple, and the giver unworthy : yet the fruit or matter is precious, comfortable and good.

The order to attain to the perfect understanding of my mind, in setting forth the same with figures and letters,

shall largely appear in this book : which I have not only done
to make plain unto your Honour, the year, month, and day ;
but also, to all others that hereafter shall read it. For that
I do pretend [*design*], if GOD and favour will permit it, to
use the same as common to the profit of all : for which cause,
I have also placed a Preface to the Reader.

But that it may please your Honour, in respect of the pre-
mises, to extend your favourable assistance to the manifest
setting forth of this short and simple work, to the glory of the
great and mighty GOD, and to the comfort of Christians : I,
as unworthy and too bold a suitor, most humbly craveth your
Lordship's aid and supportation in the same ; especially to
bear [with] the rudeness of my unlearned style, which, alas, I
lament.

But now ceasing to trouble your Lordship any longer, this
shall be my continual prayer for you.

The wisdom of GOD direct your Honour !
The mercy of GOD give you spiritual power !
The HOLY GHOST guide and comfort
you, with all fulness of
consolation in
CHRIST JESUS !
Amen.

Your Lordship's daily orator,

THOMAS BRICE.

To the Gentle Reader, mercy and peace?

AY it please thee, gentle Reader, to take in good worth this short and simple *Register*, containing the names of divers, although not all, both men, women, and virgins, &c., who, for the profession of CHRIST their Captain, have been most miserably afflicted, tormented, and [im]prisoned ; and, in fine, either died by some occasion in prison, or else erected [*gone to heaven*] in the charret [*fiery chariot*] of ELIAS, since the 4th day of February, 1555, to the 17th day of November, 1558, wherein (according to the determination of our most merciful Father) our long wished for and most noble Queen, ELIZABETH, was placed Governess and Queen, by general Proclamation ; to the great comfort of all true English hearts.

This I commit to thy friendly acceptation and favourable scanning, gentle Reader, and albeit, I doubt not but some, of godly zeal, both wise and learned, will not neglect, hereafter, to set forth so worthy a work, namely, of the martyrdom and patient sufferings of CHRIST's elect Members ; and also of the tyrannical tragedies of the unmerciful Ministers of SATAN : yet, at the request of a dear friend, to whom love and Nature hath linked me, I could not, without ingratitude, deny his lawful desire, attempting the same ; also, rather because it might be manifest to the eyes of the world, and also put the learned, of godly zeal, in memory more amply to enlarge ; and, at their good discretion, to set forth the same. Pardon my rudeness, therefore, I beseech thee ! considering that will in the unable is to be esteemed. Look not upon the baseness of the metre ! the true number whereof cannot easily be observed in such a gathering of names : but, with lifted eyes of the mind, meditate upon the omnipotent power of GOD ! which hath given and wrought such constancy in His children, in these our days, that even in fiery flambes [*flames*] and terrible torments, they have not ceased to invocate and extol the name of their Creator, Redeemer, and Comforter, according to the saying of the cxlviii. *Psalm*, "Young men and maidens, old men and children" have set forth His worthy and excellent praise. So that the same just and righteous GOD, who, for our sins, corrected us, and gave us over into the hands of the most bloody and viperous generation, to be eaten like bread : hath now, of His mercy alone, "exalted the horn of His people." Therefore all His saints shall praise Him.

Farewell !

T. B.

The manner how to understand the letters and figures.

[A specimen of a Stanza of the *Register* as originally given by BRICE, will help the reader to understand the unnecessarily complicated form in which he put it ; and also the following Instructions, which were omitted in subsequent impressions.

Three stanzas occupy each page of the original edition. They are printed like this.

63	1 5 5 8 March.	c ✠
28 28	When that JOHN DEWNESHE and HUGH FOXE, In Smithfield, cruel death sustained, As fixèd foes to Romish rocks ; And CUTHBERT SYMSON also slain. When these did worthily receive their death, We wished for our ELIZABETH.	
		7

A comparison of this Stanza, with its fellow at page 283, will show our method of reproducing this text.]

I N PRIMUS, the figures, which are always four in number, are placed in the middle of the two strykes [*strokes, or rules*], which go between the verses, within two short strikes ; signify the year wherein those persons were slain under them contained.

And where you see a little cross, ✠, on the outside of the outmost line, it signifieth the changing of the year [*i.e., on the 25th March*], as from 1554 to 1555 ; and in such manner.

The letters which stand in the little square place, on the right side of the book, signified the month wherein they died ; and for the plainer understanding thereof I have used twelve letters, for the twelve months : that is, A, for January ; B, for February ; C, for March ; D, for April ; E, for May ; F, for June ; G, for July ; H, for August ; I, for September ; K, for October ; L, for November ; M, for December.

But where one letter standeth in the little square place ; and another is placed under it between the two lines before the verse be ended ; it signified the changing of the month : so that the person or persons, where against the letter so changed doth stand, was put to death in that month which that letter doth signify.

And whereas, in the third Verse [*or Stanza, p. 270*], and no-where else, there standeth figures on the right side, between the two lines ; that giveth to understand that HUNTER, HIGBYE, PICKET, and KNIGHT, which are placed in one line, were burnt at three sundry days.

The figures which standeth in the little square place, on the left side of the book, is but the sum of the Verses. But those which stand between the two lines on the left side of the book, signified the day of the month, wherein that person or persons died, where against those figures stand.

The figures, which stand without both the lines, on the top of the right side, signifieth the folio or number of the sides ; but the figures which stand underneath the nether strike, between the two lines, is the number of persons murdered on that side [*i.e., of the page*].

This is done, gentle Reader ! that thou shouldest under-stand the year, month, and day wherein every person died ; according to the knowledge that I have learned.

Also, in some places, where you shall see a name or names

stand without figures; that signifieth the certain day to be
unknown.   Some, therefore, perchance, will judge much
rashness in me to write with ignorance; to whom, with
reverence, I answer, that as I received the names registered
and gathered by a good gentleman : even so, at a friend's
desire, I have put them in metre, in this little book, thinking
that, by pleasantness of reading, and easiness [*cheapness*] of
price, they might be the more largely blown and known.

For my desire is that all men should participate [in] this
my travail : and were the author and inditing half so
worthy as the matter; then would I most earnestly wish and
desire that it might be conveyed and delivered to the Queen's
Majesty's own hands.   Wherein Her Grace might see, what
unmerciful Ministers had charge over the poor sheep; who,
wolfishly, at their wills, devoured the same : and, also, what
ruin and decay of Her Grace's subjects (that might have
been), they have brought to pass.   Therein might Her Grace
see, as in a glass, how that bloodthirsty generation, neither
spared hore [*hoary*] headed and ancient age, which all men
ought to honour; neither youth, nor middle age; neither
wife, nor widow; young man, nor tender virgin.   But like
the unnatural eggs of ASTYAGES that tyrant, destroy, and
spill the blood of all : besides stocking [*putting in the stocks*],
racking [*putting on the rack*], and whipping of the younger
sort; whom shame would not suffer to kill, as some are well
enough known, and I am not altogether ignorant [of].

Should such tyrannical tragedies be kept one hour, from
the hands of so noble and virtuous a Governess? whose
princely and natural heart, I doubt not, should have occasion
thereby to be, in both kinds, both heavy and joyful : heavy,
for the innocent blood spilt; but joyful for the praises of her
GOD, and that our GOD shall be honoured thereby, while
the world doth endure.   I doubt whether [*doubt not but*] Her
Grace, inwardly wrapt up with PAUL and JOHN in divine science,
will brast [*burst*] out and say, " O happy LATIMER ! CRAN-
MER ! HOOPER ! ROGERS ! FARRER ! TAYLOR ! SAUNDERS !
PHILPOT ! CARDMAKER ! BRADFORD ! &c. ; you members of
CHRIST ! you faithful Fathers and preaching Pastors ! you,
that have not defiled yourselves with abomination, but have
washed your garments white in the blood of the Lamb ! you,
that in fiery torments, with STEPHEN, have called upon the

name of your Redeemer, and so finished you lives! you that
are now clothed in white garments of innocency, with crowns
of consolation, and palms of victory in your hands, following the Lamb withersoever He goeth!" Or else, in anguish
of soul, sighingly to say, "O thou tyrannous and unmerciful world! thou monstrous and unnatural generation! what
devil inflamed thy mind such malicious mischief? to torment and shed the blood of such innocent livers, perfect
preachers and worthy counsellors, learned ministers, diligent
divines, perfect personages, and faithful shepherds. They
were constant Confessors before, but thou (with the Roman
Emperor) thoughtest to prevent the determination of GOD,
in making them Martyrs, to be the sooner with their CHRIST,
whom they so much talked of. O cruel NEROS! that could
kill, through malice, such worthy men, as have often preached
to our dear father [HENRY VIII.] and brother [EDWARD VI.]
the everlasting gospel of GOD. Could neither honourable
age, innocent single life, chaste matrimony, inviolate virginity,
nor yet pity move you to cease shedding of blood! Alas, too
much unnaturalness!"

Whether the sight of this simple book, I say, should bring
to her Grace's natural heart, the passions of heaviness or joy,
I doubt: but I think rather both.

Therefore, would to God! it were worthy to enter into the
hands of so noble and natural a Princess and Queen; whom
the LORD, of His eternal and foreseeing determination, hath
now placed in this royal dignity: to the redress of such unnatural and bloody facts, as in this book are contained.

But forasmuch as some imperfection is, and may easily be
in this Gathering; I commend it to thy goodness, gentle
Reader! beseeching thee, not to be precise in perusing the
day; for it may, that, either through my negligence, or [that
of] some other writing [*manuscript*] before me, we may miss
so narrow a mark.

Such as it is, I commend
unto thee! only, judge
well!

The Book to the Reader.

ERUSE with patience, I thee pray !
My simple style, and metre base.
The works of GOD, with wisdom weigh !
The force of Love, the strength of Grace.

Love causèd GOD, His grace to give,
To such as should for Him be slain.
Grace wrought in them, while they did live,
For love, to love their CHRIST again.

Now Grace is of such strength and might,
That nothing may the same withstand.
Grace putteth death and hell to flight,
And guides us to the Living Land.

The force of Love also is such,
That fear and pain it doth expel ;
Love thinketh nothing over much ;
Love doth all earthly things excel.

Thus Love and Grace of GOD began
To work in them, to do His will :
These virtues' force wrought Love in man,
That fear was past, their blood to spill.

FINIS.

The Register of the Martyrs.

1555.

FEBRUARY

HEN raging reign of tyrants
stout,
Causeless, did cruelly conspire
To rend and root the Simple
out,
With furious force of sword and
fire;
When man and wife were put to death:
We wished for our Queen ELIZABETH.

FEBRUARY   4   When ROGERS ruefully was brent;
        8 When SAUNDERS did the like sustain;
          When faithful FARRAR forth was sent
          His life to lose, with grievous pain;
     22 When constant HOOPER died the death:
          We wished for our ELIZABETH.

FEBRUARY   9   When ROWLAND TAYLOR, that Divine,
          At Hadley, left this loathsome light;
    24 When simple LAWRENCE, they did pine,
    22 With HUNTER, HIGBY, PIGOT, and KNIGHT;
    23 When CAUSUN, constantly, died the death:
          We wished for our ELIZABETH.

1555.

MARCH   5   When TOMKINS, tyranny did abide,
Having his hand, with torchlight brent;

        7 When LAWRENCE, WHITE, and DIGGELL died,
With earnest zeal and good intent;

    14 When WILLIAM FLOWER was put to death:
We wished for our ELIZABETH.

APRIL   2   When AWCOCKE, in Newgate prisoner,
His latter end, with joy, did make;

   11 When JOHN WARREN and CARDMAKER,
Kissed each other at the stake;

   24 When MARCH, the Minister, was put to death:
We wished for our ELIZABETH.

JUNE   When WILLIAM COWLEY, for offence,
   4 Was forthwith hanged at Charing Cross;
Buried; then burned, of fond pretence;
Thus carion carcass they did toss:
When such insipients put men to death,
We wished for our ELIZABETH.

JUNE   10   When worthy WATTES, with constant cry,
Continued in the flaming fire;

   11 When SIMSON, HAWKES, and JOHN ARDLIE
Did taste the tyrant's raging ire;

   11 When CHAMBERLAINE was put to death:
We wished for our ELIZABETH.

JUNE   12   When blessèd BUTTER and OSMANDE,
With force of fire, to death were brent;

   12 When SHITTERDUN, sir FRANKE, and BLANDE,
   12 And HUMFREY MIDDLETON of Kent;

    1 When MINGE, in Maidstone, took his death:
We wished for our ELIZABETH.

1555.

JULY   When BRADFORD, beautified with bliss,
   1 With young JOHN LEAST, in Smithfield, died;
          When they, like brethren, both did kiss,
          And in the fire were truly tried;
          When tears were shed for BRADFORD's death :
          We wished for our ELIZABETH.

JULY   12 When DIRICK HARMAN lost his life ;
          12 When LAUNDER, in their fume, they fried ;
          12 When they sent EVERSON from strife,
             With moody minds, and puffèd pride ;
          12 When WADE, at Dartford, died the death :
             We wished for our ELIZABETH.

JULY   21   When RICHARD HOOKE, limbless and lame,
             At Chichester, did bear the cross ;
          22 When humble HALL, for CHRISTes name,
             Ensued the same, with worldly loss ;
          23 When JOAN POLLEY was burnt to death :
             We wished for our ELIZABETH.

JULY   23   When WILLIAM AILEWARDE, at Reading,
             In prison died of sickness sore ;
          23 When ABBES, which feigned a recanting
             Did wofully weep, and deplore ;
          23 When he, at Bury, was done to death :
             We wished for our ELIZABETH.

AUGUST   23   When DENLY died, at Uxbridge town,
             With constant care to CHRISTes cause ;
          23 When WARREN's widow yielded down
             Her flesh and blood, for holy laws ;
             When she, at Stratford, died the death :
             We wished for our ELIZABETH.

1555.

AUGUST   23   When LAURENCE, COLLIER, COKER, and
                STERE,
            At Canterbury, were causeless slain,   [fire,
       23   With HOPPER and WRIGHTE; Six in one
            Converted flesh to earth again;
       24   When ROGER CORRIAR was done to death:
            We wished for our ELIZABETH.

AUGUST   26   When TANKERFIELDE, at St. Albans,
       26   And WILLIAM BAMFORD, spent his blood;
            When harmful hearts, as hard as stones,
       30   Burnt ROBERT SMITH and STEPHEN HAR-
            WO[O]D;
       29   When PATRICK PATTINGHAM died the death:
            We wished for our ELIZABETH.

AUGUST   31   When JOHN NEWMAN, and THOMAS FUSSE,
            At Ware, and Walden, made their end;
       30   When WILLIAM HAILES, for CHRIST JESUS,
            With breath and blood did still contend;
       31   When he, at Barnet, was put to death:
            We wished for our ELIZABETH.

AUGUST   31   When SAMUELL did firmly fight,
            Till flesh and blood, to ashes went;
        3   When constant COB, with faith upright,
            At Thetford, cruelly was brent:
            When these with joy did take their death;
            We wished for our ELIZABETH.

SEPTEMBER   2   When WILLIAM ALLEN, at Walsingham,
            For truth was tried in fiery flame;
        3   When ROGER COOE, that good old man!
            Did lose his life, for CHRISTES name;
            When these, with others, were put to death:
            We wished for our ELIZABETH.

1555.

SEPTEMBER 6   When BRADBRIDGE, STRETER, and BUR-
               WARDE,
     6 TUTTIE, and GEORGE PAINTER of Hyde,
       Unto their duty, had good regard;
       Wherefore in one fire, they were fried:
       When these, at Canterbury, took their death;
       We wished for our ELIZABETH.

SEPTEMBER   When JOHN LESSE, prisoner in Newgate,
     10 By sickness turned to earth and clay;
       When wicked men, with ire and hate,
     13 Burnt THOMAS HEYWARDE, and GOREWAY;
     13 When TINGLE, in Newgate, took his death:
       We wished for our ELIZABETH.

SEPTEMBER 14   When RICHARD SMITH in Lollards'
               Tower;
     15 ANDROWES and KYNG, by sickness, died;
       In fair fields they had their bower,
       Where earth and clay doth still abide:
       When they, in this wise, did die the death;
       We wished for our ELIZABETH.

SEPTEMBER 19   When GLOVER, and CORNELIUS
       Were fiercely brent at Coventry;
     4 When WOLSEY and PIGOT, for CHRIST JESUS
       At Ely, felt like cruelty.
     19 When the poor bewept Master GLOVER's
       We wished for our ELIZABETH.   [death,

OCTOBER   When learnèd RIDLEY, and LATIMER,
     16 Without regard, were swiftly slain;
       When furious foes could not confer
       But with revenge and mortal pain.
       When these two Fathers were put to death:
       We wished for our ELIZABETH.

1555.

OCTOBER 13 When worthy WEB, and GEORGE ROPER,
In ELIAS' car to heaven were sent;

13 Also when GREGORY PAINTER,
The same straight path and voyage went;
When they, at Canterbury, took their death;
We wished for our ELIZABETH.

DECEMBER 7 When godly GORE in prison died,

14 And WISEMAN in the Lollards' Tower:

18 When Master PHILPOT, truly tried,
Ended his life with peace and power;
When he kissèd the chain, at his death,
We wished for our ELIZABETH.

1556.

JANUARY 27 When THOMAS WHITWELL, and BARTLET
GREENE,

27 ANNIS FOSTER, JOAN LASHEFORDE, and
BROUNE,

27 TUTSUN, and WINTER; these Seven were
seen,
In Smithfield, beat their enemies down;
Even Flesh and Devil, World and Death:
We wished for our ELIZABETH.

JANUARY 31 When JOHN LOWMAS and ANN ALBRIGHT,

31 JOAN SOALE, JOAN PAINTER, and ANNIS
SNOD,
In fire, with flesh and blood did fight;
When tongues of tyrants laid on lode;
When these, at once, were put to death,
We wished for our ELIZABETH.

1556.

FEBRUARY   When two women in Ipswich town,
19 Joyfully did the fire embrace;
When they sang out with cheerful sound,
Their fixèd foes for to deface;
When NORWICH NO-BODY put them to death,
     We wished for our ELIZABETH.

MARCH   12   When constant CRANMER lost his life
And held his hand into the fire;
When streams of tears for him were rife,
And yet did miss their just desire:
When Popish power put him to death,
     We wished for our ELIZABETH.

MARCH   24   When SPENCER and two brethren more,
Were put to death at Salisbury;
Ashes to earth did right restore,
They being then joyful and merry:
When these, with violence, were burnt to
     We wished for our ELIZABETH.   [death,

APRIL   2   When HULLIARDE, a Pastor pure,
At Cambridge, did this life despise;
2 When HARTPOOLES death, they did procure
To make his flesh a sacrifice;
When JOAN BECHE, widow, was done to
     We wished for our ELIZABETH.   [death:

APRIL   10   When WILLIAM TIMMES, AMBROSE, and
             DRAKE,
10 SPURGE, SPURGE, and CAVELL duly died,
Confessing that, for CHRISTes sake,
They were content thus to be tried:
[* BONNER.]   10 When * LONDON LITTLE-GRACE put them to
     We wished for our ELIZABETH.   [death,

1556.

APRIL   28 When lowly LISTER, NICOLL, and MASE,
           28 JOHN HAMMON, SPENCER, and YREN also,
              At Colchester, in the Postern Place,
              Joyfully to their death did go ;
         5 When two, at Gloucester, were put to death :
              We wished for our ELIZABETH.

MAY   When MARGARET ELIOT, being a maid,
          13 After condemning, in prison died ;
          15 When lame LAVAROCKE, the fire assayed,
          15 And blind APRICE with him was tried :
              When these two impotents were put to
                 death,
              We wished for our ELIZABETH.

MAY   16 When KATHERINE HUT did spend her
                 blood
          16 With two maids, ELIZABETH and JOAN ;
              When they embraced both reed and wood,
              Trusting in CHRIST His death alone :
              When men unnatural drew these to death,
              We wished for our ELIZABETH.

MAY   21 When two men and a sister dear,
              At Beccles were consumed to dust ;
          31 When WILLIAM SLECHE, constant and clear,
              In prison died, with hope and trust ;
              When these, our brethren, were put to death,
              We wished for our ELIZABETH.

JUNE   6 When JOHN OSWOLD, and THOMAS REEDE,
          6 HARLAND, MILWRIGHT, and EVINGTON ;
              With blazing brands their blood did bleed
              As their brethren before had done.
              When tyranny drave these to death,
              We wished for our ELIZABETH.

1556.

JUNE   20   When WHOD the Pastor, with THOMAS
               At Lewes, lost this mortal gain ;   [MILLES
               Compassed with spears, and bloody bills,
               Unto the stake for to be slain :
          23   When WILLIAM ADHERAL did die the death,
               We wished for our ELIZABETH.

JUNE   27   When JA[C]KSON, HOLYWEL, and WYE,
          27   BOWIER, LAWRENCE, and ADDLINGTON ;
          27   When ROTH, SEARLES, LION, and HURST
                  did die ;
          27   With whom, two women to death were done :
               When DORIFALL, with them, was put to death,
               We wished for our ELIZABETH.

JUNE   27   When THOMAS PARRET, prisoner,
          30   And MARTIN HUNTE died in the King's
                  Bench ;
               When the young man at Leicester,
               And CLEMENT died, with filthy stench ;
          25   When CARELESS, so took his death :
               We wished for our ELIZABETH.

JULY   16   When ASKUE, PALMER, and JOHN GWIN
               Were brent with force, at Newbury ;
               Lamenting only for their sins,
               And in the LORD were full merry :
               When tyrants merciless, put these to death,
               We wished for our ELIZABETH.

JULY   18   When JOHN FORMAN, and mother TREE,
   [* Grinstead.] At * Grenstede, cruelly were slain ;
          18   When THOMAS DUNGATE, to make up three,
               With them did pass from woe and pain :
               When these, with others, were put to death ;
               We wished for our ELIZABETH.

1556.

AUGUST 20   When the weaver at Bristow died,
And, at Derby, a wedded wife;
When these with fiery flames were fried,
For CHRISTES cause, losing their life;
When many others were put to death,
  We wished for our ELIZABETH.

SEPTEMBER 24   When RAVENSDALE and two brethren more,
To earthly ashes were consumed;
25 A godly glover would not adore
Their filthy idol; whereat they fumed;
When he, at Bristol, was put to death,
  We wished for our ELIZABETH.

SEPTEMBER 26   When JOHN HORNE, with a woman wise,
At Newton, under hedge were killed,
Stretching their hands with lifted eyes,
And so their years, in earth fulfilled;
When these, with violence, were put to death,
  We wished for our ELIZABETH.

SEPTEMBER   When DUNSTON, CLARKE, and POTKIN's
wife,
WILLIAM FOSTER, and ARCHER also,
In Canterbury, did lose their life
By famishment; as the talk do go.
When these, alas, thus took their death,
  We wished for our ELIZABETH.

OCTOBER   When three, within one castle died,
And in the fields were layed to rest.
When at Northampton, a man was tried
Whether GOD or Mammon he loved best.
When these, by tyranny, were put to death,
  We wished for our ELIZABETH.

1557.

JANUARY   2 When THOMAS FINALL and his man,
              2 FOSTER and three good members more,
                  Were purgèd with their fiery fan
                  At Canterbury, with torments sore.
                  When they with cheerfulness took their death,
                    We wished for our ELIZABETH.

JANUARY   When two at Ashford, with cruelty,
                  For CHRISTES cause, to death were brent;
              2 When, not long after, two, at Wye,
                  Suffered for CHRIST His Testament:
                  When wily wolves put these to death,
                    We wished for our ELIZABETH.

APRIL   2 When STANLY's wife, and ANNIS HYDE,
                  STURTLE, RAMSEY, and JOHN LOTHESBY
                  Were content, torments to abide,
                  And took the same right patiently;
                  When these, in Smithfield, were done to
                    We wished for our ELIZABETH.   [death,

MAY   2 When WILLIAM MORANT and STEVEN
                      GRATWICK
                  Refused, with falsehood to be beguiled,
                  And for the same, were burnèd quick,
                  With fury, in Saint George's Field;
                  When these, with others were put to death,
                    We wished for our ELIZABETH.

JUNE   16 When JOAN BRADBRIDGE, and a blind maid,
          16 APPELBY, ALLEN, and both their wives;
          16 When MANNING's wife was not afraid,
                  But all these Seven did lose their lives.
                  When these, at Maidstone, were put to death,
                    We wished for our ELIZABETH.

1557.

JUNE   19   When JOHN FISCOKE, PERDUE, and
                 WHITE ;
    19   BARBARA, widow ; and BENDEN's wife ;
    19   With these, WILSON's wife did firmly fight,
         And for their faith, all lost their life ;
         When these, at Canterbury, died the death,
           We wished for our ELIZABETH.

JUNE   22   When WILLIAM MAINARDE, his maid and
    22   MARGERY MORIES, and her son ;   [man ;
    22   DENIS, BURGES, STEVENS, and WO[O]DMAN ;
    22   GLOVE's wife, and ASHDON's, to death were
         done ;   [death,
         When one fire, at Lewes, brought to them
           We wished for our ELIZABETH.

JULY   When AMBROSE died in Maidstone Gaol,
         And so set free from tyrant's hands ;
    2   When SIMON MILNER they did assail,
    2   Having him, and a woman in bands ;
         When these, at Norwich, were done to death,
           We wished for our ELIZABETH.

JULY   2   When ten, at Colchester, in one day,
         Were fried with fire, of tyrants stout ;
         Not once permitted truth to say,
         But were compassed with bills about :
         When these, with others, were put to death,
           We wished for our ELIZABETH.

JULY   2   When GEORGE EGLES, at Chelmsford
         Was hangèd, drawn, and quarterèd ;   [town,
         His quarters carried up and down,
         And on a pole they set his head.
         When wrestèd law put him to death,
           We wished for our ELIZABETH.

1557.

JULY   5   When THURSTON's wife, at Chichester,
         5   And BOURNER's wife, with her also;
      20   When two women at Rochester,
      20   With father FRIER were sent from woe:
      23   When one, at Norwich, did die the death,
           We wished for our ELIZABETH.

AUGUST   10   When JOYCE BOWES, at Lichfield died,
           Continuing constant in the fire;
           When fixèd faith was truly tried,
           Having her just and long desire.
           When she, with others were put to death,
           We wished for our ELIZABETH.

AUGUST   17   When RICHARD ROOTH and RALPH GLAITON,
      17   With JAMES AUSCOO and his wife
           Were brent with force at Islington,
           Ending this short and sinful life;
           When they with cheerfulness, did take their
           We wished for our ELIZABETH.   [death;

OCTOBER   18   When SPARROW, GIBSON, and HOLLING-DAY,
           In Smithfield, did the stake embrace;
           When fire converted flesh to clay,
           They being joyful of such grace:
           When lawless liberty put them to death,
           We wished for our ELIZABETH.

DECEMBER 22   When JOHN ROUGHE, a Minister meek,
      22   And MARGARET MERING, with courage died:
           Because CHRIST only they did seek,
           With fire of force, they must be fried;
           When these, in Smithfield, were put to death,
           We wished for our ELIZABETH.

1558.

MARCH   28   When that JOHN DEWNESHE and HUGH
            FOXE,
            In Smithfield, cruel death sustained,
            As fixèd foes to Romish rocks ;
  28   And CUTHBERT SYMSON also slain.
            When these did worthily receive their death,
            We wished for our ELIZABETH.

MARCH   When DALE deceased in Bury gaol,
            According to GOD's ordinance ;
            When widow THURSTON they did assail ;
            And brought ANN BONGER to Death's Dance ;
            When these, at Colchester, were done to
            We wished for our ELIZABETH.   [death,

APRIL   9   When WILLIAM NICOLL, in Ha[ve]rfor[d]-
            Was trièd with their fiery fire :   [west,
  20   When SYMON fought against the best,
  20   With GLOVER, and THOMAS CARMAN ;
            When these, at Norwich, did die the death,
            We wished for our ELIZABETH.

MAY   26   When WILLIAM HARRIS, and RICHARD
            DAY ;   [brent :
  26   And CHRISTIAN GEORGE with them was
            Holding their enemies at a bay
            Till life was lost, and breath all spent ;
            When these, at Colchester, were put to
            We wished for our ELIZABETH.   [death,

JUNE   27   When SOUTHAN, LAUNDER, and RICARBIE ;
  27   HOLLYDAY, HOLLANDE, PONDE, and FLOOD,
            With cheerful look and constant cry,
  27   For CHRISTes cause, did spend their blood :
            When these in Smithfield were put to death,
            We wished for our ELIZABETH.

1558.

JUNE   When THOMAS TYLER passed this place :
                    And MATTHEW WITHERS also died.
                    Though suit were much, yet little grace
                    Among the Rulers could be spied :
                    In prison, patiently, they took their death,
                        We wishing for ELIZABETH.

JULY   10   When RICHARD YEMAN, Minister,
                    At Norwich, did his life forsake ;
              19 When Master BENBRIKE, at Winchester,
                    A lively sacrifice did make.
                    When these, with others, were put to death,
                        We wished for our ELIZABETH.

JULY   14   When WILLIAM PECKES, COTTON, and
                            WREIGHT,
                    The Popish power did sore invade ;
                    To Burning School, they were sent straight,
              14 And with them went, constant JOHN SLADE :
                    When these, at Brainford, were put to death,
                        We wished for our ELIZABETH.

NOVEMBER   4   When ALEXANDER GECHE was brent,
              4 And with him ELIZABETH LAUNSON ;
                    When they with joy, did both consent
                    To do as their brethren had done ;
                    When these, at Ipswich, were put to death,
                        We wished for ELIZABETH.

NOVEMBER   5   When JOHN DAVY, and eke his brother,
              5 With PHILIP HUMFREY kissed the cross ;
                    When they did comfort one another
                    Against all fear, and worldy loss ;
                    When these, at Bury, were put to death,
                        We wished for our ELIZABETH.

NOVEMBER.   When, last of all (to take their leave!),
        [11] At Canterbury, they did some consume,
             Who constantly to CHRIST did cleave;
             Therefore were fried with fiery fume:
             But, six days after these were put to death,
                 GOD sent us our ELIZABETH!

             Our wished wealth hath brought us peace.
             Our joy is full; our hope obtained;
             The blazing brands of fire do cease,
             The slaying sword also restrained.
             The simple sheep, preserved from death.
                 By our good Queen, ELIZABETH.

             As Hope hath here obtained her prey,
             By GOD's good will and Providence;
             So Trust doth truly look for stay,
             Through His heavenly influence,
             That great GOLIATH shall be put to death
                 By our good Queen, ELIZABETH.

             That GOD's true Word shall placèd be,
             The hungry souls, for to sustain;
             That Perfect Love and Unity
             Shall be set in their seat again:
             That no more good men shall be put to death;
                 Seeing GOD hath sent ELIZABETH.

             Pray we, therefore, both night and day,
             For Her Highness, as we be bound.
             O LORD, preserve this Branch of Bay!
             (And all her foes, with force confound)
             Here, long to live! and, after death,
                 Receive our Queen, ELIZABETH!
                     Amen.

Apoc. 6.   *How long tarriest thou, O LORD, holy and true!*
to judge, and avenge our blood on them that dwell on the earth.
                 F I N I S .

The wishes of the Wise,
Which long to be at rest;
To GOD, with lifted eyes,
They call to be redressed.

HEN shall this time of travail cease
    Which we, with woe sustain?
When shall the days of rest and peace,
    Return to us again?

When shall the mind be movèd right
    To leave this lusting life?
When shall our motions and delight
    Be free from wrath and strife?

When shall the time of woful tears
    Be movèd unto mirth?
When shall the aged, with grey hairs,
    Rejoice at children's birth?

When shall Jerusalem rejoice
    In Him, that is their King?
And Sion's hill, with cheerful voice,
    Sing psalms with triumphing?

When shall the walls erected be,
    That foes, with fury, 'fray?
When shall that perfect Olive Tree,
    Give odour like the Bay?

When shall the Vineyard be restored,
    That beastly boars devour?
When shall the people, late abhorted,
    Receive a quiet hour?

When shall the SPIRIT more fervent be,
    In us that want good will ?
When shall Thy mercies set us free
    From wickedness and ill ?

When shall the serpents, that surmise
    To poison Thine Elect,
Be bound to better exercise,
    Or utterly reject ?

When shall the blood revengèd be,
    Which on the earth is shed ?
When shall sin and iniquity
    Be cast into the bed ?

When shall that Man of Sin appear
    To be, even as he is ?
When shall thy babes and children dear
    Receive eternal bliss ?

When shall that painted Whore of Rome
    Be cast unto the ground ?
When shall her children have their doom,
    Which virtue would confound ?

When shall Thy Spouse, and Turtle Dove
    Be free from bitter blast ?
When shall Thy grace, our sins remove,
    With pardon at the last ?

When shall this life translatèd be,
    From fortune's fickle fall ?
When shall True Faith and Equity
    Remain in general ?

When shall Contention and Debate,
    For ever slack and cease ?
When shall the days of evil date,
    Be turnèd unto peace ?

When shall True Dealing rule the rost
    With those that buy and sell;
And Single Mind, in every coast,
    Among us bide and dwell?

When shall our minds wholly convert
    From wealth, and worldly gain?
When shall the movings of our heart
    From wickedness refrain?

When shall this flesh return to dust,
    From whence the same did spring?
When shall the trial of our trust
    Appearing with triumphing?

When shall the Trump blow out his blast,
    And thy dear babes revive?
When shall the Whore be headlong cast,
    That sought us to deprive?

When shall Thy CHRIST, our King, appear
    With power and renown?
When shall Thy saints, that suffer here,
    Receive their promised crown?

When shall the faithful, firmly stand?
    Before Thy face to dwell;
When shall Thy foes, at Thy left hand,
    Be cast into the hell?

Apoca. **22.**

Come, LORD JESU!

T. B.

❡ Imprinted at London, by John Kingston for
Richard Adams.

The winning of Calais by the French,

January 1558 A.D.

General Narrative of the Recapture.

By GEORGE FERRERS, the Poet.

[GRAFTON'S *Chronicle.* 1569.]

T   I

OR if ought were won by the having of St. Quentin, England got nothing at all; for the gain thereof came only to King PHILIP: but the loss of Calais, Hammes, and Guisnes, with all the country on that side of the sea, which followed soon after, was such a buffet to England as [had] not happened in more than an hundred years before; and a dishonour wherewith this realm shall be blotted until GOD shall give power to redubbe it with some like requital to the French.

At this time, although open hostility and war were between England and France, yet, contrary to the ancient custom afore used, the town of Calais and the forts thereabouts were not supplied with any new accrues [*reinforcements*] of soldiers; which negligence was not unknown to the enemy, who, long before, had practised [*plotted*] the winning of the said town and country. The French King therefore (being sharply nettled with the late loss of St. Quentin and a great piece of his country adjoining, and desirous of revenge) thought it not meet to let slip this occasion; and having presently a full army in a readiness to employ where most advantage should appear, determined to put in proof, with all speed, the enterprise of Calais; which long, and many times before, was purposed upon.

This practice [*design*] was not so secret but that the Deputies of Calais and Guisnes had some intelligence thereof; and informed the Queen [MARY] and her Council accordingly: nevertheless, either by wilful negligence there, or lack of credit by the Queen's Council here, this great case was so slenderly regarded as no provision of defence was made until it was somewhat too late.

The Duke of GUISE [*known as, Le Balafré*], being General of the French army, proceeded in this enterprise with marvellous policy. For approaching the English frontier [*known in our history as the English Pale*], under colour to victual Boulogne and Ardes; he entered upon the same, on a sudden [*on 1st January*, 1558]; and took a little bulwark [*fortification*] called Sandgate, by assault. He then divided his army into two parts, sending one part with certain great pieces of artillery along the downs [*sandhills*] by the sea-side towards Risbank [*or Ruisbank, a detached fort in Calais harbour. See this Vol. p.* 304]; and the other part, furnished also with battery pieces, marched straight forth to Newnham [*or Newhaven*] Bridge : meaning to batter the two forts, both at one time. Which thing he did with such celerity, that coming thither very late in the evening, he was master of both by the next morning.

At the first shot discharged at Newnham Bridge, the head of the Master Gunner of that piece [*fort*], whose name was HORSELEY, was clean stricken off. The Captain [*NICHOLAS ALEXANDER*] considering the great power of the French army; and having his fort but slenderly manned to make sufficient resistance, fled to Calais. And by the time he was come thither, the other part of the French army that went by the seaside, with their battery, had won Risbank; being abandoned [*by Captain JOHN HARLESTONE*] to their hands.

The next day [*2nd of January*], the Frenchmen, with five double-cannons and three culverins, began a battery from the sandhills next Risbank, against the town of Calais; and continued the same, by the space of two or three days, until they made a little breach in the wall next unto the Water Gate, which, nevertheless, was not yet assaultable : for that which was broken in the day, was by them within the town made up again in the night, stronger than afore. But the battery was not begun there by the French because they intended to enter in that place; but rather to abuse [*deceive*] the English, to have the less regard to the defence of the Castle : which was the weakest part of the town, and the place where they were we ascertained, by their espials, to win an easy entry.

So that while our people travailed fondly to defend that counterfeit breach of the town wall, the Duke had in the mean season, planted fifteen double-cannons against the Castle. Which Castle being considered by the Rulers of the town to be of no such force as might resist the battery of cannon, by reason that it was old, and without any rampires [*ramparts*] ; it was devised to make a train with certain barrels of powder to this purpose, that when the Frenchmen should enter, as they well knew, that there they would, to have fired the said train, and blown up the Keep : and for that purpose left never a man within to defend it. But the Frenchmen, at their entry, espied the train, and so avoided the same. So that the device came to no purpose; and, without any resistance, they entered the Castle; and thought to have entered the town by that way.

But [*on the 6th of January*] by the prowess and hardy courage of Sir ANTHONY AGER[*AUCHER*],Knight[*see this Vol., pp.* 315 *sqq.*], and Marshal of the Town, with his soldiers, they were repulsed and driven back again into the Castle : and followed so hard after, that our men forced them to close and shut the Castle gate for their surety, lest it should have been recovered against them. As it was once attempted [*p.*315] by SirANTHONYAGER: whothere,with his son andheir, and a Pursuivant at Arms called CALAIS, and divers others, to the number of fifteen or sixteen Englishmen, lost their lives.

The same night, after the recule [*retreat*] of the Frenchmen, whose number so increased in the Castle, that the town was not able to resist their force ; the Lord WENTWORTH, Deputy of Calais, sent a Pursuivant called GUISNES, unto the Duke of GUISE, requiring composition; which, after long debate, was agreed to, upon this sort.

> First. That the town, with all the great artillery, victuals and munition, should be freely yielded to the French King.
>
> The lives of the inhabitants only saved; to whom safe conduct should be granted, to pass where they listed.
>
> Saving the Lord Deputy, with fifty others, such as the Duke should appoint, to remain prisoners; and be put to their ransom.

The next morning [*7th of January*], the Frenchmen entered and possessed the Town : and forthwith all the men, women, and children, were commanded to leave their houses, and to go into the two churches, of Our Lady, and Saint Nicholas; upon pain of death. Where they remained a great part of that day, and one whole night, and until three o'clock at afternoon the next day [*8th*] : without either meat or drink.

And while they were thus in the churches, the Duke of GUISE, in the name of the French King, in their hearing, made a Proclamation straitly charging and commanding all and every person that were inhabitants of the Town of Calais, having about them any money, plate, or jewels to the value of [*but*] one groat [*4d.*] to bring the same forthwith, and lay it down on the high altars of the said churches, upon pain of death: bearing them in hand [*inducing them to think*] also that they should be searched.

By reason of which Proclamation, there was made a great

and sorrowful Offertory. And while they were at this offering within the churches, the Frenchmen entered into their houses, and rifled the same ; where was found inestimable riches and treasure, but specially of ordnance, armour, and other munition.

About two o'clock, the next day at afternoon, being the 7th of January ; all the Englishmen, except the Lord Deputy and the others reserved for prisoners, were suffered to pass out of the town in safety ; being guarded through the army by a number of Scottish Light Horsemen.

There were in this town of Calais, 500 English soldiers ordinarily, and no more : and of the townsmen, not fully 200 fighting men : a small garrison for the defence of such a town !   And there were in the whole number of men, women, and children, as they were counted when they went out of the gate, 4,200 persons.

But the Lord WENTWORTH, Deputy of Calais ; Sir RALPH CHAMBERLAIN, Captain of the Castle ; [JOHN] HARLESTONE, Captain of Risbank ; NICHOLAS ALEXANDER, Captain of Newn[h]ambridge ; EDWARD GRIMSTONE, Controller ; with others of the chief of the town, to the number of fifty, as aforesaid, such as it pleased the Duke of GUISE to appoint, were sent prisoners into France.

Thus have ye heard the discourse of the Overthrow and Loss of the Town of Calais ; the which enterprise was begun and ended in less than eight days, to the great marvel of the world, that a town of such strength, and so well furnished of all things as that was, should so suddenly be taken and conquered : but most specially, in the winter season ; what time all the country about, being marsh ground, is commonly overflown with water.

The said town was won from the French by King EDWARD III. in the time of PHILIP DE VALOIS, then French King : and, being in the possession of the Kings of England, 211 years ; was, in the time of PHILIP and MARY, King and Queen of England, lost within less than eight days being the most notable fort that England had.

For the winning whereof, King EDWARD aforesaid, in the 21st year of his reign [1346], was fain to continue a siege one whole year or more : wherefore it was judged of all men, that it could not have so come to pass, without some secret treachery.

Here is also to be noted, that when Queen MARY and her Council heard, credibly, of the Frenchmen's sudden approach to that town; she, with all possible speed, but somewhat too late, raised a great power for the rescue thereof : which, if wind and weather had served, might, haply, have brought succour thither in time. But such terrible tempests then arose, and continued the space of four or five days together, that the like had not been seen before in the remembrance of man; wherefore some said "That the same was done by necromancy, and that the Devil was raised up, and become French:" the truth whereof is known to GOD. But very true it is that no ship could brook the seas, by reason of those extreme storms and tempests. And such of the Queen's ships as did adventure the passage, were so shaken and torn, with the violence of the weather; as they were forced to return with great danger, and the loss of all their tackle and furniture.

Thus by the negligence of the Council at home, conspiracy of traitors elsewhere, force and false practice of enemies, helped by the rage of most terrible tempests of contrary winds and weather; this famous Fort of Calais was brought again to the hands and possession of the French.

So soon as this Duke of GUISE, contrary to all expectation, had, in a few days, gained this strong town of Calais, afore thought impregnable, and had put the same in such order as best seemed for his advantage: proud of the spoil, and pressing forward upon his sudden fortune, without giving long time to the residue of the Captains of the forts there to breathe on their business; the 13th of the same month, with all provision requisite for a siege, he marched with his army from Calais into the town and fort of Guisnes, five miles distant from thence.

Of which town and castle, at the same time, there was as Captain, a valiant Baron of England, called WILLIAM, Lord GREY of Wilton [See this Vol. p. 319]: who, not without cause suspecting a siege at hand; and knowing the town of Guisnes to be of small force (as being without walls or bulwarks, and only compassed with a trench), before the Frenchmen's arrival, caused all the inhabitants of the town

to advoid [*depart*]; and so many of them as were apt to
bear arms, he caused to retire into the Castle. Which was
a place well fortified, with strong and massy Bulwarks
[*redoubts or batteries*] of brick: having also a high and mighty
tower, of great force and strength, called the Keep.

The town being thus abandoned, the Frenchman had the
more easy approach to the Castle; who, thinking to find
quiet lodging in those vacant houses, entered the same without any fear: and being that night, at their rest as they
thought, a chosen band of soldiers, appointed by Lord GREY,
issued out by a postern of the said Castle, and slew no small
number of their sleepy guests. The rest, they put out of
their new lodgings; and (maugre the Duke and all the French
power) consumed all the houses of the town with fire. That
notwithstanding, the said Duke, with all diligence, began his
trenches: and albeit the shot of the great artillery from the
Castle was terrible, and gave him great impeachment; yet
did he continue his work without intermission, and, for
example's sake, wrought in his own person as a common
pioneer or labourer. So that, within less than three days,
he brought, to the number of thirty-five battery pieces, hard
to the brim [*edge*] of the Castle ditch, to batter the same on
all sides, as well right forth as across. But his principal
battery, he planted against the strongest bulwark of all,
called Mary Bulwark [*a detached fort*]; thinking by gaining of
the stronger, to come more easily by the weaker.

His battery being thus begun, he continued the same by
the space of two days, with such terrible thundering of great
artillery, that, by the report of [F. DE] RABUTIN a French
writer, there were, in those few days, discharged well near
to the number of 8,000 or 9,000 cannon shot.

Through the violence whereof, by the 20th of the said
month, the said great Bulwark was laid wide open, and the
breach made reasonable and easy enough for the assault;
nevertheless, the said Duke (being a man of war, and nothing
ignorant of what devices be commonly used in forts and besieged towns to entrap and damage the assailants) afore he
would put the persons of his good soldiers to the hazard of
the assault, caused the breach to be viewed once or twice by
certain forward and skilful soldiers; who, mounting the top
of the breach, brought report that the place was saultable

[*assaultable*]. Nevertheless, to make the climb more easy; he caused certain harquebussiers to pass over the ditch, and to keep the defendants occupied with shot, while certain pioneers with mattocks and shovels, made the breach more plain and easy. [*See CHURCHYARD'S account of this assault at p.* 324. *He was one of the defenders.*]

Which thing done accordingly, he gave order to Monsieur D'ANDELOT, Colonel of the French Footmen, that he, with his Bands, should be in readiness to give the assault, when sign should be given.

In which meantime, the Duke withdrew himself to an higher ground; from whence he might plainly discover the behaviour as well of his soldiers in giving the assault, as also of the defendants in answering the same. And not perceiving so many of the English part appearing for the defence, as he looked for; he gave order forthwith, that a regiment of his most forward Lance Knights [*the Reiters*] should mount the breach to open the first passage, and that Monsieur D'ANDELOT with his Bands of the French, should back them.

Which order was followed with such hot haste and desperate hardiness, that, entering a deep ditch full of water, from the bottom whereof to the top of the breach was well forty feet, without fear either of the water beneath or the fire above, they mounted the breach: and whereas the Duke had prepared divers bridges made of plank-boards, borne up with caske and empty pipes [*i.e., barrels of the size of a Pipe*] tied one to another, for his men to pass the said ditch; many of the said assailants, without care of those bridges, plunged into the water, and took the next way to come to the assault.

Which hot haste notwithstanding, the said assailants were, in this first assault, so stoutly repulsed and put back by the defendants, being furnished with great store of wild fire and fricasies for the purpose, that they were turned down headlong, one upon another, much faster than they came up: not without great waste and slaughter of their best and most brave soldiers; to the small comfort of the stout Duke, who, as is said before, stood, all this while, upon a little hill to behold this business. Wherefore, not enduring this sight any longer, as a man arraged [*enraged*], he ran among his men; so reproving some and encouraging others, that the assault was foot hot renewed with much more vehemence and fury than before:

and with no less obstinacy and desperation received by the defendants; whereby all the breach underneath was filled with French carcases.

This notwithstanding, the Duke still redoubled his forces with fresh companies; and continued so many assaults, one upon another, that at the last charge, being most vehement of all others, our men being tired, and greatly minished in the number by slaughter and bloody wounds, were, of fine [*sheer*] force, driven to avoid, and give place of entry to the enemy.

Which was not done without a marvellous expense of blood, on both sides. For, of the French part, there were slain and perished in these assaults, above the number of 800 or 900 [*CHURCHYARD says, at p.* 330 4,000]: and of the English, but little fewer [800, *p.* 329]; amongst whom the greatest loss lighted on the Spaniards, who took upon them the defence of the said Mary Bulwark: insomuch, as the report went, that of the 500 [*or rather* 450; *whereof but* 50 *were Spaniards, the rest English and Burgundians, see p.* 327] brave soldiers which King PHILIP sent thither for succour, under the conduct of a valiant Spanish Captain, called MOUNT DRAGON, there were not known to have come away any number worth the reckoning, but all were either slain, maimed or taken.

These outrageous assaults were given to the Castle of Guisnes, on St. Sebastian's day, the 20th of January aforesaid.

At the end of which day, there were also gained from the English, two other principal Bulwarks of the said Castle; which, being likewise made assaultable by battery, were taken by the Almains [? *Swiss*], who entered in by the breaches.

The Lord GREY, with his eldest son, and the chief Captains and soldiers of the said garrison, who kept the Inner Ward of the Castle, where the most high and principal Tower, called the Keep, stood; thinking themselves in small surety there (being a place of the old sort of fortification) after they saw the Utter Ward possessed by the enemy, and such a number of the most forward soldiers consumed and spent; and no likelihood of any more aid to come in time: by the advice of the most expert soldiers there, concluded for the best, to treat with the Duke for composition: according to the which advice, he sent forth two gentlemen, with this message in effect. That the Duke (being a man of war, and serving under a King) should not think it strange if the Lord GREY likewise (being a man of war, and serving his Prince, in manner) did his like deavour [*endeavour*] in well defending the place committed to his charge, so far forth, as to answer and bide the assault; considering that otherwise, he could never save his own honour, neither his truth and loyalty to his Prince. In respect whereof, according to the law of arms, he required honourable composition.

Which message, though it was well accepted of the Duke; yet he deferred his answer until the morrow. What [*At which*] time, the messengers repairing to him again, composition was granted in this sort.

First. That the Castle with all the furniture thereof, as well victuals as great artillery, powder, and other munitions of war, should be wholly rendered; without wasting, hiding, or minishment thereof.

Secondarily. That the Lord GREY, with all the Captains, Officers, and others having charge there, should remain prisoners, at the Duke's pleasure; to be ransomed after the manner of war.

Thirdly. That all the rest, as well soldiers as others, should safely depart, with their armour and baggage to what parts, it seemed them best : nevertheless, to pass, without sound of drum or trumpet, or displaying of an ensigns [*flags*] ; but to leave them behind.

These conditions being received and approved on either party, the day following, that is to wit, the 22nd day of the said month of January, all the soldiers of the said fortress, as well English as strangers, with all the rest of the inhabitants and others (except the Lord GREY, Sir ARTHUR his son, Sir HENRY PALMER Knight, MOUNT DRAGON the above named Captain of the Spaniards, and other men of charge reserved by the Composition) departed, with their bag and baggages, from thence, towards Flanders. At whose issuing forth, there was esteemed [*estimated*] to the number of 800 or 900 able men for the war : part English, part Burgundians, with a small remnant of Spaniards.

After the winning of this town and Castle, the Duke, advising well upon the place, and considering that if it should happen to be regained by Englishmen, what a noisome neighbour the same might be to Calais, now being French; and specially what impeachment should come thereby for the

passage thither from France; considering also the near
standing thereof to the French King's fortress of Ardes, so
that to keep two garrisons so nigh together should be but a
double charge, and not only needless, but also dangerous, for
the cause afore rehearsed : upon these considerations, as the
Frenchmen write, he took order for all the great artillery,
victuals, and other munition to be taken forth; and the
Castle, with all the Bulwarks and other fortifications there,
to be razed and thrown down, with all speed, and the stuff to
be carried away, and employed in other more necessary places.

Then there rested nothing, within all the English Pale on
that side, unconquered, but the little Castle or Pile called
Hammes: which, though it were but of small force, made by
art and industry of man's hand, and altogether of old work-
manship, without rampiers [*ramparts*] or Bulwarks [*redoubts*];
yet, nevertheless, by the natural situation thereof, being environed on all sides, with fens and marsh grounds, it could not
easily be approached unto: either with great ordnance for the
battery, or else with an army to encamp there, for a siege;
having but one straight passage thereto by a narrow causey
[*causeway*], traversed and cut through, in divers places, with
deep ditches always full of water. Which thing, being well
foreseen by EDWARD Lord DUDLEY, then Captain there, having as good cause to suspect a siege there as his neighbours,
had, afore the Frenchmen's coming to Guisnes, caused all the
bridges of the said causey, which were of wood, to be broken;
to give thereby the more impeachment [*obstacles*] to the French,
if they should attempt to approach the same; as, shortly
after, they did, and kept divers of the passages.

But to deliver the Duke and his soldiers from that care,
there came to him glad news from those that had charge to
watch the same causey; how the Captain, having intelligence
of the rendering of Guisnes, had conveyed himself with his
small garrison, secretly, the same night [*of the 22nd of January*]
by a secret passage over the marshes into Flanders. Whereby, the Duke, being now past care of any further siege to be
laid in all that frontier, took order forthwith to seize the said
little fort into his hands; as it was easy to do, when there
was no resistance.

When this place was once seized by the French, then
remained there none other place or strength of the English on

all that side the sea, for the safeguard of the rest of the country : whereby the French King became wholly and thoroughly Lord and Master of all the English Pale : for now, as ye have heard, there was neither town, castle, or fortress, more or less, on that side (saving Bootes Bulwark, near to Gravelines; which now, [*in* 1568] King PHILIP keepeth as his); but it was either taken away by force, or else abandoned and left open to the enemy. And, as the Frenchmen write, besides the great riches of gold and silver coin, jewels, plate, wool, and other merchandise (which was inestimable [*i.e., beyond reckoning*]) there were found 300 pieces of brass, mounted on wheels, and as many pieces of iron : with such furniture of powder, pellets [*bullets*], armour, victuals, and other munitions of war, scarcely credible.

Thus have heard the whole discourse of the Conquest of the noble town of Calais with all the English fortresses and country adjoining, made by the Duke of GUISE. The news whereof, when it came to the French King: [there is] no need to ask how joyfully it was received! not only by him and all his Court, but also universally through the whole realm of France. For the which victory, there was, as the manner is, *Te DEUM* sung, and bonfires made everywhere, as it is wont to be in cases of common joy and gladness for some rare benefit of GOD. Shortly, upon this conquest, there was a public Assembly at Paris of all the Estates of France : who frankly (in recompense of the King's charges in winning Calais and the places aforesaid, and for maintenance of his wars to be continued afterwards) granted unto him 3,000,000 of French Crowns [=*about £900,000 then = about £9,000,000 now*] ; whereof the clergy of France contributed 1,000,000 [crowns] besides their *dimes*.

And no marvel though the French did highly rejoice at the recovery of Calais out of the Englishmen's hands! For it is constantly affirmed by many that be acquainted with the affairs of France, that ever since the town was first won by the Englishmen, in all solemn Councils appointed to treat upon the state of France, there was a special person appointed to put them in remembrance, from time to time, of Calais : as it were to be wished that the like were used in England until it were regained from the French.

Now seemed every day a year, to the French King, until he

personally had visited Calais and his new conquered country. Wherefore, about the end of January, aforesaid, he took his voyage thither, accompanied with no small number of his nobility. And immediately upon his arrival there, he perused the whole town and every part thereof, from place to place : and devising with the Duke of GUISE for the better fortification thereof; what should be added to the old, what should be made new, and what should be taken away. And after order taken for that business; he placed there a noble and no less valiant Knight, called Monsieur DE THERMES, to be Captain of the town : and so departed again to France.

After the French King's departure from Calais, he made great haste for the accomplishment of the marriage moved between FRANCIS, his eldest son, called the Dauphin, and MARY STUART, daughter and sole heir of JAMES V., late King of Scotland : which Princess (if the Scots had been faithful of promise, as they seldom be) should have married with King EDWARD VI. For the breach of which promise, began all the war between England and Scotland, in the latter end of King HENRY VIII. and in the beginning of EDWARD VI.

This marriage (though it be not my matter) I thought not to omit ; for many things were meant thereby, which, thanks be to GOD ! never came to pass. But one special point was not hidden to the world, that, by the means of the same, the Realm of Scotland should, for evermore, have remained as united and incorporated to the Crown of France ; that as the Son and Heir of every French King doth succeed to the inheritance and possession of a country, called the Doulphyn [Dauphiné], and is therefore called Doulphyn [Dauphin] ; and as the Principality of Wales appertaineth to the Eldest Son of England, who is therefore called the Prince of WALES: even so, that the Dauphin and Heir of France should thereby have been King of Scotland, for evermore. Which name and title, upon this marriage, was accordingly given to FRANCIS the Dauphin and heir apparent of France, to be called " King Dauphin " : the meaning whereof was, utterly to exclude for evermore any to be King of Scotland, but only the Eldest Son of France.

This memorable marriage was solemnized in the city of Paris, the 24th day of April, 1558, with most magnificent pomp and triumph.

Lord WENTWORTH, the Lord Deputy of Calais, and the Council there.

Letter to Queen MARY, 23rd May, 1557.

[*State Papers. Foreign, MARY, Vol. X. No.* 615. In Public Record Office.]

T may please your Highness to understand that, where upon circumspect consideration and view of your Majesty's store here of munition and other habiliments of war, there is presently [*at this moment*] found not only a great want of many kinds thereof, but also such a decay in divers other things as the same are not serviceable, and will be utterly lost if they be not with speed repaired and put in better estate ; as this bearer, Master HIGHFIELD, Master of your Ordnance here [*p.* 312], can declare more amply the particularities thereof, either unto your Majesty, or unto such of your Council as shall please your Highness to direct him : we have thought it our bounden duties to be most humble suitors to your Majesty, that it would please the same to give immediate order, as well for the supplement of the said lacks, as also for your warrant to be addressed hither, for the repairing of all other things requisite to be done within his office.

And thus we continually pray Almighty GOD for the long preservation of your Highness in most prosperous estate.

From your town of Calais, the 23rd of May, 1557.

Your Majesty's
Most humble bounden and obedient subjects and servants,

WENTWORTH,	WILLIAM GREY,
RALPH CHAMBERLAIN,	A. CORNWALLIS,
EDWARD GRYMSTONE,	EUSTACE HOBYNTON.

Lords WENTWORTH and GREY, and the Council at Calais.

Report to Queen MARY, 27th December, 1557.

[*State Papers. Foreign, MARY, Vol. XI. No. 698.*

UR bounden duties most humbly remembered unto your Highness. Upon the receipt of the intelligences sent unto your Majesty this other day, from me your Grace's Deputy; I forthwith dispatched to my Lord GREY [*at Guisnes*], requiring his Lordship to repair to this town, that we might consult of the state of your Highness's places and country on this side.

So his Lordship coming hither, we have conferred together our several intelligences: and finding the same in effect to agree, it hath very much augmented our suspicion that this train [*design*] now meant by the enemy, should be made towards your Highness's country or pieces. Whereupon we, all together, have considered the state of the same; and said our opinions therein, as it may appear unto your Highness by these articles which we send herewith to your Majesty, which we have thought our duties to signify unto you. Most humbly beseeching your Highness to return unto us your pleasure therein.

So, we pray JESU, grant your Majesty long and prosperous reign.

At your town of Calais, 27th December, 1557.

Your Highness's, &c.

Our Consultation, made the 27th December, 1557.

GUISNES.

First. HAVING no supplement of men other than is presently there, we think it meetest, if the enemy should give the attempt, to abandon the Town (which could not be, without very great danger of the Castle); and defend the Turnpike, which is of the more importance, because that way only, in necessity, the relief to the Castle is to be looked for.

Item. There is great want of wheat, butter, cheese, and other victuals.

Item. It is requisite to have some men of estimation and service to be there [*i.e., at Guisnes*], that might be able to take the charge in hand; if either sickness or other accident should fortune to me the Lord GREY: which I, the said Lord GREY the rather require, by reason of Sir HENRY PALMER's hurt; being of any other person at this present utterly unfurnished.

HAMPNES CASTLE.

Item. E THINK the same sufficiently furnished of men for the sudden; albeit this hard and frosty weather, if it continue, will give the enemy great advantage: yet we put in as much water as is possible.

Of victuals, that place is utterly unprovided; except the Captain's store.

That we also thought meet to have there some man of estimation and service, for the respects contained in the article of Guisnes: which also the Lord DUDLEY requires.

NEWNAM BRIDGE.

Item. E THINK it meet, upon the occasion, to withdraw the bands [*companies of soldiers*] from the Causeway thither; and then are of opinion, the same to be sufficient to defend that piece for a season; unless the enemy shall get between this town and the bridge.

It is clean without victuals, other than the Captain's own provision.

RYSBANK.

ECAUSE that place standeth upon the sea, and by the shore side, may the enemy come in a night to it: we think it meet to appoint hither a band [*company*] of the low country [*the open district round Calais, within the English pale*] under the leading of Captain DODD.

It is altogether unfurnished of victuals, other than for the Captain's own store.

CALAIS.

HEREAS all your Majesty's pieces on this side, make account to be furnished of victuals and other necessaries from hence ; it is so, that of victuals your Highness hath presently none here : and also this town hath none, by reason that the restraint in the realm hath been so strait as the victuallers (as were wont to bring daily hither good quantities of butter, cheese, bacon, wheat, and other things) might not, of late, be suffered to have any recourse hither ; whereby is grown a very great scarcity of all such things here.

Finally. ORASMUCH as all the wealth and substance of your Majesty's whole dominion on this side, is now in your low country (a thing not unknown to the enemy) : and if with this his great power, coming down (as the bruit goeth) for the victualling of Ardes, he will give attempt on your Highness's country ; we do not see that the small number here, in respect of their force, can, by any means, defend it.

And if we should stand to resist their entry into the country [*the open district*], and there receive any loss or overthrow ; the country should nevertheless be overrun and spoiled : and besides it would set the enemy in a glory, and also be the more peril to your Highness's pieces [*towns*]. We therefore, upon the necessity, think it meet to gather all our men into strengths [*fortresses*] ; and with the same to defend your pieces to the uttermost.

Notwithstanding, all the power on this side is insufficient to defend the pieces, in case the enemy shall tarry any space in the field.

WENTWORTH,   WILLIAM GREY,
ANTHONY AUCHAR,   JOHN HARLESTON,
EDWARDE GRIMESTONE,   N. ALEXANDER,
EUSTACE HOBYNGTON.

Lord WENTWORTH, at Calais.

Letter to Queen MARY, 1 *January*, 1558, 9 *p.m.*

[*State Papers. Foreign, MARY, Vol. XII. No. 1.*

[One cannot help seeing that in this and the next letter, Lord WENT-WORTH, quite hopeless of any successful attempt, was trying to make things look as pleasant as he could to the Queen.]

T MAY PLEASE YOUR HIGHNESS, having retired the Bands from the Causeway the last night [31 *December* 1557], and placed them at the Bridge [at *Newhaven* or *Newnham*] and within the Brayes [*i.e., Calais walls*] : this morning early, I returned them to the said Causeway, to defend that passage in case the enemy would attempt to enter there ; and also to offer skirmish to take some of them, and to learn somewhat of their power.

Between nine and ten, the enemy showed in a very great bravery about six ensigns [*regiments*] of footmen, and certain horsemen ; and came from the Chalk Pits down the hill towards the Causeway. Whereupon some of ours issued and offered the skirmish ; but the enemy would in no wise seem to meddle.

During this their stillness, they caused about 200 harque-bussiers to cut over the marsh from Sandgate and get between ours and the Bridge, and then to have hotly set on them on both sides. In this time also, at a venture, I had caused your Majesty's Marshal, with the horsemen, to go abroad, and maintain the skirmish with the footmen: and by that [*time*] the Marshal came there, the enemy's harquebussiers that passed the marshes were discovered ; and ours took a very honest retire. Which the enemies on the land side perceiving, came on, both horsemen and footmen, marvellously hotly ; to whom ours gave divers onsets, continually skirmishing till they came to the Bridge, and there reposed themselves. The bridge bestowed divers shot upon the enemy, and hurt some. Of ours, thanked be GOD ! none slain nor hurt, save a man-at-arms stricken in the leg with a currion.

The alarm continued till one o'clock in the afternoon; before the end whereof our enemy's number increased: for eleven ensigns more of footmen came in sight, and three troops of horsemen.

Besides, the alarm went round about our country at that instant, even from Sandgate to Guisnes; and bands of the enemy at every passage.

They have gotten Froyton Church, and plant themselves at all the streights [*passages*] into this country. The bulwarks [? *earth works*] of Froyton and Nesle have this day done their duty very well; to whom I have this afternoon sent aid of men, and some shot and powder. Howbeit I am in some doubt of Nesle this night.

I am perfectly advertised, their number of horsemen and footmen already arrived is above 12,000; whereof little less have come in sight here. The Duke of GUISE is not yet arrived, but [is] hourly looked for with a more [*greater*] number.

This evening, I have discovered 500 waggons ladened with victuals and munition; and have further perfect intelligence, that thirty cannons be departed from Boulogne hitherwards.

They [*i.e., the French army*] are settled at Sandgate, Galley Moat, Causeway, Froyton, Calkewell, Nesle, and Syntrecase. At one o'clock after midnight, I look for them; being low water at the passage over the haven.

Thus having set all things in the best order I can, I make an end of three days' work; and leave your Majesty to consider for our speedy succour. Beseeching GOD to grant your Highness victory, with long and prosperous reign.

At your town of Calais, this New Year's Day, at nine of the night, 1557.

I have received your Majesty's letter [*of 31st December*] by [JOHN HIGHFIELD] Master of the Ordnance [at Calais], who came in this morning. The contents whereof I follow as near as I can.

Your Highness's

Most humble and obedient servant and subject,

WENTWORTH

Lord WENTWORTH at Calais.

Letter to Queen MARY, 2 January, 1558, 10 p.m.

[*State Papers, &c.*]

FTER my humble duty remembered, it may please your Highness. This last night our enemies lay still, without anything attempting in the places mentioned in my last letters; as we did well perceive, during the whole night, by great fires made in the same places.

This morning early, I put out fresh footmen to the Bridge, to relieve the watched men.

About nine a clock, the enemies in very great number approached the Bridge, and offered the skirmish: whereupon issued out some of our harquebussiers and bowmen, and kept them in play, with the help of the shot from the Bridge, more than an hour; and in the end, being overmatched with multitude, made their retire with the Turnpike, without any loss or hurt. The enemies shadowing [*sheltering*] themselves under the turnpike wall, with their curriors (which assuredly shot very great bullets, and carry far) kept themselves in such surety, as our pieces of the Bridge could not annoy them, till at eleven o'clock, certain of ours, bored holes with augers through the turnpike, and with harquebusses beat them out into the shot of ordnance, and so made them retire to the Causeway.

This forenoon, certain Swiss and Frenchmen, to the number of 500, got within the marshes between Froyton and Nesle bulwarks: and the men of the Bulwarks seeing themselves to be compassed on all sides, and seeing also that time yet served them well to depart; and (fearing they should not so do, if they tarried till they were assailed on both sides, as they could not indeed), forsook their Bulwarks, and right manfully, notwithstanding their enemies between them and home, saved themselves through the marshes. In the retire of the enemies, one COOKSON, a man-at-arms, and few other soldiers, with the countrymen, rescued most part of the booty (which was certain kine); and took three prisoners of the Captain of Abbeville's Band.

The report of this enterprise of the enemy being brought to me, fearing Colham Hill, I forthwith appointed your Majesty's Marshal with the Horsemen, and 200 footmen to repair thither; and as they should see their match, so to demean themselves. Ere these men had marched a quarter of a mile, the enemies were retired out of the country, upon occasion that wading, as they entered in, up to the girdle stead; and perceiving the water to increase, [they] thought good to make a speedy return: and nevertheless, for all their haste, went up to the breast. And if they had tarried a little longer, I had put in so much water, as I think would have put them over head and ears: and, GOD willing, at the next tide, I will take in more.

This afternoon, they have been quiet, and we, in the meantime, be occupied in cutting up of passages to let in more water about the Bridge and that part of the marshes; whereby the enemies shall have very ill watering.

I would also take in the salt water about the town [of Calais], but I cannot do it, by reason I should infect our own water wherewith we brew: and, notwithstanding all I can do, our brewers be so behindhand in grinding and otherwise, as we shall find that one of our greatest lacks. I therefore make all the haste and provision I can there, and howsoever the matter go, must shortly be forced to let in the salt water.

The three men taken to-day be very ragged, and ill-appointed. In examining, they confess that " there is great misery in their camp, and great want of money and victuals." They say (and I partly believe it, because it almost appeareth to me), "their number to be 25,000 footmen, whereof 10,000 [are] Swiss; and 10,000 horsemen. The Duke of GUISE is already among them, and the only deviser and leader of this enterprise." They say also, "a shot from the Bridgeway to the Causeway yesterday, struck off the Master of the Camp's leg, called Captain GOURDAULT."

I am also perfectly advertised, both by these men and otherwise, that they have no great ordnance yet come, but look for it daily by sea. It is eighty pieces, whereof thirty be cannons: and are laden, with munition and victuals, in 140 vessels which shall land at Sandgate; or rather I think at Boulogne, it to be taken out of great ships [there], and so again embarked at Sandgate in lesser vessels, as they have done most part of their victuals and carriage that they have hitherto occupied [*used*]. And, surely, if your Majesty's ships had been on this shore, they might either have letted [*hindered*] their voyage; or, at the least, very much hindered it: and not unlike[ly] to have distressed them, being only small boats. Their ordnance that comes, shall be conveyed in the same sort: it may therefore please your Majesty to consider it.

I have also now fully discovered their enterprise; and am (as a man may be) most sure they will first attempt upon Rysbanke; and that way chiefly assail the town. Marry! I think they lie hovering in the country, for the coming of their great artillery, and also to be masters of the sea. And therefore I trust your Highness will haste over all things necessary for us with expedition.

Under your Majesty's reformation [*correction*], I think, if you please to set the passage at liberty for all men to come that would, bringing sufficient victuals for themselves for a season; I am of opinion there would be enow, and with more speed than can be made by order. Marry! then must it well be foreseen to transport with expedition, victuals hither.

I have written to the King's Majesty [PHILIP II.] of the enemies being here: and was bold humbly to beseech his Majesty to give commission to the governors of his frontiers [that] I might, in necessity, upon my letter, have 300 or 400 harquebussiers, Spaniards, that now be placed about St. Omer; whereof I thought it my duty to advertise your Majesty, for your pleasure, whether I may write to the Governors to that effect, upon his Majesty's answer, and take them or not?

I, with the rest of the Council here, are forced to put your Majesty to some charges: for having taken in a confused number of countrymen [*i.e., peasantry within the English Pale*], we must needs reduce them to order, and the commoners also; and have therefore called them into wages, and appointed Captains of the fittest men that presently [*at this moment*] be here.

I have placed DODD with his Band in Rysbank, and the rest of the extraordinary [*i.e., volunteer*] Bands be at the Bridge, and in the Brayes of this town.

As I was making this discourse, six Ensigns [*regiments*] of footmen, and certain Bands [*troops*] of horsemen, came from Sandgate by the downs, within the sight of Rysbank : on whom, that piece, and this town also, bestowed divers shots.

This evening, they have made their approach to Rysbank, without any artillery : and, as far as I can perceive, do mind to make the assault with ladders, hurdles, &c., and other things, and that way get it.

At Calais, the 2nd of January, at ten in the night, 1557.

As I was in communication with your Mayor and Aldermen, touching the state of this town (whom I find of marvellous good courage, and ready to live and die in this town), I received letters from my Lords of the Council, of your Majesty's aid provided for us.

I fear this shall be my last letter, for that the enemy will stop my passage ; but I will do what I can tidily [*duly from time to time*] to signify unto your Majesty, our state.

> Your Majesty's most humble and obedient
> servant and subject,
>
> WENTWORTH.

JOHN HIGHFIELD, Master of the Ordnance at Calais.

To the Queen, our sovereign Lady.

[Lord HARDWICK's *Miscellaneous State Papers.* i. 114. *Ed.* 1788.]

PLEASETH it your Highness to understand the Declaration of your humblest and faithful servant JOHN HIGHFIELD, concerning the besieging and loss of your Grace's town of Calais.

First, being appointed by your most honourable Council [*i.e., the Privy Council in Calais*] to repair into England [*on the previous 23rd May, see p.* 302]; I came. And after some intelligence that the French Army drew towards the English Pale, I was commanded to return with diligence to my charge at Calais; and I arrived there on New Year's Day in the morning, the enemy being encamped about Sandgate.

The said morning, after I had delivered letters to my Lord Deputy, from your Grace's said Council, the said Lord Deputy told me how the alarm was made the night before, and also what he thought meet for me to be done for the better furniture of those fortresses which were in most danger, as the Bulwarks of the High Country [*Froyton and Nesle*], Guisnes, Newhaven Bridge, and Rysbank: and also for the defence of the Low Country, because his Lordship thought their enterprise had tended only to the spoil thereof. Then I showed that there was a sufficient store of all munitions, and that I would send to all places as need required; which was done.

Item. On Sunday following [*2nd January,* 1558], we perceived the French ordnance was brought to their camp; whereby appeared that the enemy meant to batter some place: and thereupon were two mounts repaired for the better defence. At the same time, I desired to have some pioneers appointed to help the cannoneers, who were not forty in number, for the placing and entrenching of our great ordnance; which pioneers I could never get.

The same day, the enemy forced our men to forsake the Bulwarks of the High Country. And then it was moved to my Lord Deputy that the sea might be let in, as well to drown the Causeway beyond Newhaven Bridge, as also other places about the town : wherein was answered, " Not to be necessary without more appearance of besieging," and because that "the sea being entered in, should hinder the pastures of the cattle, and also the brewing of the beer."

The same day, my Lord took order that victuals and other necessaries should be sent to Newhaven Bridge for six days; which was done.

Item. On Monday [*3rd January*] in the morning, my Lord Deputy, with the rest of the Council there, perceiving that the enemy intended to approach nearer, were in doubt whether they might abandon the Low Country : and by advice, my Lord gave order that the Bailiff of Marke should appoint the servants and women of the Low Country, with their superfluous cattle, to draw (if need happened) into the Flemish Pale ; and the said Bailiff with his best men, to repair to Marke Church, and there to abide further orders.

The same morning before day, the enemy had made their approaches, and did batter both Newhaven Bridge and the Rysbank ; which were given up before nine o'clock.

The Captain of Newhaven Bridge had word sent him that if he saw no remedy to avoid the danger, that then he should retire with his company into the Town.

The Captain of Rysbank did, about the same time, surrender ; because, as he told me since, his pieces were all dismounted, and the soldiers very loth to tarry at the breach : wherein I know no more.

But after the enemy was entered, I caused the said Rysbank to be battered ; and when my Lord saw how little it profited, he commanded to cease.

The same day, the passages being both lost, the enemy planted their ordnance on the Sand Hill, to batter the north side of the town; and then I moved my Lord to call in as many countrymen [*English peasantry*] as he could, and to appoint them Captains and their several quarters, for the relief of those which did most commonly watch and attend on the walls. Who answered, " He had determined already so to do." Howbeit the women did more labour [*watch*] about the ramparts than the said countrymen; which, for lack of order in time, did absent themselves in houses and other secret places.

The same evening, Captain SALIGUES [or SELLYN] came into Calais; whereupon the people rejoiced, hoping some succour: but after that time, it was too late to receive help by land, because the French horsemen were entered the Low Country.

Item. On Tuesday [*4th January*] in the morning, the enemy began their battery to the Town; on which side I had placed fourteen brass pieces. Howbeit, within short time, the enemy having so commodious a place, did dismount certain of our best pieces, and consumed some of the gunners, which stood very open for lack of mounds and good fortification. For if the rampart had been finished, then might divers pieces have been brought from other places; which were above sixty in number, ready mounted: but lacking convenient place, and chiefly cannoneers and pioneers, it was hard to displace the French battery. Which counter battery could not have been maintained for lack of powder. For, at the beginning, having in store, 400 barrels; I found there was spent within five days, 100.

Item. On Wednesday [*5th January*], the enemy continued their battery on the town, without great hurt done, because they could not beat the foot of the wall, for that the *contremure* was of a good height, and we reinforced the breach, in the night, with timber, wool, and other matter sufficiently; and we looked that the enemy would have attempted the assault the same evening; whereupon I caused two flankers to be made ready, and also placed two bombards, by the help of the soldiers, appointing weapons and fireworks to be in readiness at the said breach. At which time, my Lord commanded the soldiers of the garrison to keep their ordinary wards, and Master GRIMSTON to the breach with the residue of the best soldiers. And then my Lord exhorted all men to fight, with other good words as in such cases appertaineth. And my Lord told me, divers times, that "although there came no succour; yet he would never yield, nor stand to answer the loss of such a town."

Item. On Thursday [*6th January*], began one other battery to the Castle; which being a high and weak wall without ramparts, was made [as]saultable the same day. Whereupon, the Captain of the Castle desired some more help to defend this breach, or else to know what my Lord thought best in that behalf. Then, after long debating, my Lord determined to have the towers overthrown, which one SAULLE took upon him to do ; notwithstanding, I said openly that " if the Castle were abandoned, it should be the loss of the Town."

The same night, my Lord appointed me to be at the breach of the town with him : and, about eight of the clock, the enemy waded over the haven, at the low water, with certain harquebussiers, to view the breaches ; and, coming to the Castle, found no resistance, and so entered. Then the said SAULLE failed to give fire unto the train of powder [see p. 330].

Then my Lord, understanding that the enemy were entered into the Castle, commanded me to give order for battering of the Castle ; whereupon incontinent there were bent three cannons and one saker [p. 399] before the gate, to beat the bridge ; which, being in the night, did not greatly annoy.

The same time, Master Marshall [Sir ANTHONY AUCHER, see p. 292] with divers soldiers, came towards the Castle, lest the enemy should enter the town also. And after we had skirmished upon the bridge, seeing no remedy to recover the Castle, we did burn and break the said bridge : and there was a trench immediately cast before the Castle, which was [the] only help at that time.

Within one hour after, upon necessity of things, [my Lord] determined to send a trumpet with a herald, declaring that " If the Frenchmen would send one gentleman, then he would send one other in gage." Whereupon my Lord sent for me, and commanded that I should go forth of the town for the same purpose ; wherein I desired his Lordship that he would send some other, and rather throw me over the walls. Then he spake likewise to one WINDEBANKE, and to MASSINGBERD, as I remember, which were both to go unto such service.

Then my Lord sent for me again, in PEYTON's house ; and being eftsoons commanded by the Council there, I went forth with a trumpet [trumpeter], and received in a French gentleman : who, as I heard, was brought to my Lord Deputy's house, and treated upon some Articles ; which were brought, within one hour, by one HALL, merchant of the staple.

Then Monsieur D'ANDELOT entered the town with certain French gentlemen ; and the said HALL and I were brought to

Monsieur DE GUISE, who lay in the sand hills by Rysbank, and there the said HALL delivered a bill: and we were sent to Monsieur D'ESTREES' tent.

The Friday after [*7th January*], Monsieur D'ESTREES told me that my Lord Deputy had agreed to render the town with loss of all the goods, and fifty prisoners to remain.

On Saturday [*8th January*], he brought me into the town, willing me to tell him what ordnance, powder, and other houses did belong unto my office; because he would reserve the same from spoiling by the French soldiers. And after he had knowledge that all my living was on that side [*i.e., he had only his Mastership of the Ordnance at Calais*], he was content that I should depart into Flanders.

Notwithstanding, I was driven off till Wednesday, [*12th January*]. Then he said, "He would send me away, if I would promise him to make suit that his son might be returned in exchange for the Captain of the Castle," who, being prisoner, desired me also to travail in it, for he would rather give 3,000 crowns [*=£900 then=about £9,000 now*], than remain a prisoner. Whereupon I promised to inquire and labour in the same matter to the best of my power.

On my said return into the town, I found my wife, which showed me that, in my absence, she had bestowed my money and plate to the value of £600 [*=about £6,000 now*]; which was found before my coming, saving one bag with 350 crowns [*=£105=about £1,000 now*], which I offered to give unto Monsieur D'ESTREES if he would promise me, on his honour, to despatch me on horseback to Gravelines [*then held by the Spaniards*]. Which he did.

And there I met with Monsieur DE VANDEVILLE, to whom I told, that "I thought the enemy would visit him shortly"; and, among other things, I inquire where Monsieur D' ESTREES' son did lay; who told me, "He was at Bruges."

Then, at my coming to Dunkirk, there were divers Englishmen willing to serve [*i.e., in PHILIP II.'s army*]: whereupon I spake to the Captain of the town; who advised me to move it to the Duke of SAVOY.

Then I rode to Bruges, beseeching him to consider the poor men, and how willing they were to serve the King's Majesty, if they might be employed. Then he answered, that he "thought my Lord of PEMBROKE would shortly arrive at Dunkirk and then he would take order."

Further, the said Duke asked me, "After what sort the town was lost?"

I answered that "The cause was not only by the weakness of the Castle, and the lack of men; but also I thought there was some treason, for, as I heard, there were some escaped out of the town: and the Frenchmen told me, that they had intelligence of all our estate within the town."

Then I put the Duke in remembrance of Guisnes; who told me, that "he would succour the Castle, if it were kept four or five days."

Then I took leave to depart from him, and when I was going out of the house, he sent his Captain of his Guard to commit me to prison, where I have remained nine weeks, [*January—March*, 1558],without any matter laid to my charge; saving he sent to me, within fourteen days after, to declare in writing, after what sort the town was lost, which I did as nigh as I could remember.

And at the Duke's next return to Bruges, I sent him a supplication, desiring that, if any information were made against me, I might answer it in England, or otherwise at his pleasure.

[In the Public Record Office, *State Papers, Foreign, MARY,* is the following letter in French.

1558   *EMANUEL PHILIBERT, Duke of SAVOY to Queen MARY.*
March 14.   She will have been advertised that, soon after the French had entered Calais, JOHN HIGHFIELD, late Master of the Artillery
St. Omer.   there, came to Bruges. From strong suspicion that there had been an understanding between him and the French, had caused him to be arrested and detained at Bruges, where he has been until now.

Lately, while repassing through that town, was importuned by the prisoner's wife to set him free. Sends her under the charge of a French gentleman, FRANCIS DU BOURCH, the bearer.]

Whereupon he took order to send me hither [*i.e., to England*] without paying any part of my charges, which I have promised to answer.

Most humbly praying your Highness to consider my poor estate, and willing heart, which I bear, and am most bounden to your Grace's service: beseeching God to conserve your Majesty in all felicity.

JOHN FOX, the Martyrologist.

Mistress THORPE's Escape at Calais.

[Actes and Monumentes, p. 1702, Ed. 1563.]

HE worthy works of the LORD's mercy toward His people be manifold, and cannot be comprehended: so that who is he living in the earth almost, who hath not experienced the helping hand of the LORD, at some time or other upon him?

Amongst many other, what a piece of GOD's tender providence was shewed, of late, upon our English brethren and countrymen, what time Calais was taken by the tyrant GUISE (a cruel enemy to GOD's truth, and to our English nation); and yet by the gracious provision of the LORD, few, or none at all, of so many that favoured CHRIST and His Gospel, miscarried in that terrible Spoil.

In the number of whom, I know a godly couple, one JOHN THORPE and his wife, which fear the LORD and loveth His truth; who being sick the same time, were cast out into the wild fields, harbourless, desolate, and despairing of all hope of life; having their young infant moreover taken from them in the said fields, and carried away by the soldiers. Yet the LORD so wrought, that the poor woman, being almost past recovery of life, was fetched and carried, the space of well nigh a mile, by aliens whom they never knew, into a village, where she was recovered for that night.

Also the next day, coming towards England, she chanced into the same inn at the next town, where she found her young child sitting by the fireside.

Lord GREY of Wilton, Governor of Guisnes.

Letter to Queen MARY, 4th January, 1558. 7 a.m.

[State Papers. Foreign, MARY, Vol. xii. No. 711.]

Y MOST bounden duty humbly. premised to your Majesty. Whereas I have heretofore always in effect written nothing to your Highness but good, touching the service and state of your places here; I am now constrained, with woful heart, to signify unto your Majesty these ensuing.

The French have won Newhaven Bridge, and thereby entered into all the Low Country and the marshes between this [*Guisnes*] and Calais. They have also won Rysbanke, whereby they be now master of that haven.

And this last night past, they have placed their ordnance of battery against Calais, and are encamped at St. Peter's Heath before it: so that I now am clean cut off from all relief and aid which I looked to have (both out of England, and from Calais) and know not how to have help by any means, either of men or victuals.

There resteth now none other way for the succour of Calais and the rest of your Highness's pieces on this side, but a power of men out of England, or from the King's Majesty [PHILIP II.]; or from both, without delay, able to distress and keep them from victuals coming to them, as well by sea as land; which shall force them to leave their siege to the battle, or else drive them to a greater danger.

For lack of men out of England, I shall be forced to abandon the Town [*of Guisnes*], and take in the soldiers thereof for the Castle. I have made as good provision of victuals as I could, by any means, out of the country; with which, GOD willing! I doubt not to defend and keep this piece as long as any man, whosoever he be, having no better provision, and furniture of men and victuals than I have:

wherein your Grace shall well perceive that I will not fail to do the duty of a faithful subject and Captain, although the enemy attempt never so stoutly; according to the trust reposed in me.

I addressed letters presently to the King's Majesty by this bearer, most humbly desiring aid from him; according to the effect aforesaid.

I might now very evil[ly] have spared this bringer, my servant and trusty Officer here, in this time of service. Howbeit considering the great importance of his message, I thought him a meet man for the purpose; desiring your Majesty to credit him fully, and to hear him at large, even as directly as your Grace would hear me to open my mind in this complaint of imminent danger.

Thus trusting for relief and comfort forthwith from your Majesty for the safeguard of Calais, and other your pieces here; I take my leave most humbly of your Grace.

At your Highness's Castle of Guisnes, most assured English even to the death, the 4th January, 1557, at seven of the clock in the morning.

Your Majesty's most humble servant,

And obedient servant,

WILLIAM GREY.

Thomas Churchyard, the Poet.

Share in, and Eye Witness account of the Siege of Guisnes. 11th–22nd January, 1558, A.D.

[*A General Rehearsal of Wars, &c.* 1579. The title in the headline is *CHURCHYARD's Choice.*]

IR WILLIAM DRURY, now [*in* 1579] Lord Justice of Ireland, was so inclined to martial affairs, that, when foreign wars were ended, he sought entertainment at Guisnes, and those parts; which had war with the French, for King PHILLIP's Quarrel. And he, having charge, and a lusty Band of Horsemen, did many things that merit good liking.

For at that time, [there] was much ado: a Band [*regiment*] of horsemen, very well appointed and full of gentlemen, was sent from [Sir THOMAS CHENEY, K.G.] the Lord Warden [of the Cinque Ports], an honourable and a worthy gentleman, most full of nobleness; the Lord CHENEY's father, now living. In this band, and belonging to that charge, were sundry of the KEYES, gentlemen of good service: Master CRIPPES having the leading of all that company. There were sent, in like sort, from the Prince [*Sovereign, i.e., Queen MARY*]: Master WILLIAM HERBERT's (of St. Gillian) brother, called Master GEORGE HERBERT, with a Band of footmen; and one Captain BORNE, whose Lieutenant I was, at the siege of Guisnes.

These bands, a good season before Calais and Guisnes were taken, joining with other bands of Calais, did make divers journeys into Bollinnoyes [*the Boullognois, or district round Boulogne*]; and sped very well: Sir WILLIAM DRURY, at every service, deserved no little praise; and one Captain WINNIBANK, an ancient soldier, was oftentimes so forward, that he was once run through with a lance. Many Gentlemen in those services did well and worthily: and sundry times the Lord Warden's Band was to be praised.

And, at length, a voyage was made, by the consent and whole power of Calais and Guisnes, to fetch a prey from Boulogne gates; Monsieur SNARPOULE [? *SENARPONT*] then being Governor of Boulogne : but we could not handle the matter so privily, but the French, by espial, had gotten word thereof. Notwithstanding, as soldiers commonly go forward with their device, so we marched secretly all the whole night to come to our proposed enterprise : with our footmen, whereof Sir HARRY PALMER, a man of great experience, had the leading. He remained, with the whole power of [the] footmen, near the Black Neasts, as a stale [*decoy*] to annoy the enemy, and succour for such as were driven in, if any such occasion came. So the Horse Bands [*troops*] brake into the country, and pressed near Boulogne ; where there was a great number of gallant soldiers to receive them: but our horsemen, making small account of the matter, began to prey [upon] the country, and drive a booty from the face of the enemy. The French horsemen, taking their advantage, offered a skirmish, to detract time, till better opportunity served to give a charge. This courageous bickering grew so hot, that the French bands began to show; and our men must abide a shock, or retire hardily with some foil : whereupon the chiefest of our horsemen charged those of the French that were nearest danger; by which attempt, the French stayed a while. But, upon small pause, they charged our men again, and overthrew of the " Black Lances " a thirty: carrying away with them into Boulogne, eighteen gentlemen, prisoners. This skirmish began at seven o'clock in the morning; and lasted, in very great service, till a leven [*eleven*]. From this overthrow, came divers soldiers, sore wounded, to our Foot bands [*companies*] ; whose heaviness made the valiant sort pluck up their hearts, and seek a revenge.

Then, albeit, that Foot Captains and gentlemen seldom leave their Bands, and venture beyond their charge (a rule to be much regarded!), yet the stoutest Captains and gentlemen found means to horse themselves on cart horses and victuallers' nags : and put certain scarfs, in manner of guidons [*standards*] on staves' [*spears'*] ends ; showing those guidons under a hill in several sorts, sometimes appearing with twenty men, sometimes with fifty. And, last of all, made show of all our number, which was not fifty; and so, with a courageous cry, set upon the enemy (leaving some of these devised guidons behind on the hill top), and charged them with such a fury that they left their booty, and stood to their defence : but, in fine, were forced to retire, for by the little stay we held the enemy in, our footmen had leisure to march ; the sound of whose drums gave no great courage to the French. For they thereon, gave back, and left some of their best soldiers behind them ; whom we brought to Guisnes : driving the prey before us, that was gotten in the morning, lost in a skirmish, and recovered again at noon. At this service, were Sir WILLIAM DRURY, Captain ALEXANDER of Newnham Bridge, Captain CRIPPES, Captain KEYES, and three of his brethren, Captain GEORGE HERBERT, and sundry others, in like manner, that merit good respect.

Our power met many times together ; and did much hurt in the Boullognois. We besieged Fines Castle, and wan it : and Blossling Church, and overthrew it ; and killed all the men that we found therein, because Sir HARRY PALMER was there hurt through the arm, with a shot.

A long season, our fortune was good ; till, at length, by some oversight or mishap (Let the blame fall where it ought !) we lost Calais and Guisnes.

But a little, I pray you ! give me leave to touch truly the Siege of Guisnes : not because I had some charge there ; but because sundry reports hath been raised thereof, by those that never thoroughly knew or understood the matter.

The very truth is, after Calais was won, and that all hope was taken from us of any succour out of England, our General, the honourable Lord GREY [of Wilton], that is dead [he died in 1562], and Master LEWIS DIVE [p. 327], his Lieutenant, Sir HARRY PALMER, and all the Captains of Guisnes, determined to abide the worst that Fortune or the French could do.

And the day [13th of January, 1558] of the first approach the enemy made, we offered a hot and stout skirmish ; but being driven in by an over great power, though our whole people were 1,300 men, and kept the Town awhile. But considering the Castle to be strongest, and doubting [fearing] that by a Cambozade or sudden assault, the town might be won, for it was but weak ; we retired our whole power into

the Castle: and so manned the base Court, the Braies, and
Bulwarks, the Keep, the Catte, the Heart of the Castle, and
all that was necessary, with double men.

At the present siege, there came out of Flanders, fifty
valiant Spaniards; and a band of Burgundians, Monsieur
DIEFFKIE, being their Captain. Monsieur MOUNT DRAGON
was leader of the Spaniards: who were placed in the Braies;
where Captain LAMBERT had some shot [*harquebussiers*] to
succour them.

The Burgundians were placed in Mary Bulwark; with
Captain BORNE's Band, whose Lieutenant I was. Against
this Bulwark, which was thought impregnable, the [Frenchmen's]
great battery was planted: albeit, three or four days
[*15th–18th January, see pp. 296-97*] were spent (we held the
enemy such play), before the battery was planted.

One day, we issued [forth], and set upon Monsieur [*i.e., the
Duke*] DE GUISE, as he was in a place called Mill Field,
viewing the ground; and had taken him, had he not left his
cloak behind him: of the which white cloak, one of our
Gentlemen had hold of. And though he was succoured, we
brought away some of his company: and retired with little
loss or none at all. [Sir ARTHUR], the Lord GREY that now
is [1579], was at the hard escape of Monsieur DE GUISE.

We set upon a great troop of horsemen, not long before
this, that came from the spoil of Calais; and took numbers
of them. I had, for my part, a couple of fair horses and a
prisoner. At both these services, were old Captain ANDREA,
Captain JOHN SAVAGE, and a sufficient number of lusty soldiers.

We made divers sallies, but that prevailed not. For the
battery went off, and many other great cannons did beat at
the high towers; the stones whereof did marvellously annoy
us: and the shot was so great; and the enemy had gotten
such great advantage of ground, that we could not walk, nor
go safely any way within the Castle. For our General and
Sir HARRY PALMER sitting on a form, devising for our commodity,
were in such danger, that a cannon shot took
away the form, and brake Sir HARRY PALMER's leg; of which
hurt, he died in Paris after. And a great shot took off
Master WAKE's head, as he was sleeping under a great tree.
So sundry, that thought themselves safe, were so dribbed at
with cannon shot, that they never knew who did hurt them.

Well, the time drew on, after the breach was made, we
must defend the assault that was given to Mary Bulwark ;
which stood out[side] of the Castle, and far from succour of
any : because the gate was rammed up; and we could not
pass into the Castle but by the way, first, along the Braies,
and then, between two gates.   Which way, the enemy had
espied : and placed many great shot, full upon that passage.

Now [*i.e.*, 18*th January*, 1558] Monsieur DIFFKIE, Captain
BORNE, Captain OSWOLD LAMBERT [*with their companies*], and
the fifty Spaniards, [*to the number in all of about 450 men*] were
forced to abide the assault; which began at eleven o'clock,
and lasted till night.   MOUNT DRAGON came into Mary Bulwark, and three gentlemen more ; and stood stoutly to our
defence : two of whom were slain.   My Captain's head was
smitten off with a cannon's shot : and unto our Band were left
no more but one Master HOLFORD and I, to guide the whole
company.   And Captain DIFFKIE was wounded to the death,
whose Band fought manfully in the revenge of their Captain.
The old Captain ANDREA, covetous of fame, was desirous
to have our fellowship : but he had no Band [*company*] nor
people to do us pleasure.   Captain LAMBERT was crossed
[*struck*] with a great shot ; and mine armour, with the breaking of a great piece, was stricken flat upon my body ; but [it]
being unbraced, I might continue the service.   Which
service, in mine opinion, was so terribly handled by the
French (Monsieur D'ANDELOT being the leader of the
assault), that both Englishman, Burgundian, and Spaniard,
at that Bulwark, had enough to do to keep the enemy out :
and, as I believe, at this assault, we lost 150 good soldiers.

But the night coming on, the French surceased their fury,
and yet kept themselves closely, under the top of the breach,
where our shot nor flankers could do them no harm : for all
our great ordnance was dismounted, long before the enemy
made any approach for the giving of an assault.

The next day [*the 19th of January*], within three half hours,
the battery had beaten the breach so bare (it moulded away,
like a hillock of sand) that we [*reduced now to about 300 men*]
were forced to fight on our knees.   Having been kept waking
all the night before, with false allarummes [*alarms*] ; our men
began to faint, and wax weary of working at the breach : but
we defended Mary Bulwark so well all that dangerous day,

that the French lost 1,000 soldiers, by their own confession, at the same service; and yet the assault endured to the very dark night, with as much cruelty as could be devised. And always when the enemy's first men did wax feeble with labour; there was a second and new relief of fresh bands to continue the assault: so that, as long as the daylight served, it seemed by the fight, a bloody broil hath no end, nor season to take breath in; which certainly would have daunted any heart living.

The next night, was so plied with politic practices, that we had scarcely leisure to take any rest or sustentation. And, indeed, with overwatching, some of our men fell asleep "in the middle of the tale" and time of greatest necessity to debate and argue of those things that pertained to life and liberty, and to avoid utter servitude and shame [*i.e.*, *they slept in the course of the fight*].

And now we, that were without the Castle, might hear great business and stir throughout the whole body and heart of the piece [*fortress*].

For, the next morning [20*th of January*, 1558], which was the third day we were assaulted, our General looked for a general assault, and to be roundly assailed: as, of troth, he was. In the meanwhile, we might speak one to another afar off, and our friends answered us over the wall; for nearer together, we might not come: and for succour or aid to our soldiers in Mary Bulwark, we hoped not after. Every man was occupied with his own business and charge; that no one person might be spared from his place.

Well, as GOD would permit, the poor Spaniards [in the Braie] and such Burgundians as were left alive in Mary Bulwark, fell to make a counterscarf, to beat out the enemy from the Braie, when the Bulwark should be won: as it was likely to be lost, the breach was so bare, and the entry for the enemy was so large; for, in a manner, they might assault our Bulwark round about, on all sides. And they did lodge at the very edge of the breach, to the number of 2,000, of their bravest Bands: minding to assail us, as soon as the day began to peep out of the skies.

Which they performed, when the third day approached. For a general assault was given to every place of the Castle: which assault endured till the very night came on. The

French, in this assault, wan the Base Court; and were ready to set fire under the gate, and blow it up with powder.

Monsieur D'ANDELOT, in his own person, with 2,000 soldiers, entered the Mary Bulwark; who slew the Spaniards in the Braie: and forced, as many Burgundians and English as were left alive, which were but 15 (Captain ANDREA, Captain LAMBERT, and MYSELF; with twelve common soldiers) out of 400, to leap down into the dykes, and so to scramble for their lives; and creep into a hole of a brick wall that my Lord GREY had broken out to receive such as escaped from the assault. But when we had entered the hole in the wall, the French followed at our heels; and we, to save our lives, turned again, bending pikes against the passage, and so shot off one hargaboze [*harquibus*]: by which means, the enemy followed no further.

And yet we were in as great distress as before. For we were between two gates: and at the gate we should have entered, were two great cannon, ready charged to be shot off, to drive them back that would have set fire on the gate. And the cry and noise was so great and terrible, on all sides, that we could not be heard to speak. But, as GOD would, Master LEWIS DIVE [*p.* 323] (now, a man of worship in Bedfordshire) heard my voice. Then I plied the matter so sore, for life: so that, with much ado, Master DIVE received us into the heart of the Castle. And yet, in the opening of the gate, the French were like to enter pelley melley [*pell mell*] with us, if a cannon shot had not made place, whiles the gate was a shutting.

But now, we were no sooner come before my Lord GREY: but all the soldiers cried, "Yield up the Castle, upon some reasonable composition!" And when the soldiers saw they could not have the Castle yielded; they threatened "to fling my Lord GREY over the walls": and that was determined; if my Lord had not prevented [*forestalled*] them with a policy. Whereupon the Captains were called together; and there, they agreed to send me to Monsieur DE GUISE, with an offer, that "If we might all march, with bag and baggage, ensign displayed, and six pieces of ordnance: we would yield the Castle into the hands of the French."

Now it was night, and I must be let out at Master HARRY NORWITCH his Bulwark; but neither Drum nor Trumpet

went with me : because a Trumpeter was slain as he sounded
to have a parley ; and, as I heard say, a Drum[mer] that
would have followed me, was shot in the leg. But there was
no remedy. I must wade over the water, in which there lay
certain galthroppes, as they term them, which were great
boards, full of long spikes of iron ; on the which, having good
boots and a stay in my hand, I was taught daintily to tread :
and the night was so dark, that the enemy might not take any
good mark of me, albeit they shot divers times.

So, with some hazard, and no great hope to attain that I was
sent for, I was taken by the watch ; and brought to Monsieur
De Guise's tent, where the Duke D'Aumale and many great
Estates were in presence.

My message being said, with due reverence made : the
Duke told me, that "all our ordnance was dismounted, and
that thereby our malice was cut off ; and we could not do
his camp any annoyance. Wherefore," said he, " this was a
stout brag, to seek a capitulation with such advantage upon."

I replied to his Excellency, and told, " We had flankers
[guns with a cross fire] and other great pieces, which would
not be discovered till the next assault : " declaring likewise,
" Our soldiers had sworn rather to die in their [own] defence,
than not to march away, like mine men of war."

The noblemen, on this mine answer, bade me " Return !
and with the rest of the Castle, to do the worst they could !"

So I departed, and the Duke of Guise beholding, as he
thought, we were resolved to see the uttermost of fortune ;
called me back again : and fell to questions and arguments
with me, such as I liked not [i.e., he tried to bribe Churchyard in some way] ; but other answer did I not make, than
you have heard before. Wherewith, he called for some meat ;
and made me to sit down.

After I had a little refreshed myself, I demanded to know
his pleasure.

Who straightways told me, " There was no help to be had ;
but to become all captives and prisoners to the French King."

" Not so, Sir," I answered ; " and that should the next
assault make trial of."

Then, he went to talk with the Noblemen ; and there, they
concluded, " That the soldiers should march away with bag
and baggage : and the Captains and Officers should remain

prisoners:" which I knew would not be liked: and so desired to be sent to my Lord GREY.

But when I came into the Castle, and the soldiers had gotten word that they might march away at their will : they came to me, and threatened me with great words, commanding me, "To make despatch, and yield up the fort !" For they said, "Since the matter is in talk, and likely to be brought to a good purpose; they would cut my throat, if I made not, hastily, an end of the case." And thereupon had they made a great hole in a wall ; and so they thrust me out among the Almains, who rudely handled me.

But my Lord GREY, at my departure, bade me tell the Duke, that the Almains were about to break into the Castle, and to set the gate afire: and my Lord said, " He would shoot off his great ordnance among them; if the Law of Arms were not better observed ! "

But, in the meantime, at another place was entered Monsieur DE TRE [*D'ESTREES*] Master of the [French] Ordnance; and [Sir ARTHUR] the Lord GREY that now is, was sent to the Camp, for the pawn [*security*] of Monsieur D'ESTREES.

But I was come to Monsieur DE GUISE before those things were finished: and had told him my message. And he, like a noble Prince and faithful Captain, rode to the gate (causing me to mount behind Master HARRY DUDLEY); where the Almains were busily occupied about some naughty practice : and, with a great truncheon, he stroke divers of the Almains and others, to make them retire; and laying [a] load [*i.e., of blows*] about him, he made such way, that the gate was free, and the capitulation was, at leisure, talked of.

But I was not suffered to enter any more into the Castle; and so stayed as a prisoner.

Notwithstanding, look what promise Monsieur DE GUISE made, it was so well kept and observed that our soldiers marched away, with all their wealth, money, and weapons. And great wealth was borne by them from Guisnes: insomuch that divers poor soldiers were made thereby, for all [the] days of their life after. And this is to be noted. There was great honour in the Duke of GUISE. For the Bands [*originally* 1,300 *p.* 298; *but now about* 500, *having lost* 800, *see below*] that parted [*departed*] (either sick or sound, hurt or whole) were honestly conveyed, and truly dealt withal ; even as long as they were in any danger, albeit they had great sums of money and treasure with them: and the General with his Captains and Officers were courteously used, so long as they were in the Duke of Guise his camp.

And, to say the truth, I think our peace was not so dishonourable, as some report. For

Succour, had we no hope of.

The next assault had overthrown us.

The whole members [*i.e., the external fortifications*] of the Castle were cut off from us.

There remained but the bare body of the Castle in our custody.

The enemy's cannons did beat us from the breach *on the inside*.

The Castle was subject to every shot; both from the Keep, the Catte, and the Mary Bulwark.

The French possessed all the special places of our strength and comfort.

The best and chiefest of our soldiers were slain, or lay maimed in most miserable state.

And we had lost 800 men in these assaults and services; which did their duty so well, that the enemy confessed that they had lost 4,000, before we could be brought to any *parley* or composition.

But some of our Officers, by craft and cunning, escaped homewards out of the Frenchmen's hands; came to Court, and made up their Bands [*companies*] again; to the great reproach of those that meant no such matters. So, by that subtilty and shift, they that escaped got a pay or some reward of the Prince: and those that abode out the brunt and hazard of the bloody broil, were left in prison.

And the world thought, by seeing so many come home, we had lost but a few at the siege of Guisnes; which is otherwise to be proved and affirmed for a truth; when true trial [*inquiry*] shall be made.

Calais was lost before, I cannot declare how. But well I wot, Sir Anthony Ager, a stout gentleman, and a valiant Knight, there lost his life: and one Captain Saule was terribly burnt with powder, in making a train to destroy the enemy

John Fox, the Martyrologist.

The death of Queen Mary.

[*The Ecclesiastical History* ii. 2296, *Ed.* 1570].

Ow then after these so great afflictions falling upon this realm from the first beginning of Queen Mary's reign, wherein so many men, women, and children were burned; many imprisoned, and in prisons starved, divers exiled, some spoiled of goods and possessions, a great number driven from house and home, so many weeping eyes, so many sobbing hearts, so many children made fatherless, so many fathers bereft of their wives and children, so many vexed in conscience, and divers against conscience constrained to recant, and, in conclusion, never a good man in all the realm but suffered something during all the time of this bloody persecution. After all this, I say, now we are come at length, the LORD be praised! to the 17th day of November, which day, as it brought to the persecuted members of CHRIST rest from their careful mourning, so it easeth me somewhat likewise of my laborious writing; by the death, I mean, of Queen MARY. Who, being long sick before, upon the said 17th day of November, 1558, about three or four a clock in the morning, yielded her life to nature, and her kingdom to Queen ELIZABETH, her sister.

As touching the manner of whose death, some say that she died of a tympany [*dropsy*]; some, by her much sighing before her death, supposed she died of thought and sorrow. Whereupon her Council seeing her sighing, and desirous to know the cause, to the end they might minister the more ready consolation unto her, feared, as they said, that "She took that thought for the King's Majesty her husband, which was gone from her."

To whom she answering again, "Indeed," said she, "that

may be one cause; but that is not the greatest wound that pierceth my oppressed mind!" but what that was, she would not express to them.

Albeit, afterwards, she opened the matter more plainly to Master RYSE and Mistress CLARENTIUS [*p.* 362] (if it be true that they told me, which heard it of Master RYSE himself); who (then being most familiar with her, and most bold about her) told her that "They feared she took thought for King PHILIP's departing from her."

"Not that only," said she, "but when I am dead and opened; you shall find Calais lying in my heart," &c.

And here an end of Queen MARY and her persecution. Of which Queen, this truly, may be affirmed, and left in story for a perpetual Memorial or Epitaph, for all Kings and Queens that shall succeed her, to be noted, that before her, never was read in story of any King or Queen in England, since the time of King LUCIUS, under whom, in time of peace, by hanging, heading, burning, and prisoning, so much Christian blood, so many Englishmen's lives were spilled within this realm, as under the said Queen MARY, for the space of four years, was to be seen; and I beseech the LORD may never be seen hereafter.

JOHN FOX, the Martyrologist.

The Imprisonment of the Princess ELIZABETH.

John Fox, the Martyrologist.

The Imprisonment of the Princess Elizabeth.

[*Actes and Monumentes, &c., p.* 1710. *Ed.* 1563.]

IRST, therefore, to begin with her princely birth, being born at Greenwich, *anno* 1534 [1533], of the famous and victorious Prince, King HENRY VIII., and of the noble and most virtuous Lady, Queen ANNE her mother; sufficiently is committed to the story before. Also of the solemn celebration of her baptism in the said town, and Grey Friar's Church, of Greenwich; having to her godfather, THOMAS CRANMER, Archbishop of Canterbury.

After that, she was committed to godly tutors and governors. Under whose institution her Grace did so greatly increase, or rather excel in all manner of virtue and knowledge of learning, that I stand in a doubt whether is more to be commended in this behalf, the studious diligence of them that brought her up, or the singular towardness of her own princely nature to all virtuous disposition; so apt and so inclinable: both being notwithstanding the gifts of GOD, for which we are all bound to give Him thanks. What tongue is it that Her Grace knoweth not? What language she cannot speak? What liberal art or science, she hath not learned? And what virtue wherewith her noble breast is not garnished? In counsel and wisdom, what Councillor will go beyond Her Majesty?

If the goodness of nature, joined with the industry of Her Grace's institution, had not been in her marvellous, how many things were there, besides the natural infirmity of that sex, the tenderness of youth, the nobility of estate, allurements of the world, persuasions of flatterers, abundance of wealth and pleasures, examples of the Court, enough to carry her Grace away after the common fashion and rule of many other Ladies, from gravity to lightness, from study to ease, from wisdom to vanity, from religion to superstition, from godliness to gawishness, to be pricked up with pride, to be garish in apparel, to be fierce in condition?

Eloquently is it spoken, and discreetly meant of TULLY, the eloquent orator: "To live," saith he, "a good man in other places, is no great matter: but in Asia, to keep a sober and temperate life, that is a matter indeed praiseworthy!" So here, why may I not affirm without flattery, that [which] every man's conscience can testify? In that age, that sex, in such State and fortune, in so great occasions, so many incitements: in all these, to retain so sober conversation, so temperate condition, such mildness of manners, such humbleness of stomach, such clemency in forgiving, such travailing in study: briefly, in the midst of Asia, so far to degenerate from all Asia; it hath not lightly been seen in Europe! Hitherto, it hath been seen in very few. Whereby it may appear not only what education, or what Nature may do; but what GOD, above Nature, hath wrought in her noble breast, adorning it with so worthy virtues.

Of which her princely qualities and virtuous disposition, such as have been conversant with her youth can better testify. That which I have seen and read, I trust I may boldly repeat without suspicion either of feigning or flattery. For so I have read, written, and testified of Her Grace by [according to] one, both learned and also that can say something in this matter. Who in a certain book, by him set forth, entreating of Her Grace's virtuous bringing up, what discreet, sober, and godly women she had about her; speaketh, namely, of two points in Her Grace to be considered. One concerning her moderate and maidenly behaviour; the other one concerning her training up in learning and good letters. Declaring, first, for her virtuous moderation of life, that seven years after her father's death [*i.e. in* 1553], she had so little pride of stomach, so little delight in glistering gazes of the world, in gay apparel, rich attire, and precious jewels, that in all that time [*i.e., through her brother* EDWARD's *reign*] she never looked upon those, that her father left her (and which other Ladies commonly be so fond upon) but only once; and that against her will. And, moreover, after that, so little gloried in the same, that there came neither gold nor stone upon her head, till her sister enforced her to lay off her former soberness, and bear her company in her glistening gains : yea, and then, she so ware it, as every man might see that her body bare that which her heart misliked. Wherein the virtuous prudence of this Princess, not reading but following the words of PAUL and PETER, well considered True Nobility to consist not in circumstances of the body, but in substance of the heart ; not in such things which deck the body, but in that which dignifieth the mind, shining and blazing more bright than pearl or stone, be it never so precious.

Again, the said author, further proceeding in the same matter, thus testifieth, that he knew a great man's daughter receiving from the Lady MARY, before she was Queen, goodly apparel of tinsel, cloth of gold and velvet, laid on with parchment lace of gold. When she saw it she said, " What shall I do with it ? "

" Marry ! " said a gentlewoman, " wear it ! "

" Nay ! " quoth she, " that were a shame ! To follow my Lady MARY, against GOD's Word; and leave my Lady ELIZABETH, which followeth GOD's Word."

Let noble Ladies and gentlewomen here learn either to give, or to take good example given : and if they disdain to teach their inferiors, in well doing; yet, let it not shame them, to learn of their betters.

Likewise also at the coming in of the Scottish Queen [in 1551], when all the other Ladies of the Court flourished in their bravery, with their hair frounced and curled, and double curled; yet she altered nothing; but to the shame of them all, kept her old maidenly shamefastness.

Let us now come to the second point, declaring how she hath been trained in learning; and that not vulgar and common, but the purest and the best, which is most commended at these days, as the Tongues, Arts, and GOD's Word. Wherein she so exceedingly profited, as the foresaid author doth witness, that being under twenty years of age [*i.e., before* 1554], she was not, in the best kind of learning, inferior to those that all their life time had been brought up in the Universities, and were counted jolly fellows.

And that you may understand that there hath not been,

nor is in her, learning only without nature, and knowledge without towardness to practice; I will tell what hath been heard of her first schoolmaster [JOHN AYLMER], a man very honest and learned: who reported of her, to a friend of his, that "He learned every day more of her, than she of him." Which when it seemed to him a mystery, as indeed it was, and he therefore desired to know his meaning therein, he thus expounded it: " I teach her words," quoth he, " and she, me things. I teach her the tongues to speak; and her modestly and maidenly life teacheth me words to do. For," saith he, "I think she is the best inclined and disposed of any in all Europe."

It seemed to me a goodly commendation of her, and a witty saying of him.

Likewise [CASTIGLIONE] an Italian, which taught her his tongue (although that nation lightly praise not out of their own country), said once to the said party, that " He found in her two qualities, which are never lightly yokefellows in one woman; which were a singular wit, and a marvellous meek stomach."

If time and leisure would serve to peruse her whole life past, many other excellent and memorable examples of her princely qualities and singular virtues might here be noted; but none, in my mind, more worthy of commendation, or that shall set forth the fame of her heroical and princely renown more to all posterity, than the Christian patience, and incredible clemency of her nature showed in her afflictions, and towards her declared enemies. Such was then the wickedness and rage of that time, wherein what dangers and troubles were among the inferior subjects of this realm of England, may be easily gathered when such a Princess, of that Estate, being a King's daughter, a Queen's sister, and Heir Apparent to the Crown, could not escape without her cross.

And therefore, as we have hitherto discoursed [of] the afflictions and persecutions of the other poor members of CHRIST, comprehended in this History before; so likewise, I see no cause why the communion of Her Grace's afflictions also, among the other saints of CHRIST, ought to be suppressed in silence: especially seeing the great and marvellous workings of GOD's glory, chiefly in this Story, appeareth above all the rest.

And though I should, through ingratitude or silence, pass over the same; yet the thing itself is so manifest, that what Englishman is he which knoweth not the afflictions of Her Grace to have been far above the condition of a King's daughter: for there was no more behind, to make a very IPHIGENIA of her, but her offering up upon the altar of the scaffold.

In which her storms and tempests, with what patience Her Highness behaved herself, although it be best known to them who, then being her adversaries, had the minding [*imprisoning*] of her. Yet this will I say, by the way, that then she must needs be in her affliction, marvellous patient: which sheweth herself now, in this prosperity, to be utterly without desire of revenge; or else she would have given some token, ere this day, of remembrance, how she was handled.

It was no small injury that she suffered, in the Lord Protector's days, by certain venomous vipers! But to let that pass! was it no wrong, think you! or small injury that she sustained, after the death of King EDWARD, when they sought to defeat her and her sister from their natural inheritance and right to the Crown?

But to let that pass likewise! and to come more near to the late days of her sister, Queen MARY. Into what fear, what trouble of mind, and what danger of death was she brought?

First, with great solemnity, with bands of harnessed men [*i.e., in arms and armour*] (Happy was he that might have the carrying of her!) to be fetched up, as the greatest traitor in the world; clapped in the Tower: and, again, to be tossed from thence, from prison to prison, from post to pillar. At length, also prisoner in her own house; and guarded with a sort [*number*] of cutthroats, which ever gaped for the spoil of the same, that they might have been fingering of somewhat.

Which Story, if I should set forth at large, through all the particulars and circumstances of the same, and as the just occasion of the history requireth; peradventure, it would move offence to some, being yet alive. Yet notwithstanding, I intend, by the grace of CHRIST, therein to use such brevity and moderation as may be to the glory of GOD, the discharge of the Story, the profit of the reader, and hurt to none: suppressing the names of some, whom here, although I could recite, yet I thought not to be more cruel in hurting their name, than the Queen hath been in pardoning their life.

Therefore, now to enter into the description of the matter. First, to declare her undeserved troubles; and then, the most happy deliverance out of the same, this is the Story.

N THE beginning of Queen Mary's reign, mention is made before, how the Lady ELIZABETH, and the Lord COURTNEY were charged with false suspicion of [being being concerned in] Sir THOMAS WYATT'S rising [*in January*, 1554, *see p.* 207 *sqq.*]

Whereupon, Queen MARY, whether for that surmise, or for what other cause I know not, being offended with the said Lady ELIZABETH her sister, at that time lying in her house at Ashridge [*near Great Berkhampstead*], sent to her two Lords [*or rather WILLIAM, Lord HOWARD, Sir EDWARD HASTINGS, afterwards Lord HASTINGS of Loughborough; and Sir THOMAS CORNWALLIS*], and Sir JOHN WILLIAMS, afterwards Lord [WILLIAMS] of Thame, with their retinue, and troop of horsemen, to the number of 250, who at their sudden and unprovided [*unexpected*] coming [*on the 11th February*, 1554], found her at the same time, sore sick in bed, and very feeble and weak of body.

Whither, when they came; ascending up to Her Grace's Privy Chamber, willed there, one of her Ladies whom they met, to declare unto Her Grace that "There were certain Lords come from the Court, which had a message from the Queen."

Her Grace having knowledge thereof, was right glad of their coming: howbeit, being then very sick, and the night far spent, which was at ten of the clock, requested them by the messenger, that they would resort thither in the morning.

To this, they answered, and by the said messenger sent word again, that "They must needs see her; and would do so, in what case soever she were in." Whereat, the Lady being aghast, went to shew Her Grace their words; but they hastily following her, came rushing as soon as she, into Her Grace's chamber, unbidden.

At whose so sudden coming into her bedchamber, Her Grace being not a little amazed, said unto them, "My Lords!

is the haste such, that it might not have pleased you to come to-morrow, in the morning ? "

They made answer, that " They were right sorry to see Her Grace in that case."

" And I," quoth she, " am not glad to see you here, at this time of the night ! "

Whereunto, they answered that " They came from the Queen to do their message and duty ; which was to this effect, that the Queen's pleasure was that she should be at London, the 7th [? 12th] day of that present month."

Whereunto, she said, " My Lords ! no creature [can be] more glad than I, to come to Her Majesty ; being right sorry that I am not in case at this time, like to wait on her ; as you yourselves, my Lords ! do see and can well testify ! "

" Indeed, we see it true," quoth they, " that you do say ; for which we are very sorry : albeit we let you to understand that our Commission is such, and so straineth us, that we must needs bring you with us, either quick or dead."

Whereat she being amazed, sorrowfully said that " Their commission was very sore ! but yet, notwithstanding, she hoped it to be otherwise, and not so straight."

" Yes, verily ! " they answered.

Whereupon the Lords calling for two physicians, Doctor OWEN and Doctor WENDIF, demanded of them, " Whether she might be removed from thence, with life or not ? " whose answer and judgement was this, " That there was no impedimen to their judgement to the contrary ; but that she might travel without danger of life."

In conclusion, they willed her to prepare against the morning, at nine of the clock, to go with them, declaring that " they had brought with them, the Queen's litter for her."

After much talk, the Lords declaring how there was no prolonging of times and days, so departed to their chamber ; being entertained and cheered as appertained to their Honours.

On the next morrow [12th February], at the time prescribed, they had her forth as she was, very faint and feeble ; and in such case as she was ready to swoon three or four times between them. What should I speak here that [which] cannot well be expressed ! What a heavy house there was to behold the unreverent and doleful dealing of the Lords; but especially the careful fear and captivity of their innocent Lady and mistress.

Now to proceed in their journey. From Ashridge, all sick in the litter, she came to Redborne; where she was guarded all night.

From thence, to St. Albans, to Sir RALPH ROWLET's house; where she tarried that night all heavy, both feeble in body, and comfortless in mind.

From that place, they passed to Master DODD's house, at Mimms [*near Potters' Bar*]; where they also remained that night.

And so from thence, she came to Highgate: where she, being very sick, tarried that night and the next day: during which time of her abode, there came many pursuivants and messengers from the Court unto the Lords; but what about, I cannot tell.

From that place, she was conveyed to the Court; where by the way came to meet her, many gentlemen to accompany Her Highness, which were very sorry to see her in that case: but especially a great multitude of people that were standing by the way; who then flocking about her litter, lamented and greatly bewailed her estate.

Now when she came to the Court, Her Grace was there straightways shut up, and kept as close prisoner for a fortnight, seeing neither Queen, nor Lord, nor friend at that time; but only then, the Lord Chamberlain, Sir JOHN GAGE, and the Vice-Chamberlain, which were attendant upon the doors.

About which time, Sir WILLIAM ST. LO was called before the Council; to whose charge was laid, that he knew of WYATT's rebellion: which he stoutly denied, protesting that he was a true man, both to God and his Prince, defying all traitors and rebels. But being straitly examined, was, in conclusion, committed to the Tower.

The Friday before Palm Sunday [*16th March*], [STEPHEN GARDINER] the Bishop of WINCHESTER, with nineteen others of the Council (who shall be here nameless, as I have promised) came unto Her Grace, from the Queen's Majesty; and burdened [*accused*] her with WYATT's conspiracy: which she utterly denied, affirming that "she was altogether guilt-less therein."

They being not contented with this, charged Her Grace with the business made by Sir PETER CAREW and the rest of the Gentlemen of the West Country; which she also utterly denying, cleared her innocency therein.

In conclusion, after long debating of matters, they declared unto her, that "It was the Queen's will and pleasure that she should go unto the Tower, while the matter were further tried and examined."

Whereat, she being aghast, said that "She trusted the Queen's Majesty would be a more gracious Lady unto her; and that Her Highness would not otherwise conceive of her, but that she was a true woman." Declaring furthermore to the Lords, that "She was innocent in all those matters, wherein they had burdened her, and desired them therefore to be a further mean to the Queen her sister, that she, being a true woman in thought, word, and deed, towards Her Majesty, might not be committed to so notorious and doleful a place": protesting that she would request no mercy at her hand, if she should be proved to have consented unto any such kind of matter as they laid unto her charge. And therefore, in fine, desired their Lordships to think of her what she was; and that she might not so extremely be dealt withal for her truth.

Whereunto, the Lords answered that "There was no remedy. For that the Queen's Majesty was fully determined that she should go unto the Tower"; wherewith the Lords departed, with their caps hanging over their eyes [*this was a purposed sign of disrespect*].

But not long after, within the space of an hour or a little more, came four of the foresaid Lords of the Council, with the Guard, who warding the next chamber to her, secluded all her Gentlemen and yeomen, Ladies and gentlewomen; saving that for one Gentleman Usher, three Gentlewomen, and two Grooms of her Chamber, were appointed in their rooms, three other men, and three waiting women of the Queen's, to give attendance upon her; that none should have access to her Grace.

At which time, there were a hundred of Northern soldiers, in white coats, watching and warding about the gardens all

that night : a great fire being made in the midst of the Hall;
and two certain Lords watching there also with their Band
and company.

Upon Saturday, being Palm Sunday Eve [*17th March*], two
certain Lords of the Council, whose names here also we do
omit [*but who were the Marquis of WINCHESTER and the Earl
of SUSSEX*], came and certified Her Grace that "forthwith
she must go unto the Tower! the barge being prepared for
her, and the tide now ready, which tarrieth for nobody."
    In heavy mood, Her Grace requested the Lords, that " She
might tarry another tide ; " trusting that the next would be
more joyous and better [*because in the day time*].
    But one of the Lords [*i.e.*, WINCHESTER] replied that
" Neither tide nor time was to be delayed ! "
    And when Her Grace requested him, that she might be
suffered to write to the Queen's Majesty, he answered that
" He durst not permit that ; " adding that, " in his judgement it would rather hurt than profit Her Grace in so doing."
    But the other Lord, who was the Earl of SUSSEX, more
courteous and favourable, kneeling down, told Her Grace
that " She should have liberty to write, and, as he was a true
man, he would deliver it to the Queen's Highness ; and
bring an answer of the same, whatsoever came thereof."
    Whereupon she wrote ; albeit she could not, nor might
not speak with her ; to her great discomfort, being no offender
against Her Majesty.

[*The actual letter written by the Princess, at this moment, is in the State
Paper Office.* Domestic, MARY, Vol. IV. No. 2.

The Lady ELIZABETH to the Queen.

    If any ever did try this old saying, that *A King's word was more than
another man's oath,* I most humbly beseech your Majesty to verify it in
me ; and to remember your last promise, and my last demand, that " I be
not condemned without answer and due proof," which it seems that I now
am : for, without cause proved, I am, by your Council, from you, commanded to go to the Tower, a place more wonted for a false traitor than a
true subject, which, though I know I desire it not, yet, in the face of all
this realm, [it] appears proved. While I pray to GOD I may die the
shamefullest death that ever any died afore, if I may mean any such thing !
and to this present hour I protest before GOD (who shall judge my truth,
whatsoever malice shall devise), that I never practised, counselled, nor
consented to anything that might be prejudicial to your person any way,
or dangerous to the State by any means. And therefore, I humbly be-

seech your Majesty to let me answer afore yourself and not suffer me to trust to your Councillors ; yea, and that afore I go to the Tower, if it be possible, if not, before I be further condemned. Howbeit, I trust assuredly your Highness will give me leave to do it, afore I go ; that thus shamefully, I may not be cried out on, as I now shall be : yea, and without cause !

Let conscience move your Highness to take some better way with me than to make me be condemned in all men's sight afore my desert known ! Also I most humbly beseech your Highness to pardon this my boldness, which innocency procures me to do ; together with hope of your natural kindness which I trust will not see me cast away, without desert : which what it is, I would desire no more of GOD but that you truly knew ; but which thing, I think and believe you shall never by report know ; unless by yourself you hear.

I have heard of many, in my time, cast away for want of coming to the presence of their Prince ; and, in late days, I heard my Lord of SOMERSET say that "If his brother [*The Admiral* THOMAS *Lord* SEYMOUR] had been suffered to speak with him, he had never suffered ; but persuasions were made to him so great that he was brought in belief that he could not live safely if the Admiral lived, and that made him give consent to his death." Though these persons are not to be compared to your Majesty ; yet, I pray GOD, as evil persuasions persuade not one sister against the other ! and all for that they have heard false report, and not hearken to the truth not known.

Therefore, once again, kneeling with humbleness of heart, because I am not suffered to bow the knees of my body ; I humbly crave to speak with your Highness : which I would not be so bold as to desire, if I knew not myself most clear, as I know myself most true.

And as for the traitor WYATT, he might peradventure, write me a letter ; but, on my faith, I never received any from him. And as for the copy of the letter sent to the French King, I pray GOD may confound me eternally if ever I sent him word, message, token, or letter, by any means ! And to this truth, I will stand in to my death.

Your Highness's most faithful subject, that hath been from the beginning, and will be to my end,   E L I Z A B E T H.

I humbly crave but only one word of answer from yourself.]

And thus the tide [*season*] and time passed away for that time, till the next day, being Palm Sunday, when, about nine of the clock, these two came again, declaring that "it was time for Her Grace to depart."

She answered, "If there be no remedy, I must be contented ; " willing the Lords to go on before.

And being come forth into the garden, she did cast up her eyes towards the window ; thinking to have seen the Queen, which she could not. Whereat she said, " She marvelled much, what the Nobility of the realm meant ; which, in that sort, would suffer her to be led forth into captivity, the LORD knew whither ! for she did not."

After all this, she took her barge, with the two aforesaid Lords, three of the Queen's Gentlewomen, and three of her own, her Gentleman Usher, and two of her Grooms : lying and hovering upon the water, an hour; for that they could not shoot the Bridge [*the tide used to rush through the narrow spaces of old London bridge, with the force of a mill-race*] : the bargemen being very unwilling to shoot the same so soon as they did, because of the danger thereof. For the stern of the boat struck upon the ground, the fall was so big, and the water was so shallow.

Then Her Grace desired of the Lords, that "She might not land at the stairs where all traitors and offenders customably used to land" [*called the Traitor's Gate*].

They answered that "it was past their remedy; for that otherwise they had in commandment."

"Well," said she, "if it be so, my Lords! I must needs obey it : protesting before all your Honours, that here now steppeth as true a subject as ever was, towards the Queen's Highness. And before thee, O GOD! I speak it; having none other friends, but only Thee!"

The Lords declared unto her that "there was no time then to try the truth."

"You have said well, my Lords!" quoth she, "I am sorry that I have troubled you!"

So then they passed on [*i.e., through the Traitor's Gate*], and went into the Tower : where were a great company of harnessed men, and armed soldiers warding on both sides : whereat she being amazed, called the Lords to her, and demanded "the cause, why those poor men stood there?"

They declared unto her, that "it was the use and order of the place so to do."

"And if it be," quoth she, "for my cause; I beseech you that they may be dismissed."

Whereat, the poor men kneeled down, and with one voice, desired GOD to preserve Her Grace; who, the next day, were released of their cold coats.

After this, passing a little further, she sat down upon a cold stone, and there rested herself.

To whom, the Lieutenant [*Lord CHANDOS, see p.* 176]then being, said, "Madam, you were best to come out of the rain! for you sit unwholesomely."

She then replying, answered again, "Better sitting here, than in a worse place! For, GOD knoweth! I know not whither you will bring me!"

With that, her Gentleman Usher wept. She demanded of him, "What he meant so uncomfortably to use her, seeing she took him to be her comforter, and not her dismayer: especially for that she knew her truth to be such, that no man should have cause to weep for her." But forth she went into the prison.

The doors were locked and bolted upon her; which did not a little discomfort and dismay Her Grace. At what time, she called to her gentlewoman for her book [*i.e., her Bible*], desiring GOD, "Not to suffer her to build her foundation upon the sands, but upon the rocks! whereby all blasts of blustering weather should have no power against her."

After the doors were thus locked, and she close shut up; the Lords had great conference how to keep ward and watch, every man declaring his opinion in that behalf, agreeing straightly and circumspectly to keep her: while that one of them, I mean the Lord of SUSSEX, swearing, said, "My Lords! let us take heed! and do no more than our Commission will bear us! whatsoever shall happen hereafter. And, further, let us consider that she was the King our Master's daughter! and therefore let us use such dealing, that we may answer unto it hereafter, if it shall so happen! For just dealing," said he, "is always answerable."

Whereunto the other Lords agreed that it was well said of him: and thereupon departed.

It would make a pitiful and strange story, here by the way, to touch and recite what examinations and rackings of poor men there were, to find out the knife that should cut her throat! what gaping among the Lords of the Clergy to see the day, wherein they might wash their goodly white rochets in her innocent blood? But especially the Bishop of WINCHESTER, STEPHEN GARDINER, then Lord Chancellor, and ruler of the rost.

Who then, within few days after [*March*, 1554], came unto her, with divers other of the Council, and examined her of of the talk that was at Ashridge, betwixt her and Sir JAMES A CROFT concerning her removing from thence to Donnington Castle, requiring her to declare, "What she meant thereby?"

At the first, she, being so suddenly taken, did not well remember any such house : but within a while, well advising herself, she said, "Indeed, I do now remember that I have such a place : but I never lay in it, in all my life. And as for any that hath moved me thereunto, I do not remember."

Then to enforce the matter, they brought forth Sir JAMES A CROFT.

The Bishop of WINCHESTER demanded of her, "What she said to that man ?"

She answered that, "She had little to say to him, or to the rest that were then prisoners in the Tower. But my Lords!" quoth she, "you do examine every mean prisoner of me! wherein, methinks, you do me great injury! If they have done evil, and offended the Queen's Majesty, let them answer to it accordingly. I beseech you, my Lords! join not me in this sort with any of these offenders! And as concerning my going unto Donnington Castle, I do remember Master HOBY and mine Officers, and you Sir JAMES A CROFT! had such talk : but what is that to the purpose, my Lords! but that I may go to my own houses at all times?"

The Lord of ARUNDEL, kneeling down, said, "Your Grace saith true! and certainly we are very sorry that we have so troubled you about so vain matters."

She then said, "My Lords, you did sift me very narrowly! But well I am assured, you shall do no more to me, than GOD hath appointed : and so, GOD forgive you all!"

At their departing, Sir JAMES A CROFT kneeled down, declaring that "He was sorry to see the day in which he should be brought as a witness against Her Grace." "But, I assure your Grace," said he, "I have been marvellously tossed and examined touching your Highness; which, the Lord knoweth! is strange to me. For I take GOD to record! before all your Honours! I do not know anything of that crime that you have laid to my charge! and will thereupon take my death, if I should be driven to so straight a trial."

That day or thereabouts, divers of her own Officers, who had made provision for her diet, brought the same to the utter [*outer*] gate of the Tower; the common rascal soldiers receiving it: which was no small grief unto the Gentlemen, the bearers thereof.

These were not the Officers of the Tower; but such as went in white and green.

Wherefore they required to speak with [Sir JOHN GAGE] the Lord Chamberlain, being then Constable of the Tower: who, coming before his presence, declared unto his Lordship that "they were much afraid to bring Her Grace's diet, and to deliver it unto such common and desperate persons as they were, which did receive it; beseeching His Honour to consider Her Grace, and to give such order that her viands might at all times be brought in by them which were appointed thereunto."

"Yea, sirs!" said he, "who appointed you this office?"

They answer, "Her Grace's Council!"

"Council!" quoth he, "there is none of them which hath to do, either in that case, or anything else within this place; and, I assure you! for that she is a prisoner, she shall be served with the Lieutenant's men, as the other prisoners are."

Whereat the Gentlemen said that "They trusted for more favour at his hands! considering her personage," saying that "They mistrusted not, but that the Queen and her Council would be better to Her Grace than so!" and therewith shewed themselves to be offended at the ungrateful [*harsh*] words of the Lord Chamberlain, towards their Lady and Mistress.

At this, he sware, by GOD! stroking himself on the breast; that "If they did either frown or shrug at him; he would set them where they should see neither sun nor moon!"

Thus taking their leave, they desired GOD to bring him into a better mind towards Her Grace, and departed from him.

Upon the occasion whereof [*there being always a fear of poisoned food*], Her Grace's Officers made great suit unto the Queen's Council, that some might be appointed to bring her diet unto her; and that it might no more be delivered in to the common soldiers of the Tower: which being reasonably considered, was by them granted. Thereupon were appointed one of her Gentlemen, her Clerk of the Kitchen, and her two Purveyors, to bring in her provisions once a day. All which was done. The warders ever waiting upon the bringers

thereof (and the Lord Chamberlain himself, being always
with them), circumspectly and narrowly watched and
searched what they brought; and gave heed that they should
have no talk with any of Her Grace's waiting servants; and
so warded them both in and out.

At the said suit of her Officers, were sent, by the commandment of the Council, to wait upon Her Grace, two Yeomen
of her Chamber, one of her Robes, two of her Pantry and
Ewry, one of her Buttery, another of her Cellar, two of her
Kitchen, and one of her Larder: all which continued with
her, the time of her trouble.

Here the Constable (being at the first not very well pleased
with the coming in of such a company against his will) would
have had his men still to have served with Her Grace's men:
which her servants, at no hand, would suffer; desiring his
Lordship to be contented, for " that order was taken that no
stranger should come within their offices."

At which answer, being sore displeased, he brake out into
these threatening words: " Well," said he, " I will handle
you well enough ! "

Then went he into the kitchen, and there would needs
have his meat roasted with Her Grace's meat; and said
" His cook should come thither, and dress it."

To that, Her Grace's Cook answered, " My Lord ! I will
never suffer any stranger to come about her diet, but her
own sworn men, so long as I live ! "

He said, "They should ! "

But the Cook said, " His Lordship should pardon him for
that matter ! "

Thus did he trouble her poor servants very stoutly: though
afterward he were otherwise advised, and they were more
courteously used at his hands. And good cause why ! For
he had good cheer, and fared of the best; and Her Grace
paid well for it.

Wherefore he used himself afterwards more reverently
towards Her Grace.

After this sort, having lain a whole month there, in close
prison; and being very evil at ease therewithal; she sent
[*in April*] for the Lord Chamberlain and Lord CHANDOS
[*see p.*345]to come and speak with her.

Who coming, she requested them that " She might have

liberty to walk in some place, for that she felt herself not well."

To the which, they answered that "They were right sorry that they could not satisfy Her Grace's request; for that they had commandment to the contrary, which they durst not in any wise break."

Furthermore, she desired of them, "If that could not be granted; that she might walk but into the 'Queen's Lodgings.'"

"No, nor that!" they answered, "could, by any means, be obtained, without a further suit to the Queen and her Council."

"Well," said she, "my Lords! if the matter be so hard that they must be sued unto, for so small a thing; and that friendship be so strait, God comfort me!"

And so they departed: she remaining in her old dungeon still; without any kind of comfort, but only GOD.

The next day after, the Lord CHANDOS came again unto Her Grace, declaring unto her that "He had sued unto the Council for further liberty. Some of them consented thereunto. Divers others dissented, for that there were so many prisoners in the Tower. But in conclusion, they did all agree that Her Grace might walk into those 'Lodgings'; so that he and the Lord Chamberlain, and three of the Queen's Gentlewomen did accompany her: and the windows were shut, and she not suffered to look out at any of them." Wherewith, she contented herself; and gave him thanks for his goodwill in that behalf.

Afterwards, there was liberty granted to Her Grace to walk in a little garden, the doors and gates being shut up; which, notwithstanding, was as much discomfort unto her, as the walk in the garden was pleasant and acceptable. At which times of her walking there, the prisoners on that side straightly were commanded not to speak, or look out at the windows into the garden, till Her Grace were gone out again: having in consideration thereof, their keepers waiting upon them for that time.

Thus Her Grace, with this small liberty, contented herself in GOD, to whom be praise therefore.

During this time, there used a little boy, the child of a man in the Tower, to resort to their chambers, and many

times to bring Her Grace flowers; which likewise he did to
the other prisoners that were there. Whereupon naughty
and suspicious heads thinking to make and wring out some
matter thereof, called, on a time, the child unto them, promising him figs and apples, and asking, "When he had been
with the Earl of DEVONSHIRE?" not ignorant of the child's
wonted frequenting unto him.

The boy answered that "He would go by-and-by thither."

Further they demanded of him, "When he was with the
Lady ELIZABETH?"

He answered, "Every day!"

Furthermore they examined him, "What the Lord DEVON-
SHIRE sent by him to Her Grace?"

The child said, "I will go [and] know what he will give to
carry to her." Such was the discretion of the child, being
yet but three years of age.

"This same is a crafty boy!" quoth the Lord Chamberlain; "what say you, my Lord CHANDOS?"

"I pray you, my Lord! give me the figs ye promised me!"

"No, marry," quoth he, "thou shalt be whipped if thou
come any more to the Lady ELIZABETH, or the Lord
COURTNEY!"

The boy answered, "I will bring the Lady, my Mistress,
more flowers!"

Whereupon the child's father was commanded to permit
the boy no more to come into their chambers.

And the next day, as Her Grace was walking in the garden,
the child, peeping in at a hole in the door, cried unto her,
saying, "Mistress! I can bring you no more flowers!"
Whereat, she smiled, but said nothing; understanding
thereby, what they had done.

Wherefore, afterwards, the Lord Chamberlain rebuked his
father highly; commanding him to put him out of the house.

"Alas, poor infant!" quoth the father.

"It is a crafty knave!" quoth the Lord Chamberlain.
"Let me see him here no more!"

The 5th day of May [1554], the Constable was discharged
of his office of the Tower; one Sir HENRY BEDINGFIELD being
placed in his room. A man unknown to Her Grace, and
therefore the more feared: which so sudden [a] mutation
was unto her, no little amaze.

He brought with him a hundred soldiers in blue coats; wherewith she was marvellously discomforted; and demanded of such as were about her, "Whether the Lady JANE's scaffold were taken away or not?" fearing, by reason of their coming, least she should have played her part.

To whom, answer was made, that "The scaffold was taken away; and that Her Grace needed not to doubt [*fear*] any such tyranny, for GOD would not suffer any such treason against her person."

Wherewith, being contented, but not altogether satisfied, she asked, "What Sir H. BEDINGFIELD was? and whether he was of that conscience or not, that if her murdering were secretly committed to his charge, he would see the execution thereof?"

She was answered that "They were ignorant what manner of man he was." Howbeit they persuaded her that GOD would not suffer such wickedness to proceed.

"Well!" quoth she, "GOD grant it be so! For Thou! O GOD! art the withdrawer and mollifier of all such tyrannous hearts and acts! and I beseech Thee! to hear me thy creature! which am Thy servant and at Thy commandment! trusting by Thy grace ever so to remain."

About which time, it was spread abroad, that Her Grace should be carried from thence; by this new jolly captain and his soldiers; but whither, it could not be learned. Which was unto Her Grace a great grief, especially for that such a kind of company was appointed to her guard: requesting rather to continue there still, than to be led thence with such a rascal company.

At last, plain answer was made by the Lord CHANDOS, that "There was no remedy; but from thence she must needs depart to the Manor of Woodstock, as he thought."

Being demanded of her, "For what cause?"

"For that," quoth he, "the Tower is like[ly] further to be furnished."

Whereat she, being more greedy, as far as she durst, demanded, "wherewith!"

He answered, "With such matter as the Queen and Council were determined in that behalf: whereof he had no knowledge." And so departed.

In conclusion, the 16th day of May she was removed from the Tower : the Lord Treasurer [*the Marquis of* WINCHESTER] being then there, for the lading of her carts, and discharging the Place of the same.

Where Sir HENRY BEDINGFIELD, being appointed her goaler, did receive her with a company of rakehells to guard her ; besides the Lord of DERBY's Band [*servants*] wafting in the country about, for the moonshine in the water[!]. Unto whom, at length came, my Lord [WILLIAMS] of Thame, joined in Commission, with the said Sir HENRY for the safe guiding of her to prison. And they together conveyed Her Grace to Woodstock, as hereafter followeth.

The first day [*16th May*], they conducted her to Richmond, where she continued all night : being restrained of her own men, which were laid out in chambers ; and Sir HENRY BEDINGFIELD his soldiers appointed in their rooms, to give attendance on her person.

Whereat she, being marvellously dismayed, thinking verily some secret mischief a working towards her, called her Gentleman Usher, and desired him with the rest of his company to pray for her, "For this night," quoth she, "I think to die."

Whereat he being stricken to the heart, said, "GOD forbid that any such wickedness should be pretended [*intended*] against your Grace ! "

So comforting her as well as he could, he at last burst out in tears ; and went from her down into the court where were walking the Lord [WILLIAMS] of Thame, and Sir HENRY BEDINGFIELD ; and he staying aside the Lord of Thame, who had proffered to him much friendship, desire to speak with him a word or two.

Unto whom, he familiarly said, "He should with all his heart."

Which when Sir HENRY standing by, heard, he asked, "What the matter was ? "

To whom the Gentleman Usher answered, "No great matter, sir, but to speak with my Lord a word or two ! "

Then when the Lord of Thame came to him he spake in this wise, "My Lord ! you have always been my good Lord, and so I beseech you to remain. Why I come to you at this time, is to desire your Honour, unfeignedly to declare unto

Z   I me, whether any danger is meant unto my Mistress this night or not ? that I and my poor fellows may take such part as [it] shall please GOD to appoint.   For certainly we will rather die, than she should secretly and innocently miscarry."

"Marry," said the Lord of Thame, "GOD forbid that any such wicked purpose should be wrought ! and rather than it should be so, I, with my men, are ready to die at her feet also."

And so, GOD be praised ! they passed that doubtful night, with no little heaviness of heart.

The next day [*17th May*] passing over the water [*i.e.*, *the Thames*] at Richmond, going towards Windsor ; Her Grace espied certain of her poor servants standing on the other side, which were very desirous to see her.   Whom, when she beheld, turning to one of her men standing by, said, "Yonder, I see certain of my men ; go to them ! and say these words from me, *Tanquam ovis !* "

So, she passing forward to Windsor, was lodged there that night, in the Dean of Windsor's house : a place indeed more meet for a priest, than a Princess.

And from thence [*on 18th May*] Her Grace was guarded and brought the next night, to Master DORMER's house ; where much people standing by the way, some presented to her one gift, and some another.   So that Sir HENRY was greatly moved thereat, and troubled the poor people very sore, for shewing their loving hearts in such a manner ; calling them "Rebels ! " and " Traitors ! " with such like vile words.

Besides, as she passed through the villages, the townsmen rang the bells, as being joyful of her coming ; thinking verily it had been otherwise than it was indeed : and as the sequel proved after, to the poor men.   For immediately the said Sir HENRY hearing the same, sent his soldiers hither : who apprehended some of the ringers, setting them in the stocks, and otherwise uncourteously misused some others for their good wills.

On the morrow [*19th May*] Her Grace passed from Master DORMER's, where was, for the time of her abode, a straight watch kept ; came to the Lord of Thame his house [*at Thame*] where she lay all the next night ; being very princely enter-tained, both of Knights and Ladies, gentlemen and gentle-women. Whereat Sir HENRY BEDINGFIELD gronted [*grunted*] and was highly offended, saying unto them that "They could not tell what they did, and were not able to answer to their doings in that behalf; letting them to understand that she was the Queen's Majesty's prisoner, and no otherwise; advising them therefore to take heed, and beware of after claps!"

Whereunto, the Lord of Thame answered him in this wise, that "He was well advised of [in] his doings, being joined in Commission as well as he," adding with warrant, that "Her Grace might, and should, in his house, be merry."

After this, Sir HENRY went up into a chamber, where were appointed for Her Grace, a chair, two cushions, and a foot-carpet, very fair and prince-like; wherein presumptuously he sat, calling for BARWICK, his man, to pull off his boots: which as soon as it was known among the ladies and gentles, every one musing thereat, did laugh him to scorn; and observed his indiscreet manners in that behalf, as they might very well.

When supper was done, he called my Lord, and willed him that all the Gentlemen and Ladies should withdraw themselves; every one to his lodging: marvelling much that he would permit there such a company; considering so great a charge was committed to him.

"Sir HENRY!" quoth my Lord, "content yourself! All shall be voided, your men and all."

"Nay, my soldiers," quoth Sir HENRY, "shall watch all night."

The said Lord of Thame answered, "It shall not need."

"Well," said he, "need or need not, they shall do so," mistrusting, belike, the company; which, GOD knoweth, was without cause.

The next day [20th May] Her Grace took her journey from thence, to Woodstock; where she was enclosed, as before in the Tower of London; the soldiers guarding and warding both within and without the walls, every day to the number of three score, and, in the night, without the walls forty; during the time of her imprisonment there.

At length, she had gardens appointed for her walks, which were very comfortable to Her Grace. Always when she did recreate herself therein, the doors were fast locked up, in as straight a manner as they were in the Tower; there being at the least five or six locks between her lodging and her walks; Sir HENRY himself keeping the keys, trusted no man therewith.

Whereupon she called him "her gaoler :" and he, kneeling down, desired Her Grace not to call him so, for he was appointed there to be one of her Officers.

"From such Officers," quoth she, "good Lord, deliver me!"

And now, by way of digression, or rather of refreshing the reader (if it be lawful in so serious a story to recite a matter incident, and yet not impertinent to the same) occasion here moveth or rather enforceth me to touch briefly what happened in the same place and time, by a certain merry conceited man, being then about Her Grace. Who (noting the straight and strange keeping of his Lady and Mistress by the said Sir HENRY BEDINGFIELD, with so many locks and doors, with such watch and ward about her, as was strange and wonderful) spied a goat in the ward where Her Grace was; and (whether to refresh her oppressed mind, or to notify her straight handling by Sir HENRY; or else both), he took it up on his neck, and followed Her Grace therewith, as she was going to her lodging. Who, when she saw it, asked him, "What he would do with him?" willing him to let it alone.

Unto whom, the said party answered, "No, by Saint Mary! if it like your Grace! will I not! For I cannot tell whether he be one of the Queen's friends or not. I will, GOD willing! carry him to Sir HENRY BEDINGFIELD, to know what he is."

So, leaving Her Grace, went, with the goat on his neck, and carried it to Sir HENRY BEDINGFIELD ; who, when he saw him coming with it, asked him half angrily, "What he had there?"

Unto whom the party answered, saying, "Sir! I cannot tell what he is. I pray you, examine him! for I found him in the place where my Lady's Grace was walking, and what talk they have had, I cannot tell. For I understand him not, but he should seem to me to be some stranger : and I think verily a Welshman, for he hath a white frieze coat on his back. And forasmuch as I being the Queen's subject, and perceiving the strait charge committed to you of her keeping, that no stranger should have access to her, without sufficient license : I have here found a stranger (what he is, I cannot tell) in the place where Her Grace was walking ; and, therefore, for the necessary discharge of my duty, I thought it good to bring the said stranger to you to examine, as you see cause." And so he set him down.

At which his words, Sir HENRY BEDINGFIELD seemed much displeased, and said, " Well ! well ! you will never leave this gear, I see." And so they departed.

Now to return to the matter from whence we have digressed.

After Her Grace's being there a time [*i.e., about a year*], she made suit to the Council, that she might be suffered to write to the Queen ; which, at last, was permitted to Her Grace. So that Sir HENRY BEDINGFIELD brought her pen, ink, and paper ; and standing by her, while she wrote, which he very straitly observed ; always, she being weary, would carry away her letters, and bring them again when she called for them.

In the finishing thereof, he would have been messenger to the Queen of the same ; whose request Her Grace denied, saying, " One of her own men should carry them ; and that she would neither trust him, nor none of his thereabouts."

Then he answering again, said, " None of them durst be so bold," he trowed, " to carry her letters, being in her present case ! "

" Yes," quoth she, " I am assured I have none so dishonest that would deny my request in that behalf ; but will be as willing to serve me now as before."

" Well," said he, " my Commission is to the contrary ; and may not suffer it."

Her Grace, replying again, said, " You charge me very often with your Commission ! I pray GOD you may justly answer the cruel dealing ye deal with me ! "

Then he kneeling down, desired Her Grace to think and consider how he was a servant, and put in trust there by the Queen to serve Her Majesty : protesting that if the case were hers, he would as willingly serve Her Grace, as now he did the Queen's Highness.

For the which answer, Her Grace thanked him, desiring GOD that she might never have need of such servants as he was : declaring further to him that his doings towards her were not good or answerable, but more than all the friends he had, would stand by ; for in the end, she plainly told him, they would forsake him.

To whom, Sir HENRY replied, and said that "There was no remedy but his doings must be answered; and so they should, trusting to make a good account thereof."

The cause which moved Her Grace so to say, was for that he would not permit her letters to be carried, four or five days after the writing thereof. But, in fine, he was content to send for her Gentleman from the town of Woodstock, demanding of him, "Whether he durst enterprise the carriage of Her Grace's letters to the Queen or not?"

And he answered, "Yea, sir! That I dare, and will, with all my heart."

Whereupon, Sir HENRY, half against his stomach, took them to him, to the effect aforesaid.

Then, about the 8th of June [1555] came down Doctor OWEN and Doctor WENDIF, sent by the Queen to Her Grace, for that she was sickly; who ministering to her, and letting her blood, tarried there, and attended on Her Grace five or six days: who being well amended, they returned again to the Court, making their good report to the Queen and Council, of Her Grace's behaviour and humbleness towards the Queen's Highness; which Her Majesty hearing, took very thankfully. But the Bishops thereat repined, looked black in the mouth, and told the Queen, they "marvelled she submitted not herself to Her Majesty's mercy, considering that she had offended Her Highness."

Wily champions, ye may be sure! and friends at a need! GOD amend them!

About this time, Her Grace was requested by a secret friend, "to submit herself to the Queen's Majesty; which would be very well taken, and to her great quiet and commodity."

Unto whom, she answered that "She would never submit herself to them whom she had never offended! For," quoth she, "if I have offended, and am guilty; I then crave no mercy, but the law! which I am certain I should have had, ere this, if it could be proved by me. For I know myself, I thank GOD! to be out of the danger thereof, wishing that I were as clear out of the peril of my enemy; and then I am sure I should not be so locked and bolted up within walls and doors as I am. GOD give them a better mind! when it pleaseth Him."

About this time [*i.e., after the Queen's marriage on 3rd July 1554*] was there a great consulting among the Bishops and gentlemen, touching a marriage for Her Grace : which some of the Spaniards wished to be with some stranger, that she might go out of the realm with her portion. Some saying one thing, and some another.

A Lord [*Lord* PAGET] being there, at last said that "the King should never have any quiet common wealth in England; unless her head were stricken from the shoulders."

Whereunto the Spaniards answered, saying, "GOD forbid that their King and Master should have that mind to consent to such a mischief!" This was the courteous answer of the Spaniards to the Englishmen speaking, after that sort, against their own country.

From that day, the Spaniards never left off their good persuasions to the King, that the like honour he should never obtain as he should in delivering the Lady ELIZABETH's Grace out of prison : whereby, at length, she was happily released from the same.

Here is a plain and evident example of the good nature and clemency of the King and his Councillors towards Her Grace. Praised be GOD therefore ! who moved their hearts therein.

Then hereupon, she was sent for, shortly after, to come to Hampton Court.

In her imprisonment at Woodstock, these verses she wrote with her diamond, in a glass window.

> *Much suspected by me,*
> *Nothing proved can be,*
> *Quoth* ELIZABETH *the prisoner.*

[In the Second Edition of his *Actes*, &c., published in 1570 under the fresh title of *Ecclesiastical History, p.* 2,294; JOHN FOX gives the following additional information of the Woodstock imprisonment.

And thus much touching the troubles of Lady ELIZABETH at Woodstock.

Whereunto this is more to be added, that during the same time the Lord [WILLIAMS] of Thame had laboured for the Queen, and became surety for her, to have her from Woodstock to his house, and had obtained grant thereof. But (through the procurement either of Master BEDINGFIELD, or by the doing of [the Bishop of] WINCHESTER, her mortal enemy), letters came over night, to the contrary: whereby her journey was stopped.

Thus, this worthy Lady, oppressed with continual sorrow, could not be permitted to have recourse to any friends she had; but still in the hands of her enemies, was left desolate, and utterly destitute of all that might refresh a doleful heart, fraught full of terror and thraldom. Whereupon no marvel, if she hearing, upon a time, out of her garden at Woodstock, a certain milkmaid singing pleasantly, wished herself to be a milkmaid, as she was: saying that " Her case was better, and life more merry than hers, in that state she was.]

Sir HENRY BEDINGFIELD and his soldiers, with the Lord [WILLIAMS] of Thame, and Sir RALPH CHAMBERLAIN guarding and waiting upon her, the first night [*July* 1555] from Woodstock, she came to Rycot.

The next night to Master DORMER's; and so to Colebrook, where she lay all that night at the *George*. By the way, coming to the said Colebrook, certain of her gentlemen and yeomen, to the number of three score met Her Grace, much to all their comforts: which had not seen Her Grace of long season before, neither could: but were commanded, in the Queen's name, immediately to depart the town," to Her Grace's no little heaviness and theirs, who could not be suffered once to speak with from them. So that night all her men were taken her, saving her Gentleman Usher, three gentlewomen, two Grooms, and one of her Wardrobe; the Soldiers watching and warding round-about the house, and she shut up close within her prison.

The next day Her Grace entered Hampton Court on the back side, unto the Prince's Lodgings. The doors being shut to her; and she, guarded with soldiers as before, lay there a fortnight at the least, ere ever any had recourse unto her.

At length, came the Lord WILLIAM HOWARD, who marvellously honourably used Her Grace: whereat she took much comfort, and requested him to be a means that she might speak with some of the Council.

To whom, not long after came the Bishop of WINCHESTER, the Lord of ARUNDEL, the Lord of SHREWSBURY, and Secretary PETRE; who, with great humility, humbled themselves to Her Grace.

She again likewise saluting them, said, "My Lords! I am glad to see you! For, methinks, I have been kept a great while from you, desolately alone. Wherefore I would desire you to be a means to the King's and Queen's Majesties, that I may be delivered from prison, wherein I have been kept a long space, as to you, my Lords, is not unknown!"

When she had spoken, STEPHEN GARDINER, the Bishop of WINCHESTER kneeled down, and requested that "She would submit herself to the Queen's Grace; and in so doing he had no doubt but that Her Majesty would be good unto her."

She made answer that "rather than she would do so, she would lie in prison all the days of her life:" adding that "she craved no mercy at Her Majesty's hand, but rather desired the law, if ever she did offend her Majesty in thought, word, or deed. And besides this, in yielding," quoth she, "I should speak against myself, and confess myself to be an offender, which I never was towards Her Majesty; by occasion whereof, the King and Queen, might ever hereafter conceive an ill opinion of me: and, therefore, I say, my Lords! it were better for me to lie in prison for the truth, than to be abroad and suspected of my Prince."

And so they departed, promising to declare her message to the Queen.

On the next day [*July* 1555] the Bishop of WINCHESTER came again unto Her Grace, and kneeling down, declared that "The Queen marvelled that she should so stoutly use herself, not confessing to have offended; so that it should seem the Queen's Majesty wrongfully to have imprisoned Her Grace."

"Nay," quoth my Lady ELIZABETH, "it may please her to punish me, as she thinketh good."

"Well," quoth GARDINER, "Her Majesty willeth me to tell you, that you must tell another tale ere that you be set at liberty."

Her Grace answered that "She had as lief be in prison with honesty and truth, as to be abroad suspected of Her Majesty. And this that I have said, I will stand to. For I will never belie myself!"

The Lord of WINCHESTER again kneeled down, and said, "Then your Grace hath the vantage of me and the other Lords, for your long and wrong imprisonment."

"What vantage I have," quoth she, "you know; taking

GOD to record, I seek no vantage at your hands, for your so dealing with me. But GOD forgive you, and me also!"

With that, the rest kneeled, desiring Her Grace that "all might be forgotten," and so departed, she being fast locked up again.

A sevennight after [*July* 1555], the Queen's Majesty sent for Her Grace, at ten of the clock in the night, to speak with her. For she had not seen her in two years before. Yet for all that, she was amazed at the so sudden sending for, thinking it had been worse for her, than afterwards proved; and desired her gentlemen and gentlewomen to "pray for her! for that she could not tell whether ever she should see them again or not."

At which time, coming in with Sir HENRY BEDINGFIELD and Mistress CLARENCIUS [*p.* 332], Her Grace was brought into the garden, unto a stairs' foot, that went into the Queen's Lodging; Her Grace's gentlewomen waiting upon her, her Gentleman Usher and his grooms going before with torches. Where her gentlemen and gentlewomen being all commanded to stay, saving one woman; Mistress CLARENCIUS conducted her to the Queen's bedchamber, where Her Majesty was.

At the sight of whom, Her Grace kneeled down, and desired GOD to "preserve Her Majesty! not mistrusting, but that she should try herself as true a subject towards Her Majesty as ever any did," and desired Her Majesty even so to judge of her; and said "she should not find her to the contrary; whatsoever false report otherwise had gone of her."

To whom, the Queen answered, "You will not confess your offence; but stand stoutly in your truth! I pray GOD! it may so fall out."

"If it do not," quoth she, "I request neither favour nor pardon at your Majesty's hands."

"Well," said the Queen, "you stiffly still persevere in your truth! Belike, you will not confess but that you have wrongly punished!"

"I must not say so, if it please your Majesty! to you!"

"Why, then," said the Queen, "belike you will to others."

"No, if it please your Majesty!" quoth she, "I have borne the burden, and must bear it. I humbly beseech your Majesty to have a good opinion of me, and to think me to be your true subject; not only from the beginning, hitherto; but for ever, as long as life lasteth."

And so they departed [*separated*], with very few comfortable words of the Queen in English. But what she said in Spanish, GOD knoweth! It is thought that King PHILIP was there, behind a cloth [*tapestry*], and not shewn; and that he shewed himself a very friend in that matter, &c.

Thus Her Grace departing, went to her lodging again; and the sevennight after, was released of Sir HENRY BEDING-FIELD, "her gaoler," as she termed him, and his soldiers.

So Her Grace, set at liberty from imprisonment, went into the country, and had appointed to go with her, Sir THOMAS POPE, one of Queen MARY's Councillors; and one of her Gentleman Ushers, Master GAGE; and thus straitly was she looked to, all Queen MARY's time.

And this is the discourse of Her Highness's imprisonment.

Then there came to Lamheyre, Master JERNINGHAM, and NORRIS, Gentleman Usher, Queen MARY's men; who took away from Her Grace, Mistress ASHELEY to the Fleet, and three others of her gentlemen to the Tower; which thing was no little trouble to Her Grace, saying, that "she thought they would fetch all away at the end." But God be praised! shortly after was fetched away GARDINER, through the merciful providence of the LORD's goodness, by occasion of whose opportune decease [13*th November*, 1555], the life of this so excellent Prince that is the wealth of England, was preserved.

After the death of this GARDINER; followed the death also, and dropping away of others, her enemies; whereby, by little and little, her jeopardy decreased, fear diminished, hope of more comfort began to appear, as out of a dark cloud; and though as yet Her Grace had no full assurance of perfect safety, yet more gentle entertainment daily did grow unto her, till the same day, which took away the said Queen MARY, brought in the same her foresaid sister, Lady ELIZABETH in to the right of the Crown of England. Who, after so long restrainment, so great dangers escaped, such blusterous storms overblown, so many injuries digested and wrongs sustained: the mighty protection of our merciful GOD, to our no little safeguard, hath exalted and erected, out of thrall, to liberty; out of danger, to peace and rule; from dread, to dignity; from misery, to majesty; from mourning, to ruling; briefly, of a prisoner, hath made her a Prince; and hath placed her in her royal throne, being placed and proclaimed Queen with as many glad hearts of her subjects, as ever was any King or Queen in this realm before, or ever shall be (I think) hereafter.

In whose advancement, and this her princely governance, it cannot sufficiently be expressed what felicity and blessed happiness this realm hath received, in receiving her at the LORD's almighty and gracious hand. For as there have been divers Kings and Rulers over this realm, and I have read of some; yet could I never find in English Chronicles, the like that may be written of this our noble and worthy Queen, whose coming in was not only so calm, so joyful, so peaceable, without shedding of any blood; but also her reigning hitherto (reign now four years and more) hath been so quiet, that yet (the LORD have all the glory!) to this present day, her Sword is a virgin, spotted and polluted with no drop of blood.

In speaking whereof, I take not upon me the part of the Moral, or of the Divine Philosopher, to Judge of things done; but only keep me within the compass of an Historiographer, declaring what hath been before; and comparing things done, with things now present, the like whereof, as I said, is not to be found lightly in Chronicles before. And this, as I speak truly, so would I to be taken without flattery; to be left to our posterity, *ad sempiternam clementiæ illius memoriam.*

In commendation of which her clemency, I might also here add, how mildly Her Grace, after she was advanced to her Kingdom, did forgive the said Sir HENRY BEDINGFIELD; suffering him, without molestation, to enjoy goods, life, lands, and liberty. But I let this pass.

Thus hast thou, gentle Reader! simply but truly described unto thee, the time, first, of the sorrowful adversity of this our most Sovereign Queen that now is; also, the miraculous preserving her in so many straights and distresses: which I thought here briefly to notify, the rather for that the wondrous works of the LORD ought not to be suppressed; and that also Her Majesty, and we her poor subjects likewise, having thereby a present matter always before our eyes, be admonished how much we are bound to His Divine majesty, and also to render thanks to Him condignly for the same.

THE PASSAGE

*of our most dread Sovereign
Lady, Queen ELIZABETH,
through the City of Lon-
don to Westminster,
the day before her
Coronation.*

Anno. 1558.

Cum privilegio.

The Receiving of the Queen's Majesty.

PON Saturday, which was the 14th day of January, in the year of our Lord God, 1558 [*i.e.*, 1559], about two of the clock, at after noon, the most noble and Christian Princess, our most dread Sovereign Lady, ELIZABETH, by the grace of GOD, Queen of England, France, and Ireland, Defender of the Faith, &c., marched from the Tower, to pass through the City of London, towards Westminster: richly furnished, and most honourably accompanied, as well with Gentlemen, Barons, and other the Nobility of this realm, as also with a noble train of goodly and beautiful Ladies, richly appointed.

And entering the City, was of the people received marvellous entirely, as appeared by the assembly's prayers, wishes, welcomings, cries, tender words, and all other signs: which argue a wonderful earnest love of most obedient subjects towards their Sovereign. And, on the other side, Her Grace, by holding up her hands, and merry countenance to such as stood afar off, and most tender and gentle language to those that stood nigh to Her Grace, did declare herself no less thankfully to receive her people's good will, than they lovingly offered it unto her.

To all that "wished Her Grace well!" she gave "Hearty thanks!" and to such as bade "GOD save Her Grace!" she said again, "GOD save them all!" and thanked with all her heart. So that, on either side, there was nothing but gladness! nothing but prayer! nothing but comfort!

The Queen's Majesty rejoiced marvellously to see that so exceedingly shewed towards Her Grace, which all good Princes have ever desired; I mean, so earnest Love of Subjects, so evidently declared even to Her Grace's own person, being carried in the midst of them. The people, again, were wonderfully ravished with the loving answers and gestures of their Princess; like to the which, they had before tried, at her first coming to the town, from Hatfield. This Her Grace's loving behaviour preconceived in the people's heads, upon these considerations, was then thoroughly confirmed; and indeed implanted a wonderful hope in them touching her worthy government in the rest of her reign.

For in all her Passage, she did not only shew her most gracious love towards the people in general; but also privately, if the baser personages had either offered Her Grace any flowers or such like, as a signification of their good will; or moved to her any suit, she most gently (to the common rejoicings of all lookers on, and private comfort of the party) stayed her chariot, and heard their requests. So that, if a man should say well, he could not better term the City of London that time, than a Stage wherein was shewed the wonderful Spectacle of a noble hearted Princess towards her most loving people; and the people's exceeding comfort in beholding so worthy a Sovereign, and hearing so prince-like a voice; which could not but have set the enemy on fire, (since the virtue is in the enemy always commended) much more could not but inflame her natural, obedient, and most loving people; whose weal leaneth only upon her Grace, and her government.

Thus, therefore, the Queen's Majesty passed from the Tower [*see as to her former dismal visit in March,* 1554, *at p.* 345], till she came to Fanchurch [*Fenchurch*]: the people on each side, joyously beholding the view of so gracious a Lady, their Queen; and Her Grace no less gladly noting, and observing the same.

Near unto Fanchurch, was erected a scaffold richly furnished; whereon stood a noise of instruments; and a child, in costly apparel, which was appointed to welcome the Queen's Majesty, in the whole City's behalf.

Against which place, when Her Grace came, of her own will she commanded the chariot to be stayed; and that the noise might be appeased, till the child had uttered his welcoming Oration, which he spake in English metre, as here followeth.

O peerless Sovereign Queen! Behold, what this thy town
Hath thee presented with, at thy First Entrance here!
Behold, with how rich hope, she leadeth thee to thy Crown!
Behold, with what two gifts, she comforteth thy cheer!

The First is Blessing Tongues! which many a "Welcome!"
    say.   [sky!
Which pray, thou may'st do well! which praise thee to the
Which wish to thee long life! which bless this happy day!
Which to thy Kingdom "Heapes!" [Hips!], all that in
    tongues can lie.

The Second is True Hearts! which love thee from their root!
Whose Suit is Triumph now, and ruleth all the game,
Which Faithfulness has won, and all untruth driven out;
Which skip for joy, when as they hear thy happy name!

Welcome, therefore, O Queen! as much as heart can think.
Welcome again, O Queen! as much as tongue can tell,
Welcome to joyous Tongues, and Hearts that will not shrink!
"GOD, thee preserve!" we pray; and wish thee ever well!

At which words of the last line, the people gave a great shout; wishing, with one assent, as the child had said.

And the Queen's Majesty thanked most heartily, both the City for this her gentle receiving at the first, and also the people for confirming the same.

Here was noted in the Queen's Majesty's countenance, during the time that the child spake, besides a perpetual attentiveness in her face, a marvellous change in look, as the child's words touched either her person, or the people's

Tongues and Hearts: so that she, with rejoicing visage, did evidently declare that the words took no less place in her mind, than they were most heartily pronounced by the child, as from all the hearts of her most hearty citizens.

The same Verses were fastened up in a table [*painted board. Table is the Elizabethan word for picture*] upon the scaffold; and the Latin thereof likewise, in Latin verses, in another table, as hereafter ensueth.

> *Urbs tua quæ ingressu dederit tibi munera primo,*
> *O Regina! parem non habitura, vide!*
> *Ad diadema tuum, te spe quam divite mittat,*
> *Quæ duo letitiæ det tibi dona, vide!*
> *Munus habes Primum, Linguas bona multa Precantes,*
> *Quæ te quum laudant, tum pia vota sonant,*
> *Fœlicemque diem hunc dicunt, tibi secula longa*
> *Optant, et quicquid denique lingua potest.*
> *Altera dona feres, vera, et tui Amantia Corda,*
> *Quorum gens ludum jam regit una tuum:*
> *In quibus est infracta fides, falsumque perosa,*
> *Quæque tuo audito nomine læta salit.*
> *Grata venis igitur, quantum Cor concipit ullum!*
> *Quantum Lingua potest dicere, grata venis!*
> *Cordibus infractis, Linguisque per omnia lætis*
> *Grata venis! salvam te velit esse DEUS!*

Now when the child had pronounced his oration, and the Queen's Highness so thankfully received it; she marched forward towards Gracious [*Gracechurch*] Street, where, at the upper end, before the sign of the *Eagle*, the city had erected a gorgeous and sumptuous Ark, as here followeth.

A Stage was made which extended from one side of the street to the other, richly vawted [*vaulted*] with battlements, containing three ports [*gates*]; and over the middlemost was advanced three several stages, in degrees [*tiers*]. Upon the lowest stage, was made one seat royal; wherein were placed two personages representing King HENRY VII., and ELIZABETH his wife, daughter of King EDWARD IV. Both of these two Princes sitting under one Cloth of Estate, in their seats;

no otherwise divided, but that th[e] one of them, which was King HENRY VII., proceeding out of the House of LANCASTER, was enclosed in a red rose; and the other, which was Queen ELIZABETH, being heir to the House of YORK, enclosed with a white rose : each of them royally crowned and decently apparelled, as pertaineth to Princes, with sceptres in their hands, and one vawt [*vault*] surmounting their heads, wherein aptly were placed two tables, each containing the title, of those two Princes. And these personages were so set, that the one of them joined hands with the other, with the ring of matrimony perceived on the finger.

Out of the which two roses sprang two branches gathered into one : which were directed upward to the second stage or degree; wherein was placed one representing the valiant and noble Prince, HENRY VIII., who sprang out of the former stock, crowned with a crown imperial. And by him sate one representing the right worthy Lady, Queen ANNE; wife to the said HENRY VIII., and mother to our most sovereign Lady, Queen ELIZABETH that now is. Both apparelled with sceptres and diadems, and other furniture due to the estate of a King and Queen: and two tables surmounting their heads, wherein were written their names and titles.

From their seat also, proceeded upwards one branch directed to the third and uppermost stage or degree, wherein likewise was planted a seat royal; in the which was set one representing the Queen's most excellent Majesty, ELIZABETH, now our most dread Sovereign Lady, crowned and apparelled as the other Princes were.

Out of the forepart of this pageant was made a standing for a child, which, at the Queen's Majesty's coming, declared unto her the whole meaning of the said pageant.

The two sides of the same were filled with loud noises of music.

And all empty places thereof, were furnished with sentences concerning Unity. And the whole pageant was garnished with red and white roses; and in the forefront of the same pageant, in a fair wreath, was written the name and title of the same, which was

THE UNITING OF THE TWO HOUSES OF YORK AND LANCASTER.

This pageant was grounded upon the Queen Majesty's name.

For like as the long war between the two Houses of YORK and LANCASTER then ended, when ELIZABETH, daughter of EDWARD IV., matched in marriage with HENRY VII., heir to the House of LANCASTER; so since that the Queen's Majesty's name was ELIZABETH, and forasmuch as she is the only heir of HENRY VIII., which came of both Houses as the knitting up of concord: it was devised that like as ELIZABETH was the first occasion of concord; so She, another ELIZABETH, might maintain the same among her subjects. So that Unity was the end, whereat the whole device shot; as the Queen's Majesty's name moved the first ground.

This pageant now against the Queen's Majesty's coming, was addressed [set forth] with children representing the fore-named personages; with all furniture due unto the setting forth of such a well-meant matter, as the argument declared, costly and sumptuously set forth, as the beholders can witness.

Now, the Queen's Majesty drew near unto the said pageant, and forasmuch as the noise was great, by reason of the press of people, so that she could scarce hear the child which did interpret the said pageant; and her chariot was passed so far forward that she could not well view the personages representing the Kings and Queens above named; she required to have the matter opened unto her, and what they signified, with the End of Unity, and Ground of her Name, according as is before expressed.

For the sight whereof, Her Grace caused her chariot to be removed back; and yet hardly could she see, because the children were set somewhat with the farthest in.

But after that Her Grace understood the meaning thereof, she thanked the City, praised the fairness of the work, and promised that " She would do her whole endeavour for the continual preservation of concord!" as the pageant did import.

The child appointed in the standing above named, to open the meaning of the said pageant, spake these words unto Her Grace.

The two Princes that sit under one Cloth of State :
The Man in the red rose; the Woman in the white :
HENRY the SEVENTH, and Queen ELIZABETH his mate,
By ring of marriage, as man and wife unite.

Both heirs to both their bloods : to LANCASTER, the King,
The Queen, to YORK; in one the two Houses do knit.
Of whom, as Heir to both, HENRY the EIGHTH did spring,
In whose seat, his true Heir, thou, Queen ELIZABETH! dost
　　sit !

Therefore as civil war and shed of blood did cease;
When these two Houses were united into one :
So now, that jar shall stint and quietness increase,
We trust, O noble Queen! thou wilt be cause alone!

　　The which also were written in Latin verses. And both
drawn in two tables upon the forefront of the said pageant,
as hereafter followeth.

> *Hii quos jungit idem solium, quos annulus idem :*
> *Hæc albente nitens, ille rubente rosa :*
> *SEPTIMUS HENRICUS rex, regina ELIZABETHA,*
> *Scilicet Hæredes gentis uterque suæ.*
> *Hæc EBORACENSIS, LANCASTRIUS ille dederunt*
> *Connubio e geminis quo foret una domus.*
> *Excipit hos hæres HENRICUS copula regum*
> *OCTAVUS, magni regis imago potens.*
> *Regibus hinc succedis avis regique parenti*
> *Patris justa Hæres ELIZABETHA tui.*

❡ SENTENCES PLACED THEREIN, CONCERNING UNITY.

> *Nullæ concordes animos vires domant.*
> *Qui juncti terrent, dejuncti timent.*
> *Discordes animi solvunt, concordes ligant.*
> *Augentur parva pace, magna bello cadunt.*
> *Conjunctæ manus fortius tollunt onus.*
> *Regno pro mœnibus æneis civium concordia.*
> *Qui diu pugnant, diutius lugent.*
> *Dissidentes principes, subditorum lues.*

Princeps ad pacem natus, non ad arma datur.
Filia concordiæ copia, neptis quies.
Dissentiens respublica hostibus patet.
Qui idem tenent, diutius tenent.
Regnum divisum facile dissolvitur.
Civitas concors armis frustra tentatur.
Omnium gentium consensus firmat fidem.
&c.

These Verses and other pretty Sentences were drawn in void places of this pageant, all tending to one end, that quietness might be maintained and all dissention displaced : and that by the Queen's Majesty, Heir to Agreement, and agreeing in name with her which tofore had joined those Houses, which had been the occasion of much debate and Civil War with this realm (as may appear to such as well search Chronicles ; but be not to be touched in this Treatise, only declaring Her Grace's Passage through the City, and what provision the City made therefore).

And ere the Queen's Majesty came within hearing of this pageant, as also at all the other pageants ; she sent certain to require the people to be silent, for Her Majesty was disposed to hear all that should be said unto her.

When the Queen's Majesty had heard the child's oration and understood the meaning of the pageant at large ; she marched forward towards Cornhill, always received with like rejoicing of the people.

And there, as Her Grace passed by the Conduit, which was curiously trimmed against that time, adorned with rich banners, and a noise of loud instruments upon the top thereof : she espied the second pageant. And because she feared, for the people's noise, that she should not hear the child which did expound the same, she inquired what that pageant was, ere that she came to it. And there understood, that there was a child representing Her Majesty's person, placed in a Seat of Government, supported by certain Virtues which suppressed their contrary Vices under their feet : and so forth, as, in the description of the said pageant, shall hereafter appear.

This pageant, standing in the nether end of Cornhill, was extended from one side of the street to the other; and, in the same pageant was devised three gates, all open: and over the middle part thereof was erected one Chair or Seat royal, with Cloth of Estate to the same appertaining, wherein was placed a child representing the Queen's Highness, with consideration had for place convenient for a table, which contained her name and title.

And in a comely wreath, artificially and well devised, with perfect sight and understanding to the people, in the front of the same pageant, was written the name and title thereof which is

THE SEAT OF WORTHY GOVERNANCE.

Which Seat was made in such artificial manner, as to the appearance of the lookers on, the forepart seemed to have no stay; and therefore, of force, was stayed by lively [*living*] personages. Which personages were in number four, standing and staying the forefront of the same Seat royal, each having his face to the Queen and the people; whereof every one had a table to express their effects. Which are Virtues, namely, PURE RELIGION, LOVE OF SUBJECTS, WISDOM, and JUSTICE; which did tread their contrary Vices under their feet: that is to wit, PURE RELIGION did tread upon IGNORANCE and SUPERSTITION, LOVE OF SUBJECTS did tread upon REBELLION and INSOLENCY, WISDOM did tread upon FOLLY and VAINGLORY, JUSTICE did tread upon ADULATION and BRIBERY. Each of these personages, according to their proper names and properties, had not only their names in plain and perfect writing set upon their breasts, easily to be read of all: but also every of them was aptly and properly apparelled; so that his apparel and name did agree to express the same person, that in title he represented. This part of the pageant was thus appointed and furnished.

The two sides over the two side ports had in them placed a noise of instruments [*i.e., a band of players*]; which, immediately after the child's speech, gave a heavenly melody.

Upon the top or uppermost part of the said pageant stood the Arms of England, royally portraitured; with the proper beasts to uphold the same. One representing the Queen's

Highness sat in this Seat, crowned with an imperial crown: and before her seat was a convenient place appointed for one child, which did interpret and apply the said pageant as hereafter shall be declared.

Every void place was furnished with proper Sentences commending the Seat supported by the Virtues; and defacing the Vices, to the utter extirpation of rebellion, and to everlasting continuance of quietness and peace.

The Queen's Majesty approaching nigh unto this pageant, thus beautified and furnished in all points, caused her chariot to be drawn nigh thereunto, that Her Grace might hear the child's oration, which was this:

While that Religion True shall Ignorance suppress,
And with her weighty foot, break Superstition's head;
While Love of Subjects shall Rebellion distress,
And with Zeal to the Prince, Insolency down tread;

While Justice can Flattering tongues and Bribery deface;
While Folly and Vainglory, to Wisdom yield their hands:
So long, shall Government not swerve from her right race,
But Wrong decayeth still, and Righteousness upstands.

Now all thy subjects' hearts, O Prince of peerless fame!
Do trust these virtues shall maintain up thy throne!
And Vice be kept down still, the wicked put to shame;
That good with good may joy, and naught with naught may
  moan!

Which Verses were painted upon the right side of the same pageant; and in Latin thereof, on the left side, in another table, which were these.

Quæ subnixa alte solio regina superbo est,
 Effigiem sanctæ Principis alma refert,
Quam Civilis Amor fulcit, Sapientia firmat,
 Justicia illustrat, Religioque beat
Vana Superstitio et crassæ Ignorantia frontis

Pressæ sub Pura Religione jacent.
Regis Amor domat Effrænos, animosque rebelles
Justus Adulantes, Donivorosque terit.
Cum regit Imperium sapiens, sine luce sedebunt
Stultitia, atque hujus numen inanis honor.

Beside these Verses, there were placed in every void room of the pageant, both in English and Latin, such Sentences as advanced the Seat of Governance upholden by Virtue.

The ground of this pageant was that, like as by Virtues (which do abundantly appear in Her Grace), the Queen's Majesty was established in the Seat of Government; so she should sit fast in the same, so long as she embraced Virtue, and held Vice under foot. For if Vice once got up the head, it would put the Seat of Government in peril of falling.

The Queen's Majesty, when she had heard the child, and understood the pageant at full, gave the City also thanks there; and most graciously promised her good endeavour for the maintenance of the said virtues, and suppression of vices.

And so marched on, till she came against the Great Conduit in Cheap; which was beautified with pictures and sentences accordingly, against Her Grace's coming thither.

Against Soper Lane's end was extended from the one side of the street to the other, a pageant which had three gates, all open.

Over the middlemost whereof, were erected three several stages, whereon sat eight children, as hereafter followeth. On the uppermost, one child; on the middle, three; on the lowest, four; each having the proper name of the Blessing that he did represent, written in a table, and placed above his head.

In the forefront of this pageant, before the children which did represent the Blessings, was a convenient standing cast out for a child to stand, which did expound the said pageant unto the Queen's Majesty; as was done in the other before. Every of these children were appointed and apparelled according to the Blessing, which he did represent.

And on the forepart of the said pageant was written, in fair letters, the name of the said pageant, in this manner following.

THE EIGHT BEATITUDES, EXPRESSED IN THE FIFTH CHAPTER OF THE GOSPEL OF SAINT MATTHEW, APPLIED TO OUR SOVEREIGN LADY QUEEN ELIZABETH.

Over the two side posts was placed a noise of instruments. And all void places in the pageant were furnished with pretty Sayings commending and touching the meaning of the said pageant; which were the Promises and Blessings of Almighty GOD made to His people.

Before the Queen's Highness came into this pageant, she required the matter somewhat to be opened unto her; that Her Grace might the better understand what should, afterward, by the child, be said unto her. Which was so, that the City had there erected the pageant with eight children, representing the Eight Blessings touched in the Fifth Chapter of *St. Matthew*; whereof every one, upon just considerations, was applied unto Her Highness. And that the people thereby put Her Grace in mind, that as her good doings before, had given just occasion why that these Blessings might fall upon her; that so, if Her Grace did continue in her goodness, as she had entered, she should hope for the fruit of these Promises, due unto them that do exercise themselves in the Blessings.

Which Her Grace heard marvellously graciously, and required that the chariot might be removed towards the pageant, that she might perceive the child's words: which were these, the Queen's Majesty giving most attentive ear, and requiring that the people's noise might be stayed.

Thou hast been eight times blest! O Queen of worthy fame!
By Meekness in thy spirit, when care did thee beset!
By Mourning in thy grief! by Mildness in thy blame!
By Hunger and by Thirst, and justice couldst none get!

By Mercy showed, not felt! by Cleanness of thy heart!
By seeking Peace always! by Persecution wrong!, [smart!
Therefore, trust thou in GOD! since He hath helped thy
That, as His Promise is, so He will make thee strong!

When these words were spoken, all the people wished that "As the child had spoken, so GOD would strengthen Her Grace against all her adversaries!" whom the Queen's Majesty did most gently thank, for their so loving wish.

These Verses were painted on the left side of the said pageant; and other, in Latin, on the other side, which were these:

> *Qui lugent hilares fient, qui mitia gestant*
> *   Pectora, multa soli jugera culta metent.*
> *Justitiam esuriens sitiensve replebitur, ipsum*
> *   Fas homini puro corde videre DEUM.*
> *Quem alterius miseret Dominus miserebitur hujus,*
> *   Pacificus quisquis, filius ille DEI est.*
> *Propter justitiam quisquis patietur habetque*
> *   Demissam mentem, cælica regna capit.*
> *Huic hominum generi terram, mare, sidera vovit*
> *   Omnipotens, horum quisque beatus erit.*

Besides these, every void place in the pageant was furnished with Sentences touching the matter and ground of the said pageant.

When all that was to be said in this pageant was ended; the Queen's Majesty passed on forward in Cheap side.

At the Standard in Cheap, which was dressed fair against the time, was placed a noise of trumpets, with banners and other furniture.

The Cross, likewise, was also made fair and well trimmed. And near unto the same, upon the porch of Saint Peter's Church door, stood the Waits of the City; which did give a pleasant noise with their instruments, as the Queen's Majesty did pass by. Who, on every side, cast her countenance, and wished well to all her most loving people.

Soon after that Her Grace passed the Cross, she had espied the pageant erected at the Little Conduit in Cheap; and incontinent required to know what it might signify. And it was told Her Grace, that there was placed TIME.

"TIME!" quoth she, "and Time hath brought me hither!"

And so forth the whole matter was opened to Her Grace, as hereafter shall be declared in the description of the pageant. But when in the opening, Her Grace understood that the *Bible* in English, should be delivered unto her by Truth (which was therein represented by a child), she thanked the City for that gift, and said that she would oftentimes read over that book; commanding Sir John Parrat, one of the knights which held up her canopy, to go before, and to receive it : but learning that it should be delivered unto Her Grace, down by a silken lace, she caused him to stay.

And so passed forward till she came against the Aldermen, in the high end of Cheap, tofore the Little Conduit; where the Companies of the City ended, which began at Fanchurch [*Fenchurch Street*] and stood along the streets, one by another, enclosed with rails hanged with cloths, and themselves well apparelled with many rich furs, and their Livery Hoods upon their shoulders, in comely and seemly manner ; having before them sundry persons well apparelled in silks and chains of gold, as Whifflers and Guarders of the said Companies : besides a number of rich hangings (as well of tapestry, arras, cloths of gold, silver, velvet, damask, satin, and other silks) plentifully hanged all the way, as the Queen's Highness passed from the Tower through the City. Out at the windows and penthouses of every house did hang a number of rich and costly banners and streamers, till Her Grace came to the upper end of Cheap.

And there by appointment, the Right Worshipful Master Ranulph Cholmeley, Recorder of the City, presented to the Queen's Majesty, a purse of crimson satin, richly wrought with gold ; wherein the City gave unto the Queen's Majesty a thousand marks in gold [= £666 = *about* £5,000 *now*]; as Master Recorder did declare briefly unto the Queen's Majesty. [*Compare the similar usual gift to her Mother 25 years before, in this Vol. p.* 16]. Whose words tended to this end, that "The Lord Mayor, his brethren and commonalty of the City, to declare their gladness and good will towards the Queen's Majesty, did present Her Grace with that gold ; desiring Her Grace to continue their good and gracious Queen, and not to esteem the value of the gift, but the mind of the givers."

The Queen's Majesty, with both her hands took the purse, and answered to him again marvellously pithily; and so pithily that the standers by, as they embraced entirely her gracious answer, so they marvelled at the couching thereof: which was in words truly reported these. "I thank my Lord Mayor, his brethren, and you all! And whereas your request is, that I should continue your good Lady and Queen: be ye ensured that I will be as good unto you, as ever Queen was to her people! No will in me can lack! neither, do I trust, shall there lack any power! And persuade yourselves that, for the safety and quietness of you all, I will not spare, if need be, to shed my blood! GOD thank you all!"

Which answer of so noble a hearted Princess, if it moved a marvellous shout and rejoicing, it is nothing to be marvelled at; since both the heartiness thereof was so wonderful, and the words so jointly knit.

When Her Grace had thus answered the Recorder, she marched towards the Little Conduit; where was erected a pageant, with square proportion, standing directly before the same Conduit, with battlements accordingly. And in the same pageant were advanced two hills or mountains of convenient height.

The one of them, being on the north side of the same pageant, was made cragged, barren, and stony; in the which was erected one tree, artificially made, all withered and dead, with branches accordingly. And under the same tree, at the foot thereof, sat one, in homely and rude apparel, crookedly, and in mourning manner, having over his head in a table, written in Latin and English, his name, which was

RUINOSA RESPUBLICA,

A DECAYED COMMON WEAL.

And upon the same withered tree, were fixed certain tables wherein were written proper Sentences, expressing the causes of the Decay of the Common weal.

The other hill, on the south side, was made fair, fresh, green, and beautiful; the ground thereof full of flowers and beauty. And on the same was erected also one tree, very fresh and fair; under which, stood upright one fresh personage, well apparelled and appointed; whose name also was written, both in English and in Latin, which was

RESPUBLICA BENE INSTITUTA,
A FLOURISHING COMMON WEAL.

And upon the same tree also, were fixed certain tables containing Sentences, which expressed the causes of a Flourishing Common weal.

In the middle, between the said hills, was made artificially, one hollow place or cave, with door and lock enclosed; out of which, a little before the Queen's Highness's coming thither, issued one personage, whose name was TIME (apparelled as an old man, with a scythe in his hands, having wings artificially made), leading a personage, of less stature than himself, which was finely and well apparelled, all clad in white silk; and directly over her head was set her name and title, in Latin and English, *TEMPORIS FILIA,* THE DAUGHTER OF TIME.

Which two, so appointed, went forward, towards the south side of the pageant.

And on her breast was written her proper name, *VERITAS,* TRUTH; who held a book in her hand, upon the which was written, *Verbum Veritatis, The Word of Truth.*

And out of the south side of the pageant, was cast a standing for a child, which should interpret the same pageant.

Against whom, when the Queen's Majesty came, he spake unto Her Grace these words:

This old man with the scythe, old Father TIME they call:
And her, his daughter TRUTH, which holdeth yonder book;
Whom he out of his rock hath brought forth to us all,
From whence, these many years, she durst not once outlook.

The ruthful wight that sitteth under the barren tree,
Resembleth to us the form when Common weals decay;
But when they be in state triumphant, you may see
By him in fresh attire, that sitteth under the bay.

Now since that TIME again, his daughter TRUTH hath
    brought ;
We trust, O worthy Queen ! thou wilt this Truth embrace !
And since thou understandest the good estate and nought ;
We trust Wealth thou wilt plant, and Barrenness displace !

But for to heal the sore, and cure that is not seen,
Which thing the Book of Truth doth teach in writing plain ;
She doth present to thee, the same, O worthy Queen !
For that, that words do fly, but writing doth remain.

When the child had thus ended his speech, he reached
his book towards the Queen's Majesty; which, a little before,
TRUTH had let down unto him from the hill : which by Sir
JOHN PARRAT was received, and delivered unto the Queen.
    But she, as soon as she had received the book, kissed it ;
and with both her hands held up the same, and so laid
it upon her breast; with great thanks to the City therefore.
And so went forward toward Paul's Churchyard.

The former matter, which was rehearsed unto the Queen's
Majesty, was written in two tables, on either side the
pageant, eight verses : and in the midst, these in Latin.

> *Ille, vides, falcem læva qui sustinet uncam,*
>   *TEMPUS is est, cui stat filia VERA comes ;*
> *Hanc pater exesa deductam rupe reponit*
>   *In lucem, quam non viderat ante diu.*
> *Qui sedet a læva cultu male tristis inepto,*
>   *Quem duris crescens cautibus orbis obit*
> *Nos monet effigiæ, qua sit Respublica quando*
>   *Corruit, at contra quando beata viget,*
> *Ille docet juvenis forma spectandus amictu*
>   *Scitus, et æterna laurea fronde virens.*

The Sentences, written in Latin and English upon both
the trees, declaring the causes of both estates, were these :

❡ *C A U S E S   O F   A   R U I N O U S   C O M M O N
W E A L   A R E   T H E S E.*

Want of the Fear of GOD.	Civil disagreement.
Disobedience to rulers.	Flattering of Princes.
Blindness of guides.	Unmercifulness in rulers.
Bribery in magistrates.	Unthankfulness in subjects.
Rebellion in subjects.	

❡ *C A U S E S   O F   A   F L O U R I S H I N G
C O M M O N   W E A L.*

Fear of GOD.	Obedient subjects.
A wise Prince.	Lovers of the Common Weal.
Learned rulers.	Virtue rewarded.
Obedience to officers.	Vice chastened.

The matter of this pageant dependeth of them [*i.e., the pageants*] that went before. For, as the first declared Her Grace to come out of the House of Unity; the second, that she is placed in the Seat of Government, stayed with virtues to the suppression of vice; and therefore in the third, the Eight Blessings of Almighty GOD might well be applied unto her: so this fourth now, is to put Her Grace in remembrance of the state of the Common Weal, which TIME, with TRUTH his daughter, doth reveal: which TRUTH also, Her Grace hath received; and therefore cannot but be merciful and careful for the good government thereof.

From thence, the Queen's Majesty passed towards Paul's Churchyard.

And when she came over against Paul's School, a child appointed by the Schoolmaster thereof, pronounced a certain Oration in Latin, and certain Verses: which also were there written, as follows.

Philosophus ille divinus PLATO, inter multa præclare ac sapienter dicta, hoc posteris proditum reliquit, Rempublicam illam felicissimam fore, cui Princeps sophiæ studiosa, virtutibusque ornata contigerit. Quem si vere dixisse censeamus (ut quidem verissime) cur non terra Britannica plauderet? cur non populus gaudiam atque lætitiam agitaret ? immo, cur non hunc diem albo (quod aiunt) lapillo notaret ? quo Princeps talis nobis adest, qualem priores non viderunt, qualemque posteritas haud facile cernere poterit, dotibus quum animi, tum corporis undique felicissima. Casti quidem corporis dotes ita apertæ sunt, ut oratione non egeant. Animi vero tot tantæque, ut ne verbis quidem exprimi possint. Hæc nempe Regibus summis orta, morum atque animi nobilitate genus exuperat. Hujus pectus CHRISTI *religionis amore flagrat. Hæc gentem Britannicum virtutibus illustrabit, clipeoque justitiæ teget. Hæc literis Græcis et Latinis eximia, ingenioque præpollens est. Hac imperante, pietas vigebit, Anglia florebit, Aurea Secula redibunt. Vos igitur Angli, tot commoda accepturi,* ELIZABETHAM *Reginam nostram celeberrimam ab ipso* CHRISTO *hujus regni imperio destinatam, honore debito prosequimini. Hujus imperiis animo libentissimo subditi estote, vosque tali principe dignos præbete. Et quoniam, pueri non viribus sed precibus officium prestare possunt, nos Alumni hujus Scholæ ab ipso* COLETO, *olim Templi Paulini Decano, extructæ, teneras palmas ad cœlum tendentes* CHRISTUM *Opt. Maxi. precaturi sumus, ut tuum celsitudinem annos* NESTOREOS *summo cum honore Anglis imperitare faciat, matremque pignoribus charis beatam reddat. Amen.*

> *Anglia nunc tandem plaudas, lætare, re sulta,*
> *Presto jam vita est, præsidiumque tibi.*
> *En tua spes venit tua gloria, lux, decus omne*
> *Venit jam solidam quæ tibi prestat opem.*
> *Succurretque tuis rebus quæ pessum abiere.*
> *Perdita quæ fuerant hæc reparare volet*
> *Omnia florebunt, redeunt nunc aurea secla.*
> *In melius surgent quæ cecidere bona.*
> *Debes ergo illi totam te reddere fidam,*
> *Cujus in accessu commoda tot capies.*
> *Salve igitur dicas, imo de pectore summo.*
> *ELIZABETH Regni non dubitanda salus,*
> *Virgo venit, veniatque optes comitata deinceps.*

2 B   I

Pignoribus charis, læta parens veniat.
Hoc DEUS omnipotens ex alto donet Olympo,
Qui cælum et terram condidit atque regit.

Which the Queen's Majesty most attentively hearkened unto. And when the child had pronounced, he did kiss the Oration, which he had there fair written in paper, and delivered it unto the Queen's Majesty, which most gently received the same.

And when the Queen's Majesty had heard all that was there offered to be spoken ; then Her Grace marched toward Ludgate : where she was received with a noise of instruments ; the forefront of the Gate being finely trimmed against Her Majesty's coming.

From thence, by the way, as she went down toward Fleet Bridge, one about Her Grace, noted the City's charge, that " there was no cost spared."

Her Grace answered, that " She did well consider the same, and that it should be remembered ! " An honourable answer, worthy a noble Prince : which may comfort all her subjects, considering there can be no point of gentleness or obedient love shewed towards Her Grace ; which she doth not most tenderly accept, and graciously weigh.

In this manner, the people on either side rejoicing, Her Grace went forward towards the Conduit in Fleet Street, where was the fifth and last pageant, erected in the form following.

From the Conduit, which was beautified with painting, unto the north side of the street, was erected a Stage embattled with four towers, and in the same, a square plat rising with degrees.

Upon the uppermost degree was placed a Chair or royal Seat ; and behind the same Seat, in curious artificial manner, was erected a tree of reasonable height, and so far advanced above the seat as it did well and seemly shadow the same, without endamaging the sight of any part of the pageant. And the same tree was beautified with leaves as green as Art could devise, being of a convenient greatness and containing thereupon the fruit of the date tree ; and on the top of the same tree, in a table was set the name thereof, which was, *A Palm Tree.*

And in the aforesaid Seat or Chair was a seemly and meet personage, richly apparelled in Parliament robes, with a sceptre in her hand, as a Queen; crowned with an open crown: whose name and title were in a table fixed over her head in this sort, DEBORAH, *The Judge and Restorer of Israel.* Judic. 4.

And the other degrees, on either side, were furnished with six personages; two representing the Nobility, two the Clergy, and two the Comminalty. And before these personages, was written in a table,

DEBORAH, WITH HER ESTATES, CONSULTING FOR THE GOOD GOVERNMENT OF ISRAEL.

At the feet of these, and the lowest part of the pageant, was ordained a convenient room for a child to open the meaning of the pageant.

When the Queen's Majesty drew near unto this pageant; and perceived, as in the others, the child ready to speak: Her Grace required silence, and commanded her chariot to be removed nigher that she might plainly hear the child speak; which said, as hereafter followeth:

JABIN, of Canaan King, had long, by force of arms,
Oppressed the Israelites; which for GOD's People went:
But GOD minding, at last, for to redress their harms;
The worthy DEBORAH, as Judge among them sent.

In war, She, through GOD's aid, did put her foes to flight,
And with the dint of sword the band of bondage brast;
In peace, She, through GOD's aid, did always maintain right
And judgèd Israel, till forty years were past.

A worthy precedent, O worthy Queen! thou hast!
A worthy woman, Judge! a woman sent for Stay!
And that the like to us, endure always thou may'st;
Thy loving subjects will, with true hearts and tongues, pray!

388 BLUE COAT BOYS AT ST. DUNSTAN'S. [Jan. 1559.

Which verses were written upon the pageant: and the same in Latin also.

> *Quando DEI populum Canaan, rex pressit JABIN,*
> *Mittitur a magno DEBORA magna DEO :*
> *Quæ populum eriperet, sanctum servaret Judan,*
> *Milite quæ patrio frangeret hostis opes.*
> *Hæc Domino mandante DEO lectissima fecit*
> *Fœmina, et adversos contudit ense viros.*
> *Hæc quater denos populum correxerat annos*
> *Judicio, bello strenua, pace gravis.*
> *Sic, O sic, populum, belloque et pace, guberna!*
> *DEBORA sis Anglis, ELIZABETHA tuis!*

The void places of the pageant were filled with pretty Sentences concerning the same matter.

The ground of this last pageant was, that forasmuch as the next pageant before, had set before Her Grace's eyes the Flourishing and Desolate States of a Common Weal; she might by this, be put in remembrance to consult for the worthy Government of her people ; considering GOD, ofttimes, sent women nobly to rule among men, as DEBORAH which governed Israel in peace, the space of forty years ; and that it behoveth both men and women so ruling, to use advice of good counsel.

When the Queen's Majesty had passed this pageant; she marched towards Temple Bar.

But at St. Dunstan's, where the children of the Hospital [*i.e., Christ's Hospital, now known as the Blue Coat School, see p. 394*], were appointed to stand with their Governors ; Her Grace perceiving a child offered to make an oration unto her, stayed her chariot; and did cast up her eyes to heaven, as who should say, " I here see this merciful work towards the poor ; whom I must, in the midst of my royalty, needs remember." And so, turned her face towards the child, which, in Latin, pronounced an Oration to this effect.

That after the Queen's Highness had passed through the City ; and had seen so sumptuous, rich, and noble spectacles of the citizens, which declared their most

hearty receiving and most joyous welcoming of Her
Grace into the same : this one Spectacle yet rested and
remained ; which was the everlasting Spectacle of
Mercy unto the poor members of Almighty GOD, furthered by that famous and most noble Prince, King
HENRY VIII., Her Grace's Father; erected by the City
of London ; and advanced by the most godly, virtuous,
and gracious Prince, King EDWARD VI., Her Grace's dear
and loving brother. Doubting nothing of the mercy of
the Queen's most gracious clemency : by the which they
may not only be relieved and helped, but also stayed
and defended ; and therefore incessantly, they would
pray and cry unto Almighty GOD for the long life and
reign of Her Highness, with most prosperous victory
against her enemies.

The child, after he had ended his Oration, kissed the paper
wherein the same was written, and reached it to the Queen's
Majesty; who received it graciously both with words and
countenance, declaring her gracious mind towards their relief.

From thence, Her Grace came to Temple Bar, which was
dressed finely, with the two images of GOTMAGOT the Albion,
and CORINEUS the Briton ; two giants big in stature, furnished
accordingly : which held in their hands, even above the gate,
a table, wherein was written, in Latin verses, the effect of all
the pageants which the City before had erected. Which
Verses are these :

> *Ecce sub aspectu jam contemplaberis uno*
> *O Princeps populi sola columna tui !*
> *Quicquid in immensa passim perspexeris urbe*
> *Quæ cepere omnes unus hic arcus habet.*
> *Primus, te solio regni donavit aviti,*
> *Hæres quippe tui vera parentis eras.*
> *Suppressis vitiis, domina virtute, Secundus,*
> *Firmavit sedem regia virgo tuam.*
> *Tertius, ex omni posuit te parte beatam*
> *Si, qua cœpisti pergere velle, velis.*
> *Quarto, quid verum, Respublica Lapsa quid esset,*
> *Quæ Florens staret te docuere tui.*

Quinto, magna loco monuit te DEBORA, missam
Cælitus in regni gaudia longa tui.
Perge ergo Regina ! tuæ spes unica gentis !
Hæc Postrema urbis suscipe Vota tuæ.
" Vive diu ! regnaque diu ! virtutibus orna
Rem patriam, et populi spem tueare tui !
Sic, O sic petitur cœlum ! Sic itur in astra !
Hoc virtutis opus, cætera mortis erunt !"

Which Verses were also written in English metre, in a lesse[r] table, as hereafter followeth.

Behold here, in one view, thou mayst see all that plain;
O Princess, to this thy people, the only stay!
What eachwhere thou hast seen in this wide town; again,
This one Arch, whatsoever the rest contained, doth say.

The First Arch, as true Heir unto thy Father dear,
Did set thee in thy Throne, where thy Grandfather sat!
The Second, did confirm thy Seat as Princess here;
Virtues now bearing sway, and Vices beat down flat!

The Third, if that thou wouldst go on as thou began,
Declareth thee to be blessed on every side !
The Fourth did open Truth, and also taught thee when
The Common Weal stood well, and when it did thence slide!

The Fifth, as DEBORAH, declared thee to be sent
From heaven, a long comfort to us thy subjects all!
Therefore, go on, O Queen! (on whom our hope is bent)
And take with thee, this wish of thy Town as final!

" Live long ! and as long, reign ! adorning thy country
With virtues ; and maintain thy people's hope of thee!
For thus, thus heaven is won ! thus, must thou pierce the sky !
This is by virtue wrought ! All other must needs die!"

On the south side [*i.e., of Fleet Street, at Temple Bar*] was appointed by the City, a noise of singing children; and one child richly attired as a Poet, which gave the Queen's Majesty her Farewell, in the name of the whole City, by these words.

As at thine Entrance first, O Prince of high renown!
Thou wast presented with Tongues and Hearts for thy fair;
So now, sith thou must needs depart out of this Town,
This City sendeth thee firm Hope and earnest Prayer!

For all men hope in thee, that all virtues shall reign;
For all men hope that thou, none error wilt support;
For all men hope that thou wilt Truth restore again,
And mend that is amiss; to all good men's comfort!

And for this Hope, they pray thou mayst continue long
Our Queen amongst us here, all vice for to supplant!
And for this Hope, they pray that GOD may make thee strong,
As by His grace puissant, so in His truth constant!

Farewell! O worthy Queen! and as our hope is sure,
That into Error's place, thou wilt now Truth restore!
So trust we that thou wilt our sovereign Queen endure
And loving Lady stand, from henceforth, evermore!

While these words were in saying, and certain wishes therein repeated for the maintenance of Truth, and rooting out of Error; she, now and then, held up her hands to heaven-ward, and willed the people to say "Amen!"

When the child had ended, she said, "Be ye well assured, I will stand your good Queen!"

At which saying, Her Grace departed forth, through Temple Bar towards Westminster, with no less shooting [*i.e., firing of guns*] and crying of the people, than, when she entered the City, with a great noise of ordnance which the Tower shot off, at Her Grace's entrance first into Tower Street.

The child's saying was also, in Latin verses, written in a table which was hanged up there.

O Regina potens ! quum primam urbem ingredereris
Dona tibi, Linguas fidaque Corda dedit.
Discedenti etiam tibi nunc duo munera mittit,
Omina plena Spei, votaque plena Precum.
Quippe tuis Spes est, in te quod provida virtus
Rexerit, errori nec locus ullus erit.
Quippe tuis Spes est, quod ut verum omne reduces
Solatura bonas, dum mala tollis, opes.
Hac Spe freti orant, longum ut Regina gubernes,
Et regni excindas crimina cuncta tui.
Hac Spe freti orant, divina ut gratia fortem,
Et veræ fidei te velit esse basin.
Jam, Regina, vale ! et sicut nos spes tenet una,
Quod vero indueto, perditus error erit.
Sic quoque speramus quod eris Regina benigna
Nobis per regni tempora longa tui !

Thus the Queen's Highness passed through the City! which, without any foreign person, of itself, beautified itself; and received Her Grace at all places, as hath been before mentioned, with most tender obedience and love, due to so gracious a Queen, and sovereign Lady.

And Her Grace likewise, of her side, in all Her Grace's Passage, shewed herself generally an Image of a worthy Lady and Governor; but privately these especial points were noted in Her Grace, as signs of a most Prince-like courage, whereby her loving subjects may ground a sure hope for the rest of her gracious doings hereafter.

Certain Notes of the Queen's Majesty's great mercy, clemency, and wisdom used in this Passage.

 BOUT the nether end of Cornhill, toward Cheap, one of the Knights about Her Grace, had espied an ancient Citizen which wept, and turned his head back. And therewith said this Gentleman, "Yonder is an Alderman," for so he termed him, "which weepeth, and turneth his face backward! How may it be interpreted that he doth so? For sorrow! or for gladness?"

The Queen's Majesty heard him; and said, "I warrant you, it is for gladness!" A gracious interpretation of a noble courage, which would turn the doubtful to the best. And yet it was well known, that (as Her Grace did confirm the same) the party's cheer was moved, for very pure gladness for the sight of Her Majesty's person; at the beholding whereof, he took such comfort, that with tears he expressed the same.

In Cheapside, Her Grace smiled; and being thereof demanded the cause, answered, "For that she had heard one say, *Remember old King HENRY VIII!*" A natural child! which at the very remembrance of her father's name took so great a joy; that all men may well think that as she rejoiced at his name whom this Realm doth hold of so worthy memory, so, in her doings, she will resemble the same.

When the City's charge without partiality, and only the City, was mentioned unto Her Grace; she said, "It should not be forgotten!" Which saying might move all natural Englishmen heartily to shew due obedience and entireness to their so good a Queen, which will, in no point, forget any parcel of duty lovingly shewed unto her.

The answer which Her Grace made unto Master Recorder of London, as the hearers know it to be true and with melting hearts heard the same, so may the reader thereof conceive what kind of stomach and courage pronounced the same.

What more famous thing do we read in ancient histories of old time, than that mighty Princes have gently received presents offered them by base and low personages. If that be to be wondered at, as it is passingly! let me see any writer that in any one Prince's life is able to recount so many precedents of this virtue, as Her Grace shewed in that one Passage through the City. How many nosegays did Her Grace receive at poor women's hands? How ofttimes stayed she her chariot, when she saw any simple body offer to speak to Her Grace? A branch of rosemary given to Her Grace, with a supplication, by a poor woman, about Fleet Bridge, was seen in her chariot till Her Grace came to Westminster; notwithstanding the marvellous wondering of such as knew the presenter, and noted the Queen's most gracious receiving and keeping the same.

What hope the poor and needy may look for, at Her Grace's hand; she, as in all her journey continually, so in her hearkening to the poor children of Christ's Hospital, with eyes cast up unto heaven, did fully declare; as that neither the wealthier estate could stand without consideration had to the poverty, neither the poverty be duly considered unless they were remembered, as commanded to us by GOD's own mouth.

As at her first Entrance, she, as it were, declared herself prepared to pass through a City that most entirely loved her; so she, at her last Departing, as it were, bound herself by promise to continue good Lady and Governor unto that City, which, by outward declaration, did open their love to their so loving and noble Prince, in such wise as she herself wondered thereat.

But because Princes be set in their Seat by GOD's appointment, and therefore they must first and chiefly render the glory of Him from whom their glory issueth; it is to be noted in Her Grace, that, forasmuch as GOD hath so wonderfully placed her in the Seat of Government over this realm; she in all doings, doth shew herself most mindful of

His goodness and mercy shewed unto her. And amongst all other, two principal signs thereof were noted in this Passage.

First, in the Tower : where Her Grace, before she entered her chariot, lifted up her eyes to heaven, and said :

O LORD ! Almighty and everlasting GOD ! I give Thee most hearty thanks, that as Thou hast been so merciful unto me, as to spare me to behold this joyful day ! And I acknowledge that Thou hast dealt as wonderfully and mercifully with me, as Thou didst with thy true and faithful servant DANIEL, the prophet ; whom thou deliveredst out of the den, from the cruelty of the greedy and raging lions : even so, was I overwhelmed, and only by Thee ! delivered. To Thee ! therefore, only, be thanks, honour, and praise for ever ! Amen.

The second was, the receiving of the *Bible*, at the Little Conduit, in Cheap. For when Her Grace had learned that the *Bible* in English, should there be offered ; she thanked the City therefore, promised the reading thereof most diligently, and incontinent commanded that it should be brought. At the receipt whereof, how reverently, she did, with both her hands, take it ! kiss it ! and lay it on her breast ! to the great comfort of the lookers on !

GOD will undoubtedly preserve so worthy a Prince ; which, at His honour, so reverently taketh her beginning. For this saying is true, and written in the Book of Truth : " He that first seeketh the Kingdom of GOD, shall have all other things cast unto him."

Now, therefore, all English hearts, and her natural people must needs praise GOD's mercy, which hath sent them so worthy a Prince ; and pray for Her Grace's long continuance amongst us.

Imprinted at London in Fleet Street within Temple Bar, at the sign of the Hand and Star, by Richard Tottill, the .xxiii. day of January.

[1559]

Rev. WILLIAM HARRISON, B.D.
Canon of Windsor, and Rector of Radwinter.

ELIZABETH arms England, which MARY had left defenceless.

[Book II., Chap. 16 of *Description of England*, in HOLINSHED's *Chronicle*. Ed. 1587[-8]. Reprinted by F. J. FURNIVALL, M.A., for *New Shakspere Society*, *p.* 278, Ed. 1877.]

Ow well, and how strongly our country hath been furnished, in times past, with armour and artillery, it lieth not in me, as of myself to make rehearsal.

Yet that it lacked both, in the late time of Queen MARY; not only the experience of mine elders, but also the talk of certain Spaniards, not yet forgotten, did leave some manifest notice.

Upon the first, I need not stand: for few will deny it.

For the second, I have heard that when one of the greatest Peers of Spain [*evidently in Queen MARY's reign*] espied our nakedness in this behalf, and did solemnly utter in no obscure place, that " It should be an easy matter, in short time, to conquer England; because it wanted armour!" his words were then not so rashly uttered, as they were politicly noted.

For, albeit, that, for the present time, their efficacy was dissembled; and semblance made as though he spake but merrily: yet at the very Entrance of this our gracious Queen unto the possession of the Crown, they were so providently called to remembrance, and such speedy reformation sought, of all hands, for the redress of this inconveniency, that our country was sooner furnished with armour and munition from divers parts of the main [*the Continent*], besides great plenty that was forged here at home, than our enemies could get understanding of any such provision to be made.

By this policy also, was the no small hope conceived by Spaniards utterly cut off ; who (of open friends, being now become our secret enemies ; and thereto watching a time wherein to achieve some heavy exploit against us and our country) did thereupon change their purposes : whereby England obtained rest ; that otherwise might have been sure of sharp and cruel wars.

Thus a Spanish word uttered by one man at one time, overthrew, or, at the least, hindered sundry privy practices of many at another time.

In times past, the chief force of England consisted in their long bows. But now we have in manner generally given over that kind of artillery, and for long bows indeed, do practice to shoot compass for our pastime ; which kind of shooting can never yield any smart stroke, nor beat down our enemies, as our countrymen were wont to do, at every time of need. Certes, the Frenchmen and Reitters [*i.e.*, *Reiters, the German or Swiss Lance-knights*] deriding our new archery, in respect of their corslets, will not let, in open skirmish, if any leisure serve, to turn up their tails, and cry, " Shoot, English !" and all because our strong shooting is decayed, and laid in bed.

But if some of our Englishmen now lived, that served King EDWARD III. in his wars with France : the breech of such a varlet had been nailed to his back with one arrow ; and another feathered in his bowels, before he should have turned about to see who shot the first.

But as our shooting is thus, in manner, utterly decayed among us one way : so our countrymen wax skilful in sundry other points ; as in shooting in small pieces, the caliver, and handling of the pike ; in the several uses whereof, they are become very expert.

Our armour differeth not from that of other nations ; and therefore consisteth of corslets, almain rivets, shirts of mail, jacks quilted and covered with leather, fustian, or canvas over thick plates of iron that are sewed in the same. Of which, there is no town or village that hath not her convenient furniture. The said armour and munition like-

wise is kept in one several place of every town, appointed
by the consent of the whole parish; where it is always
ready to be had and worn within an hour's warning.

Sometimes also it is occupied [*used*], when it pleaseth the
magistrate, either to view the able men and take note of the
well keeping of the same; or finally to see those that are en-
rolled, to exercise each one his several weapon : at the charge
of the townsmen of each parish, according to his appointment. Certes there is almost no village so poor in England,
be it never so small, that hath not sufficient furniture in
a readiness to set forth three or four soldiers (as, one archer,
one gunner, one pike, and a bill-man), at the least. No,
there is not so much wanting as their very liveries [*uniforms*]
and caps; which are least to be accounted of, if any haste
required. So that if this good order continue, it shall be
impossible for the sudden enemy to find us unprovided.

As for able men for service, thanked be GOD! we are
not without good store. For by the Musters taken in 1574
and 1575, our number amounted to 1,172,674; and yet they
were not so narrowly taken, but that a third part of this
like multitude was left unbilled and uncalled.

What store of munition and armour, the Queen's Majesty
hath in her storehouses, it lieth not in me to yield account;
sith I suppose the same to be infinite. And whereas it was
commonly said, after the loss of Calais, that England would
never recover the store of ordnance there left and lost; the
same is proved false : since some of the same persons do
now confess that this land was never better furnished with
these things in any King's days, since the Conquest.

The names of our greatest ordnance are commonly
these :

> *Robinet*, whose weight is 200 lbs.; and it hath 1¼ inches
> within the mouth.
> *Falconet*, weighing 500 lbs., and his wideness is 2 inches
> within the mouth.
> *Falcon* hath 800 lbs., and 2½ inches within the mouth.
> *Minion* poiseth [*weigheth*] 1,100 lbs., and hath 3¼ inches
> within the mouth.
> *Sacre* hath 1,500 lbs., and is 3½ inches wide in the
> mouth.

Demi-Culverin weigheth 3,000 lbs., and hath 4½ inches within the mouth.

Culverin hath 4,000 lbs., and 5½ inches within the mouth.

Demi-Cannon, 6,000 lbs., and 6½ inches within the mouth.

Cannon, 7,000 lbs., and 8 inches within the mouth.

E. Cannon, 8,000 lbs., and 7 inches within the mouth.

Basilisk, 9,000 lbs., and 8¾ inches within the mouth.

By which proportions, also, it is easy to come by the weight of every shot, how many scores [*i.e., of yards*] it doth fly at point blank, how much powder is to be had to the same, and finally how many inches in height, each bullet ought to carry.

The names of the Great Ordnance	hath	Weight of the Shot. lbs.	Scores [of yards] of carriage.	Pounds of Powder.	Height of Bullet. Inches.
Robinet		I	0	½	I
Falconet.....................		2	14	2	1¼
Falcon		2½	16	2½	2¼
Minion		4½	17	4½	3
Sacre		5	18	5	3¼
Demi-Culverin		9	20	9	4
Culverin		18	25	18	5¼
Demi-Cannon		30	38	28	6¼
Cannon		60	20	44	7¼
E. Cannon		42	20	20	6¾
Basilisk.....................		60	21	60	8¼

As for the Armouries of some of the Nobility (whereof I also have seen a part), they are so well furnished, that within some one Baron's custody, I have seen three score or a hundred corslets at once ; besides calivers, hand-guns, bows, sheafs of arrows, pikes, bills, pole-axes, flasks, touch-boxes, targets, &c. : the very sight whereof appalled my courage.

Seldom shall you see any of my countrymen, above eighteen or twenty years old, to go without a dagger at the least, at his back or by his side ; although they be aged burgesses or magistrates of any city who, in appearance, are most exempt from brabling and contention.

Our Nobility commonly wear swords or rapiers, with their daggers; as doth every common serving man also that followeth his lord and master.

Finally, no man travelleth by the way, without his sword or some such weapon, with us; except the Minister, who commonly weareth none at all, unless it be a dagger or hanger at his side.

The True Report

of the burning of the Steeple and Church of Paul's in London.

Imprinted at London, at the
West end of Paul's Church, at the sign of the *Hedgehog,* by William Seres.

Cum privilegio ad imprimendum solum.
Anno 1561, *the* 10*th of June.*

2 C

The True Report of the burning of the Steeple and Church of Paul's in London.

N Wednesday, being the 4th day of June in the year of our Lord 1561 (and in the 3rd year of the reign of our Sovereign Lady ELIZABETH, by the Grace of God, Queen of England France and Ireland, Defender of the Faith, &c.), between one and two of the clock at afternoon, was seen a marvellous great fiery lightning; and immediately ensued a most terrible hideous crack of thunder, such as seldom hath been heard; and that, by estimation of sense, directly over the city of London. At which instant, the corner of a turret of the Steeple of St Martin's Church within Lud Gate was torn; and divers great stones casten down; and a hole broken through the roof and timber of the said Church by the fall of the same stones.

For divers persons (in time of the said tempest, being on the river of Thames; and others being in the fields near adjoining to the city) affirmed that they saw a long and spear-pointed flame of fire, as it were, run through the top of the broche [*or spire*] or shaft of Paul's Steeple; from the East, westward. And some of the parish of St Martin's, then being in the street, did feel a marvellous strong air or whirlwind, with a smell like brimstone, coming from Paul's Church; and withal heard a rush of the stones which fell from their Steeple into the Church.

Between four and five of the clock, a smoke was espied by divers to break out under the bowl of the said shaft of Paul's; and namely [*particularly*] by PETER JOHNSON, Principal Registrar to the Bishop of LONDON; who immediately brought word to the Bishop's House.

But, suddenly after, as it were in a moment, the flame brake forth in a circle, like a garland, round about the broche, about two yards, to the estimation of sight, under the bowl of the said shaft; and increased in such wise that, within a quarter of an hour, or little more, the Cross and the Eagle on the top fell down upon the South cross Ile [*Aisle*].

The Lord Mayor being sent for, and his Bretheren [the Aldermen], came with all speed possible; and had a short consultation, as in such a case might be, with the Bishop of LONDON and others, for the best way of remedy. And thither came also [Sir NICHOLAS BACON] the Lord Keeper of the Great Seal, and [WILLIAM PAULET, Marquis of WINCHESTER] the Lord Treasurer: who, by their wisdom and authority, directed as good order as in so great confusion could possibly be.

Some there were, pretending experience in wars, that counselled the remnant of the Steeple to be shot down with cannons; which counsel was not liked, as most perilous both for the dispersing [of] the fire, and [the] destruction of houses and people.

Others (perceiving the Steeple to be past all recovery; considering the hugeness of the fire, and the dropping of the lead) thought best to get ladders, and scale the Church; and with axes to hew down a space of the roof of the Church to stay the fire, at the least to save some part of the said Church: which was concluded [*decided upon*]. But before the ladders and buckets could be brought, and things put in any order (and especially because the Church was of such height that they could not scale it, and no sufficient number of axes could be had: the labourers also being troubled with the multitude of idle gazers); the most part of the highest roof of the Church was on fire.

First, the fall of the Cross and Eagle fired the South cross Ile [*Aisle*]; which Ile was first consumed. The beams and brands of the Steeple fell down on every side, and fired the other three parts : that is to say, the Chancel or Quire, the North Ile, and the body of the Church. So that, in one hour's space, the broche [or spire] of the Steeple was burnt down to the battlements ; and the most part of the highest roof of the Church likewise consumed.

The state of the Steeple and Church seeming both desperate ; my Lord Mayor was advised, by one Master WINTER of the Admiralty [i.e. Admiral Sir WILLIAM WINTER], to convert the most part of his care and provision to preserve the Bishop's Palace adjoining to the north-west end of the Church ; lest from that House, being large, the fire might spread to the streets adjoining. Whereupon the ladders, buckets, and labourers were commanded thither ; and, by great labour and diligence, a piece of the roof of the North Ile was cut down, and the fire so stayed : and, by much water, that part quenched ; and the said Bishop's House preserved.

It pleased GOD also, at the same time, both to turn, and calm, the wind : which afore was vehement ; and continued still high and great in other parts without the city.

There were above 500 persons that laboured in carrying and filling water, &c. Divers substantial citizens took pains as if they had been labourers ; so did also divers and sundry Gentlemen, whose names were not known to the Writer hereof : but amongst others, the said Master WINTER, and one Master STRANGUISH, did both take notable pains in their own persons ; and also much directed and encouraged others, and that not without great danger to themselves.

In the evening, came the Lord CLINTON, [the] Lord Admiral, from the Court at Greenwich ; whom the Queen's Majesty (as soon as the rage of the fire was espied by Her Majesty and others in the Court, of the pitiful inclination and love that her gracious Highness did bear both to the said Church and the city) sent to assist my Lord Mayor, for the suppressing of the fire : who, with his wisdom authority and diligent travail, did very much good therein.

About ten of the clock, the fierceness of the fire was past, the timber being fallen and lying burning upon the vaults of stone ; the vaults yet (GOD be thanked!) standing unperished. So as only the timber of the whole Church was consumed, and the lead molten : saving the most part of the two low Iles of the Quire, and a piece of the North Ile, and another small piece of the South Ile in the body of the Church.

Notwithstanding all which, it pleased the merciful GOD, in his wrath, to remember his mercy ; and to enclose the harm of this most fierce and terrible fire within the walls of this one Church : not extending any part of his wrath in this fire upon the rest of the city, which to all reason and sense of man was subject to utter destruction. For in the whole city, without the Church, no stick was kindled surely. Notwithstanding that, in divers parts and streets, and within the houses both adjoining and of a good distance, as in Fleet Street and Newgate Market, by the violence of the fire, burning coals of great bigness fell down almost as thick as hailstones ; and flaws of lead were blown abroad into the gardens without the city, like flaws of snow in breadth : without hurt (GOD be thanked!) to any house or person.

Many fond talks go abroad of the original cause of this. Some say, It was negligence of plumbers : whereas, by due examination, it is proved that no plumbers or other workmen laboured in the Church for six months before. Others suspect that it was done by some wicked practice of wild fire or gunpowder : but no just suspicions thereof, by any examination, can be found hitherto. Some suspect Conjurors and Sorcerers, whereof there is also no great likelihood : and if it had been wrought that way ; yet could not the Devil have done it without GOD's permission, and to some purpose of his unsearchable judgments, as appeareth in the story of JOB.

The true cause, as it seemeth, was the tempest, by GOD's sufferance. For it cannot be otherwise gathered, but that, at the said great and terrible thunderclap, when St Martin's Steeple was torn, the lightning (which by natural order smiteth the highest) did first smite the top of Paul's Steeple ;

and entering in at the small holes, which have always remained open for building scaffolds to the works, and finding the timber very old and dry, did kindle the same: and so the fire increasing, grew to a flame, and wrought the effect which followed; most terrible then to behold, and now most lamentable to look upon.

On Sunday following, being the 8th day of June [1561], the reverend [Father] in GOD [JAMES PILKINGTON] Bishop of DURHAM, at St Paul's Cross, made a learned and fruitful Sermon; exhorting the auditory to a general repentance, and namely [*especially*] to humble obedience to the laws and Superior Powers, which virtue is much decayed in these our days: seeming to have intelligence from the Queen's Highness, that Her Majesty intendeth more severity of laws shall be executed against persons disobedient, as well in causes of Religion as Civil; to the great rejoicing of his auditors.

He exhorted also his audience to take this as a general warning to the whole realm, and namely [*especially*] to the city of London, of some greater plague to follow if amendment of life in all [e]states did not ensue. He much reproved those persons which would assign the cause of this wrath of GOD to any particular [e]state of men; or that were diligent to look into other men's lives, and could see no faults in themselves: but wished that every man would descend into himself and say with DAVID, *Ego sum qui peccavi.* " I am he that hath sinned." And so forth to that effect, very godly.

He also not only reproved the profanation of the said Church of Paul's, of long time heretofore abused [*in Paul's Walk*] by walking, jangling, brawling, fighting, bargaining, &c., namely [*particularly*] in Sermon and Service time: but also answered by the way to the objections of such evil-tongued persons which do impute this token of GOD's deserved ire to alteration, or rather, Reformation of Religion; declaring out of ancient records and histories the like, yea, and greater matters, [that] had befallen in the time of superstition and ignorance.

For, in the 1st year of King STEPHEN [1135-6 A.D.] not only the said Church of Paul's was burnt: but also a great part of the city: that is to say, from London Bridge to St Clement's [Church] without Temple Bar, was by fire consumed.

And in the days of King HENRY VI., the Steeple of Paul's was also fired by lightning: although it was then stayed by diligence of the citizens; the fire being then, by likelihood, not so fierce.

Many other such like common calamities he rehearsed, which happened in other countries, both nigh to this realm and far off, where the Church of Rome hath most authority. And therefore [he] concluded the surest way to be, that every man should judge examine and amend himself; and embrace believe and truly follow the Word of GOD; and earnestly to pray to GOD to turn away from us his deserved wrath and indignation; whereof this his terrible work is a most certain warning, if we repent not unfeignedly.

The which GOD·grant may come to pass in all estates and degrees, to the glory of His name, and to our endless comfort in CHRIST our Saviour. Amen.

GOD save the Queen.

Rev. JOHN FOX, the Martyrologist.

A false fearful Imagination of fire at Oxford University.

[*Acts and Monuments*, 1576. *The passages in brackets, from* 1563 *Edition.*]

A merry and pleasant Narration, touching a false fearful Imagination of Fire raised among the Doctors and Masters of Oxford in St. Mary's church, at the recantation of Master MALARY, Master of Arts of Cambridge.

ITHERTO, [gentle reader, we have remembered a great number of lamentable and bloody tragedies of such as have been slain through extreme cruelty : now I will here set before thee again a merry and comical spectacle, whereat thou mayest now laugh and refresh thyself, which, forasmuch as it did necessarily accord with our present enterprise, I have not thought it good to pass it over with silence.]

There was one Master MALARY, Master of Arts of Cambridge, Scholar of Christ's College, who, for the like opinions to those above rehearsed, holden contrary to the Catholic determination of holy mother Church of Rome; that is, for the right truth of CHRIST's gospel, was convented before the bishops : and, in the end, sent to Oxford, there openly to recant, and to bear his faggot; to the terror of the students of that University. The time and place were appointed that he should be brought solemnly into St. Mary's church upon a Sunday; where a great number of the head Doctors and Divines and others of the University were together assembled: besides a great multitude of citizens and town dwellers, who came to behold the sight. Furthermore, because that solemnity should not pass without some effectual sermon for the holding up of the mother Church of Rome, Dr. SMITH, Reader then of the Divinity Lecture, was appointed to make the sermon at this recantation. Briefly, at the preaching of this sermon there was assembled a mighty audience of all sorts and degrees; as well of students as others. Few almost were absent who loved to hear or see any news; insomuch that there was no place almost in the whole church, which was not fully replenished with concourse and throng of people.

All things thus being prepared and set in readiness, cometh forth poor MALARY with his faggot upon his shoulder. Not long after, also, proceedeth the Doctor into the pulpit to make his sermon; the purpose and argument whereof was wholly upon the sacrament: the which Doctor, for the more confirmation and credit to his words; had provided the holy catholic cake and the sacrament of the altar, there to hang by a string before him in the pulpit. Thus the Doctor, with his god-almighty, entering his godly sermon, had scarce proceeded into the midst thereof (the people giving great silence with all reverence unto his doctrine), but suddenly was heard in the church the voice of one crying in the street, "Fire! fire!" The party who thus cried first in the street, was called HEUSTER.

[The occasion of this exclamation came by a chimney that was on fire in the town, wherein the fire, having taken hold of the soot and dry matter, burned out at the top of the chimney; and so caused the neighbours to make an outcry.]

This HEUSTER coming from Allhallows parish saw the chimney on fire, and so passing through the street by St. Mary's church, cried "Fire! fire!" as the fashion is; meaning no hurt.

[Such is the order and manner amongst the Englishmen; much diverse and contrary to that which is used among the Germans. For whensoever any fire happeneth in Germany, by and by, the bells ringing in the steeples stir up the people to help. Who immediately are all ready in armour; some go unto the walls, others beset the ways, and the residue are appointed to quench the fire. The labour is diversely divided amongst them, for whilst some fetch water in leather buckets, other some cast on the water, some climb the houses, and some with hooks pull them down; some again attend and keep watch without, riding about the fields: so that, by this means, there lacketh neither help within, neither safeguard without. But the like is not used here in England: for when any such thing happeneth, there is no public sign or token given; but the outcry of the neighbours doth stir up all the others to help. There is no public or civil order in doing of things, neither any division of labour: but every man, running headlong together, catcheth whatsoever cometh next to hand to quench the fire.]

This sound of fire being heard in the church, first of them that stood outermost next to the church door; so increased and went from one to another: that at length it came unto the ears of the Doctors, and at last to the Preacher himself. Who, as soon as they heard the matter, being amazed with sudden fear, and marvelling what the matter should mean; began to look up into the top of the church, and to behold the walls. The residue seeing them look up, looked up also. Then began they, in the midst of the audience, to cry out with a loud voice, "Fire! fire!" "Where?" saith one; "Where?" saith another. "In the church!" saith one. The mention of the church was scarcely pronounced, when, as in one moment, there was a common cry amongst them, "The church is on fire! The church is set on fire by heretics!" &c. And, albeit no man did see any fire at all; yet, forasmuch as all men cried out so, every man thought it true that they heard. Then was there such fear, concourse and tumult of people through the whole church, that it cannot be declared in words, as it was indeed.

And as in a great fire (where fire is indeed), we see many times how one little spark giveth matter of a mighty flame, setting whole stacks and piles a burning: so here, upon a small occasion of one man's word, kindled first a general cry, then a strong opinion running in every man's head within the church, thinking the church to be on fire; where no fire was at all. Thus it pleased Almighty GOD to delude these deluders: that is, that these great Doctors and wise men of the schools, who think themselves so wise in GOD's matters as though they could not err; should see, by their own senses and judgments, how blinded and infatuated they were, in these so small matters and sensible trifles.

Thus this strong imagination of fire being fixed in their heads, as nothing could remove them to think contrary; but that the church was on fire: so everything that they saw or heard increased this suspicion in them, to make it seem most true which was indeed most false. The first and chiefest occasion that augmented this suspicion, was the heretic there bearing his faggot: which gave them to imagine that all other heretics had conspired with him, to set the church on fire.

After this, through the rage of the people, and running to and fro, the dust was so raised, that it showed as it had been the smoke of fire: which thing, together with the outcry of the people, made all men so afraid; that, leaving the sermon, they began all together to run away. But such was the press of the multitude running in heaps together; that the more they laboured, the less they could get out. For while they ran all headlong unto the doors, every man striving to get out first; they thrust one another in such sort, and stuck so fast: that neither they that were without could get into the church again, neither they that were within could get out by any means. So then, one door being stopped, they ran to another little wicket on the north side, toward the college called Brasennose, thinking so to pass out. But there again was the like or greater throng. So the people, clustering and thronging together; it put many in danger, and brought many unto their end, by bruising of their bones or sides. There was yet another door towards the West, which albeit it was shut and seldom opened; yet now ran they to it with such sway, that the great bar of iron (which is incredible to be spoken) being pulled out and broken by force of men's hands: the door, notwithstanding, could not be opened for the press or multitude of people.

Much hurt done in the throng, whereof some died. Some yet are alive whose mothers' arms were there broken. [1576.]

At last, when they were there also past all hope to get out, then they were all exceedingly amazed, and ran up and down: crying out upon the heretics who had conspired their death. The more they ran about and cried out, the more smoke and dust rose in the church: even as though all things had now been on a flaming fire. I think there was never

such a tumultuous hurlyburly rising so of nothing heard of
before; nor so great a fear where was no cause to fear, nor
peril at all: so that if DEMOCRITUS, the merry philosopher,
sitting in the top of the church, and seeing all things in such
safety as they were, had looked down upon the multitude,
and beholden so great a number, some howling and weeping,
running up and down, and playing the mad men, now hither,
now thither, as being tossed to and fro with waves or tempests ;
trembling and quaking, raging and faring, without any
manifest cause; especially if he had seen those great Rabbins,
the Doctors laden with so many badges or cognisances of
wisdom, so foolishly and ridiculously seeking holes and corners
to hide themselves in ; gasping, breathing and sweating, and
for very horror being almost beside themselves : I think he
would have satisfied himself with this one laughter for all
his lifetime ; or else rather would have laughed his heart out
of his belly, whilst one said that he plainly heard the noise
of the fire, another affirmed that he saw it with his eyes,
and another sware that he felt the molten lead dropping
down upon his head and shoulders. Such is the force of
imagination, when it is once grafted in men's hearts through
fear.

In all the whole company, there was none that behaved
himself more modestly than the heretic that was Some say that
the monk's
there to do penance ; who, casting his faggot off head was
broken with
from his shoulders upon a monk's head that stood the faggot.
by, kept himself quiet, minding to take such part as the
others did.

All the others, being careful for themselves, never made an
end of running up and down and crying out. None cried out
more earnestly than the Doctor that preached (who was, as I
said, Dr. SMITH), who, in manner first of all, cried out in the
pulpit, saying, " These are the trains and subtleties of the
heretics against me: LORD have mercy upon me! LORD have
mercy upon me ! " But might not GOD, as it had been (to
speak with JOB) out of a whirlwind, have answered Job xl. 6.
again unto this preacher thus : " Thou dost now implore my
mercy, but thou thyself showest no mercy unto thy fellows
and brethren ! How doth thy flesh tremble now at the
mention of fire ! But you think it a sport to burn other simple
innocents neither do ye anything at all regard it. If burning

and to suffer a torment of fire seem so grievous a matter unto you, then you should also have the like consideration in other men's perils and dangers, when you do burn your fellows and brethren ! Or, if you think it but a light and trifling matter in them, go to now, do you also with like courage, contemn, and with like patience, suffer now the same torments yourselves. And if so be I should now suffer you with the whole church, to be burned to ashes, what other thing should I do unto you than you do daily unto your fellows and brethren ? Wherefore, since you so little esteem the death of others, be now content that other men should also little regard the death of you." With this, I say, or with some other like answer, if that either GOD, or human charity, or the common sense of nature would expostulate with them ; yea if there had been a fire indeed (as they were more feared than hurt), who would have doubted, but that it had happened unto them according to their deserts ? But now, worthy it is the noting, how the vain fear and folly of those Catholics either were deluded, or how their cruelty was reproved ; whereby they, being better taught by their own example, might hereafter learn what it is to put other poor men to the fire, which they themselves here so much abhorred.

But to return again to the description of this pageant, wherein (as I said before) there was no danger at all ; yet were they all in such fear, as if present death had been over their heads. In all this great maze and garboil, there was nothing more feared than the melting of the lead, which many affirmed that they felt dropping upon their bodies. [For almost all the churches in England are covered with lead, like as in Germany they are for the most part tiled.]

Now in this sudden terror and fear, which took from them all reason and counsel out of their minds, to behold what practices and sundry shifts every man made for himself it ; would make not only DEMOCRITUS, and HERACLITUS also, to laugh, but rather a horse well near to break his halter. But none used themselves more ridiculously than such as seemed greatest wise men, saving that in one or two, peradventure, somewhat more quietness of mind appeared ; among whom was one CLAYMUND, President of Corpus Christi College (whom, for reverence and learning's sake, I do here name), and a few other aged persons with him ; who, for their age and weakness, durst not thrust themselves into the throng amongst the rest, but kneeled down quietly before the high altar, committing themselves and their lives unto the Sacrament.

The others, who were younger and stronger, ran up and down through the press, marvelling at the incivility of men; and waxed angry with the unmannerly multitude that would give no room unto the Doctors, Bachelors, Masters, and other Graduates and Regent Masters. But as the terror and fear was common unto all men, so was there no difference made of persons or degrees; every man scrambling for himself. The violet cap, or purple gown, did there nothing avail the Doctor; neither the Master's hood, nor the monk's cowl, were there respected. Yea, if the King or Queen had been there at that present and in that perplexity; they had been no better than a common man.

After they had long striven and essayed all manner of ways, and saw no remedy, neither by force nor authority to prevail: they fell to entreating and offering of rewards; one offering twenty pounds [of good money], another his scarlet gown, so that any man would pull him out, though it were by the ears!

Some stood close unto the pillars, thinking themselves safe under the vaults of stone from the dropping of the lead: others, being without money, and unprovided of all shifts, knew not which way to turn them. One, being a President of a certain College (whose name I need not here to utter), pulling a board out from the pews, covered his head and shoulders therewith against the scalding lead; which they feared much more than the fall of the church. Now what a laughter would this have ministered unto DEMOCRITUS amongst other things, to behold there a certain grand paunch; who, seeing the doors stopped and every way closed up, thought, by another compendious means, to get out through a glass window, if it might be by any shift? But here the iron grates letted [*hindered*] him; notwithstanding his greedy mind would needs attempt, if he could haply bring his purpose to pass. When he had broken the glass, and was come to the space between the grates where he should creep out; first he thrust in his head with the one shoulder, and it went through well enough. Then he laboured to get the other shoulder after; but there was a great labour about that, and long he stuck by the shoulders with much ado; for what doth not importune labour overcome? Thus far forth he was now gotten; but, by what part of his body he did stick fast, I am not certain, neither may I feign: forasmuch as there be yet witnesses who did see these things, who would correct me, if I should do so. Notwithstanding, this is most certain, that he did stick fast between the grates, and could neither get out, nor in.

Thus this good man, being indeed a monk, and having but short hose; by the which way he supposed soonest to escape, by the same he fell into further inconvenience, making of one danger two. For, if the fire or lead had fallen on the outside, those parts which did hang out of the window had been in danger; and, contrariwise, if the flame had raged within the church, all his other parts had lien open to the fire. And as this man did stick fast in the window, so did the rest stick as fast in the doors, that sooner they might have been burned, than they could once stir or move one foot. Through the which press, at last, there was a way found, that some, going over their heads, gat out.

Here also happened another pageant in a certain monk (if I be not misadvised) of Gloucester College, whereat "Pleno ridet CALPHURNIUS ore."—HORACE. CALPHURNIUS might well laugh with an open mouth. So it happened, that there was a young lad in this tumult, who, seeing the doors fast stopped with the press or multitude, and that he had not way to get out, climbed up upon the door; and there, staying upon the top of the door, was forced to tarry still: for, to come down into the church again he durst not for fear of the fire, and to leap down toward the street he could not without danger of falling. When he had tarried there awhile, he advised himself what to do; neither did occasion want to serve his purpose: for, by chance, amongst them that got out over men's heads, he saw a monk, coming towards him, who had a great wide cowl hanging at his back. This the boy thought to be a good occasion for him to escape by. When the monk came near unto him, the boy, who was on the top of the door, came down, and prettily conveyed himself into the monk's cowl; thinking (as it came to pass indeed) that if the monk did escape, he should also get out with him. To be brief, at last the monk gat out over men's heads, with the boy in his cowl, and, for a great while, felt no weight or burden.

At the last, when he was somewhat more come to himself, and did shake his shoulders, feeling his cowl heavier than it was accustomed to be, and also hearing the voice of one speaking behind in his cowl; he was more afraid than he was before when he was in the throng: thinking, in very deed, that the evil spirit which had set the church on fire had flown into his cowl. By and by he began to play the exorcist: " In the name of GOD," said he, " and all saints, I command thee to declare what thou art, that art behind at my back! " To whom the boy answered, " I am BERTRAM's boy," said he; for that was his name. " But I," said the monk, " adjure thee, in the name of the unseparable Trinity, that thou, wicked spirit! do tell me who thou art, from whence thou comest, and that thou get thee hence! " " I am BERTRAM's boy," said he, " Good Master! let me go! " and with that his cowl began, with the weight, to crack upon his shoulders. The monk when he perceived the matter; took the boy out, and discharged his cowl. The boy took to his legs, and ran away as fast as he could.

Among others, one wiser than the rest ran with the church-door key, beating upon the stone walls; thinking therewith to break a hole through to escape out.

In the meantime those that were in the street, looking diligently about them, and perceiving all things to be without fear; marvelled at this sudden outrage, and made signs and tokens to them that were in the church to keep themselves quiet, crying to them that there was no danger.

But, forasmuch as no word could be heard by reason of the noise that was within the church, those signs made them much more afraid than they were before, interpreting the matter as though all had been on fire without the church; and for the dropping of the lead and falling of other things, they should rather tarry still within the church, and not to venture out. This trouble continued in this manner by the space of certain hours.

The next day, and also the week following, there was an incredible number of bills [*written notices*] set upon the church doors, to inquire for things that were lost in such variety

I

and number, as DEMOCRITUS might here again have had just cause to laugh. " If any man have found a pair of shoes yesterday in St. Mary's Church, or knoweth any man that hath found them, &c." Another bill was set up for a gown that was lost. Another entreated to have his cap restored. One lost his purse and girdle, with certain money ; another his sword. One inquireth for a ring ; and one for one thing, another for another. To be short, there were few in this garboil ; but that either through negligence lost, or through oblivion left something behind them.

Thus have you heard a tragical story of a terrible fire which did no hurt ; the description whereof, although it be not so perfectly expressed according to the worthiness of the matter, yet because it was not to be passed with silence, we have superficially set forth some shadow thereof: whereby the wise and discreet may sufficiently consider the rest, if any thing else be lacking in setting forth the full narration thereof.

As touching the heretic, because he had not done his sufficient penance there by occasion of this hurlyburly; therefore the next day following he was reclaimed into the Church of St. Frideswide [*Christ Church*] ; where he supplied the rest that lacked of his plenary penance.

The Spoil

of

Antwerp.

Faithfully reported by a true Englishman, who was present at the same.

November 1576.

Seen and allowed.

Printed at London by RICHARD JONES.

[The first thing here is to settle the authorship of this anonymous tract ; which was also anonymously entered at Stationers' Hall, probably from political reasons. From internal evidence at pp. 435, 441, 447, it is clear that the Writer was *not* one of the Fellowship of the English Merchant Adventurers in Antwerp ; but was an Englishman who had arrived in that city on the 22nd October 1576. Who this Writer was would seem to be clearly settled by the following extracts from documents in the State Paper Office, London.

S. P. *Foreign. Eliz.* Vols. 139-140.

915. GEORGE GASCOIGNE to Lord BURGHLEY.

From Paris, 15 September 1576.

The troubles and news of Flanders have set all the soldiers of this realm in a triumph. . . .

But now I mean to become an eyed-witness of the stir in Flanders ; and from thence your honour shall shortly (GOD willing) hear of me.

951. GEORGE GASCOIGNE to Lord BURGHLEY.

From Paris, 7 October 1576.

Whereof I trust shortly to understand more, for to-morrow (GOD willing) I go towards the Low Countries ; and mean to spend a month, [or] two, or three, as your Honours shall like, in those parts.

For I mean to spend this winter (or as long as shall be thought meet) in service of my country. I beseech your Honour to confer with Master Secretary [Sir FRANCIS WALSINGHAM] who can more at large make you privy to my intent.

955. Sir AMIAS PAULET, Ambassador for England in France, to Sir FRANCIS WALSINGHAM.

From Paris, 12 October 1576.

Master GASCOIGNE is departed towards Flanders ; having prayed me to recommend him unto you by my letters, and also to convey these letters enclosed unto you.

If this GEORGE GASCOIGNE, who, as his handwriting shows, is doubtless the Soldier-Poet, left Paris on the 8th October, he could very well have come to Antwerp, as the Writer of this narrative states, at page 149, he did, by the 22nd of that month.

GASCOIGNE the Poet was a very tall man, so that he was called "long GEORGE." This he seems to refer to at page 441 where he says, " I got up like a tall fellow."

For further confirmation of GASCOIGNE being the Author, see pp. 435-7

2. The best Plan of Antwerp, about the time of the Spanish Fury, that we have met with, is that of GEORGE BRAUN'S *Civitates Orbis Terrarum*, Vol. I., Plan 17.

3. All the dates in the following narrative are Old Style.

4. It is to be specially noted that Antwerp was a Roman Catholic city that had never, *in the least way possible*, rebelled against PHILIP II. ; and that its awful destruction was made, without the least provocation, by the soldiers of its Sovereign, that should have protected it. Its only crime was its great wealth. 5,000 merchants met in its Bourse, or Exchange, every week. It was then the Venice of the North, with about 125,000 inhabitants.

The following extract will explain the general position of affairs in Flanders about this time.

S. P. *Foreign. Eliz.* Vol. 140.

1,021. *Dr* [THOMAS] *WILSON* [*Ambassador for England in Flanders*] *to the Privy Council.*

19 November 1576.

And except despair drive the Prince [of ORANGE], I do not think that ever he will yield that to [the Duke of ANJOU, the] Monsieur [of France] which he hath in his power ; being now in better case since these late troubles than ever he was before : having Zierikzee and Haarlem again ; and Tergoes also, which he never had before.

There are in the Spaniards' possession, Antwerp ; Lierre, 8 English miles from thence ; [Den]dermonde, 18 miles distant ; and Maestricht, 50 miles distant ; and more they have not in their power. . . .

The States, so far as I can understand, have none other intention, but that the Spaniards may be sent out of the country ; and then they offer to live in all obedience to their King and Sovereign. The Spaniards will not depart except the King expressly command them. In the mean season, they do mind nothing but spoil and ravin.]

[5. The following illustrative documents, now in the State Paper Office, London, carry on the story of the Spanish Fury to a somewhat later date.

The spelling of the word GASCON is so important, that we took the opinion of several experts at the State Paper Office upon it. They were all unanimous that the word is written GASCON, and not GASTON as printed in Volume 140 of the *Calendar* of those *Foreign State Papers.* That being so and the Christian name being given as GEORGE : it is clear that THOMAS HETON, in the flurry in which he wrote the *Memorial* from the Company, wrote GEORGE GASCON phonetically for GEORGE GASCOIGNE.

6. The next two documents are the letters which the Soldier-Poet brought to England, when he got out of Antwerp on 12th November 1576, as stated at page

S. P. *Foreign. Eliz.* Vol. 140.

1,009. THOMAS HETON to Sir FRANCIS WALSINGHAM.

From Antwerp, 10 November 1576.

Right Honourable, the 3rd of this month the States' men, Horsemen and Footmen, entered this town with consent : and on the morrow, which was Sunday the 4th of this present, the Spaniards with certain Almains, out of the Castle, entered the town and drave away the States' Power and they fled as they could : the town [being] put to sack, with a pitiful slaughter and a miserable spoil.

Our House [was] entered by Twelve Spaniards, soldiers, who put me and the rest of the Company in great fear. We were put to ransom first at 12,000 crowns ; and since it it is grown one way and [an]other to 3,000 more : and what the Company have lost, that had their chambers and packhouses in the town in burghers' houses, at this present, I know not ; but they are spoiled of all.

In the name of the Company there is a letter written to the honourable [Privy] Council of our state [*See next document*] most humbly beseeching that their Honours would be a mean[s] for us to Her Majesty, as to their Honours in this case they shall think good.

If we might have had passport[s] when I revuired it, first of the States, then of Monsieur [DE] CHAMPAGNEY

Governor of this town, and after of the Lords of this town, as both by the Intercourse [of 1507] and Privileges we ought in right to have had; then had we avoided this great peril of life and miserable spoil which we have sustained.

And now I most humbly beseech you to move my good Lords that some [persons and money] may be sent over for our comfort, that we may be permitted to pass out of this town in person, and [also] such goods as we have remaining. For in this town we shall lack both victuals and fuel; and also be daily in fear of the like spoil that we have sustained.

And thus, what for the great peril that I have sustained, and the burden and charge of my Office; I must crave pardon though my writing be not as it should be.

I do perceive they [*the Spaniards*] stand here in doubt how Her Majesty will take this doing to us.

The Lord send me and my wife into England, if it be his good will.

At Antwerp, the 10th of November 1576.

THOMAS HETON.

1,010 *The Merchant Adventurers to the Privy Council.*

From Antwerp, [10] November 1576.

Right Honourable our good and gracious Lords, &c. In all humbleness these are showing to your Honours that in respect of the troubles all over this country, and especially the danger in this town of Antwerp; such of our Society as are here remaining did purpose, and some attempted, to have, in due time, removed from this place both their persons and goods; some by water and some by land, as well towards England as for Duchland [*Germany.*] And being letted [*hindered*] of their purpose and attempts both the ways, and not suffered to pass their goods out of this town; whereupon [they] sought to have had free passage and passport here, according to the Intercourse and Safe Conduct.

But after many delays, from time to time; the 3rd day of this month, our requests were plainly denied, either to be granted, or by writing answered.

So as, the 4th day, we are fallen into great peril of our lives; divers of our Company being hurt, and some slain. And by sacking of this town ever since, we are not only spoiled of our money and goods that were in private houses thereof; but also we are further forced, for ransom and safeguard of our persons and goods within the principal House of our residence here, to answer and content the Spanish soldiers and others who, in the Fury, entered our said House, accounting charges, above the sum of £5,000 Flemish.

Towards furniture [*furnishing*] whereof, we have been constrained to give them all the money and plate that was in our said House; and also to use our credit for so much as we could get besides. And yet all accounted and delivered to them doth not discharge the one half of the sum; and for the rest we have given them Bills payable at a month, and some part at two months: so as now we have not money to provide for our needful sustentation.

Wherefore we most humbly beseech your good Lordships aud Honours, of your accustomed clemencies, to have compassion upon us; and to be means to our most gracious Sovereign Lady, the Queen's Majesty, that speedy order may be given for our relief, and release out of this place: where presently [*at present*] we are void of money and credit; and shortly are like[ly] to be void of sustenance, and not able to get it for money.

The discourse of these tragedies we omit, and refer the same to be reported to your Lordships by this bringer, Master GEORGE GASCON; whose humanity, in this time of trouble, we, for our parts, have experimented.

And so leaving the further and due consideration of our case unto your Right Honourable wisdoms and clemencies; we beseech Almighty GOD to preserve your good Lordships and Honours in long health and felicity.

Written at Antwerp, this [10th] day of Novembei 1576,
By your Lordships' and Honours'
Most bound and obedient,
The Governor and Fellowship of the
English Merchant Adventurers in Antwerp,
THOMAS HETON.

7. In 1602, an anonymously written Play, based on this Narrative, was published in London, under the title, *A larum for London, or the Siege of Antwerp*, in 4to.

8. Five days after GASCOIGNE got out of Antwerp; the English Ambassador was there. No doubt he helped our Merchant Adventurers in their dire extremity.

JERONIMO DE RODAS, or RODA, was the supreme villain in command of the troops that had sacked the town; as SANCHO D'AVILA was in charge of Antwerp Castle. Doctor WILSON thus reports a conversation that he had with RODAS on the 17th November 1576, thirteen days after the massacre began. This gives us the Spanish view of the matter; and also such miserable excuse as they could possibly offer for their villany, which however is no excuse at all.

We must remember that it would be the Ambassador's policy to keep fair with RODAS, who was master of the situation for the moment.

S. P. *Foreign. Eliz.* Vol. 140.

1,021. *Dr* THOMAS WILSON *to the Privy Council.*

19 November 1576.

And now, if it please your Honours, I am to declare my coming to RODAS, who did send unto me a Safe Conduct for me and mine, upon a letter that I did write to him from Ghent the 10th of this month : and the 17th of the same, I did speak with him ; immediately after my coming to Antwerp.

And, delivering my Letters of Credit, [I] made him acquainted with all that I did at Brussels ; and that my coming [to Flanders] was for the King's benefit and honour : assuring him that if either the Estates would alienate this country [of Flanders] to any foreign Prince, or would convert it to themselves in prejudice of the King [PHILIP II.] ; Her Majesty would employ all her force to withstand such attempts.

These speeches he liked very well : and was persuaded, even by plain demonstration before my departure, that my coming was to none other end ; as it was not indeed.

Hereupon he declared unto me at large, the whole doings at Brussels, the Mutinies made by the Spaniards at Alost and elsewhere after their victory had at Zierikzee ; and blamed greatly the young heads at Brussels, and the fury of the people to use the King's Council, and to break up the door of his Palace, in such sort as they did : [*RODAS was very nearly made prisoner in the Palace at Brussels on 5th September 1576, by the Seigneur De Hèze:*] clearing the Council from all intention of evil to the town, or people, of Brussels; making a very great discourse unto me of this matter.

"Well," quoth I, "you are well revenged of the people by your late victory here in Antwerp; which hath been very bloody."

"Can you blame us?" quoth he. "Is it not natural to withstand force with force; and to kill rather than to be killed? and not to lose the King's piece committed to our charge?"

All this I granted: and praised the Spaniards for their valiant courage; that, being so few, could, with policy and manhood, overcome so many.

"But now," quoth I, " I pray you give me leave to speak a little. After you were lords of the town—which you got wholly and quietly within two hours after your issuing forth—what did you mean, to continue still killing, without mercy, people of all sorts that did bear no armour at all; and to murder them in their houses? to fire the chiefest and fairest part of the city, after you were in full and quiet possession of all? And not contented to spoil the whole town, but to ransom those that were spoiled? And to spare no Nation: although they did bear no arms at all; nor yet were dealers in any practice at all against the King's Ministers, or the Spaniards?"

His answer was, That the fury of the soldiers could not be stayed: and that it grieved him much when the city was on fire; and [that there] was no sparing to kill, when all were conquered. The soldiers of Alost were adventurers, had no Captains, desperate persons: and would not be ruled by any Proclamation or commandment that could be given or made.

"Well," quoth I, "if the Fury could not be stayed; yet the Ransoming might be forbidden; which is an act against the Law of all Nations." And therefore I required him, in the name of the Queen's Majesty, to command restitution to be made to the English Nation. . . .

To conclude, he told me, That he would be glad to do what he might for restitution; but he thought it would be hard. For that which is to be paid with Bills, which for the

Company amounteth to 5,000 crowns, at the month's end : the same [Bills], he saith, shall be discharged ; and the bonds cancelled. Further he hath promised to grant a Safe Conduct for all English Merchants to go (with their goods remaining, ships, and merchandizes), without danger, withersoever they will : not aiding, or abetting, the King's enemies.

9. We next give the opinion of the Sieur DE CHAMPAGNEY as to how the massacre came about.

In the following January, he was in England : and then presented a long Memorial in French, to our Privy Council ; in which occurs the following reference to the Spanish Fury.

S. P. *Foreign. Eliz.* Vol. 142.

1,029. *The Sieur DE CHAPAGNEY's Declaration.*

At London, in January 1577.

That he undertook the Government of Antwerp most unwillingly, at the express desire and command of the King of Spain. That, during his Government, he did all in his power to restrain the excesses of the Spaniards in the Citadel ; so far as to incur their odium and hatred. That he was unable to prevent the sack of the town, owing to the treachery of the Almain Colonels [*VAN EINDEN &c.*] of the only troops under his command ; who would not suffer the burghers to arm in their defence.

10. EDWARD GRIMESTON, in his *General History of the Netherlands to* 1608 (which is mainly based on J. F. LE PETIT's *Chronique*, printed at Dordrecht in 1601) gives the following account of the destruction of Antwerp Castle, which had been built by the Duke of ALVA.

The inhabitants of Antwerp being still in fear, by reason of their Castle, so long as the war was thus wavering, fearing they should be, at some time, again surprised (terming it a den of thieves, an invention of men full of cruelty, a nest of tyranny, a receptacle of all filthy villany abomination and wickedness) obtained leave of the States to dismantle it towards the town.

The which the burghers began the 28th of August [1577],

with such spleen as there was neither great nor small (wives
children, gentlewomen, and burghers ; and all in general) but
would pull down a piece of it ; men, women, and servants
going thither, with their Ensigns displayed, having many
victuallers on the plain before the Castle [*the Esplanade*] ; so
as it seemed a camp.   And although the masons' work was
great, strong, and thick ; yet were they not long in beating
it down on that side.

Soon after, in imitation of that of Antwerp, followed the
dismantling of the Castles of Ghent, Utrecht, Valenciennes,
Bethune, Lille, Aire, and others ; and the Citadel of Arras
was laid open towards the town.

[The following Preface occurs in the Bodleian copy of this Tract.]

To the Reader.

 SHALL earnestly require thee, gentle Reader, to correct the errors passed and escaped in printing of this pamphlet according to this Table.*

And furthermore to understand that this victory was obtained with loss of but five hundred Spaniards, or six [hundred] at the most ; of whom I heard no man of name recounted [as killed] saving only Don EMANUEL.

Thus much, for haste, I had forgotten in this treaty [*treatise*] ; and therefore thought meet to place it here in the beginning.   And therewithal to advertise thee, that these outrages and disordered cruelties done to our Nation proceeded but from the common soldiers : neither was there any of the Twelve which entered the English House [*see pp*. 446, 447], a man of any charge or reputation.   So that I hope, these extremities notwithstanding, the King their master will take such good order for redress thereof as our countrymen, in the end, shall rest satisfied with reason ; and the amity between our most gracious Sovereign and him shall remain also firm and unviolate : the which I pray GOD speedily to grant for the benefit of this realm. Amen.

* The necessary corrections have been herein made.—E. A.

The Spoil of Antwerp.

INCE my hap was to be present at so piteous a spectacle as the Sacking and Spoil of Antwerp, a lamentable example which hath already filled all Europe with dreadful news of great calamity, I have thought good, for the benefit of my country, to publish a true report thereof. The which may as well serve for profitable example unto all estates of such condition[s] as suffered in the same: as also answer all honest expectations with a mean truth set down between the extreme surmises of sundry doubtful minds; and increased by the manifold light tales which have been engendered by fearful or affectionate [*prejudiced*] rehearsals.

And therewithal if the wickedness used in the said town do seem unto the well disposed Reader, a sufficient cause of GOD's so just a scourge and plague; and yet the fury of the vanquishers do also seem more barbarous and cruel than may become a good Christian conqueror: let these my few words become a forewarning on both hands; and let them stand as a lantern of light between two perilous rocks; that both amending the one, and detesting the other, we may gather fire out of the flint and honey out of the thistle.

To that end, all stories and Chronicles are written; and to that end I presume to publish this Pamphlet; protesting that neither malice to the one side, nor partial affection to the other, shall make my pen to swerve any iote [*jot* or *iota*] from truth of that which I will set down, and saw executed.

For if I were disposed to write maliciously against the vanquishers: their former barbarous cruelty, insolences, rapes, spoils, incests, and sacrileges committed in sundry other places, might yield me sufficient matter without the lawful remembrance of this their late Stratagem. Or if I would undertake to move a general compassion by blazing abroad the miseries and calamities of the vanquished : their long sustained injuries and yokes of untollerable bondage, their continual broils in war, their doubtful dreads in peace, their accusations without cause, and condemnations without proof, might enable a dumb stone to talk of their troubles, and fetch brinish tears out of the most craggy rock to lament and bewail the burning houses of so near neighbours.

But as I said before, mine only intent is to set down a plain truth, for the satisfying of such as have hitherto been carried about with doubtful reports ; and for a profitable example unto all such as, being subject to like imperfections, might fall thereby into the like calamities.

And to make the matter more perspicuous ; I must derive the beginning of this Discourse a little beyond the beginning of the Massacre : that the cause being partially opened, the effect may be the more plainly seen.

It is then to be understood that the Sacking and Spoil of Antwerp hath been, by all likelihood, long pretended [*designed*] by the Spaniards : and that they have done nothing else but lie in wait continually, to find any least quarrel to put the same in execution. For proof whereof, their notable Rebellion and Mutiny began in the same [city, on 26th April 1574]; when their watch-word was *Fuora villiacco !* [This is apparently old Spanish for *Out with the townsfolk !*] might sufficiently bewray their malicious and cruel intent. And though it were then smoothly coloured over [*explained away*] and subtilly appeased by the crafty devisers of the same : yet the coals of the choler, being but raked up in the embers of false semblance, have now found out the wicked winds of wiliness and wrath ; which meeting together have kindled such a flame as gave open way to their detestable devices.

For the Estates of the Low Countries, being over-wearied with the intolerable burden of their tyrannies ; and having taken arms to withstand their malice and rebellious mutinies : the town of Antwerp, being left open and subject unto the Citadel, did yet remain quiet; and entered not into any martial action.

Whereat the Spaniards (being much moved ; and having not yet opportunity to work their will so colourably [*with a sufficient pretence*] as they wished) bestowed certain cannon shot out of the said Castle, and slew certain innocent souls ; with some other small harm and damage done to the edifices : thinking thereby to harden the hearts of the poor Flemings, and to make them take arms for their just defence ; whiles they thereby might take occasion to execute their unjust pretence. And this was done on the 19th, or 20th, of October [1576] last.

Now to answer all objections ; I doubt not but it will be alleged that the Castle bestowed the said cannon shot at the town ; because they of the town did not shoot at the Prince of ORANGE's ships, which lay within sight thereof : but alas it is easy to find a staff when a man would beat a dog.

For the truth is, that those ships did no greater hurt either to the town or Castle than friendly to waft up [*convoy*] all manner of grain and victuals for the sustenance of the said town : which even then began to want such provisions by reason that the said Spaniards had built a Fort on [the] Flanders side upon the same river [*the Scheldt*] ; and thereby stopped all such as brought victual to the said town ; burning and destroying the country near adjoining, and using all terror to the poor people, to the intent that Antwerp might lack provision[s].

And about the same time also, the Spaniards cut off a bridge, which was the open passage between Antwerp and Machlen [*Malines*], at a village called Walem [*Waelhem*] A manifest proof of their plain intent to distress the said town, and to shut up the same from the rest of Brabant : since they were walled in with the river on the one side ; and on that other the Spanish horsemen occupied all the country, and so terrified the poor people as they durst not bring their commodities to the same.

All this notwithstanding, the chief rulers of the said town of Antwerp appeased the people ; and put up [with] these injuries until they might be better able to redress them.

Soon after, the Spaniards, assisted by the treason of certain

2 E   I

High Duches [*Germans*], entered the town of Maestricht upon a sudden; and put the same to sack: killing and destroying great numbers of innocent people therein. A thing to be noted. For that Maestricht had never revolted; but stood quiet under their garrisons, as faithful subjects to their King [PHILIP II]: and the one half thereof pertained also unto the Bishop of LIEGE, who had yet meddled nothing at all in these actions.

The chief rulers and people of Antwerp (perceiving thereby the cruel intent of the Spaniards; and doubting [*fearing*] their Duche [*German*] garrison, which was of the Count OBERSTEIN's Regiment, as they were also which betrayed Maestricht) began to abandon the town, leaving their houses and goods behind them; and sought to withdraw themselves into some place of safer abode.

Whereat the Estates, being moved with compassion, and doubting that the town would shortly be left desolate, levied a Power of 3,000 Footmen and 800 or 1,000 Horsemen [*mostly Walloons and Germans*]; and sent the same, under the conduct of the Marquis D'HAVRÉ, the young Count [PHILIP] D'EGMONT, Monsieur DE CAPRES, Monsieur DE BERSELLE [or BERSELEN], Monsieur DE GOGINES, and other Nobles and Gentlemen, to succour and defend the town of Antwerp against the cruel pretence [*designs*] of the said Spaniards.

And they came before the Gates thereof, on Friday the 2nd of this instant [November 1576], at a Port on the east or south-east side thereof, called Kipdorp Port. Whereat the Spaniards, being enraged, discharged sundry shot of great artillery from the Castle; but to small purpose.

At last, Monsieur [FRÉDÉRIC PERRENOT, Sieur] DE CHAMPAGNEY, who was Governor of the town, and the Count OBERSTEIN, which was Colonel of the garrison, demanded of the States' [troops], Wherefore they approached the town in such order?

Who answered, That they came to enter the same as friends, and to entrench and defend it from the Spaniards: protesting further, That they would offer no manner of violent damage or injury to the persons or goods of any such as inhabited the same.

Hereupon the said Monsieur [the Sieur] DE CHAMPAGNEY

and Count OBERSTEIN went out unto them, and conferred
more privately together by the space of one hour: and
returned into the town, leaving the Estates' Power at a
village called Borgherhout.

On the morrow, being the 3rd of this instant [November
1576], they were permitted to enter, and came into the town:
21 Ensigns of Footmen and 6 Cornets of Horsemen.

Immediately after their entry, the inhabitants brought
them sacks of wool and other such provision; wherewith
they approached the Yard or plain ground which lieth before
the Castle: and, placing the same at the ends of five streets
which lie open unto the said Castle Yard [*Esplanade*],
entrenched under them with such expedition that in less
than five hours those streets' ends were all reasonably well
fortified from the Castle, for any sudden [attack].

At this time and twelve days before [*i.e. from 22nd
October* 1576], I was in the said town of Antwerp, upon
certain private affairs of mine own; so that I was enforced
to become an eyed-witness [see page 420] of their Entry [*i.e.
of the States' troops*] and all that they did: as also afterwards
—for all the Gates were kept fast shut, and I could not
depart—to behold the pitiful Stratagem which followed.

The Castle thundered with shot at the town: but it was a
very misty day; so that they could neither find their marks
very well, not yet see how the streets' ends were entrenched.

It was a strange thing to see the willingness of the inhabitants, and how soon many hands had despatched a
very great piece of work. For, before midnight, they had
made the trenches as high as the length of a pike; and
had begun one trench for a Counterskarf [*Counterscarp*]
between all those streets and the Castle Yard: the which
they perfected unto the half way from St George's Churchyard unto the water's side by St Michael's; and there
left from work, meaning to have perfected it the next
day.

That Counterscarf had been to much purpose, if it had
been finished: as shall appear by a Model [*Plan*] of the
whole place which I have annexed to this treaty [*treatise*]; by

view whereof the skillful Reader may plainly perceive the execution of every particularity.*

These things thus begun and set in forwardness; it is to be noted that the Spaniards (having intelligence of the States' Power, when it set forward from Brussels; and perceiving that it bent towards Antwerp) had sent to Maestricht, Lierre, and Alost to draw all the Power that could be made, unto the Castle of Antwerp. So that on Sunday, the 4th of this instant [November 1576], in the morning, they all met at the said Castle. And their Powers, as far as I could gather, were these:

There came from Maestricht, very near to 1,000 Horsemen, led by ALONZO DE VARGAS who is the General of the Horsemen; and 500 Footmen or more, governed by the Camp Master, FRANCESCO DE VALDEZ.

There came from Lierre, 500 Footmen or more, governed by the Camp Master, JULIANO DE ROMERO.

There came from Alost, 2,000 Footmen, which were the same that rebelled for their pay and other unreasonable demands, immediately after the Winning of Zierikzee [*J. DE RODAS, at page 426, states that these 2,000 soldiers were* "desperate men."] These had none other conductor than their *Electo* [or *Eletto, i.e., their elected Chief; at this time a man named NAVARETTE*], after the manner of such as mutiny and rebel: but were of sundry Companies, as Don EMANUEL's, and others. Nevertheless I have been so bold in the Model [*Plan*] as to set down the said Don EMANUEL for their leader: both because I think that, their mutiny notwithstanding, he led them at the exploit; and also because he was slain amongst them at their entry.

Thus the number of [the] Spaniards was 4,000 or thereabouts; besides some help that they had of the garrison within the Castle. And besides, 1,000 High Almains [*Germans*] or more; which came from Maestricht, Lierre, and those parts. And they were of three sundry Regiments:

---

* This Plan of Antwerp at the time of the Spanish Fury, drawn up from the instructions of GEORGE GASCOIGNE, is wanting in every copy of this Narrative that we have met with. We have strenuously searched for it in every direction; but without success. Its disappearance is a great loss.—E.A.

CHARLES FUGGER's, POLWILLER's, and FRONDSBERGER's:
but they were led all by CHARLES FUGGER. So that the
whole force of the Spaniards and their complices was
5,000 and upwards.

The which assembled and met at the Castle, on the said
4th day [of November 1576], about ten of the clock before
dinner: and, as I have heard credibly reported, would
neither stay to refresh themselves, having marched all night
and the day before; nor yet to confer of anything but only
of the order how they should issue and assail: protesting
and vowing neither to eat nor drink until they might eat and
drink at liberty and pleasure in Antwerp: the which vow
they performed, contrary to all men's reason and expectation.

Their order of entry into the Castle Yard [*Esplanade*], and
their approach to the trenches I did not see: for I could not
get out of the town; neither did I think it reasonable to be
Hospes in aliena republica curiosus.

Yet, as I heard it rehearsed by sundry of themselves, I
will also here rehearse it for a truth:

The Horsemen and Footmen which came from Maestricht and Lierre, came through a village on the east side of
the town called Borgerhout about ten of the clock before
noon, as beforesaid. The Governor and Estates, being
thereof advertised, sent out presently part of their Horsemen
and Footmen to discover and take knowledge of them. But
before they could issue out of the Gates, the Spaniards were
passed on the south-east side of the town ditch, and entered
at a Gate which standeth on the Counterscarf of the Castle
Yard [*Esplanade*], called the Windmill Port. There
entered the Horsemen and all the Footmen; saving the
High Almains [*Germans*] who marched round about the
Castle, by a village called Kiel; and, trailing their pikes
on the ground after them, came in at a small Postern on
the Brayes by the river, and on the west side of the Castle.

Those which came from Alost, came through the said
village called Kiel, and so, through the Castle, [and] issued
out of the same at the Fore Gate, which standeth towards
the town.

Being thus passed, and entered into the Castle Yard,
about eleven of the clock; they of Alost and of the Castle

cast themselves into four Squadrons; they of Maestricht and Lierre into two Squadrons, and their Horsemen into a Troop behind them; and the High Almains [*Germans*] into a Squadron or Battalion by the river's side.

Being thus ordered, and appointment given where every Squadron should charge and endure; they cast off certain Loose Shot [*Skirmishers*] from every Squadron, and attacked the Scarmouch [? *Piquet*]. The which continued not one hour; before they drew their Squadrons so near unto the Counterscarf and Trenches, that they brake and charged *pell mell*.

The Castle had, all this while, played at the town and trenches with thundering shot: but now, upon a signal given, ceased to shoot any more, for fear to hurt their own men; wherein I noted their good order, which wanted no direction, in their greatest fury.

The Walloons and Almains [*Germans*] which served in the Trenches, defended all this while very stoutly. And the Spaniards with their Almains continued the charge with such valour, that in fine they won the Counterscarf, and presently scaled the Trenches with great fury. The Walloons and Almains, having long resisted without any fresh relief or supply, many of them in this meanwhile being slain and hurt, were not able any longer to repulse the Spaniards: so that they entered the Trenches about twelve of the clock, and presently pursued their victory down every street.

In their chase, as fast as they gained any cross street, they flanked the same with their Musquet[eer]s until they saw no longer resistance of any Power; and they proceeded in chase, executing all such as they overtook. In this good order they charged and entered; in this good order they proceeded; and in as good order, their lackays and pages followed with firebrands and wild fire, setting the houses on fire in every place where their masters had entered.

The Walloons and Almains which were to defend the town [*being chiefly those commanded by the Marquis d'HAVRÉ*] being grown into some security by reason that their Trenches were so high as seemed invincible; and, lacking sufficient generals or directors, were found as far out of order as the

Spaniards were to be honoured for the good order and direction which they kept.

For those which came to supply and relieve the Trenches
came straggling and loose. Some came from the furthest
side of the town. Some, that were nearer, came very
fearfully! and many, out of their lodgings, from drinking
and carousing; who would scarcely believe that any
conflict was begun, when the Spaniards now met them in
the streets to put them out of doubt that they dallied
not.

To conclude, their carelessness and lack of foresight was
such that they never had a *Corps du Gard* [Block House] to
supply and relieve their Trenches; but only one in the
Market Place of the town, which was a good quarter of a
mile from their fortifications : and that also was of Almains
[*Germans commanded by that double-dyed traitor* CORNELIS
VAN EINDEN, *or* VAN ENDE]; who, when they spied the
Spaniards, did gently kneel down, letting their pikes fall,
and crying, *O liebe Spaniarden ! O liebe Spaniarden !* [" O
dear Spaniards ! " *That is,* VAN EINDEN *traitorously joined
with the invading Spaniards.*]

Now I have set down the order of their entry, approach,
charge, and assault, together with their proceeding in victory;
and that by credible report, both of the Spaniards themselves and of others who served in their company : let me
also say a little of that which I saw executed.

I was lodged in the English House, *ut supra* : and had
not gone abroad that morning by reason of weighty business
which I had in hand the same day. At dinner time [*which
was then about* 11 *a.m.*], the Merchantmen of my country,
which came out of the town and dined in my chamber,
told me, That a hot scarmouch [*skirmish*] was begun in
the Castle Yard, and that the fury thereof still increased,
About the midst of dinner, news came, That the shot was
so thick, as neither ground, houses, nor people could be
discerned for the smoke thereof: and before dinner were
fully ended, That the Spaniards were like[ly] to win the
Trenches.

Whereat I stept from the table, and went hastily up into

a high tower of the said English House: from whence I might discover fire in four or five places of the town towards the Castle Yard; and thereby I was well assured that the Spaniards indeed were entered within the Trenches.

So that I came down, and took my cloak and sword, to see the certainty thereof: and as I passed towards the Bourse [*Exchange*] I met many; but I overtook none. And those which I met were no townsmen, but soldiers; nether walked they as men which use traffic, but ran as men which are in fear.

Whereat, being somewhat grieved, and seeing the townsmen stand every man before his door with such weapons as they had; I demanded of one of them, What it meant?

Who answered me in these words, *Hélas, Monsieur, il n'y a point d'ordre; et voilà la ruine de cette ville!* [Alas, Sir, there is no order; and behold the ruin of this town!]

Ayez courage, mon ami! [Have courage, my friend!], quoth I; and so went onwards yet towards the Bourse: meeting all the way more and more [of those] which mended their pace.

At last, a Walloon Trumpeter on horseback, who seemed to be but a boy of years, drew his sword, and laid about him, crying *Où est ce que vous enfuyez, canaille? Faisons tête, pour l'honeur de la patrie!* [Where are you flying to, rascals? Make head, for the honour of our country!] Wherewith fifty or threescore of them turned head, and went backwards towards the Bourse.

The which encouraged me, *par compagnie*, to proceed.

But alas, this comfort endured but a while. For by that time I came on the farther side of the Bourse, I might see a great troop coming in greater haste, with their heads as close together as a school of young fry or a flock of sheep; who met me, on the farther side of the Bourse, towards the Market Place: and, having their leaders foremost (for I knew them by their javelins, boar spears, and staves), [they] bare me over backwards; and ran over my belly and my face, [a] long time before I could recover on foot.

At last, when I was up, I looked on every side, and seeing them run so fast, began thus to bethink me, "What,

in God's name, do I hear? which have no interest in
this action; since they who came to defend this town
are content to leave it at large, and shift for themselves."

And whilst I stood thus musing, another flock of
flyers came so fast that they bare me on my nose, and
ran as many over my back, as erst had marched over my
stomach. In fine, I got up like a tall fellow; and went
with them for company: but their haste was such as I
could never overtake them until I came at a broad cross
street, which lieth between the English House and the
said Bourse.

There I overtook some of 'them grovelling on the
ground, and groaning for the last gasp; and some others
which turned backwards to avoid the tickling of the
Spanish Musquets [*Musketeers*]: who had gotten the ends
of the said broad cross street, and flanked it both ways.
And there I stayed a while till, hearing the shot increase
and fearing to be surprised with such as might follow
in tail of us; I gave adventure to pass through the said
cross street: and, without vaunt be it spoken, passed
through five hundred shots before I could recover the
English House.

At my coming thither, I found many of the Merchants
standing before the gate: whom I would not discomfort nor dismay but said, That the Spaniards had
once entered the town, and that I hoped they were gone
back again.

Nevertheless I went to the Governor: and privily persuaded him to draw in the company; and to shut up the
gates.

The which he consented unto: and desired me, because
I was somewhat better acquainted with such matters than
the Merchants, to take charge of the key.

I took it willingly, but before I could well shut and bar
the gate, the Spaniards were now come forwards into the
same street; and passing by the door, called to come
in; bestowing five or six musquet shot at the gate,
where I answered them; whereof one came very near my
nose, and piercing through the gate, strake one of the
Merchants on the head, without any great or dangerous

hurt. But the heat of the pursuit was yet such, that they could not attend the spoil; but passed on in chase to the New Town, where they slew infinite numbers of people: and, by three of the clock, or before, returned victors; having slain, or put to flight, all their enemies.

And now, to keep promise and to speak without partiality, I must needs confess that it was the greatest victory, and the roundliest executed, that hath been seen, read, or heard of, in our Age: and that it was a thing miraculous to consider how Trenches of such a height should be entered, passed over, and won, both by Footmen and Horsemen.

For immediately after that the Footmen were gotten in, the Horsemen found means to follow: and being, many of them, Harquebussiers on horseback, did pass by their own Footmen in the streets; and much hastened both the flight of the Walloons, and made the way opener unto speedy executioners.

But whosoever will therein most extoll the Spaniards for their valour and order, must therewith confess that it was the very ordinance of GOD for a just plague and scourge unto the town. For otherwise it passeth all men's capacity to conceive how it should be possible.

And yet the disorder and lack of foresight in the Walloons did great[ly] help to augment the Spanish glory and boast.

To conclude. The Count D'OBERSTEIN was drowned in the New Town. The Marquis D'HAVRÉ and [Sieur DE] CHAMPAGNEY escaped out of the said New Town, and recovered the Prince of ORANGE's ships.

Only the young Count [PHILIP] of EGMONT was taken, fighting by St Michael's. Monsieur DE CAPRES and Monsieur DE GOGINES were also taken. But I heard of none that fought stoutly, saving only the said Count of EGMONT; whom the Colonel VERDUGO, a Spaniard of an honourable compassion and good mind, did save: with great danger to himself in defending the Count.

In this conflict there were slain 600 Spaniards, or thereabouts. And on the Thursday next following [8th November 1576], a view of the dead bodies in the town being taken, it was esteemed at 17,000 men, women, and children. [*This would be apart from those drowned in the Scheldt.*] A pitiful massacre, though GOD gave victory to the Spaniards.

And surely, as their valiance was to be much commended ; so yet I can much discommend their barbarous cruelty in many respects. For methinks that as when GOD giveth abundance of wealth, the owner ought yet to have regard on whom he bestow it : even so, when GOD giveth a great and miraculous victory, the conquerors ought to have great regard unto their execution. And though some, which favour the Spanish faction, will alledge sundry reasons to the contrary : yet, when the blood is cold and the fury over, methinks that a true Christian heart should stand content with victory ; and refrain to provoke GOD's wrath by [the] shedding of innocent blood.

These things I rehearse the rather, because they neither spared *Age nor Sex, Time nor Place, Person nor Country, Professson nor Religion, Young nor Old, Rich nor Poor, Strong nor Feeble :* but, without any mercy, did tyrannously triumph, when there was neither man nor means to resist them.

For *Age and Sex, Young and Old ;* they slew great numbers of young children ; but many more women more than four score years of age.

For *Time and Place ;* their fury was as great ten days after the victory, as at the time of their entry ; and as great respect they had to the Church and Churchyard, for all their hypocritical boasting of the Catholic Religion, as the butcher had to his shambles or slaughter house.

For *Person and Country,* they spared neither friend nor foe, Portugese nor Turk.

For *Profession and Religion,* the Jesuits must give their ready coin ; and all other Religious Houses, both coin and plate : with all short ends that were good and portable.

The *Rich* was spoiled because he had; and the *Poor* were hanged because they had nothing. Neither *Strength* could prevail to make resistance, nor *Weakness* move pity for to refrain their horrible cruelty.

And this was not only done when the chase was hot; but, as I erst said, when the blood was cold; and they [were] now victors without resistance.

I refrain to rehearse the heaps of dead carcases which lay at every Trench where they entered; the thickness whereof did in many places exceed the height of a man.

I forbear also to recount the huge numbers drowned in the New Town: where a man might behold as many sundry shapes and forms of man's motion at [the] time of death as ever MICHAEL ANGELO did portray in his Tables of Doomsday [*Picture of the Last Judgment*].

I list not to reckon the infinite number of poor Almains [*Germans*], who lay burned in their armour. Some [with] the entrails scorched out, and all the rest of the body free. Some [with] their head and shoulders burnt off; so that you might look down into the bulk and breast, and there take an anatomy of the secrets of Nature. Some [were] standing upon their waist; being burnt off by the thighs. And some no more but the very top of the brain taken off with fire; whiles the rest of the body did abide unspeakable torments.

I set not down the ugly and filthy polluting of every street with the gore and carcases of horses; neither do I complain that the one lacked burial, and the other flaying, until the air, corrupted with their carion, infected all that yet remained alive in the town.

And why should I describe the particularity of every such annoyance as commonly happens both in camps and castles where martial feats are managed?

But I may not pass over with silence the wilful burning and destroying of the stately Town House, and all the muniments and records of the city: neither can I refrain to tell their shameful rapes and outrageous forces presented unto sundry honest dames and virgins.

It is also a ruthful remembrance, that a poor English

Merchant, who was but a servant, having once redeemed
his master's goods for 300 crowns, was yet hanged until
he were half dead, because he had not 200 more to give
them. And the halter being cut down, and he come to
himself again ; [he] besought them on knees, with bitter
tears, to give him leave to seek and try his credit and
friends in the town, for the rest of their unreasonable
demand. At his return, because he sped not, as indeed no
money was then to be had, they hung him again outright :
and afterwards, of exceeding courtesy, procured the Friars
Minor to bury him.

To conclude. Of the 17,000 carcases which were viewed
on the Thursday : I think, in conscience, 5,000, or few
less, were massacred after their victory ; because they
had not ready money wherewith to ransom their goods
at such prices as they pleased to set on them. At least,
all the World will bear me witness, that ten days after,
whosoever was but pointed at, and named to be a Walloon,
was immediately massacred without further audience or
trial.

For mine own part, it is well known that I did often
escape very narrowly ; because I was taken for a Walloon.
And on Sunday, the 11th of this instant [November 1576],
which was the day before I gat out of the town, I saw three
poor souls murdered in my presence, because they were
pointed [at] to be Walloons : and it was well proved,
immediately [after], that one of them was a poor artificer,
who had dwelt in the town eight years before, and [had]
never managed arms, but truly followed his occupation.

Furthermore, the seed of these and other barbarous facts
brought forth this crop and fruit, That, within three days,
Antwerp, which was one of the richest towns in Europe,
had now no money nor treasure to be found therein, but only
in the hands of murderers and strumpets. For every Don
DIEGO must walk, jetting up and down the streets, with
his harlot by him, in her chain and bracelets of gold.
And the notable Bourse, which was wont to be a safe
assembly for merchants and men of all honest trades, had
now none other merchandise therein but as many dicing
tables as might be placed round about it, all the day long.

Men will boast of the Spaniards, that they are the best and most orderly soldiers in the World: but, sure[ly], if this be their order, I had rather be accounted a *Besoigner* [French for *an indigent beggar*] than a brave soldier in such a Band: neither must we think, although it hath pleased GOD (for some secret cause only known to his divine Majesty) to yield Antwerp and Maestricht thus into their hands; that he will spare to punish this their outrageous cruelty, when his good will and pleasure shall be to do the same. For surely their boasting and bragging of iniquity is over great to escape long unscourged.

I have talked with sundry of them; and demanded, Why they would command that the Town House should be burned?

And their answer was, Because it was the place of assembly where all evil counsels were contrived.

As though it were just that the stocks and stones should suffer for the offence of men. But such is their obstinate mind and arrogancy that, if they might have their will, they would altogether raze and destroy the towns, until no one stone were left upon another. Neither doth their stubborn blindness suffer them to perceive that in so doing they should much endamage the King their Master; whom they boast so faithfully to honour, serve, and obey.

As for the injuries done by them unto our own Nation particularly; I will thus set down as much as I know.

We were quiet in the House appointed for the Mansion of English Merchants, under safe Conduct, Protection, and Placard [*Placcaet = Proclamation*] of their King: having neither meddled any way in these actions; nor by any means assisted the Estates of the country with money, munition, or any kind of aid. Yea, the Governor [THOMAS HETON] and Merchants, foreseeing the danger of the time, had often demanded passport[s] of the King's Governors and Officers to depart.

And all these, with sundry other allegations, we propounded and protested unto them before they entered the English House; desiring to be there protected, according to our Privileges and Grants from the King their Master;

and that they would suffer us there to remain, free from
all outrage spoil or ransom, until we might make our estate
known unto [SANCHO D' AVILA] the Castellan [of Antwerp
Castle] and other Head Officers which served there for the
said King.

All which notwithstanding; they threatened to fire the
House unless we would open the doors: and, being once
suffered to enter, demanded presently the ransom of 12,000
crowns of the Governor. Which sum, being not indeed in
the House, neither yet one-third part of the same; they
spared not with naked swords and daggers to menace the
Governor, and violently to present him death; because
he had not wherewith to content their greedy minds.

I will not boast of any help afforded by me in that
distress: but I thank the Lord GOD! who made me an
instrument to appease their devilish furies. And I think
that the Governor and all the Company will confess that I
used mine uttermost skill and aid for the safeguard of their
lives, as well as [of] mine own.

But in the end, all eloquence notwithstanding; the
Governor [THOMAS HETON], being a comely aged man
and a person whose hoary hairs might move pity and
procure reverence in any good mind; especially the upright-
ness of his dealing considered: they enforced him, with
great danger, to bring forth all the money, plate, and jewels
which were in the House; and to prepare the remnant of
12,000 crowns at such days and times as they pleased to
appoint.

And of the rest of our Nation, which had their goods
remaining in their several packhouses and lodgings elsewhere
in the town; they took such pity that four they slew,
and divers others they most cruelly and dangerously hurt:
spoiling and ransoming them to the uttermost value that
might be made, or esteemed, of all their goods. Yea, a
certain one, they enforced to ransom his goods twice; yea,
thrice: and, all that notwithstanding, took the said goods
violently from them at the last.

And all these injuries being opened unto their chief
Governors in time convenient; and whiles yet the whole
sum, set for [the] several ransoms of our countrymen and
the English House in general, were not half paid; so that

justice and good order might partly have qualified the
former rigours proferred by the soldiers : the said Governors
were as slow and deaf, as the others were quick and light,
of hearing to find the bottom of every bag in the town.
So that it seemeth they were fully agreed in all things :
or, if any contention were, the same was but [a] strife who,
or which, of them might do greatest wrongs.   Keeping the
said Governor and Merchants there still, without grant of
passport or safe conduct, when there are scarcely any
victuals to be had for any money in the town ; nor yet
the said Merchants have any money to buy it, where it is.
And as for credit ; neither credit nor pawn can now find coin
in Antwerp.

In these distresses, I left them the 12th of this instant
November 1576 ; when I parted from them : not as one who
was hasty to leave and abandon them in such misery ; but
to solicit their rueful causes here, and to deliver the same
unto Her Majesty and [the Privy] Council in such sort as I
beheld it there.

And this is, in effect, the whole truth of the Sacking and
Spoil of so famous a town.   Wherein is to be noted—that
the Spaniards and their faction being but 5,000 ; the
Trenches made against them of such height as seemed
invincible ; the Power within the town, 15,000 or 16,000
able fighting men well armed, I mean the townsmen ready
armed being counted : it was charged, entered, and won in
three hours ; and before six hours passed over, every house
therein sacked, or ransomed at the uttermost value.

The which victory (being miraculous and past man's capacity
to comprehend how it should be possible) I must needs
attribute unto GOD's just wrath poured upon the inhabitants
for their iniquity, more than to the manhood and force of the
Spaniards.   And yet I mean not to rob them of their
deserved glory ; but to confess that both their order and
valour in charging and entering was famous : and had they
kept half so good order, or shewed the tenth part of such
manly courage, in using their victory and parting of their
spoil ; I must then needs have said that CÆSAR had never
any such soldiers.   And this must I needs say for them that,
as their continual training in service doth make them expert

in all warlike stratagem[s]; so their daily trade in spoiling hath made them the cunningest ransackers of houses, and the best able to bring a spoil unto a quick market, of any soldiers or master thieves that ever I heard of.

But I leave the scanning of their deeds unto GOD, who will bridle their insolency when he thinketh good and convenient. And let us also learn, out of this rueful tragedy, to detest and avoid those sins and proud enormities which caused the wrath of GOD to be so furiously kindled and bent against the town of Antwerp.

Let us also, if ever we should be driven to like occasion, which GOD forbid! learn to look better about us for good order and direction; the lack whereof was their overthrow. For surely the inhabitants lacked but good guides and leaders: for (having none other order appointed, but to stand every man armed in readiness before his door) they died there, many of them, fighting manfully; when the Wallooners and High Duches [*Germans*] fled beastly.

Let us also learn to detest the horrible cruelties of the Spaniards, in all executions of warlike stratagems; lest the dishonour of such beastly deeds might bedim the honour wherewith English soldiers have always been endowed in their victories.

And finally let us pray to GOD for grace to amend our lives, and for power and foresight to withstand the malice of our enemies: that remaining and continuing in the peaceable protection of our most gracious Sovereign, we may give Him the glory; and all due and loyal obedience unto Her Majesty, whom GOD now and ever prospect and preserve. Amen.

Written the 25th day of November 1576,
by a true Englishman, who was
present at this piteous Massacre,
ut supra.

A very true Report of the apprehension
and taking of that arch-Papist EDMUND
CAMPION, the Pope his right hand; with
Three other lewd Jesuit Priests, and
divers other Lay people, most
seditious persons of like sort.

Containing also a controlment of a most untrue former
book set out by one A. M., *alias* ANTHONY MUNDAY,
concerning the same : as is to be proved and justified
by GEORGE ELLIOT, one of the Ordinary
Yeomen of Her Majesty's Chamber,

Author of this Book, and chiefest cause of the
finding of the said lewd and seditious people, great
enemies to GOD, their loving Prince,
and country.

Veritas non quærit angulos.

Imprinted at London at the *Three Cranes* in the
Vintry by THOMAS DAWSON.
1581.

[The *Edinburgh Review* of April 1891, in an article on *The Baffling of the Jesuits*, states

" Until Father PARSONS landed at Dover on June 11 [and Father CAMPION on June 25], 1580; no Jesuit had ever been seen in England. IGNATIUS LOYOLA had been dead just twenty-five years, and two of his associates in founding the Society of JESUS were still alive. LOYOLA during his lifetime had admitted only a single Englishman into the order, a lad of nineteen, of whom we know nothing but that his name was THOMAS LITH, and that he was admitted to the novitiate in June 1555. During the next ten years, six more Englishmen entered the order, two of them being men of some mark—JASPER HEYWOOD, formerly Fellow of All Souls'; and THOMAS DARBYSHIRE, who had been Archdeacon of Essex and a Canon of St Paul's. In the next decade, about the same number of English recruits joined the society; three, and three only, were scholars of any reputation—PARSONS, CAMPION, and HENRY GARNET. When the Jesuit Mission to England started, there were not thirty English Jesuits in the world."

At Vol. I., p. 130, is a letter written from Goa, 10 Nov. 1579, by THOMAS STEVENS, one of these English Jesuits.

The arrest and execution of EDMUND CAMPION—in Latin, EDMUNDUS CAMPIANUS—was one of the most important events in our political history during the year 1581. It made a profound impression throughout Western Europe, and occasioned the publication of many tracts in various languages. For further information on this subject, the Reader is referred to *EDMUND CAMPION, A Biography,* by RICHARD SIMPSON. London, 1867-8; and also to Mr JOSEPH GILLOW's *Biographical Dictionary of the English Catholics,* now in progress.

The following account of the arrest by the man who made it, is printed from a copy of the extremely rare original edition that is now in Lambeth Palace Library [Press Mark, xxx. 8. 17.]. It was printed [? privately printed] in 1581 ; but it was not entered at Stationers' Hall. It was clearly produced before the execution of CAMPION, on the 1st of December of that year; to which there is no allusion in it; but apparently not very much earlier, for the Writer says at page 465 " Some men may marvel that I would be silent so long."

By this act of patriotism ; GEORGE ELLIOT earned the titles, among the Roman Catholics, of JUDAS ELLIOT, and of ELLIOT ISCARIOT. It is however only fair to him to state what moved him to go hunting after Priests, Jesuits, etc.

ANTHONY MUNDAY, in his *Discovery of EDMUND CAMPION and his Confederates, &e.*, published on 29th January 1582, in giving an account of CAMPION's trial, states :

GEORGE ELLIOT, one of the Ordinary Yeomen of Her Majesty's Chamber, upon his oath, gave forth in evidence, as followeth :

That he, living here in England among certain of that sect, fell in acquaintance with one PAYNE, a Priest ; who gave him to understand of a horrible treason intended against Her Majesty and the State, which he did expect shortly to happen.

The order, how, and after what manner, in brief is thus :

That there should be levied a certain company of armed men ; which, on a sudden, should enterprise a most monstrous attempt. A certain company of these armed men should be prepared against Her Majesty, as many against my L[ord] of L[EICESTER], as many against my L[ord] T[reasurer, Lord BURGHLEY], as many against Sir F[RANCIS] W[ALSINGHAM], and divers others whose names he doth not well remember.

The deaths of these noble personages should be presently fulfilled : and Her Majesty used in such sort as [neither] modesty nor duty will suffer me to rehearse. ^{Meaning the} But this should be the general cry everywhere, ^{Queen of} " Queen MARY ! Queen MARY ! " ^{Scots. [A.M.]}

It was also appointed and agreed upon, Who should have this Man of Honour's room, and who should have that Office. Everything was determined. There wanted nothing but the coming over of such Priests and others as were long looked for.

Upon this report, the aforenamed GEORGE ELLIOT took occasion to question with this PAYNE, How they could find in their hearts to attempt an act of so great cruelty ; considering how high an offence it should be to GOD, besides great danger might arise thereby.

Whereto PAYNE made answer, That the killing [of] Her Majesty was no offence to GOD, nor the uttermost cruelty they could use to her, nor [to] any that took her part: but that they might as lawfully do it as to a brute beast. And himself would be one of the foremost in the executing [of] this villanous and most traitorous action.

A most traitorous and villanous answer. Of every true subject to be read with due reverence of the person. [A.M.]

In *Lansd. MS.* 32, No. 60, in the British Museum, there is a paper to the same effect, signed by G. E. [GEORGE ELLIOT]. It is headed *Certain Notes and Remembrances concerning a Reconciliation, &c.*; and bears marginal notes by Lord BURGHLEY.

It will probably be new to most readers that ELLIOT's arrest of CAMPION was a pure matter of accident. ELLIOT went to Lyford Manor House more particularly in search of PAYNE the Priest, and found CAMPION there by chance. The Jesuit had been secretly, but securely, wandering through the land from one Roman Catholic household to another, for more than a year; despite the *utmost* efforts of the English Government to put their hands on him: and at last he becomes their prisoner almost by a pure accident.

CAMPION was lodged in the Tower on the 22nd July 1581. Two days later, ANTHONY MUNDAY's *Brief Discourse of the taking of EDMUND CAMPION &c.*, was entered at Stationers' Hall [ARBER, *Transcript &c.*, II. 397]. It was therefore very hurriedly written, and mainly from information supplied by Master HUMPHREY FOSTER, High Sheriff of Berkshire: who, being himself a Roman Catholic, had been very slack at the capture of CAMPION [p. 462]; but who, for his own protection, puts a better face on things in MUNDAY's hurriedly written *Discourse, &c*

To the Christian Reader, GEORGE ELLIOT wisheth all due reverence.

OME experience, Christian Reader, that I have gathered by keeping company with such seditious people as CAMPION and his associates are, partly moveth me to write this book; and partly I am urged thereunto (although my wisdom and skill be very slender to set down and pen matter of less moment than this) for that I (being one of the Two in Commission at that time from Her Highness's most honourable Privy Council for the apprehending of the said seditious CAMPION and such like; and the chiefest cause of the finding out of the said lewd people, as hereafter more at large appeareth) do think it a great abuse that the most part of Her Majesty's loving subjects shall be seduced to believe an untruth; and myself and he which was in Commission with me (whose name is DAVID JENKINS, one of the Messengers of Her Majesty's Chamber) very vilely slandered with a book set out by one ANTHONY MUNDAY concerning the apprehension of the said lewd people—which, for the truth thereof, is almost as far different from truth as darkness from light; and as contrary to truth as an egg is contrary in likeness to an oyster.

And therefore considering I am able to report a truth for the manner of the finding and taking of the said seditious persons; although fine skill be far from me to paint it out: hoping the wise will bear with my want therein, and esteem a true tale, be it never so bluntly told, rather than a lie, be it never so finely handled—I have emboldened myself to take this treatise in hand; wherein, God willing, I will describe nothing but truth; as by the sequel shall appear. Which is this:

That about four years past [?1578], the Devil (being a crafty fox and chief Patron doubtless of the Pope's Prelacy ; having divers and many Officers and inferior substitutes to the Pope, his chief Vicar ; and intending by them to increase the kingdom of this Antichrist) dispersed his said Officers in divers places of this realm : where, like vagrant persons (refusing to live within the lawful government of their country) they lead a loose life ; wandering and running hither and thither, from shire to shire and country [County] to country, with such store of Romish relics, Popish pelf, trifles, and trash as were able to make any Christian heart, that hath seen the trial of such practices as I have done, even for sorrow to bleed. Only thereby to draw the Queen's Majesty's subjects their hearts and faiths both from GOD and Her Highness ; as namely, by delivering unto them *Bulls* from Rome, *Pardons, Indulgences,* Medals, *Agnus DEI,* hallowed grains and beads, crucifixes, painted pictures, and such other paltry : every part whereof they will not let [*stop*] to say to be matters very necessary for salvation.

By reason whereof, most loving Reader, I myself, about that time [1578], by the space of one quarter of a year together, was deeply bewitched and drawn into their darkness, as the blindest bayard of them all. But at the last, even then (by GOD's great goodness, mighty providence, and especial grace) all their enchantments, witchcrafts, sorceries, devilish devices and practices were so broken and untied in me ; and the brightness of GOD's divine majesty shining so surely in my heart and conscience : that I perceived all their doings to be, as they are indeed, only shows without substance, manifest errors and deceitful juggling casts, and none others.

Notwithstanding I determined with myself, for certain causes which I omit, to sound the depth of their devilish drifts, if I might ; and the rather therefore used and frequented their company : whereby appeared unto me not a few of their ungracious and villanous false hearts, faiths, and disloyal minds, slanderous words, and most vile treasons towards my most excellent and noble mistress, the Queen's Majesty, and towards divers of her most honourable Privy Council ; in such sort as many times did make mine eyes to gush out with tears for very sorrow and fear to think of it.

Wherefore, lately [*about 14th May* 1581], I made my humble submission unto the Right Honourable Her Highness's Privy Council, for my unlawful living as aforesaid. At whose hands I found such honourable dealing, and by their means such mercy from Her Majesty, that I wish with all my heart all the Papists, which are subjects born to Her Highness, to run the same course that I have done : and then should they easily see what difference there is between the good and merciful dealing of our most gracious loving and natural Prince ; and the great treacheries of that great enemy to our country, the Pope. For Her Highness freely forgiveth offenders ; but the Pope pardoneth for money. Her Grace's hands are continually full of mercy, ready to deliver enough freely to any that will desire and deserve it : and the Pope his great clutches and fists are ready to deliver nothing but devilish devices and paltry stuff of his own making, to set country and country together by the ears ; and yet for these, hath he money.

Truly it is a most lamentable case that ever any Christian should be seduced and drawn from the true worshipping of GOD, and their duty to their Prince and country ; as many are by the Pope and his Satanical crew. I beseech GOD turn their hearts, and grant us all amendment ; which can neither be too timely, if it were presently ; nor never too late, whensoever it shall happen : unless wilfully they proceed in their dealings, which GOD forbid. For *humanum est errare, perseverare belluinum.*

Shortly after my submission and reconciliation, as aforesaid, it pleased my Lords of Her Highness's most honourable Privy Council to grant the Commission that I before spake of, to myself and to the said DAVID JENKINS, for the apprehension of certain lewd Jesuit Priests and other seditious persons of like sort, wheresoever we should happen to find them within England. Whereupon we determined a certain voyage [*journey*] : in which EDMUND CAMPION the aforesaid Jesuit and others were by us taken and brought to the Tower of London, in manner as hereafter followeth.

The true manner of taking of EDMUND CAMPION and his associates.

T happened that after the receipt of our Commission aforesaid, we consulted between ourselves, What way were best to take first? For we were utterly ignorant where, or in what place, certainly to find out the said CAMPION, or his compeers. And our consultation was shortly determined: for the greatest part of our travail and dealings in this service did lie chiefly upon mine own determination, by reason of mine acquaintance and knowledge of divers of [the] like sect.

It then presently came to my remembrance of certain acquaintance which I once had with one THOMAS COOPER a Cook, who, in November [1578] was two years, served Master THOMAS ROPER of [Orpington in] Kent; where, at that time, I in like manner served: and both of us, about the same month [November 1578], departed the said Master ROPER his service; I into Essex, and the said COOPER to Lyford in Berkshire, to one Master YATE. From whence, within one half year after [*before May* 1579], I was advertised in Essex, that the said Cook was placed in service; and that the said Master YATE was a very earnest Papist, and one that gave great entertainment to any of that sect.

Which tale, being told me in Essex two years before [1579] we entered [on] this journey, by GOD's great goodness, came to my memory but even the day before [13th July 1581] we set forth. Hereof I informed the said DAVID JENKINS, being my fellow in Commission, and told him it would be our best way to go thither first: for that it was not meant that we should go to any place but where indeed I either had acquaintance; or by some means possible in our journey, could get acquaintance. And told him we would dispose of our journey in such sort as we might come to the

said Master YATE's upon the Sunday about eight of the
clock in the morning: "where," said I, "if we find the said
Cook, and that there be any Mass to be said there that day,
or any massing Priest in the house; the Cook, for old
acquaintance and for that he supposeth me to be a Papist,
will bring me to the sight thereof."

And upon this determination, we set from London [on
Friday] the 14th day of July last; and came to the said
Master YATE's house, the 16th of the same month, being
Sunday, about the hour aforesaid.

Where, without the gates of the same house, we espied
one of the servants of the house, who most likely seemed, by
reason of his lying aloof, to be as it were a Scout Watcher,
that they within might accomplish their secret matters more
safely.

I called the said servant, and enquired of him for the
said THOMAS COOPER the Cook.

Who answered, That he could not well tell, whether he
were within or not.

I prayed him that he would friend me so much as to see;
and told him my name.

The said servant did so, it seemed; for the Cook came
forth presently unto us where we sat still upon horseback.
And after a few such speeches, as betwixt friend and friend
when they have been long asunder, were passed; still sitting
upon our horses, I told him That I had longed to see him;
and that I was then travelling into Derbyshire to see my
friends, and came so far out of my way to see him. And
said I, "Now I have seen you, my mind is well satisfied;
and so fare you well!"

"No," saith he, "that shall you not do before dinner."

I made the matter very earnest to be gone; and he, more
earnest and importune to stay me. But in truth I was as
willing to stay as he to have me.

And so, perforce, there was no remedy but stay we must.
And having lighted from horseback; and being by him
brought into the house, and so into the buttery, and there
caused to drink: presently after, the said Cook came and
whispered with me, and asked, Whether my friend (meaning
the said JENKINS) were within the Church or not? Therein
meaning, Whether he were a Papist or no?

To which I answered, "He was not; but yet," said I, "he is a very honest man, and one that wisheth well that way."

Then said the Cook to me, "Will you go up?" By which speech, I knew he would bring me to a Mass.

And I answered him and said, "Yea, for God's sake, that let me do : for seeing I must needs tarry, let me take something with me that is good."

Some men blame me for dissembling the matter as I did : but to do my Prince and country service, I hold it lawful to use any reasonable policy. For the Field is not always won by strength. And so we left JENKINS in the buttery; and I was brought by the Cook through the hall, the dining parlour, and two or three other odd rooms, and then into a fair large chamber : where there was, at the same instant, one Priest, called SATWELL, saying Mass; two other Priests kneeling by, whereof one was CAMPION, and the other called PETERS *alias* COLLINGTON [*or rather* COLLETON]; three Nuns, and 37 other people.

When SATWELL had finished his Mass; then CAMPION he invested himself to say Mass, and so he did : and at the end thereof, made holy bread and delivered it to the people there, to every one some, together with holy water; whereof he gave me part also.

And then was there a chair set in the chamber something beneath the Altar, wherein the said CAMPION did sit down; and there made a Sermon very nigh an hour long : *I had once my Commission in my hand to have dealt with them myself alone in the Chamber. If I had, I pray you judge what had happened unto me.* the effect of his text being, as I remember, "That Christ wept over Jerusalem, &c." And so applied the same to this our country of England for that the Pope his authority and doctrine did not so flourish here as the same CAMPION desired.

At the end of which Sermon, I gat down unto the said JENKINS so soon as I could. For during the time that the Masses and the Sermon were made, JENKINS remained still beneath in the buttery or hall; not knowing of any such matter until I gave him some intelligence [of] what I had seen.

And so we departed, with as convenient expedition as we might, and came to one Master FETTIPLACE, a Justice of the Peace in the said country [*County*]: whom we made privy of our doings therein; and required him that, according to the tenour of our Commission, he would take sufficient Power, and with us thither.

Whereupon the said Justice of Peace, within one quarter of an hour, put himself in a readiness, with forty or fifty men very well weaponed: who went, in great haste, together with the said Master FETTIPLACE and us, to the said Master YATE his house.

Where, at our coming upon the sudden, being about one of the clock in the afternoon of the same day, before we knocked at the gates which were then (as before they were continually accustomed to be) fast shut (the house being moated round about; within which moat was great store of fruit trees and other trees, with thick hedge rows: so that the danger for fear of losing of the said CAMPION and his associates was the more doubted); we beset the house with our men round about the moat in the best sort we could devise: and then knocked at the gates, and were presently heard and espied; but kept out by the space of half an hour.

In which time, as it seemeth, they had hidden CAMPION and the other two Priests in a very secret place within the said house; and had made reasonable purveyance for him as hereafter is mentioned: and then they let us into the house.

Where came presently to our sight, Mrs YATE, the good wife of the house; five Gentlemen, one Gentlewoman, and three Nuns: the Nuns being then disguised in Gentlewomen's apparel, not like unto that they heard Mass in. All which I well remembered to have seen, the same morning, at the Masses and Sermon aforesaid: *One Nun got away in country maid's apparel.* yet every one of them a great while denied it. And especially the said Mistress YATE; who could not be content only to make a plain denial of the said Masses and the Priests: but, with great and horrible oaths, forsware the same, betaking herself to the Devil if *Mistress YATE proferred us a good sum of money to have given over the search.* any such there were; in such sort as, if I had not seen them with mine own eyes, I should have believed her.

But knowing certainly that these were but bare excuses, and that we should find the said CAMPION and his compeers if we made narrow *Master YATE was then, as he is still, in prison in Reading, for Papistry.* search; I eftsoons put Master FETTIPLACE in remembrance of our Commission: and so he, myself, and the said JENKINS Her Majesty's Messenger, went to searching the house; where we found many secret corners.

Continuing the search, although with no small toil, in the orchards, hedges, and ditches, within the moat and divers other places; at the last [we] found out Master EDWARD YATE, brother to the good man of the house, and two countrymen called WEBLIN and MANSFIELD, fast locked together in a pigeon house : but we could not find, at that time, CAMPION and the other two Priests whom we specially sought for.

It drew then something towards evening, and doubting lest we were not strong enough ; we sent our Commission to one Master FOSTER, High Sheriff of Berkshire ; and to one Master WISEMAN, a Justice of Peace within the same County ; for some further aid at their hands.

The said Master WISEMAN came with very good speed unto us the same evening, with ten or twelve of his own men, very able men and well appointed : but the said Master FOSTER could not be found, as the messenger that went for him returned us answer.

And so the said house was beset the same night with at the least three score men well weaponed ; who watched the same very diligently.

And the next day, being Monday [17th July 1581], in the morning very early, came one Master CHRISTOPHER LYDCOT, a Justice of Peace of the same shire, with a great sort [*company*] of his own men, all very well appointed : who, together with his men, shewed such earnest loyal and forward service in those affairs as was no small comfort and encouragement to all those which were present, and did bear true hearts and good wills to Her Majesty.

The same morning, began a fresh search for the said Priests ; which continued with very great labour until about ten of the clock in the forenoon of the same day : but the said Priests could not be found, and every man [was] almost persuaded that they were not there.

Yet still searching, although in effect clean void of any hope for finding of them, the said DAVID JENKINS, by GOD's great goodness, espied a certain secret place,* which

* In MUNDAY'S *Brief Discourse, &c.* [24 July 1581] there is a description of this " secret place " ; which may be correct as to its situation in the Manor House at Lyford :

A chamber, near the top of the house ; which was but very simple : having in it a large great shelf with divers tools and instruments both he quickly found to be hollow; and with a pin of iron which he had in his hand much like unto a harrow tine, he forthwith did break a hole into the said place: where then presently he perceived the said Priests lying all close together upon a bed, of purpose there laid for them; where they had bread, meat, and drink sufficient to have relieved them three or four days together.

Master Lyd- cot was then hard by.

The said JENKINS then called very loudly, and said, "I have found the traitors!"; and presently company enough was with him: who there saw the said Priests [that], when there was no remedy for them but *nolens volens*, courteously yielded themselves.

Shortly after came one Master READE, another Justice of the Peace of the said shire, to be assistant in these affairs.

Of all which matters, news was immediately carried in great haste to the Lords of the Privy Council: who gave further Commission that the said Priests and certain others their associates should be brought to the Court under the conduction of myself and the said JENKINS; with commandment to the Sheriff to deliver us sufficient aid forth of his shire, for the safe bringing up of the said people.

First myself rode post to the Court; and, after me, the said Messenger.

After that the rumour and noise for the finding out of the said CAMPION, SATWELL, and PETERS *alias* COLLINGTON, was in the said house something assuaged; and that the sight of them was to the people there no great novelty: then was the said High Sheriff sent for once again; who all that while had not been seen in this service. But then came, and received into his charge the said Priests and certain others from that day until Thursday following.

The fourth Priest which was by us brought up to the Tower, whose name is WILLIAM FILBIE,

ANTHONY MUNDAY saith, The Sheriff and his men gave him instructions for the setting out of the said untrue book.

upon it, and hanging by it; which they judged to belong to some crossbow maker. The simpleness of the place caused them to use small suspicion in it: and [they] were departing out again; but one in the company, by good hap, espied a chink in the wall of boards whereto this shelf was fastened, and through the same he perceived some light. Drawing his dagger, he smit a great hole in it; and saw there was a room behind it: whereat the rest stayed, searching for some entrance into it; which by pulling down a shelf they found, being a little hole for one to creep in at.

was not taken with the said CAMPION and the rest in the said house : but was apprehended and taken in our watch [*on the* 17*th*], by chance, in coming to the said house to speak with the said PETERS [*or* COLLETON], as he said ; and thereupon [was] delivered likewise in charge to the Sheriff, with the rest.

Upon Thursday, the 20th day of July last [1581], we set forwards from the said Master YATE his house towards the Court, with our said charge ; being assisted by the said Master LYDCOT and Master WISEMAN, and a great sort [*company*] of their men ; who never left us until we came to the Tower of London. There were besides, that guarded us thither, 50 or 60 Horsemen ; very able men and well appointed : which we received by the said Sheriff his appointment.

We went that day to Henley upon Thames, where we lodged that night.

And about midnight we were put into great fear by reason of a very great cry and noise that the said FILBIE made in his sleep ; which wakened the most that were that night in the house, and that in such sort that every man almost thought that some of the prisoners had been broken from us and escaped ; although there was in and about the same house a very strong watch appointed and charged for the same. The aforesaid Master LYDCOT was the first that came unto them : and when the matter was examined, it was found no more but that the said FILBIE was in a dream ; and, as he said, he verily thought one to be a ripping down his body and taking out his bowels.

The next day, being Friday [21st July 1581], we set forward from Henley. And by the way received commandment by a Pursuivant from the Lords of the Privy Council, that we should stay that night at Colebrook ; and the next day after, being Saturday, to bring them through the city of London unto the Tower, and there to deliver them into the charge of Sir OWEN HOPTON Knight, Her Majesty's Lieutenant of the same ; which accordingly we did.

And this is, in effect, the true discourse [of] that was used in the apprehension of the said CAMPION and his associates.

Some men may marvel that I would be silent so long for the setting out of the manner of their takings; considering I find myself aggrieved with the same untrue report set out before by the said A. M[UNDAY]. In good faith I meant nothing less than to take any such matter in hand, if so great an untruth had not been published against us that were doers in those affairs; and besides hitherto divers other weightier business has partly hindered me therein.

But now at the last, although very late, I have rudely set down the verity in this matter: thinking it better to tell a true tale by leisure, than a lie in haste; as the said A. M., by his former book, hath done to his own discredit, the deluding of Her Majesty's liege people, and the slander of some which have intermeddled in the said cause.

The names of those that were taken and brought up to
the Tower of London, as aforesaid.

1. EDWARD CAMPION,   .   .   Jesuit and Priest.

2. THOMAS SATWELL [*alias* FOORD],
3. JOHN PETERS *alias* COLLINGTON
   [*or more properly* COLLETON], } Priests.
4. WILLIAM FILBIE,   .   .   .

5. EDWARD YATE,   .   .   .
6. EDWARD KEYNES,   .   .   .
7. HUMPHREY KEYNES,   .   .
8. JOHN COTTON,   .   .   . } Gentlemen.
9. WILLIAM ILSLEY [*or* HILDESLEY],
10. JOHN JACOB [*or* JAMES],   .   .

11. JOHN MANSFIELD,   .   .   . } Husbandmen and
12. WILLIAM WEBLIN [*or* WEBLEY], } Neighbours thereby.

INCE the committing of the persons before-named to the Tower as aforesaid, there hath been, for my service done in those and such like affairs, no small nor few brags, threatenings, curses, and evil wishes given out against me by such as, · if they were known, deserve both little liberty and small favour. CAMPION, when he first saw me after his apprehension, said unto me, That my service done in the taking of him would be unfortunate to me. And in our journey towards the Tower, he advised me to get out of England for the safety of my body.

Some of my friends have doubted [*feared*] lest that sort of lewd people would. do their good wills to hurt me by some secret device, as conjuration, witchcraft, or such like; the which I rather think to be true, for that, shortly after the foresaid business ended, it pleased GOD to visit me with some sickness after I was gone to bed at night; which indeed for two or three hours handled me something hardly. But, GOD I take to witness, I never was of that opinion that it came to me by any other means but only by riding post two or three journies about the business aforesaid.

Yet, within one day or two after my sickness, there came to a neighbour's house [to] where I lodged in Southwark, one Mistress BEYSAUNT, a widow, whose abode is most about St. Mary Overies, and at the last by report smelleth of Papistry, and asked the good wife of the house for me, and what she had lately heard of me.

She answered, She knew me not ; nor nothing she had heard of me.

Then said Mistress BEYSAUNT, " The very truth is, it is he that took CAMPION and the rest of the company that are in the Tower ; and was the cause that Master ROPER and divers other good men are troubled : and the last day," saith she, " he did fall mad in the street, and was carried so into his lodging ; and is not like[ly] to escape with life. I pray you inquire further of him, and let me have knowledge thereof." It seemeth she was privy to some secret practice against me.

So that hereby I may plainly see that the Papists take great care for me : but whether it be for my weal or woe, and what her meaning was, let the world judge. But let the Devil, the Pope, and them do what they can ; my faith standeth so sure on CHRIST JESUS my Saviour, that through him I defy them all.

There hath been great murmuring and grudging against me about the committing of the aforesaid Master THOMAS ROPER ; and many faults have been found for the same.

What I did therein I mean not here to recite : but my dealings in those causes are known to such as before whom I think the fault finders dare not shew their faces. But whatsoever I did against him, I would have done against mine own father ; the case standing as it did. Yet such find-faults, to make the matter seem more odious to the World against me, do not stick to report and say, That the said Master ROPER hath brought me up from my childhood to this day at his only charges. Which is so false as GOD is true. For although I was his servant ; I continued with him, in all, not past one year.

But to conclude. A great number of such like untruths have been published against me, and no few bold brags ; as report goeth. I could name some if I would : but I let them pass ; unless I be commanded to the contrary by such as have authority to deal with me therein. GOD grant them amendment, I mean not towards myself ; or else make their doings known in such sort as they may have their deservings ; or at least be put to the mercy of Her Majesty : to whose Highness, JESUS send long life, a prosperous reign, with all joy and felicity !

GEORGE ELLIOT.

Imprinted at London at the *Three Cranes* in the Vintry,

by THOMAS DAWSON.

1581.

On 12 March 1582, there was entered for publication at Stationers' Hall [ARBER, *Transcript &c.*, II. 408.] *A brief Answer made unto two seditious Pamphlets.* By A. M. [ANTHONY MUNDAY.] The *Preface to the Reader* is however dated " From Barbican, the 22 of March 1582."

We give here the beginning of this *Answer*; the side notes being, of course, the comments of ANTHONY MUNDAY.

OT long after I had published [on 22 January 1582] my book called *The Discovery of CAMPION;* there came unto my hands a seditious pamphlet in the French tongue, intituled *The History of the Death which the Reverend Father, Master EDMUND CAMPION Priest, of the Society of the name of JESUS, and others have suffered* in England for the Catholic, or Romish, religion ^{Not for their religion; but} or faith, the 1st December 1581; adding underneath ^{for High} *Translated out of English into French.* ^{Treason. [A.M.]}

When I had thoroughly perused this book, noting the traitorous effects and slanderous speeches therein contained, receiving the judgment likewise of divers learned and godly men : as well to correct the manifest untruths wherewith this pamphlet is notably stuffed, as also that the godly and virtuous may discern their apparent impudency and wicked nature; I resolved myself to shape a brief *Answer* to such a shameless libel; myself being therein untruly and maliciously abused.

First, our nameless historiographer, because he would aim his course after some odd manner of conveyance, ^{The manner of} taketh occasion to begin his book with the taking ^{the aforesaid traitorous} of CAMPION, his bringing to the Tower, what ^{book. [A.M.]} happened in his time of stay there, and lastly his martyrdom (as he termeth it) with two other holy and devout Priests; and, in this manner continuing his unadvised labour, he beginneth as hereafter followeth :

GEORGE ELLIOT (*sometime servant to Master THOMAS ROPER; and since belonging to a Gentlewoman, the widow of SIR WILLIAM PETRE: in whose service he made show to be a sound and good Catholic*) *not long since committed a murder,*

To build upon hearsay proveth but a slender foundation. [A.M.]

as men say: for which offence, fearing the danger that was like[ly] to ensue, he went and submitted himself to one of the chief Lords in the Court; and, the better to win his favour, on his own behalf promised to deliver into his hands the Father EDMUND CAMPION.

This promise, saith he, *was received; and unto the said GEORGE and an Officer, was delivered Commission to take and apprehend the said EDMUND CAMPION.*

Then went they on their way, and coming into Berkshire to [the] *house of one Master YATE; GEORGE ELLIOT met with the Cook of the house with whom he was very well acquainted, because they had before both served one Master.*

His Master was then in the gaol at Reading. Judge then how CAMPION could be within "with his Master." [A.M.]

The Cook, thinking no ill, began to tell him many things; and that Father CAMPION was in the house with his Master.

Upon which report, GEORGE sent his fellow to the Justice, who was a very great Calvinist. And he in mean while was brought into the house by the said Cook: where, like another JUDAS, traitor and disloyal, he first attended the sacrifice of the Mass which was celebrated that day by the Father EDMUND, as also a Sermon which he made. In which time behold a good man came running, willing them to take heed of a present treason.

Scantly was all carried away that had served for the Mass and the Sermon; but the Justice was there arrived with [a] *very great force, besetting the house round about, that none should escape away.*

After very diligent search through all the chambers and other more secret places; they were determined to return, as not finding anything, until they were advertised (either by GEORGE, who had understood it of the Cook; or by some other) of a certain corner, more dark and subtle; where they found the Father EDMUND and two other Priests hidden: who, the same day, with Gentlemen and other persons, were sent up to London; a spectacle of great joy unto their adversaries.

This much of our French historian's words, I thought

good in this place to set down : because the disproof
thereto annexed may discover what truth all
they of this sect frequent in any of their actions.

By that which followeth, written by GEORGE ELLIOT *himself; consider the truth of this report.* [A.M.]

This aforenamed GEORGE ELLIOT came home
unto my lodging [? in Barbican, see page 469; and
in February 1582]; where I shewed him the slanders
that were used of him in the French book.

Whereupon, taking good advice, and noting the circumstances that so highly touched him ; upon his conscience,
he delivereth this unreprovable Answer.

GEORGE ELLIOT *his Answer, to clear himself of the former untrue Objections.*

BOUT three years since [? 1578] it was my fortune to serve Master THOMAS ROPER of
[Orpington in] Kent. With whom I had not
stayed past eleven weeks, but PAYNE the Priest
(of whom mention is made [see page 453] in the
Discovery of CAMPION set forth by the Author of this book
[*i.e.* ANTHONY MUNDAY]) inticed me [in November 1578]
from thence to serve my Lady PETRE, to whom the said
PAYNE served craftily as Steward of her house.

With her I continued almost two years [? Nov. 1578–
Nov. 1580]. In which time, being myself bent
somewhat to that religion, frequenting the company of a number of Papists, I perceived their
dealings to be, as they are indeed, full of wicked
treasons and unnatural dispositions, too bad to
be named. The conceit whereof (examining

Who frequenteth their company shall find all their dealings disloyal and traitorous. [A.M.]

first my duty to GOD, next my love to my Princess
[*Sovereign*], and last the care of my country,) by the
grace and permission of GOD, offered me so great dis-
liking of their dealings that, so warily and conveniently
as I might, I weaned my affection from their abominable
infection : nevertheless using their companies still, for that
it gave me the better occasion to see into the depth of their
horrible inventions.

From my Lady PETRE, in November was twelvemonth [1580], by entreaty I came to Master ROPER's again. With whom I continued till Whitsuntide last [14th May 1581], when my conscience hardly digesting such a weighty burden as with their devices and practices it was very sore ladened ; I was constrained to give over that slavish kind of life, and humbly committed my reconciliation to the Right Honourable and my good Lord, the Earl of LEICESTER : to whom I made known the grievous estate of my life which, for the space of four years, I had endured amongst them.

Now whereas it hath pleased my adversary to set down that I

> *committed a murder, and to avoid the danger of law offered* to the aforesaid my good Lord *to deliver unto him* EDMUND CAMPION, *thereby to obtain my pardon.*

How untrue this is, his Honour very well knoweth ; and so do a number more besides. For, in truth, I neither, as then, knew CAMPION, had never seen him in all my life, nor knew where or in what place he was, it is very unlike[ly] then I should make him any such promise. But that he may learn another time to order his matters with more truth and discretion ; I will set down both how I went, with what Commission, and to what intent : and then let him have judgment according to the credit of his Work :

(marginal note: It is very unlike[ly]that he, which never saw CAMPION in all his life, nor knew where he was, could make any promise to bring him forth. [A.M.])

When I had revealed the traitorous speeches of PAYNE the Priest (how, and after what manner, you may read in the book [by ANTHONY MUNDAY] before expressed [see page 453]) I was demanded, If I knew where he was at that time ?

I could not make any certain answer.

Whereupon I was demanded again, If I would do my endeavour to search him out ?

Whereto, according to my bounden duty, I agreed right willingly.

Then was I appointed, in company with DAVID JENKINS, one of the Messengers of Her Majesty's Chamber; and to us was delivered a Warrant to take and apprehend, not any one man, but *all Priests, Jesuits, and such like seditious persons,* as in our journey we should meet withal. Neither was CAMPION, PAYNE, or any one man named in the Warrant : for that as the one was judged hard to be found ; so it was uncertain where to find him [that] I knew well enough.

I saw the Warrant myself; and neither was CAMPION, PAYNE, or any one named therein : but all Priests, Jesuits, and such seditious persons. [A.M.]

Wherefore remembering, when I served Master ROPER, that there was one THOMAS COOPER a Cook, who served him likewise, and also knew the aforesaid PAYNE ; to him I thought good to go, because I had understanding that he dwelt at Lyford in Berkshire with one Master YATE who was a very earnest Papist and gave great entertainment to all of that sect : thinking as it might so fall out that we either might find the said PAYNE there, or else understand where he was. And considering the generality [*comprehensiveness*] of our Warrant, some other Priests might chance to be there ; in respect that he was such a host for all of that disposition.

When we came to Lyford, and had talked with this aforesaid THOMAS COOPER ; we were framing ourselves to depart thence, not having been within the house at all. But he desiring us to stay dinner, we alighted and went in with him ; he not telling me that

> CAMPION *was there with his Master*

for he [*Master YATE*] was then in the gaol at Reading ; or any other Priest : though it hath pleased our nameless Author to write so.

When we were within the house, this COOPER brought us into the buttery : where he, whispering me in the ear, demanded, If my fellow were within the Church or no? as much to say as, Whether he was a Papist or no?

A holy kind of Church, whereof the Devil is Vicar. [A.M.]

I answered, " He was not ; yet nevertheless," quoth I, " he is a very honest man, and one that wisheth well that way."

Then said the Cook, " Will you go up ? "

Hereby I understood that he would bring me to a Mass.

Whereto I consenting, leaving DAVID JENKINS in the buttery, he brought me up : where, after one SATWELL *alias* FOORD had said Mass, CAMPION prepared himself to say Mass. And there was the first time that ever I saw CAMPION in all my life : not having heard by any that he was there in the house, before I was brought up into the chamber.

As concerning how he was taken, how he was brought up to London, and how all things passed in that service ; I have already set down in my book imprinted : which conferring with his false report, you shall find it as much to differ as truth doth from falsehood.

This have I thought good here to set down, in the reproof of him who hath published such a manifest untruth : and as concerning what I have reported to be spoken by PAYNE, I am ready at all times to justify it with my death, that they are his words according as he spake them.

By me GEORGE ELLIOT.

1589.

Est natura hominum novitatis avida.

THE SCOTTISH QUEEN's

Burial at Peterborough,

upon Tuesday, being Lammas Day

[1st August] 1587.

LONDON.

Printed by A. J. [ABEL JEFFES] for EDWARD VENGE;
and are to be sold at his shop
without Bishops Gate.

The following is a truer account of the actual interment:

On Sunday, being the 30th of July, 1587, in the 29th year of the reign of ELIZABETH the Queen's Majesty of England, there went from Peterborough Master WILLIAM DETHICK, *alias* Garter Principal King of Arms, and five Heralds, accompanied by 40 horse and men, to conduct the body of MARY, late Queen of Scots, from Fotheringhay Castle in Northamptonshire (which Queen had remained prisoner in England nineteen years): having for that purpose, brought a royal coach drawn by four horses, and covered with black velvet; richly set forth with escutcheons of the Arms of Scotland, and little pennons round about it.

The body (being enclosed in lead; and the same coffined in wood) was brought down, and reverently put into the coach.

At which time, the Heralds put on their Coats of Arms, and bareheaded, with torches' light, brought the same forth of the Castle, about ten of the clock at night: and so conveyed it to Peterborough [eleven] miles distant from Fotheringhay Castle.

Whither being come, about two of the clock on the Monday morning [31st July]; the body was received most reverently at the Minster Door of Peterborough, by the Bishop, Dean and Chapter, and [ROBERT COOKE] *Clarenceux* King at Arms.

And, in the presence of the Scots which came with the same, it was laid in a Vault prepared for the same, in the Quire of the said Church, on the south side; opposite to the tomb of Queen KATHARINE [of Arragon], Dowager of Spain, the first wife of King HENRY the Eighth.

The occasion why the body was forthwith laid into the Vault, and not borne in the Solemnity; was because it was so extreme[ly] heavy, by reason of the lead, that the Gentlemen could not have endured to have carried it, with leisure, in the solemn proceeding: and besides, [it] was feared that the solder might rip; and, [it] being very hot weather, might be found some annoyance.

A Remembrance of the Order and Manner of the Burial of MARY, Queen of Scots. Printed in *Archæologia*, I., 155 [for 355], 1770.

The following additional details are given in the Account drawn up by [Doctor RICHARD FLETCHER] the Dean of Peterborogh. See S. GUNTON, *History of the Cathedral of Peterburgh*, p. 78. Ed. 1686.

The body, with the closures, weighed nine hundred weight; which being carried, and attended orderly by the said persons, was committed to the ground in the Vault appointed: and immediately the Vault was covered, saving a small hole left open for the Staffs to [be] broken into.

There were at that time, not any Offices of the Church Service done: the Bishop being ready to have executed therein. But it was by all that were present, as well Scottish as others, thought good and agreed, that it should be done at the day and time of Solemnity.]

The Scottish Queen's Burial at Peterborough,

upon Tuesday, being Lammas Day

[1st August], 1587.

ER body was brought in a coach, about
100 attending thereon, from Fotheringhay
Castle, upon Sunday [30th July], at night.
[RICHARD HOWLAND] the Bishop of
PETERBOROUGH, [RICHARD FLETCHER]
the Dean [of Peterborough], the Prebends,
and the rest [of the Chapter] met the same
at the Bridge; being not far from the
town: and so conveyed it to the Bishop's Palace, and from
thence upon Tuesday being Lammas Day, [it] was carried to
the Church, where she was buried * on the south side of the
Hearse by torchlight.

The Hearse [*or Catafalque*] was made field-bed wise; the
valance of black velvet, with a gold fringe; [and] the top of

---

* There is a Memorial entered on the wall of the Cathedral of Peterborough, for one [named ROBERT SCARLET] who, being Sexton thereof,
interred two Queens therein (KATHARINE Dowager and MARY of Scotland); more than fifty years interceding betwixt their several sepultures.
This vivacious Sexton also buried two generations; or the people in
that place twice over. Thus having built many houses (so I find graves
frequently called *domus æternales*) for others : some, as it was fitting,
performed this last office unto him. [He died on 2nd July 1594,
æt. 98.] THOMAS FULLER, *Worthies, &c.*, ii. 293., Ed. 1662.

the imperial covered with baize. About it, were set ten Posies [of the Motto of the Arms of Scotland], *In my defence, GOD me defend!* with ten Scutcheons great and little; and, at the top, a double one with a crown imperial thereupon. The Supporters [were] Unicorns, with 100 pennons or little flags. It was impaled with baize; and in it [were] fourteen stools, with black velvet cushions.

Upon the pillars supporting the imperial of the Hearse, the which were all covered with velvet, were fixed Scutcheons: bearing either [the] Red Lion alone; or else parted with the Arms of France, or with the arms of the Lord LENOX.

The Church and Chancel were hanged with baize and Scutcheons, as at other funerals.

[Here must be inserted some additional information:

Upon Monday, in the afternoon, came to Peterburgh, all the Lords and Ladies and other Assistants appointed; and at the Bishop's Palace was prepared [at Queen ELIZABETH's expense] a great supper for them: where all, at one table, supped in the Great Chamber; [it] being hanged with black.

Dean R. FLETCHER, in S. GUNTON's *History*, &c., p. 78, Ed. 1686.

On Tuesday, being the 1st of August, in the morning, about eight of the clock, the Chief Mourner, being [BRIDGET RUSSELL] the Countess of BEDFORD [*now the Widow of her third husband*], was attended upon by all the Lords and Ladies; and brought into the Presence Chamber within the Bishop's Palace: which [Chamber], all over, was hanged with black cloth.

· She was, by the Queen's Majesty's Gentlemen Ushers, placed somewhat under a Cloth of Estate [*canopy*] of purple velvet: where, (having given to the [*Gentlemen representing, on this occasion, the*] Great Officers, their Staffs of Office (viz. to the Lord Steward; Lord Chamberlain; the Treasurer, and Comptroller [of the Household]), she took her way into the Great Hall.

A Remembrance of the Order, &c. Archæologia, I., 155 [for 355], 1770].

The Mourners came out of the Bishop's Palace; being set in order by the Heralds thus:

First 100 Releevants; poor old women, for the most part widows: in black cloth gowns, with an ell of white holland over their heads; which they had for their labour, and nine shillings apiece in money. These divided themselves in the body of the Church; and stood half on the one side, and half on the other: and there stood during the whole Solemnity.

At the Church door, the Singing Men and Quiristers met the Mourners with a *Psalm*; and led them the way into the Chancel, continuing singing, with the Organ, until the Sermon began.

Then followed two Yeomen, viz.: the Sheriff [of Northamptonshire]'s Bailiff and the Bailiff of Peterborough; with black staves.

And after them [100 poor men, in] Mourning Coats.

Then Sir GEORGE SAVILE, in a Mourning gown, carrying the great Standard: viz. a Cross on a Field azure; the Streamer, a Unicorn argent in a Field of guiles; a Posy written, *In my defence, GOD me defend!*

Then followed Mourning Cloaks, two by two, a great number: whereof the first were the late Queen's Officers.

And after them, Mourning Gowns.

Among these Officers of her House was [Monsieur DU PREAU] a French Jesuit, her Confessor, with a golden crucifix about his neck; which he did wear openly: and being told, That the people murmured and disliked at it; he said, He would do it, though he died for it. Thus we may see how obdurate their hearts are in malice; and how obstinate they shew themselves in the vain toys and superstitious trifles of their own imaginations.

Then [RICHARD FLETCHER] the Dean [of Peterborough].

Next the two Bishops: [RICHARD HOWLAND] of PETERBOROUGH, and [WILLIAM WICKHAM, of] LINCOLN.

[CHARLES WILLOUGHBY,] the Lord WILLOUGHBY of Parham;

[LEWIS MORDAUNT,] the Lord MORDAUNT [of Turvey];

[HENRY COMPTON,] the Lord COMPTON;

Sir THOMAS CECIL [*afterwards* Lord BURLEGH, *and later* Earl of EXETER]:

All four, in gowns, with White Staffs; representing the [Lord] Steward; [the Lord] Chamberlain; [the] Treasurer, and [the] Controller [of the Queen's Household].

After these, 16 Scots and Frenchmen; which had been Officers in her [*Queen MARY's*] House.

Then Sir ANDREW NOEL alone, carrying the Banner of Scotland.

Then [WILLIAM, *afterwards* Sir WILLIAM, SEGAR] Percullis the Herald [*Portcullis Pursuivant*] bearing the Crown [*or Helmet*] and Crest: thereon a red lion rampant crowned, holding a sword the point upward; the Helmet overmanteled guiles powdered ermine.

Then the Target [*or Shield*, borne by JOHN RAVEN,] *Rouge Dragon* [*Pursuivant*];

The Sword by [HUMPHREY HALES] York [Herald];

The Coat of Arms by [ROBERT GLOVER,] Somerset Herald.

Then [ROBERT COOKE] *Clarenceux* [King at Arms] with a Gentleman at Arms [*or rather, a Gentleman Usher*].

Then followed the Coffin [*empty of course*], covered with a pall of velvet; six Scutcheons fixed thereon, upon the head whereof stood a Crown of Gold.

Six Gentlemen bare [*the supposed*] corpse, under a velvet canopy borne by these four Knights:

> Sir THOMAS MANNERS,
> Sir JOHN HASTINGS,
> Sir JAMES HARINGTON,
> Sir RICHARD KNIGHTLEY.

Eight Banerols [*a Banner, about a yard square, borne at the funerals of great persons*] borne by eight Squires; four on either side of the Coffin.

After the [*supposed*] corpse, came the Head Mourner [BRIDGET RUSSELL,] the Countess of BEDFORD; assisted by the two Earls [JOHN MANNERS,] of RUTLAND and [HENRY CLINTON, of] LINCOLN: [LUCY,] the Lady St. JOHN of Basing bearing her train.

Then followed, by two and two, other Ladies:

[WILLIAM DETHICK gives us a fuller List of these Ladies than
this Tract.   The brackets show those who went together.

ELIZABETH MANNERS, the Countess of RUTLAND.)
ELIZABETH CLINTON, the Countess of LINCOLN.   )
ANNE, the [? Dowager] Lady TALBOT.)
The Lady MARY SAVILE.   )
ELIZABETH, the Lady MORDAUNT.   )
CATHARINE, the Lady St. JOHN of Bletsoe.)
THEODOSIA, Wife of Sir THOMAS MANNERS.)
DOROTHY, Wife of Sir THOMAS CECIL.   )
ELIZABETH, Wife of Sir EDWARD MONTAGU.)
MABEL, Wife of Sir ANDREW NOEL.   )
Mistress ALINGTON.   )
A Scottish Gentlewoman.)]
The other Gentlemen.

The ten Scottish and French Women of the [late] Queen's
[Household]: with black attire on their heads, of Taffaty
before; and behind, White Lawn hanging down, like French
Hoods.

They, with the Scottish and French men, did all go out
before the Sermon, except Master MELVIN [i.e. ANDREW
MELVILLE; and also BARBARA MOWBRAY] who stayed; and
came in when it was ended.

The Head Mourner and the [twelve] Ladies, with the two
Earls assistant were placed within the Hearse [*or Catafalque*].

The two Knights, with their Banners, were set at the East
end of the Hearse, without the pale: and the eight Squires,
with their Bannerols, four of a side, in like manner without
the pale.

All the rest of the Mourners were carried up by a Herald
above the Hearse; and placed of each side, the women next
the altar.

The Bishop and the Dean [of Peterborough] stood at the
altar, with two gilded basons.

All which being placed and set, and the Church quiet;

2H   I

[WILLIAM WICKHAM,] the Bishop of LINCOLN began his Sermon [out of *Psalm* xxxix. 5–7].*

And in his prayer [when he gave thanks for such as were translated out of this Vale of Misery, he] used these words:

"Let us bless GOD for the happy dissolution of MARY, late the Scottish Queen and Dowager of France. Of whose life and departure, whatsoever shall be expected, I have nothing to say: for that I was unacquainted with the one; and not present at the other. Of Her Majesty's faith and end, I am not to judge. It is a charitable saying of the Father LUTHER 'Many [a] one liveth a Papist; and dieth a Protestant.' Only this I have been informed, That she took her death patiently; and recommended herself wholly to JESUS CHRIST."

The Sermon ended, a long piece of velvet and a cushion were carried and laid before the Countess [of BEDFORD], to go and kneel upon; hard before the Bishop [of PETER-BOROUGH]'s feet.

Then, by [Garter,] the King of Heralds, were carried the four Officers with their White Staffs; and placed two at the top of the stairs under the Bishop, and two beneath them.

Then the two principal Heralds [Garter and *Clarenceux*] fetched up the Countess; the two Earls [of RUTLAND and LINCOLN] leading her, and the Lady St. JOHN [of Basing] bearing up her train.

There she kneeled awhile.

And then all returned to their places.

This was the First Offering [for Queen ELIZABETH].

Not[e] that BRAKENBURY went this time before her [*the Countess of BEDFORD*].

The two Earls [were] placed without the pale [of the Hearse], before the Countess.

One of the Kings of Heralds fetched from the Hearse, the Coat Armour; brought it down to the other King of Heralds;

---

* In the discourse of his Text, he only dealt with general doctrine, of the vanity of all flesh. *Dean R FLETCHER.*

and he delivered it to the two Earls. They carried it, obeisance being done to the Countess, to the Bishop [of PETERBOROUGH]; and kissed it in delivering of it. A third Herald took it of the Bishop; and laid it down on the altar.

The Sword, the Target, the Helmet, Crown, and Crest, in like sort was all done by the two Earls : kissing their hands before them.

Then were the two Banners carried, by one after another, severally by those that brought them; and so set upon the altar, leaning to the wall.

The other eight Bannerols were put into the Hearse as they stood.

Then went the Countess [of BEDFORD], Master JOHN MANNERS [acting as Vice Chamberlain,] holding up her train the second time; and offered alone [for herself] to the Bishop.

Then the Ladies and Gentlemen, by two and two, went up and offered.

Then the [four] Officers with White Staffs offered.

And, last of all, came there a Herald to the pulpit; and fetched the Bishop of LINCOLN.

And then the most part of the Mourners departed, in the same order they came in : and towards the door of the Chancel, stood the Scottish women, parted on both sides; and as the English Ladies passed, they kissed them all.

Then over the Vault, where the body lay; [RICHARD FLETCHER] the Dean [of Peterborough] read the ordinary words of [the] Burial [Service].

And this being done : the four Officers brake their White Staffs over their heads; and threw them into the Vault.

[Dean FLETCHER's *The Manner of the Solemnity, &c.*, concludes thus :

And so they departed to the Bishop's House : where was

a great feast appointed accordingly [at Queen ELIZABETH's expense*].

The concourse of people was of many thousands.

And, after dinner, the Nobles departed away; every one towards his own home.

The Master of the [Queen's] Wardrobe paid to the Church, for breaking of the ground in the Quire, and making the grave, £10; and for Blacks of the Quire and Church, £20.*]

F I N I S.

* The total of Queen ELIZABETH'S expenses for this Funeral amounted to £321, 14s. 6d.

T[HOMAS] D[ELONEY].

Three Ballads on the Armada fight.

[Original broadsides, in British Museum. C. 18. e. 2/62–64.]

A joyful new Ballad declaring the happy obtaining of the great
Galleazzo, *wherein Don* PEDRO DE VALDEZ *was the chief;*
through the mighty power and providence of GOD : *being a*
special token of His gracious and fatherly goodness towards us;
to the great encouragement of all those that willingly fight in the
defence of His Gospel and our good
Queen of England.

To the tune of *Monsieur's Almain.*

[Entered at Stationers' Hall, 10th August, 1588 ; see *Transcript*, ii. 495. *Ed.* 1875.]

NOBLE England,
    fall down upon thy knee !
And praise thy GOD, with thankful heart,
    which still maintaineth thee !
The foreign forces
    that seek thy utter spoil,
Shall then, through His especial grace,
    be brought to shameful foil.
With mighty power,
    they come unto our coast ;
To overrun our country quite,
    they make their brags and boast.

In strength of men
  they set their only stay ;
But we, upon the LORD our GOD
  will put our trust alway !

Great is their number
  of ships upon the sea ;
And their provision wonderful :
  but, LORD, Thou art our stay !
Their armèd soldiers
  are many by account ;
Their aiders eke in this attempt
  do, sundry ways, surmount.
The Pope of Rome,
  with many blessèd grains,
To sanctify their bad pretence,
  bestoweth both cost and pains,
But little land
  is not dismayed at all !
The LORD, no doubt ! is on our side,
  which soon will work their fall.

In happy hour,
  our foes we did descry !
And under sail, with gallant wind,
  as they came passing by.
Which sudden tidings
  to Plymouth being brought ;
Full soon our Lord High Admiral,
  for to pursue them sought.
And to his train
  courageously he said,
" Now, for the LORD, and our good Queen,
  to fight be not afraid !
Regard our Cause !
  and play your parts like men !

The LORD, no doubt! will prosper us
    in all our actions then."

This great *Galleazzo*
    which was so huge and high,
That, like a bulwark on the sea
    did seem to each man's eye.
There was it taken,
    unto our great relief,
And divers nobles, in which train
    Don PEDRO was the chief.
Strong was she stuffed
    with cannons great and small,
And other instruments of war,
    Which we obtainèd all.
A certain sign
    of good success, we trust :
That GOD will overthrow the rest,
    as he hath done the first.

Then did our Navy
    pursue the rest amain,
With roaring noise of cannons great,
    till they, near Calais came.
With manly courage
    they followed them so fast ;
Another mighty Galleon
    did seem to yield at last :
And in distress
    for safeguard of their lives,
A flag of truce, they did hand out,
    with many mournful cries.
Which when our men
    did perfectly espy
Some little barks they sent to her,
    to board her quietly.

But these false Spaniards
  esteeming them but weak,
When they within their danger came,
  their malice forth did break :
With chargèd cannons
  they laid about them then,
For to destroy those proper barks
  and all their valiant men.
Which when our men
  preceivèd so to be ;
Like lions fierce, they forward went
  to 'quite this injury ;
And boarding them
  with strong and mighty hand,
They killed the men, until their Ark
  did sink in Calais sand.

The chiefest Captain
  of this Galleon so high,
Don HUGO DE MONCALDO, he
  within this fight did die :
Who was the General
  of all the Galleons great,
But through his brains, with powder's force,
  a bullet strong did beat.
And many more,
  by sword, did lose their breath,
And many more within the sea
  did swim, and took their death.
There might you see
  the salt and foaming flood,
Died and stained like scarlet red
  with store of Spanish blood.

This mighty vessel
  was threescore yards in length,

Most wonderful, to each man's eye,
  for making and for strength.
In her were placed
  a hundred cannons great,
And mightily provided eke
  with bread-corn, wine, and meat.
There were of oars
  two hundred, I ween.
Threescore feet and twelve in length
  well measured to be seen ;
And yet subdued,
  with many others more :
And not a ship of ours lost !
  the LORD be thanked therefore !

Our pleasant country,
  so beautiful and so fair,
They do intend, by deadly war,
  to make both poor and bare.
Our towns and cities,
  to rack and sack likewise,
To kill and murder man and wife
  as malice doth arise ;
And to deflour
  our virgins in our sight ;
And in the cradle cruelly
  the tender babe to smite.
GOD's Holy Truth,
  they mean for to cast down,
And to deprive our noble Queen
  both of her life and crown.

Our wealth and riches,
  which we enjoyèd long ;
They do appoint their prey and spoil
  by cruelty and wrong.

To set our houses
  a fire on our heads;
And cursedly to cut our throats
  As we lie in our beds.
Our children's brains
  to dash against the ground,
And from the earth our memory
  for ever to confound.
To change our joy
  to grief and mourning sad,
And never more to see the days
  of pleasure we have had.

But GOD Almighty
  be blessed evermore!
Who doth encourage Englishmen
  to beat them from our shore,
With roaring cannons
  their hasty steps to stay,
And with the force of thundering shot,
  to make them fly away;
Who made account,
  before this time or day,
Against the walls of fair London
  their banners to display.
But their intent,
  the LORD will bring to nought,
If faithfully we call and cry
  for succour as we ought.

And yours, dear brethren!
  which beareth arms this day,
For safeguard of your native soil;
  mark well, what I shall say!
Regard your duties!
  think on your country's good!

And fear not in defence thereof,
 to spend your dearest blood !
Our gracious Queen
 doth greet you every one !
And saith, " She will among you be
 in every bitter storm !
Desiring you
 true English hearts to bear
To GOD ! to her ! and to the land
 wherein you nursèd were ! "

LORD GOD Almighty !
 (which hath the hearts in hand,
Of every person to dispose)
 defend this English land !
Bless Thou, our Sovereign
 with long and happy life !
Endue her Council with Thy grace !
 and end this mortal strife !
Give to the rest
 of commons more and less,
Loving hearts ! obedient minds !
 and perfect faithfulness !
That they and we,
 and all, with one accord,
On Sion hill, may sing the praise
 of our most mighty LORD.
       T. D.

FINIS.

Printed by JOHN WOLFE
for EDWARD WHITE
1588.

*The Queen's visiting of the Camp at Tilbury, with her
entertainment there.*

To the tune of *Wilson's wild.*

[Entered at Stationers' Hall, 10th August, 1588; see *Transcript,* ii. 495. *Ed.* 1875.]

ITHIN the year of CHRIST our Lord,
    a thousand and five hundred full,
And eighty-eight by just record,
    the which no man may disannul;
And in the thirtieth year remaining,
    of good Queen ELIZABETH's reigning .
A mighty power there was prepared
    By PHILIP, then the King of Spain,
Against the Maiden Queen of England;
    Which in peace before did reign.

Her royal ships, to sea she sent
    to guard the coast on every side;
And seeing how her foes were bent,
    her realm full well she did provide
With many thousands so prepared
    as like was never erst declared;
Of horsemen and of footmen plenty,
    whose good hearts full well is seen,
In the safeguard of their country
    and the service of our Queen.

In Essex fair, that fertile soil
    upon the hill of Tilbury,
To give our Spanish foes the foil
    in gallant camps they now do lie,
Where good order is ordained,
    and true justice eke maintained
For the punishment of persons
    that are lewd or badly bent.
To see a sight so strange in England,
    'Twas our gracious Queen's intent.

And on the eighth of August, she
    from fair St. James's, took her way,
With many Lords of high degree,
    in princely robes and rich array;
And to barge upon the water
    (being King HENRY's royal daughter!)
She did go, with trumpets sounding,
    and with dubbing drums apace,
Along the Thames, that famous river,
    for to view the Camp a space.

When she, as far as Gravesend came,
    right over against that pretty town,
Her royal Grace with all her train
    was landed there with great renown.
The Lords, and Captains of her forces,
    mounted on their gallant horses,
Ready stood to entertain her,
    like martial men of courage bold
" Welcome to the Camp, dread Sovereign ! "
    Thus they said, both young and old.

The Bulwarks strong, that stood thereby,
    well guarded with sufficient men,
Their flags were spread courageously,
    their cannons were dischargèd then.
Each gunner did declare his cunning
    for joy conceivèd of her coming.
All the way her Grace was riding,
    on each side stood armèd men,
With muskets, pikes, and good calivers,
    for her Grace's safeguard then.

The Lord General of the field
    had there his bloody Ancient borne,
The Lord Marshal's colours eke
    were carried there, all rent and torn,

The which with bullets was so burned
    when in Flanders he sojourned.
Thus in warlike wise they marched,
    even as soft as foot could fall ;
Because her Grace was fully minded
    perfectly to view them all.

Her faithful soldiers, great and small,
    as each one stood within his place,
Upon their knees began to fall
    desiring GOD, to " save her Grace ! "
For joy whereof, her eyes were filled
    that the water down distilled ;
" LORD bless you all, my friends ! " she said,
    " but do not kneel so much to me ! "
Then sent she warning to the rest,
    they should not let such reverence be.

Then casting up her Princely eyes
    unto the hill with perfect sight,
The ground all covered, she espies,
    with feet of armèd soldiers bright :
Whereat her royal heart so leaped,
    on her feet upright she stepped.
Tossing up her plume of feathers
    to them all as they did stand,
Cheerfully her body bending,
    waving of her royal hand.

Thus through the Camp she passèd quite,
    in manner as I have declared.
At Master RICH's, for that night,
    her Grace's lodging was prepared.
The morrow after her abiding,
    on a princely palfrey riding ;
To the Camp, she came to dinner,
    with her Lords and Ladies all.

The Lord General went to meet her,
 with his Guard of Yeomen tall.

The Sergeant Trumpet, with his mace,
 And nine with trumpets after him,
Bareheaded went before Her Grace
 in coats of scarlet trim.
The King of Heralds, tall and comely,
 was the next in order duly,
With the famous Arms of England
 wrought with rich embroidered gold
On finest velvet, blue and crimson,
 that for silver can be sold.

With maces of clean beaten gold,
 the Queen's two Sergeants then did ride,
Most comely men for to behold,
 in velvet coats and chains beside.
The Lord General then came riding,
 and Lord Marshal hard beside him,
Richly were they both attired
 in princely garments of great price;
Bearing still their hats and feathers
 in their hands, in comely wise.

Then came the Queen, on prancing steed,
 attired like an angel bright;
And eight brave footmen at her feet
 whose jerkins were most rich in sight.
Her Ladies, likewise of great honour,
 most sumptuously did wait upon her,
With pearls and diamonds brave adorned,
 and in costly cauls of gold:
Her Guards, in scarlet, then rode after,
 with bows and arrows, stout and bold.

The valiant Captains of the field,
   mean space, themselves in order set;
And each of them, with spear and shield,
   to join in battle did not let.
With such a warlike skill extended,
   as the same was much commended.
Such a battle pitched in England
   many a day hath not been seen.
Thus they stood in order waiting
   for the presence of our Queen.

At length, her Grace most royally
   receivèd was, and brought again.
Where she might see most loyally
   this noble host and warlike train.
How they came marching all together,
   like a wood in winter's weather,
With the strokes of drummers sounding,
   and with trampling horses; then
The earth and air did sound like thunder
   to the ears of every man.

The warlike army then stood still,
   and drummers left their dubbing sound;
Because it was our Prince's will
   to ride about the army round.
Her Ladies, she did leave behind her,
   and her Guard, which still did mind her,
The Lord General and Lord Marshal
   did conduct her to each place.
The pikes, the colours, and the lances,
   at her approach, fell down apace!

And then bespake our noble Queen,
   " My loving friends and countrymen!
I hope this day the worst is seen,
   that in our wars, ye shall sustain!

But if our enemies do assail you,
   never let your stomachs fail you !
For in the midst of all your troops ;
   we ourselves will be in place !
To be your joy, your guide and comfort ;
   even before your enemy's face ! "

This done, the soldiers, all at once,
   a mighty shout or cry did give !
Which forcèd from the azure skies
   an echo loud, from thence to drive ;
Which filled her Grace with joy and pleasure :
   and riding then from them, by leisure,
With trumpets' sound most loyally,
   along the Court of Guard she went :
Who did conduct Her Majesty
   unto the Lord Chief General's tent.

Where she was feasted royally
   with dainties of most costly prices
And when that night approaching nigh,
   Her Majesty, with sage advice,
In gracious manner, then returned
   from the Camp where she sojourned
And when that she was safely sit
   within her barge, and passed away ;
Her Farewell then, the trumpets sounded ;
   and the cannons fast did play !

                    T. D.

FINIS.

Imprinted at London by JOHN WOLF

for EDWARD WHITE. 1588.

21

A new Ballet of the strange and most cruel whips, which the
Spaniards had prepared to whip and torment English men and
women : which were found and taken at the overthrow of certain
of the Spanish ships, in July last past, 1588.

To the tune of *The valiant Soldier.*

[Entered at Stationers' Hall, 31 August, 1588 ; see *Transcript,* ii. 498. *Ed.* 1875.]

LL you that list to look and see
    what profit comes from Spain,
And what the Pope and Spaniards both
    preparèd for our gain.
Then turn your eyes and bend your ears,
    and you shall hear and see
What courteous minds, what gentle hearts,
    they bear to thee and me !

They say "they seek for England's good,
    and wish the people well ! "
They say "they are such holy men,
    all others they excel ! "
They brag that " they are Catholics,
    and CHRIST's only Spouse !
And whatsoe'er they take in hand,
    the holy Pope allows ! "

These holy men, these sacred saints,
    and these that think no ill :
See how they sought, against all right,
    to murder, spoil, and kill !
Our noble Queen and country first
    they did prepare to spoil,
To ruinate our lives and lands
    with trouble and turmoil.

And not content, by fire and sword,
    to take our right away;
But to torment most cruelly,
    our bodies, night and day.
Although they meant, with murdering hands,
    our guiltless blood to spill;
Before our deaths, they did devise
    to whip us, first, their fill.

And for that purpose had prepared
    of whips such wondrous store,
So strangely made, that, sure, the like
    *was never seen before.
For never was there horse, nor mule,
    nor dog of currish kind,
That ever had such whips devised
    by any savage mind!

One sort of whips, they had for men,
    so smarting, fierce, and fell,
As like could never be devised
    by any devil in hell:
The strings whereof with wiry knots,
    like rowels they did frame,
That every stroke might tear the flesh,
    they laid on with the same.

And pluck the spreading sinews from
    the hardened bloody bone,
To prick and pierce each tender vein,
    within the body known;
And not to leave one crooked rib
    on any side unseen,
Nor yet to leave a lump of flesh,
    the head and foot between.

And for our silly women eke,
   their hearts with grief to clog ;
They made such whips, wherewith no man
   would seem to strike a dog.
So strengthened eke with brazen tags
   and filed so rough and thin,
That they would force at every lash,
   the blood abroad to spin.

Although their bodies sweet and fair
   their spoil they meant to make,
And on them first their filthy lust
   and pleasure for to take :
Yet afterwards such sour sauce
   they should be sure to find,
That they should curse each springing branch
   that cometh of their kind.

O Ladies fair, what spite were this !
   your gentle hearts to kill !
To see these devilish tyrants thus
   your children's blood to spill.
What grief unto the husband dear !
   his loving wife to see
Tormented so before his face
   with extreme villainy.

And think you not, that they which had
   such dogged minds to make
Such instruments of tyranny,
   had not like hearts to take
The greatest vengeance that they might,
   upon us every one ?
Yes, yes ! be sure ! for godly fear
   and mercy, have they none !

Even as in India once they did
    against those people there
With cruel curs, in shameful sort,
    the men both rent and tare ;
And set the ladies great with child
    upright against a tree,
And shot them through with piercing darts :
    such would their practice be !

Did not the Romans in this land
    sometimes like practice use
Against the Britains bold in heart,
    and wondrously abuse
The valiant king whom they had caught,
    before his queen and wife,
And with most extreme tyranny,
    despatched him of his life ?

The good Queen BOADICEA,
    and eke her daughters three ;
Did they not first abuse them all
    by lust and lechery ;
And, after, stripped them naked all,
    and whipped them in such sort,
That it would grieve each Christian heart
    to hear that just report ?

And if these ruffling mates of Rome
    did Princes thus torment ;
Think you ! the Romish Spaniards now
    would not shew their descent ?
How did they, late, in Rome rejoice,
    in Italy and Spain ;
What ringing and what bonfires !
    what *Masses* sung amain !

What printed books were sent about
    as fillèd their desire,
How England was, by Spaniards won,
    and London set on fire!
Be these the men, that are so mild!
    whom some so holy call!
The LORD defend our noble Queen
    and country from them all!

T. D.

FINIS.

Imprinted at London, by THOMAS ORWIN and
THOMAS GUBBIN; and are to be sold in
Paternoster Row, over against
the *Black Raven*,
1588.

INDEX

Edinburgh: Printed by T. and A. CONSTABLE